MW01232949

Alabama: The Bicentennial

200 Years of
Athletes, Authors, Agriculture, Artists, Autos, Achievers, Aviation, Armed Forces, Astronauts Advocates for freedom

John H. Merrill
Tom Ward

Churchill Press

A special thanks goes to ALFA and the Alabama Power Company for generous donations to help place books in every school in Alabama with fourth grade classrooms.

ALFA®
FARMERS
ALABAMA FARMERS FEDERATION

ALABAMA POWER
A SOUTHERN COMPANY
Always on.SM

First Edition

Dedication

This book is dedicated to my parents,
Horace and Mary Merrill,
who gave me a love for Alabama,
our people, and our history!

I also dedicate this book to my wife, Cindy.
She has helped me love our people, our history,
and our state better than anyone I've ever known.

John H. Merrill
2019

Gratitude

Thanks to the following people, who are listed in alphabetical order and whose help was foundational to this project:

Thanks to the Alabama Department of Archives and History, and specifically to Director Steve Murray, for helping this project benefit so many. Thanks also to Georgia Ann Hudson for her contribution about the state Archives, and to Mary Beth Wasden for her help in facilitating the details of coordinating this.

Thanks to David Azbell for sharing priceless stories and fascinating photographs.

Thanks to Joe Bellafato and Felicia Hammonds, for once again making the process of layout and printing efficient and pleasant.

Thanks to Greg Butrus for wise counsel and his contribution of the Paul Butrus profile.

Thanks to Dr. Wayne Flynt for his time, expertise, unmatched perspective on the totality of our state's history, and personal example of existential living.

Thanks to Tommy Ford, an accomplished editor, author, and historian. Your perspective, editing ability, and personal knowledge of so many of the people profiled in this project made it a better book.

Thanks to the educators who enlighten, challenge, inspire, and guide our state's students as part of your daily careers.

Thanks to Dr. Jane Geiger, for wise counsel and an attentive ear during seemingly endless hours of talking through ideas and reciting newly learned trivia. Thanks also for your finishing-carpenter role, artfully editing and offering wordsmithing suggestions that were helpful, meaningful, and for being the kindest person I know.

Thanks to the Kiwanis Club of Homewood and Mountain Brook, with the variety of perspectives of ideas that came even beyond the question and answer time. You truly made this a better book.

Thanks to Doug Marshall for wise counsel, a contagious spirit of service to others, and most of all, for a friendship for which I am profoundly grateful.

Thanks to Jake Reiss, book promoter extraordinaire, for connecting me with others, suggesting resources, opining on names for profiles, and wise counsel on the ripeness of a book project.

Thanks to Greg Robinson for great friendship, advice, counsel, and stories. Thanks to Bradley Robinson for research assistance, suggestions, and enthusiasm.

Thanks to Terry Schrimscher for so many discussions of the book's content, and for introducing me to the fascinating story of Miles Copeland.

Thanks to TuscaBlue, and specifically Spencer Kyser, for their enlargements of the book cover.

Thanks to the University of Alabama Department of History and specifically former professors William Barnard, Russell Bryant, and Forest McDonald for inspiring my love and recitation of history.

Thanks to Betty and Gary Ward, for endless hours with this manuscript, with all the proofreading, editing, fact-checking, suggestions, and ideas. Thanks also for so many enjoyable conversations about its ultimate content. They were great fun. Thanks also for being the godliest Alabamians I've ever known.

Thanks to Elizabeth, Mary Frances, Thomas, and Sarah Margaret Ward. Thanks for wonderful ideas for the book and for priceless encouragement. Everything I write, ultimately, is in part for you. Thanks also to Thomas for outstanding research and interview time and to Sarah Margaret for starting this project by suggesting a different type of history book.

Thanks to Andrew N. Williams John W. Williams for outstanding research, and thanks also to Melinda and Brad for ideas, support, and encouragement.

Thanks to Sue Wilson, whose contributions to this book occurred many years ago in Advanced Placement English class at Holt High School in the 1984-85 school year. Your class brought the art of storytelling, and authors like Voltaire, into my life in ways that never would have been foreseen.

This is a departure from the alphabetical order, but thanks to the Honorable John H. Merrill for the privilege of doing this book as co-authors. All the meetings, innumerable e-mails, and those quick messages about including this person or that fact have now become a book that brings a fresh and relatable perspective, to present and future generations of the state that we both call home.

Tom Ward
2019

Table of Contents

AUTHORS

Creators. Founders. Innovators. Writers.

Mary Anderson
Inventor of the windshield wiper
Greene County

When most people are stuck in traffic, they might search for a distraction or grumble some regrettable words. For Mary Anderson of Greene County, she used the time to change driving forever.

During a slow ride, Anderson invented the windshield wiper.

In 1902, while visiting New York City, Anderson rode in a streetcar. The reason for the slow journey was that the driver of the streetcar, in which Anderson was a passenger, had to keep stopping the vehicle to get out and clean snow off the windshield. Anderson, according to the story passed down through later generations, began composing a drawing of her brilliant idea that would become the windshield wiper. As she designed it, the first windshield wiper was operated by a pull-handle located near the steering wheel.

The next year, on November 10, 1903, Anderson's application for a U.S. Patent for her "Window Cleaning Device" was approved, but no businesses were interested in her invention. Why not? Theories abound, but interestingly, soon after her patent expired, car companies began including similarly constructed windshield wipers in new vehicles.

Mother Angelica
Founder, EWTN Network
Jefferson County

A classic story of faith-filled compassion and outreach was born in Alabama and became a global ministry.

And it all happened because of a little girl who grew up in poverty.

Mother Angelica has been the subject of books, articles, television shows, and audio tapes. She was the founder of both the Eternal World Television Network (that still thrives in Birmingham), and the Shrine of the Most Blessed Sacrament (in Hanceville, Cullman County, Alabama).

The amazing journey began, sadly, when John Rizzo abandoned his wife and five-year-old daughter, Rita, leaving the girl and mom to live in poverty. At age 21, against the wishes of her mom, Rita joined the Order of Poor Clares in Ohio. She assumed the name Sister Mary Angelica.

Roughly a decade later, Sister Mary Angelica became inspired by the growing Civil Rights Movement of the 1950s, and sought to pursue her vision of a community of faith appealing to Southern African Americans. Ultimately, she connected with Archbishop Thomas Toolen of Mobile, who encouraged her to direct her attention toward Birmingham. Determined to finance the venture, she and her fellow Poor Clares made and sold fishing lures to raise the needed funds. With the proceeds from the fishing lures, a house was purchased in the Irondale area of Birmingham. With subsequent additional private funding, the Lady of the Angels Monastery was established and dedicated in 1962.

While her gifts of leadership and visionary thinking had become obvious to anyone dealing with her, Angelica's greatest earthly gift, communicating godly and biblical messages to ordinary people, soon became known far beyond her adopted home of Alabama.

The powerful and easily understood messages from Mother Angelica were distributed in the form of books, 45 rpm records, and ultimately through the Eternal Word Television Network based in Irondale. According to information provided by its website, the network is "the largest religious media network in the world. EWTN's 11 networks broadcast in multiple languages 24 hours a day, seven days a week to over 268 million television households in more than 145 countries and territories."

The seemingly endless multimedia platforms used by the EWTN to reach the world include satellite television, iHeart Radio, the world's largest Catholic website, 500 radio affiliates, a worldwide shortwave radio network, and two global wire services.

Pictured on the previous page: Top, left: Birmingham native and Pulitzer Prize winning author Howell Raines. Top, center: CBS news correspondent and bestselling author, Morgan County native Jan Crawford. Top, right: Calhoun County native and Pulitzer Prize winning author Rick Bragg. Middle row: from left to right, three staples of Alabama life that were founded by its people, Jack's restaurants, Southern Living magazine, and Milo's Famous Sweet Tea. Bottom, left: the Innovation Depot has become an incubator for new ideas and businesses. Bottom, right, the greatest American novel, To Kill A Mockingbird, was authored by Monroe County's own Nelle Harper Lee.

Douglas Arant
Co-founder, Bradley Arant
Jefferson County

It is only fitting that the largest and oldest existing law firm in Alabama is named in part after one of its greatest attorneys.

The record is clear; Douglas Arant spent his life doing things the right way, and giving of himself to his country, state, and community.

Long before he became a name partner in the firm now known as Bradley Arant Boult and Cummings, Douglas Arant proved early in life that he was a young man of elite intellect with a heart for service. Born on a Lee County farm to parents of limited means, Arant earned a scholarship to the University of Virginia. He left school to serve in the First World War, ultimately earning the rank of Second Lieutenant. After the war, he returned to Virginia, where he earned bachelor's and master's degrees before entering the Yale Law School.

Yale University was the venue where Arant first showed his potential for national prominence, graduating magna cum laude and serving as the editor-in-chief of the Yale Law Journal.

Returning to his homeland of Alabama, Arant joined the law firm of Tilman, Bradley and Baldwin that would become the firm known by the brand name of Bradley Arant.

Although an accomplished lawyer, Arant was known for his ability to see a linear path from society as it was, toward a society as it could be. He sponsored the first African American as a member of the Birmingham Bar, the future Alabama Supreme Court Justice Oscar W. Adams, Jr. Arant was invited by President Kennedy to convene with 243 other attorneys in Washington, in the summer of 1963, as part of a group challenged by the young president to take the battle for civil rights from the streets to the courtrooms.

Arant served on countless boards of organizations, was elected the President of the Alabama State Bar, and was named Birmingham's Lawyer of the Year. The state of Alabama still benefits from his visionary legal practice and the firm that still bears his name.

John Archibald
Pulitzer Prize winning author
Jefferson County

When the 2018 Pulitzer Prize for Commentary was awarded to Alabama's John Archibald, his name became part of American journalism history. While all Pulitzer Prizes carry enormous prestige, the Pulitzer for Commentary boasts an illustrious list of past winners, including great American legends such as George F. Will, Murray Kempton, William Safire, and Thomas Friedman.

For Archibald, that moment was merely the latest step of a journey that has produced compelling columns and unique perspectives gained from all corners of Alabama. From his childhood as the son of a Methodist preacher, to his life as a columnist and father, that journey has empowered him to learn and tell the stories of the state's people and the issues of the day. Part of Archibald's success arises from the fact that he doesn't merely conduct research for his columns; he goes out to the places where the news, stories, and scandals happen. Those stories have led him from interviewing rural Alabamians to pursuing facts about those in the corridors of government power. Sometimes, those stories have even exposed the abuse of that power, as with the scandal leading to the resignation of Alabama Governor Robert Bentley.

Archibald's investigative work on the 2015 Bentley scandal continued the theme of exposing malfeasance that has become his personal trademark since his college years. After graduating from Banks High School in Birmingham, Archibald ultimately enrolled at The University of Alabama and began writing for the student newspaper, *The Crimson White*. During his years on the campus in Tuscaloosa, Archibald zealously pursued news stories on what he found to be a systemic imbalance of power within the student body. That placed him in opposition to a political machine that typically controlled the student government and produced many of the state's future leaders. That same determination has defined his reporting, opinion columns, and path to the Pulitzer Prize.

Archibald's wife, Alecia, was his colleague on *The Crimson White* staff and has become an accomplished reporter and magazine editor.

Often controversial and never boring, the opinion columns by Archibald in *The Birmingham News* and the *Alabama Media Group* have gained national attention, earned him regular interviews in the national media, and propelled him to the elite realm of journalism.

Joe Azbell
Author, columnist, politico
Montgomery County

Amazingly, both Dr. Martin Luther King, Jr., and George C. Wallace called him a friend. Each relied on him during crucial moments in their careers, and he came through for them. He met presidents and celebrities. Several who pursued the presidency sought his help, and some of them won. He knew Hank Williams (the first one), George Bush, Ronald Reagan, Richard Nixon, and just about every celebrity who came through the state.

And he wasn't even from Alabama. At least not originally.

Azbell ran away from his childhood home in Texas at a young age. So where did he hide out from school officials or law enforcement during the day? He cleverly figured out that the one place they would never look for runaways was in the library. So he camped out there during the day, reading and learning.

At the age of five, he had already begun shining shoes and selling newspapers. "I learned that if you could look at a man, you could tell if he would let you shine his shoes," he explained.

As a reporter and columnist, Azbell possessed some type of sixth-sense about what was newsworthy and what readers cared about. As the city editor of *The Montgomery Advertiser*, Azbell wrote the article announcing the impending Montgomery Bus Boycott. Rather than putting it in the section reserved for black people, Azbell placed the article as the lead story on the front page, where all readers would see it. According to Dr. King, the boycott might not have succeeded if Azbell had not strategically placed the article to achieve the greatest impact.

One can only imagine how King's life would have been different if the boycott had failed.

King publicly called Azbell a good friend, as did the legendary Rev. E. D. Nixon, the originator of the boycott, and in many ways the founder of the Civil Rights Movement. Nixon once signed a photo for Azbell, inscribing "Joe Azbell did more for blacks than any white man in America."

Many years later, Azbell had the honor of serving as an honorary pallbearer at Nixon's funeral.

As for Governor Wallace, his path was also greatly influenced by Azbell. The Wallace presidential campaign theme in 1972 was "Send them a message," a slogan chosen by Azbell. Azbell played a key role in the governor's presidential campaigns, and had the unfortunate job of dealing with the media, even while fighting his own grief, in the aftermath of the 1972 assassination attempt on Wallace in Maryland.

Through the decades Azbell's columns in *The Montgomery Advertiser* maintained a large loyal readership, entertained with his vast collection of stories as well as his political reporting.

And then there was the time that he was fired from a job, then rehired with a pay raise within a few hours. When the funeral of singer Hank Williams was drawing a large crowd in 1953, Azbell ordered *The Montgomery Advertiser* to stop the presses. He had the front cover redesigned, adding the story of the country music legend's funeral. Azbell's boss stormed into the office and fired him for costing the paper a lot of money to publish a story no one cared about.

By the end of the day, with over 20,000 mourners in town, the special edition featuring the Williams story had sold out. Realizing the error of their ways, the management at the *Advertiser* pleaded with Azbell to return. Joe Azbell left the *Advertiser* in 1968, joining the *Montgomery Independent* and authoring weekly columns until 1995. His last column was published the week after he died.

Azbell's son, David, has become a political force in his own right. The young Azbell has seemingly inherited his father's gifts for political messaging and reading people. The younger Azbell, like his father, has crafted messaging and communications for both governors and presidential candidates. David was the press secretary for Governor Bob Riley, served as an advisor to Republican presidential nominee Senator John McCain, served as press secretary to Governor Fob James, and as the last spokesman for George C. Wallace. He authored, along with Mike Hubbard, then Alabama Speaker of the House, *Storming The Statehouse*, an account of the Republican takeover of Alabama politics in 2010. He has orchestrated countless successful candidacies and referendum votes, providing strategies, tactics, and messaging.

Joe Azbell, as a lover of history, would no doubt be thrilled by his son's collection of memorabilia and political artifacts that make his Montgomery office almost as much of a museum as office space. The office has become an unofficial tourist destination for political junkies and amateur historians. David enjoys thousands of followers for his writing on social media. Although not a reporter, David Azbell's thousands of loyal Facebook followers have empowered him to keep his dad's tradition of political and historical stories alive for future generations.

Rev. Frank Barker
Co-founder, Presbyterian Church of America
Jefferson County

Maybe it began during his years in the skies as a jet pilot for the U.S. Navy. For almost 60 years, Dr. Frank M. Barker has spent his entire career soaring and helping others to do the same.

Born in Birmingham, Barker studied at Auburn University, where he earned a degree in textile engineering (1953) before entering the U.S. Navy. After four years of soaring to the skies, he enrolled in Columbia University, where he earned the Bachelor of Divinity and the Master of Theology degrees.

The next major event of his career was described by the church history of Briarwood Presbyterian Church:

Ordained in 1960 by Birmingham Presbytery of the Presbyterian Church in the United States, Dr. Barker became the Pastor of a recently gathered group of Presbyterians who were soon to be organized as the Briarwood Presbyterian Church. From a congregation of 35 members, meeting in a storefront building in 1960, Briarwood grew to a membership of over 4,000.

The theme of soaring to new heights continued in 1973, when Barker became one of the rare people who not only served as the founding pastor of a church, but also of a major church denomination, the Presbyterian Church in America (P.C.A.). Barker and his Briarwood church hosted the first and founding meeting of the PCA, which now includes over 1,500 churches.

Even in the decades following his retirement, Barker has continued the Saturday morning Bible studies at his home, and serves as head of the Department of Old Testament at Birmingham Theological Seminary.

Julia Tarrant Barron
Founder, Judson College and Howard College
Perry County

What do Samford University, Judson College, and *The Alabama Baptist* newspaper have in common?

All three were founded by an extraordinary woman, Julia Tarrant Barron.

Born Julia Tarrant in South Carolina, Julia moved with her family during childhood to the area called Elyton at the time. Tarrant City, in metropolitan Birmingham, is named for her family. At age 23, she married fellow South Carolina native William Barron, and the couple moved to Marion, Alabama (Perry County). William Barron was a highly successful businessman, but by Julia's 28th birthday, William had died and she had become a widow.

Julia Tarrant Barron was blessed with vast resources and an equally large reservoir of generosity. She donated the land for the new sanctuary of her church, Siloam Baptist Church of Marion. According to the Alabama Women's Hall of Fame, she convened a meeting at her home that

Catchin' BASS
& takin' names

The commercial bass fishing industry began in Alabama

It was the first major bass fishing tournament of the year.

Actually, it was the first major bass fishing tournament...ever.

In June of 1967, Montgomery insurance salesman Ray Scott hosted the First All-American Invitational Bass Tournament at Beaver Lake in Arkansas. Scott saw the almost limitless potential of a sport that few, especially in the media, took seriously. He organized the tournament, set strict rules to give credibility to the event, and established prizes for the winning fisherman.

Today, the organization Scott founded, Bass Anglers Sportsman Society (BASS), has become the world's largest fishing organization. Just as Scott foresaw, bass fishing has become a multibillion dollar sport. BASS now includes television programs, websites, magazines, instructional programs, and of course the world-famous tournaments.

The ESPN network purchased the organization and used it as the core of its outdoors programming. In 2011, an ownership group headed by Alabama native and publishing executive Don Logan purchased the organization and moved its headquarters to Birmingham.

In 2018, the BASS organization celebrated its 50th anniversary, all thanks to Ray Scott's ability to see the potential that had escaped the attention of the world.

Blount County's Gerald Swindle has become one of the outstanding anglers in all of BASS fishing. He has twice been named 2016 Toyota Bassmaster Angler of the Year (2004 and 2016), and won the Southern Open points championship in 2011.

The Locust Fork native has also become known as one of the funniest anglers in the business, keeping fans and reporters entertained with his humor.

resulted in the establishment of Judson College in Marion, a Christian school created for women. Largely for the benefit of her son, John Thomas Barron, she was instrumental in founding a Christian college in Birmingham, Howard College (later renamed Samford University). John Thomas Barron was, fittingly, the first graduate of Howard College in 1846.

Julia also founded *The Alabama Baptist*, a newspaper for Baptists in the state, along with her pastor, Milo P. Jewett.

Unfortunately, the Civil War begat Reconstruction and the implosion of many rural economies. Julia's hometown of Marion was no exception. The once wealthy Julia Barron lived her remaining years in poverty. According to the Alabama Women's Hall of Fame, her pastor asked her about living in poverty after giving away so much of what she owned.

Her answer revealed the true measure of a great person.

"I only wish I had more to give."

John "Big Daddy" Bishop
Founder, Dreamland BBQ
Tuscaloosa County

It was the year everything changed in Tuscaloosa.

When 1958 began, football championships stood in the distant past, and there wasn't much happening in the Jerusalem Heights area of Tuscaloosa. Before the year's end, the University of Alabama hired Bear Bryant as its football coach and John "Big Daddy" Bishop founded the Dreamland BBQ restaurant in Jerusalem Heights.

A professional brick mason, Bishop decided to start his own business to better support his family, but couldn't decide whether to open a mortuary or a restaurant. As legend has it, he prayed fervently for God to reveal the correct path, and soon thereafter had a dream that instructed him to open a restaurant right next door to his home.

Obeying that dream, Big Daddy Bishop turned it into a reality and made the word "dream" a part of the name.

The rest, as they say, is history, and history has been kind to Bishop and his family ever since. For decades, Dreamland has been known for serving only ribs and white sliced bread at their original Jerusalem Heights location. In the early days, as many don't know, they sold everything from postage stamps to sandwiches. Eventually, the ribs & bread menu became a national sensation, with television broadcasters, famous personalities, political leaders, national reporters, world famous athletes, tourists, and just about everyone else coming to the land of Big Daddy's dream and indescribably good sauce.

Dreamland now enjoys multiple locations and an expanded menu while remaining true to its mission of delicious ribs and honoring the dream of the man who asked God to help him provide for his family.

Rick Bragg
Pulitzer Prize winning author
Calhoun County

Rick Bragg has enjoyed a rare career in which the Pulitzer Prize was only the beginning of his many successes. Raised in the area of Piedmont, Alabama (Calhoun County), Bragg has joined William Faulkner and Harper Lee as history's great scribes about all things from the Deep South. His debut novels became national best-sellers, establishing him as an elite author. The subject matter of his writing has typically arisen from his life, his complicated family, and his beloved Piedmont. Bragg tells the story of the unbounded love, unparalleled work ethic, and unsurpassed Southern cooking that defined his mother, Margaret. He describes, sometimes unsparingly, his fallen father, an absentee parent who struggled with addiction, trauma from the Korean War, and economic despair.

His books *All Over But the Shoutin*, *Ava's Man*, and *The Prince of Frogtown* are widely considered as classics of modern Southern literature.

Bragg has authored other books including a 2018 cookbook stuffed with recipes lovingly crafted by his mom. Ironically, she owned neither a recipe book nor notes about her own recipes. Loaded with great recipes and even better stories, the book artfully celebrates the distinctively Southern food culture.

As the world learned from his columns in *Southern Living* magazine, Bragg's literary career began when he would compose prose or write recited words from Mark Twain in notebooks meant for academic classes. He often did so during school time that was also meant for those classes. Officially though, his career began when he was hired as a reporter for *The Anniston Star*. A meteoric rise followed, landing him at the *St. Petersburg Times* and then at the *New York Times*. Bragg's coverage of the 1995 bombing of the Murrah Federal Building in Oklahoma City earned him the Pulitzer Prize for Feature Writing.

Many have written about Southern culture, but few have managed to do so as artfully, provincially, and humorously as Rick Bragg.

Bill Britt
Founder, Alabama
Political Reporter

Bill Britt has been called the premier political investigative reporter in the state. He has been named one of Alabama's top political reporters. The national political website, ballotpedia.org, named him one of the "top influencers" in the state of Alabama.

Britt serves as editor in chief of *Alabama Political Reporter*, a news website covering political news in the state. He also hosts a weekly television show, "The Voice of Alabama Politics." Britt developed and grew *Alabama Political Reporter* to become a primary source for the state's political news, pioneering the online politics industry in the state. Susan Britt serves as associate editor, as well as a weekly panelist on the television show.

Bill and Susan lived comfortably in New York until shortly after September 11, 2001, when they decided to return to their southern roots and their aging parents.

Their website and television show have become a weekly staple for political junkies across Alabama.

Harry Brock
Founder, Compass Bank
Jefferson County

Through innovative thinking and a dynamic personality, Harry Brock transformed banking in the state of Alabama and laid the foundation for Birmingham to become an interstate banking hub.

After co-founding a bank in the 1960s, Brock helped join together two banks to form a registered bank holding company, Central and State National Corporation of Alabama, in 1971. Then Brock went to work seeking to reform state banking laws and influenced the passage of the Statewide Bank Merger bill of 1980. That allowed banks to open branches beyond county lines, and paved the way for Brock's Central Bank to become a growing financial institution with the type of lending power that would benefit customers throughout the state.

In 1987, Brock led Central Bank to acquire a bank in Texas and became the first state bank to own a bank in another state. Renaming the newly expanded bank as Compass Bank, Brock spearheaded the growth that made Birmingham a regional banking center with multiple holding company banks in the Brock model.

Fittingly, the Brock School of Business at Samford University is named in memory of Brock, who was a pioneer in the growth of banking and who had also served as Chairman of the Samford University Board of Trustees.

Brock was inducted into the Alabama Academy of Honor in August,1983 and the Alabama Business Hall of Fame in October, 1993. He received an honorary doctorate from Samford University in 1994.

The Bromberg family
Founders, Bromberg Jewelers
Jefferson County

The year 1836 brought plenty of memorable events, such as Sam Houston's election as President of the Republic of Texas and the creation of the Wisconsin Territory. A number of famous people passed away that year, such as one of America's founding fathers and Presidents, James Madison, along with Betsy Ross (who sewed the first American flag). In Alabama, a Prussian immigrant named Frederick Bromberg established a jewelry business based on quality products and personal service.

Today, Alabama's oldest business operation is also the state's oldest family-operated business. It's almost hard to imagine that Bromberg's was founded while James Madison and Betsy Ross were still alive, but the longevity of the family business stands as a tribute to the successful vision of Frederick Bromberg over 150 years ago.

Frederick Bromberg somehow maintained his initial success, even as American society was ripped apart by the Civil War. His son, also named Frederick, continued the store's success, and his four sons helped guide the business through the Great Depression and beyond. The business expanded to Birmingham from the original location in Mobile (which ultimately closed, leaving Birmingham as the hub of the business).

Beginning in the 1950s, Bromberg's began expanding their operations by acquiring local jewelry businesses in other communities. Today, Bromberg's offers many items from the top designers, as well as custom-designed pieces from their master jewelers. The family has also continued its leadership beyond the business world, producing leaders such as Frank Bromberg, Jr., who served on the University of Alabama System Board of Trustees and helped lead the three campuses to unprecedented growth.

The Bruno family
Founders, Bruno's grocery
Jefferson County

By the time Joe Bruno opened his first grocery store in downtown Birmingham, he already had six years of experience under his belt.

Also, he was only 18 years old.

Bruno founded his grocery store in 1932, and as one writer described, it would have fit into a meat locker. Humble beginnings didn't matter much to Joe, one of eight children of Sicilian immigrants. Hard work, fair prices, and unmatched service brought success and then a second location.

As Bruno's expanded, Joe brought his brothers into what had become the family business. The brothers worked hard, played by the rules, and gave back to the public even while providing the best groceries at the best prices.

Before long, the Bruno's family included many more people than Joe and his brothers. They opened additional stores under the names Food World and Consumer Warehouse. By the family's 50th anniversary in the grocery business, they operated over 50 grocery stores in multiple states, with an additional 40 stores of their drug store chain, Big B Drugs.

Joe retired in 1977 and served as chairman emeritus of the store chain. Brother Angelo became chairman with Angelo's son, Ron, serving as President and CEO. In 1991, tragedy struck the family, as Joe's brothers Angelo and Lee were killed when a corporate plane crashed in Georgia. Also killed in the plane were Sam Vacarella, senior vice president of merchandise; Edward C. Hyde, vice president of store operations; R. Randy Paige Jr., vice president of personnel; Karl Mollica, director of produce; Mary Faust, senior vice president of Bruno's advertising agency, Steiner-Bressler; and pilots John Tesney and Rob Stamps.

Ultimately, the Bruno family sold the massive company that had become their signature business, but their family name lives in the public eye through the seemingly endless gifts of resources, time, and leadership through the past 80 years. The groups and causes supported by the Bruno family and the Joseph S. Bruno Charitable Foundation would fill the pages of another book, but one organization has kept them in the food business, the Urban Food Project. "The project operates a local food distribution system that improves production, purchasing and delivery of healthy local food to Birmingham restaurants, wholesalers and retailers," according to the foundation's website.

In 1995, Anne Bruno LaRussa founded Oasis Counseling, "one of the few women's counseling centers in the state, providing services to women throughout their life span, from the very young to the very wise," as described by its website.

Jack Caddell
Founder, Jack's restaurants
Jefferson County

Most people in Alabama know Jack Caddell by his first name, even if they don't know who he was.

That's because Jack's Family Restaurants, founded in Homewood in 1960, has fed countless people from Alabama and beyond.

Jack Caddell started his restaurant in Homewood, the first fast-food place in Alabama, by using the simple concept of inexpensive food items such as hamburgers (15 cents), fries (15 cents), and shakes (20 cents). He cleverly marketed his business by using leading local celebrities such as Bozo the Clown, Cousin Cliff, and Romper Room Jane, who appealed to children and families.

Through it all, Jack's motto for his employees never changed: "Smiling Faces, Friendly Service."

Today, hungry Southerners can find Jack's Family Restaurants in more than 145 locations in Alabama, Tennessee, Mississippi and Georgia.

That's why they can't wait to go back-back-back to Jack-Jack-Jack's for more-more-more.

TRIVIA

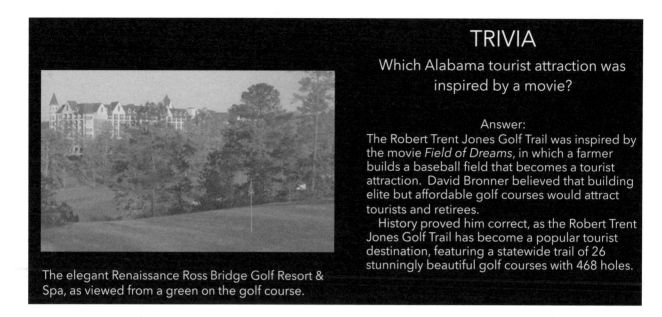

Which Alabama tourist attraction was inspired by a movie?

The elegant Renaissance Ross Bridge Golf Resort & Spa, as viewed from a green on the golf course.

Answer:
The Robert Trent Jones Golf Trail was inspired by the movie *Field of Dreams*, in which a farmer builds a baseball field that becomes a tourist attraction. David Bronner believed that building elite but affordable golf courses would attract tourists and retirees.

History proved him correct, as the Robert Trent Jones Golf Trail has become a popular tourist destination, featuring a statewide trail of 26 stunningly beautiful golf courses with 468 holes.

Truman Capote
Best-selling author
Monroe County

Authors, as the saying goes, should write what they know. For Truman Capote, the ability to compose compelling prose with dramatic flair flowed from his turbulent youth.

Born in New Orleans with the name Truman Streckfus Persons, Truman endured the divorce of his parents during his childhood. His parents, and especially his custodial mother, often left him with cousins in Monroeville, Alabama. The small town became an anchor of stability for young Truman, who badly needed one. After his mom remarried, Truman was adopted by his stepfather, and took his last name, Capote.

The Monroeville cousins had a next-door neighbor named Harper Lee, who became his lifelong friend and later his perceived rival. It would be difficult to overstate the importance of Monroeville on the life of Capote. The peaceful town, the stability of the cousins with whom he lived, and the friendship with Lee empowered confidence and creativity in young Truman. Years later, Harper Lee accompanied Capote to Kansas on interviews for the article about the murders of four people. The account would become the foundation for *In Cold Blood*, the book that revolutionized the literature of dramatic nonfiction.

Between his Monroeville childhood and the adult success, Capote moved to New York City with his parents, enrolling in schools in New York, then Greenwich, Connecticut, and then again in New York. Although considered a bright and talented writer, Capote paid little attention to academics. He actually had to repeat the 12th grade after making frequent trips to Manhattan nightclubs with socialites including Gloria Vanderbilt and playwright Eugene O'Neill's daughter, Oona.

Capote pursued his literary career, and composed works that have become classics, such as *Breakfast At Tiffany's*, *Other Voices, Other Rooms*, and, of course, *In Cold Blood*. In his later years, Capote endured personal and health issues, but remained one of the most socially prominent artists of the twentieth century.

Notwithstanding his personal difficulties, Capote remains a glamorous and influential presence in the history of American literature, thanks in no small part to Harper Lee and Monroeville, Alabama.

Milo & Beatrice Carlton
Founders, Milo's restaurants
Jefferson County

The journey began on a hot summer afternoon, on Birmingham's north side, near the Carraway Methodist Hospital, in August of 1946. Former U.S. Army chef Milo Carlton had returned from World War II, and he was putting his culinary skills to work to open his brand new restaurant, appropriately named Milo's.

Although he was a talented cook, Milo needed several jobs filled, including bookkeeper, someone to deal with vendors, someone to run the cash register, someone to monitor the quality control of the food and the popular sweet tea, and someone to get the food to the customers and make sure they were happy.

Thankfully for Milo, his bride Beatrice was able to handle all of those jobs, and the restaurant saw immediate success. The secret sauce that transforms hamburgers, along with the delicious sweet tea, became the signature items on the menu.

Their son, Ronnie, conceived the excellent idea to franchise the restaurant. The result of Ronnie's idea is that Milo's has become a restaurant with 15 locations in the Birmingham metro area and Tuscaloosa.

In 2002 the family sold the restaurants and focused on their famously successful sweet tea business. The family now sells the tea in Milo's restaurants, in grocery stores, and in convenience stores. A large facility in Bessemer now houses the Milo's sweet tea operation, and the number of loyal customers grows each year. The business is now run by Tricia Wallwork, the CEO of Milo's Tea, who is also the granddaughter of Milo and Beatrice Carlton.

The Carraway family
Carraway Methodist Hospital
Jefferson County

He knew they needed help, and he decided to act. Dr. Charles Carraway understood that the coal miners living in northern Birmingham needed adequate medical care. In 1908, Dr. Carraway opened a 16-bed clinic beside his home. Carraway had been inspired by William and Charles Mayo, who brought multiple physicians into one practice in Minnesota for their Mayo Clinic. Modeling his own facility after Mayo, he formed the first multi-specialty practice in Alabama.

Dr. Carraway also helped found what would become Blue Cross Blue Shield of Alabama (then known as Hospital Service Corporation) and the state's first surgical training program.

Carraway Hospital became one of the region's leading healthcare facilities, and the blue star atop the hospital became both a landmark and source of pride in the northern part of the city.

After Dr. Carraway suffered a stroke in 1957, his son, Dr. Ben Carraway, was chosen as the new Chief Executive Officer. The younger Carraway began a massive building program for the hospital, which had now become Carraway Methodist Hospital. During his tenure as leader, the hospital expanded from 257 to 617 beds. In the 1980s, he kept the hospital on the cutting edge with improvements such as a Lifesaver emergency helicopter service, a trauma center, a hyperbaric oxygen therapy department, and a wound care center.

In 1993, the third generation of Carraway leadership was realized, as Dr. Robert Carraway succeeded his grandfather and father. Although the youngest Carraway physician brought great progress to the hospital, two issues hurt the hospital financially. First, Carraway's selfless devotion to the patients caused hardship, as the hospital routinely treated those with no means to pay and offered sizable discounts to ministers. Also, despite the growth and dynamic leadership, the reality of economics on the north side of town finally overcame the infrastructure, leadership, and talented doctors. The hospital was losing money at an unacceptable rate, and Carraway Hospital was sold to a medical group called Physicians Medical Center Carraway.

History will remember the Carraway family of doctors for providing excellent care and selfless devotion to their patients, and to their beloved Birmingham.

George Washington Carver
Inventor, educator
Macon County

George Washington Carver's path into the history books began in his infancy, when he was kidnapped. Owned by the Carver family from Missouri, he was taken by slave raiders, along with his mother and sister. They were sold at auction, but Moses Carver, the legal owner of George and his family, paid a professional to find and retrieve them. The hunter only found little George, whom he purchased by exchanging one of Moses Carver's horses.

Thereafter, Moses Carver and his wife, Susan, raised George and his brother James on their Missouri farm as if they were their own children. Because of George's physical frailties, Susan kept him inside the home and spent time teaching him how to read and write, sew, do laundry, cook, and prepare herbal medicines. Even as a child, George developed the nickname "The Plant Doctor" because of his interest and work with cultivating plants and protecting them from insects.

In his teenage years, George left the Carver home, living a nomadic lifestyle and taking classes at various schools. Carver ultimately enrolled at Iowa State University, where he earned bachelors and graduate degrees. His studies under the the highly regarded mycologist (fungal scientist) L. H. Pammel made him an attractive candidate for a faculty position after he earned his graduate degree.

Carver entertained several offers for teaching positions, but accepted the offer of Booker T. Washington at the Tuskegee Institute (now Tuskegee University). At Tuskegee, Carver revolutionized farming practices as well as the peanut and sweet potato industries. He discovered that cotton exhausted the soil of certain nutrients, but that peanuts and sweet potatoes replenished the soil and made it suitable for cotton just a few years later.

The only problem with the crop rotation was that it created a surplus of peanuts and sweet potatoes, which Carver decided to remedy. He developed new uses for different crops, especially peanuts, by creating medicines from peanuts, as well as milk, paper, Worcestershire sauce, soaps, punches, cooking oils, cosmetics and stains for wood. Carver might be most famous for his work with peanut butter.

When Carver passed away in 1943, at the age of 78, he became the first non-U.S. president in American history to be honored with a national monument, when President Franklin D. Roosevelt commissioned the George Washington Carver monument.

The world will always benefit from the knowledge and discoveries of George Washington Carver and his team at Tuskegee University in Macon County, Alabama.

Trivia

Which Auburn University graduate holds over 400 patents for his inventions?

Harry Knowles grew up in Birmingham and graduated from Ensley High School. His father held six patents for technical inventions, and his half-brother was an early pioneer in the development of hearing aids.

After graduating from Auburn in 1961, Harry Knowles became one of the greatest inventors since Thomas Edison. Most of his inventions came in the realms of bar code and laser technology. Over 400 patents were granted for his inventions.

Amazingly, his contributions to the world of science did not end there. He founded the Knowles Science Teaching Foundation that trains, supports, and mentors teachers across America.

Mark Childress
Best-selling novelist
Monroe County

In 1993, *Crazy in Alabama* became one of America's best-selling novels, making the national lists and earning the honor of one of the Ten Best Novels of the year. The anthem of Southern eccentricity, the book has been translated into no less than eight different languages. The story has also been made into a movie, premiering at the New Orleans Film Festival.

For author Mark Childress, the novel wasn't his first to make the Ten Best Novels of a given year, and it wasn't his first great seller, but it has become his signature work. Childress had the good fortune to have been born in Monroeville, Alabama, the launching pad for some of America's greatest novelists. After moving several times during his childhood, Childress eventually graduated from the University of Alabama in 1978 and became a reporter for *The Birmingham News*. His gift for storytelling was not lost on readers, and he rose quickly in his profession, becoming the features editor of *Southern Living* magazine.

Ultimately, Childress submitted to his life's calling and left the prominent magazine to concentrate on his budding career as a novelist.

Most of Childress' fiction portrays Southern culture and society in the twentieth century. He deftly develops characters who possess eccentricities that create endless openings for his trademark humor and plot twists. Other honors for Childress, beyond the best-seller lists and Top Ten Novels awards, include the Distinguished Alumni Award and the Thomas Wolfe Award from the University of Alabama, and the Alabama Library Association's Writer of the Year in 1994.

Jan Crawford
National television reporter
Morgan County

News watchers across America and beyond learn about national politics, and especially the court system, from Morgan County's own Jan Crawford.

A graduate of Brewer High School, Crawford emerged as a leading journalist at the University of Alabama. There, she developed her skills with the student newspaper, *The Crimson White*. After her Tuscaloosa years, she graduated from the University of Chicago School of Law and chose a career in journalism.

Crawford has emerged as a leading national reporter for CBS News, appearing on Face the Nation, the CBS Evening News, and CBS News Sunday Morning.

In its coverage of presidential elections and supreme court confirmations, CBS has turned to its star reporter for enlightened analysis and well-sourced reporting.

Beyond the realm of reporting, Crawford also became a *New York Times* bestselling author with her book, *Supreme Conflict: The Inside Story of the Struggle for Control of the United States Supreme Court*, published in 2007.

Emory Cunningham
Founder, Southern Living magazine
Walker and Jefferson Counties

It was time, he decided, to tell the other side of the story.

In the late 1950s, Americans typically received their news from the evening news broadcasts of the three major networks, along with newspapers. For a few years, Emory Cunningham and his wife Jeanne lived in Chicago because of his job. During that time, they watched the national media berate, belittle, and belie the Deep South and its people. Although unsavory things were happening there (and elsewhere), the media, he believed, was painting an image of the entire region and its people with a broad brush.

Fortunately for the Deep South, Cunningham was also a part of the media, having moved to Chicago for his job with *Progressive Farmer* magazine. It was during the Chicago years that Cunningham, who was raised on his family's farm in Kansas, Alabama, decided to tell the other side of the story.

Cunningham decided to launch a new magazine, through the parent company *Progressive Farmer*, that would celebrate life in the Deep South. He decided to name it *Southern Living*, and he believed in his heart and considerably strong intellect that the magazine would be well received in the South and beyond.

There was only one problem; the *Progressive Farmer* executives were not interested, at least initially.

Southern Living was a big idea with a big vision for his company's growth, but big things were nothing new to Cunningham, who was a whopping 14 pounds at birth. Although it took years to make his dream a reality, Cunningham launched *Southern Living*, a magazine that became its own industry of various magazines, cookbooks, and other publications. Even during explosive growth, Cunningham's dynamic vision and leadership guided the company. He personally designed the conceptual design of the Southern Progress headquarters in Birmingham, and negotiated the company's acquisition by Time Warner without attorneys.

Cunningham's leadership extended beyond the publishing industry, including service to his alma mater as Chairman, Auburn University Board of Trustees.

Coffee family
North Alabama pioneers
Lauderdale County

John Coffee founded the City of Florence, became a business partner of future President Andrew Jackson, and served as a Brigadier General in the United States Army.

He also helped determine the borders of Alabama, Mississippi, and Tennessee.

The founding and development of Florence came after his years as a war hero, when Coffee formed the Cypress Land Company to develop land in Northwest Alabama. He acquired investors who trusted and believed in his ability, such as Jackson, Alabama's future governor Thomas Bibb, and a future associate justice of the United States Supreme Court, John McKinley.

Coffee's wife, Mary Donelson Coffee, was the niece of Andrew Jackson's wife Rachel. President Jackson developed many ties to the state of Alabama, but none were closer than his relationship to the Coffee family.

John and Mary had nine children. Their son, Alexander Coffee, carved out his own path to success and wealth. He founded the Globe Factory, a partnership whose holdings included mills producing cotton thread, cloth and grist for corn meal.

Alexander's daughter Mary (from his first wife) married Edward A. O'Neal Jr., son of Alabama governor Edward A. O'Neal. That marked the merger of two of the state's most important families. His second marriage produced a daughter, Eliza, who died at age 25. The Eliza Coffee Memorial Hospital in Florence was named after her.

Hugh Daniel
Founder, Daniel Construction
Jefferson County

In downtown Birmingham, the Daniel building still stands prominently on 20th Street, the main artery between the business district and the Southside area. Hugh Daniel Drive connects Highway 280 with a host of homes, subdivisions, golf courses, and horse farms in Shelby County.

In the world of charitable giving, the Daniel Foundation of Alabama has become an important benefactor for causes in the Birmingham area and beyond.

So how and why did the Daniel name become so prominent?

Hugh Daniel, the patriarch of today's Daniel family, was a visionary builder.

Daniel first built the foundation of knowledge for his career, graduating from The Citadel as valedictorian of the class of 1929. In 1934, he joined his brother in Daniel Construction, which was all about building new creations. The next year, he decided to build a new business, opening a Daniel Construction office in Birmingham. After the company completed two shipyard constructions during World War II, Daniel joined the U.S. Navy, serving as a lieutenant in the Civil Engineering Corps.

Daniel's creativity and love for building extended beyond physical structures, as he also co-founded and built Central Bank, which today is known as BBVA Compass Bank.

Forever a builder, Daniel assumed leadership roles in existing community organizations and helped them soar to even greater success. Some of those included the Birmingham Committee of 100, Chamber of Commerce, Baptist Hospitals Foundation, Birmingham Museum of Art, the Southern Research Institute, the Birmingham Symphony Association, and the Board of Trustees of Birmingham-Southern College.

Morris Dees
Southern Poverty Law Center
Montgomery County

Morris Dees has become one of the world's most recognized names in the realm of civil justice. As an attorney, he has won landmark cases and multi-million dollar lawsuits. Many idealists speak of changing the world, but Morris Dees has actually done it through his tireless work on behalf of the downtrodden and forgotten.

But it didn't start out that way.

Dees shared a career path similarly situated to two other giants of public service, Clifford Durr and Millard Fuller. All three earned law degrees, began professional lives in the mainstream of society's elite, and then abandoned their careers for the service of the less fortunate.

Joining his friend Millard Fuller, Dees originally founded a marketing company (Fuller & Dees), made it extremely profitable, then sold it to the parent company of the *Los Angeles Times*.

For Dees, the deciding factor in selling the company was the inspiring book by Clarence Darrow: *The Story of My Life*. It was time, he decided, to devote his career to a cause higher than himself.

Dees co-founded the Southern Poverty Law Center, an organization that uses the judicial system, education, publications, the Civil Rights Memorial Center, and other means to combat hate groups, remedy situations involving miscarriages of justice, and educate the public on the benefits of tolerance.

The Southern Poverty Law Center has become a top source of public information for tracking the formation, growth, and activities of hate groups. The center's press releases on this subject typically gain national attention. These efforts, especially in the arena of the judicial system, have slowed or even crippled the activities of hate groups.

Seemingly unaffected by controversy, Dees remains a top public face of the fight for civil rights in the 21st century.

Drummond family
International coal mining
Walker and Jefferson Counties

One brilliant man in Sipsey turned three mules into the foundation of a multi-billion dollar global empire.

H. E. Drummond used his three mules as collateral for a $300 loan from the Walker County Bank. With those funds, he founded H.E. Drummond Coal Company, and changed Walker County forever. As Alabama celebrates its bicentennial, Drummond has expanded the scope of its company's success to multiple ventures outside the realm of coal mining, including real estate development in Alabama, Florida, and California. Although the Drummond sons are publicly identified with the company, H. E. Drummond's daughters were active board members, and Barbara Drummond Thorne became a longtime trustee of Samford University, where a prominent building is named in her memory.

The journey of a family and a business empire presents a compelling story...

By the Numbers

3...H. E. Drummond used his three mules as collateral for the loan to start the H. E. Drummond Coal Company.

0...The number of places in the world where Drummond does not have the capacity to ship coal to customers. Their wholly owned subsidiaries make Drummond a one-stop operation from the mining to the actual delivery.

1956...The year that H. E. Drummond passed away suddenly, and his sons quickly moved to take up the mantle of their father's successful leadership. Son Don Drummond became company president, and his brother Segal became vice president of sales and finance.

1...After graduating from the University of Alabama in 1961, Garry Neil Drummond became the first engineer hired by Drummond Coal. The company now employs approximately 325 engineers.

1970...The year that Drummond reached its first agreement to supply coal to the nation of Japan. Since that historic agreement, Drummond has become an international force in the coal industry.

90...In the decade of the nineties, Drummond acquired mines in the nation of Columbia and in Wyoming.

Marshall Durbin
Founder, Marshall Durbin company
Jefferson County

Marshall Durbin was a creator, a founder, a visionary, and a man unaffected by the hurdles of doubt or fear.

He founded a real estate business, but the stock market crash of 1929 and the Great Depression left him unable to make a good income. Undeterred in his confidence, he borrowed $500 from a friend and opened a fish stand in his hometown of Birmingham. He added poultry and opened a second stand two years later.

Soon, he discarded fish and focused on poultry, expanding his operations in a three-story building in Birmingham that contained refrigeration equipment.

Durbin, still a creator, gradually began adding facilities

in Jasper, Haleyville, and other locations in Alabama and beyond. Marshall Durbin, Jr., explained the secret of his father's success:

"His principal business philosophy was hard work and lots of it. In the early years, he would be on the streets making personal calls to hotels and restaurants at 4 a.m., calling on the chefs in person. There was a lot of competition, and often the company that got the business was the first one there. He always tried to be the first one there."

Durbin was a founder, not only for his own benefit, but for his industry. He co-founded the National Broiler Council, the Alabama Poultry and Egg Association, and the National Broiler Marketing Association.

At his passing, in 1971, Marshall Durbin was succeeded by his son, Marshall, Jr. The result became an expanded operation, and by 1996 the company was producing 111 million chickens per year.

Zelda Fitzgerald
Acclaimed author
Montgomery County

Perhaps no two Americans personified the roaring 1920s more than novelist F. Scott Fitzgerald and his wife, fellow author Zelda Sayre Fitzgerald.

Zelda's upbringing didn't exactly lend itself to a future of wild parties and a decadent lifestyle. She was the youngest child of an Alabama Supreme Court Justice, Anthony Dickinson Sayre.

One summer, she met a young officer and aspiring author stationed at Camp Sheridan. His name was F. Scott Fitzgerald, and they immediately began dating and partying.

The couple famously made international headlines as they lived in America and in France. Zelda became the ultimate embodiment of the 1920s woman, rising above the stifling norms of the past, forging her own identity as a socialite and an author in her own right.

The Fitzgeralds partied in New York, Paris and the French Riviera. They partied in Montgomery. They even partied frequently in Selma, in the brownstone mansion that still stands imposingly on Lapsley Steet.

Unfortunately, the seemingly endless supply of alcohol and partying gave rise to serious health issues for them both. F. Scott Fitzgerald passed away at 44 and Zelda at 47.

From the night the two met in Montgomery, they began the journey that would make them the signature couple of an entire era. Thanks to the generosity of prominent Alabama attorney Julian McPhillips, Zelda's Montgomery home now houses a museum dedicated to preserving the legacy of F. Scott and Zelda Fitzgerald.

Steve Flowers
Author, political guru
Pike County

Anyone wanting to understand Alabama politics can look no further than the career, interviews, and writings of the great Steve Flowers.

Each week, the column about Alabama politics by Flowers appears in over 60 newspapers, with a circulation just a little south of half-million readers.

Undefeated in his political career, Flowers served five terms in the Alabama House of Representatives. During his service Flowers was voted the Most Outstanding Member, and the Most Ethical Member of that body. In his first year, he was voted the outstanding freshman member by *Alabama Magazine*. Flowers honed political skills during his formative years in his hometown of Troy, as a 12-year-old page in the Legislature, and later as a student leader at the University of Alabama.

After leaving elective office, Flowers has continued winning in the world of politics. In addition to his highly successful weekly column, he co-authored one of the great books on the state's rich political history: *Of Goats & Governors: Six Decades of Colorful Alabama Political Stories*.

Flowers hosts a weekly radio show, and has analyzed Alabama politics for national television audiences on CBS, ABC, PBS, Fox, CNN, Bloomberg and the BBC (British Broadcasting Network).

Dr. Wayne Flynt
Author, historian
Lee and Calhoun Counties

He has become one of the Deep South's most highly acclaimed scholars. His admirers include, well, just about anyone who has ever read his books, heard his speeches, or learned of his impeccable reputation.

Dr. Wayne Flynt was hired by Auburn University in 1977 (from Samford University), and has remained there for the duration of his career and retirement. That long-term stability has served as a stark contrast to his nomadic childhood, during which his hometown was wherever his father's sales jobs took the family that year.

To his great delight, Flynt was able to settle in and enjoy one high school, Anniston High School, where he thrived as a leader and debate champion. His debate partner was the future United States Senator Donald Stewart.

Although recruited by the University of Alabama's national championship debate coach Annabel Hagood, Flynt pursued his education at Howard College (now Samford University). While a student at Howard, Flynt organized a reading program for African-American youngsters in the Homewood suburb of Birmingham. He also helped organize a voter registration drive for African Americans. Both endeavors sparked the disapproval of leaders from the college's board of trustees and prominent alumni.

Unlike many of his fellow believers in the Civil Rights Movement, Flynt did not arrive at his opinions through the influences of others, the speeches of dynamic leaders, or as a form of rebellion. Flynt studied the Holy Bible at a depth normally not undertaken by teenagers, and found that the words of Jesus Christ were incongruent with the racism, segregation, discrimination, condescension, and even hate that he saw in the culture of the Deep South. Even some leaders of Christian churches, he concluded, said, did, and taught things that directly opposed the teachings of Christ and the Bible as a whole.

A deeply spiritual youngster, Flynt was propelled to action by his Bible, just as he still is. That was why he risked the ire of college leaders with his voters drive and the tutoring program.

Frustrated by both the culture and the climate of strife, Flynt and his wife, Dorothy Ann ("Dartie"), moved to Tallahassee, Florida, where he successfully pursued a master's and doctorate from Florida State University. He loved many people in Alabama, but chose not to return there as a resident.

Everything changed, however, when he read a certain book.

He read the great American novel, *To Kill A Mockingbird,*

which was written by Alabama native, Nelle Harper Lee. Inspired by the powerful story, flawless writing and challenges posed by the novel, Flynt gained a renewed love for his home state and ultimately moved back. After spending time at Samford University, Flynt was hired by Auburn University in 1977.

Even beyond his compelling lectures, Dr. Flynt has become the state's premier historian over the past 40 years. His success arises in part from his writing about the people and events that historians so often overlook. While other academics concentrate on the famous, powerful, or wealthy, Flynt has often told the stories of poor working people and lower middle class workers who worked hard, played by the rules, and defined the culture and values of the society.

Each of his books has become a valuable addition to the state's recorded history. His most recent work before Alabama's bicentennial celebration was an exploration of the remarkable correspondence between Flynt and Harper Lee, the great American novelist whose signature work convinced Flynt to return to Alabama.

Harper Lee, who became one of Dr. Flynt's biggest fans, described his writing as both a national treasure and works of art.

Flynt's philosophy of "living existentially" arises from his biblically-based belief that each day is a gift from God, that our existence and purpose arises from serving God, and that the way in which we treat our fellow humans matters greatly.

Millard Fuller
Founder, Habitat for Humanity
Chambers County

Millard Fuller found success as a self-made millionaire before his 30th birthday. To his great surprise, he discovered that the success and wealth had cost him happiness and fulfillment in his life, family, and marriage.

Fuller, a native of Chambers County, Alabama, had graduated from the University of Alabama School of Law and Auburn University. He and Morris Dees had founded a marketing firm together (Fuller & Dees). Both men, as history would reveal, possessed extraordinary talent and intellect. Together, they had acquired great wealth. That wealth, as it turned out, had caused more harm than good.

It was time, Fuller and wife Linda decided, to give it all away.

They decided to devote their lives to their God, and they chose service to others as their worship. Selling their possessions and giving them to the poor, they affiliated with various ministries, including a low-cost housing charitable venture in Zaire (now named the Democratic Republic of the Congo). Returning back to the states, they created an organization that would repeat their success in Africa and benefit people who needed the dignity and safety of a home.

The result? Habitat for Humanity has made a powerful impact in America and beyond, helping less fortunate families and fostering community spirit among helpers in local communities.

In awarding the Presidential Medal of Freedom to Mr. Fuller, President Bill Clinton called Habitat for Humanity "the most successful continuous community service project in the history of the United States."

Habitat for Humanity has expanded its mission to include such services as shelter for disaster victims, education, and partnerships in the wake of catastrophes.

Trivia

Which Alabamian became the first female CEO of an American oil company?

Vicki Hollub, a graduate of McAdory High School and the University of Alabama, has served as the CEO and president of Occidental Petroleum since 2016.

She became the first female to lead a major American oil company. Hollub has also been honored, in 2016, as a Distinguished Engineering Fellow from the University of Alabama's College of Engineering. In college she earned bachelor's of science degree and added on a concentration in mineral resources and fuels.

"Big Bob" Gibson
Founder, Bob Gibson BBQ
Morgan County

They called him Big Bob for a reason. It was the 1920s, and Bob Gibson stood at an imposing 6-foot-4, and at least 300 pounds. That's big by today's standards, but he was a colossal figure in 1925, the year when he first began serving his delicious bar-b-q.

That was when Big Bob took some wooden planks (made from oak trees) and nailed them to a tree in his backyard in Decatur, Alabama (Morgan County). He dug his first bar-b-q pit by hand, and began doing what he loved best - serving the best bar-b-q around.

When he first started serving delicious food from that plank table nailed to a tree, Gibson was a railroad worker, and cooking was a hobby. As the number of customers grew, he realized that had to change and he entered the bar-b-q business as a full-time adventure. He could artfully prepare bar-b-q, and his unusual white sauce became known far beyond the Decatur area.

As great as his food became, his outsized presence and gregarious personality made him a personal attraction for customers as well. Big Bob Gibson made bar-b-q an event rather than merely a meal. That was one reason that so many customers kept returning, and was also a reason that all five of his children followed him into the bar-b-q business. Bob Gibson, Jr., Catherine McLemore, David Gibson, Ruth Hopkins, and Velma Hampton all successfully opened restaurants, making their customers invariably happy and well-fed.

Thankfully, it didn't stop there. Big Bob's grandson, Don McLemore, and his wife Carolyn, continued the family tradition of Big Bob's bar-b-q. The fourth generation of the family emerged when Big Bob's great-granddaughter Amy and husband Chris Lilly made the family tradition their career.

But the family hasn't merely done things the same old way. Don McLemore and Chris Lilly decided that their restaurants needed a red bar-b-q sauce that matched their family's delicious and legendary white sauce. In 1997 they made that dream a reality, and since then the Big Bob Gibson's red sauce has won the Memphis in May World Championship Barbecue Cook-off twice. In 1998, Big Bob Gibson's Championship Red Sauce was named "The Best Sauce on the Planet" over 500 commercial sauce entries at the American Royal International Barbecue Sauce Contest.

From a homemade oak-plank table in the 1920s to world championships in the 21st century, a family tradition has become the pride of Decatur, Alabama.

Winston Groom

Pulitzer Prize winning author
Mobile County

Mobile's Winston Groom became one of America's great novelists, and then one of its excellent historians. He has won the Pulitzer Prize. His books have sold millions of copies in America and beyond. A classic modern movie was based on one of his books.

No matter the subject, it seems that Winston Groom has written it, and written it well. He has written about the Vietnam war and racial strife. He has authored crime novels, cookbooks, and books about college football, our world wars, and most famously about a simpleton named Forrest Gump who understood the profound truth that life is like a box of chocolates.

After high school in Mobile (at Mobile's University Military School), Groom attended the University of Alabama and joined the Delta Tau Delta fraternity. He also joined the ROTC program at the university. After college, Groom found himself in Vietnam, with the U.S. Army Fourth Infantry Division, on a tour of duty in 1966 and 1967. The war left a lasting and profound effect on Groom, who has often written about it.

Groom began his post-war career as a reporter, but ultimately moved to New York and pursued a career as a novelist. In the late 1970s and early 1980s, Groom wrote four books, with *Conversations with the Enemy* nominated for the Pulitzer Prize.

In 1986, his best known work, *Forrest Gump*, was published. The book did not succeed immediately, but after the movie of the same title was released in 1994, the book sold almost two million copies. *Forrest Gump* is the story about the title character who is intellectually and cognitively limited but finds himself center-stage in many of America's biggest moments of the 1960s and1970s. Groom's character becomes a war hero, wins college football games, discovers the Watergate burglars, inspires the yellow "have a nice day" face, becomes a ping pong champion, and unknowingly becomes a major shareholder of Apple.

His next book, *Gone the Sun* (1988) won the Pulitzer Prize. *Gone the Sun* tells the story of a Vietnam veteran who returns home to Alabama, becomes a newspaper editor, and learns much more about people than he would have imagined.

Groom's most recent works have taken the form of nonfiction novels, kind of a Harper Lee meets Truman Capote style.

In addition to the Pulitzer Prize, Groom has been inducted into the Alabama Writers Hall of Fame, and has received the Harper Lee Award as the Distinguished Writer of the Year.

Each day, many thousand of Alabamians and travelers on Interstate 65 through Chilton from elsewhere see the giant peach as they drive by. It's actually a water tower, but the monument calls attention to the famous Chilton County peaches that have inspired restaurants, tourist stops, festivals, beauty contests, and delicious snacks.

But it almost didn't happen.

The Chilton County peach industry began in the late 19th century, soon after the town of Thorsby was founded by Theodore Thorson and John Peterson. The first sizable peach crop was harvested in 1898, and the industry that would one day define Chilton County was up and running.

Until it wasn't.

The state's prohibition laws forced the local wineries to close, and insect problems had badly affected the harvests. By 1913, both Thorson and Peterson had each given up and moved away.

Local growers persevered through difficult times, and soon, the almost biblical plague of the boll weevil caused the destruction of cotton crops and created the need to diversify farming practices. That, along with newly developed pesticides, made the harvest of peaches more attractive. By 1915, the yield of peaches in Chilton County was 2,640,000 bushels.

A variety of circumstances caused the peach industry to ebb and flow in Chilton County, but eventually, the people of Clanton and surrounding areas learned to promote their signature crop to the public.

Travelers can stop and enjoy freshly harvested peaches, peach ice cream, creative recipes featuring peaches, souvenirs, festivals, and of course the giant peach just off the northernmost Clanton exit off of Interstate 65.

By 2015, the Chilton County annual peach harvest exceeded 11 million pounds.

Walt Guthrie

Political cartoonist
Jefferson County

During his two decades as a leading political cartoonist and satirist at the *Birmingham Post-Herald*, no politician or malfeasor was safe from his sometimes scalding rebukes. Even from his days as the lead cartoonist at the University of Alabama's student newspaper, *The Crimson White*, Guthrie's style was as uninhibited as the content of his work.

After the *Post-Herald* ceased operations, Guthrie served as co-editor and co-publisher of *Rant Magazine*. Eventually, he became a leading independent movie director in the Atlanta area.

Though both Guthrie and the *Birmingham Post-Herald* have left the Alabama political arena, his zealous efforts to shine the light of public scrutiny on the state's leaders made a lasting impact.

Francis Hare

Legal pioneer
Jefferson & Wilcox Counties

Francis Hare was a man far ahead of his time. He pioneered the 21st century personal injury law practice in the mid 20th century.

Born in Lower Peach Tree, Alabama (Wilcox County), he was raised by his uncle and namesake, Judge Francis Hare, in Monroeville after he was orphaned. Hare became a national figure early in his career, as one of the first lawyers in America to focus his practice on representing personal injury victims.

Hare founded the law firm of Hare Wynn, and the Alabama Trial Lawyers Association. Perhaps his signature case was the nationally known and still cited Ford Pinto litigation, in which the Ford Motor Company was held liable for knowingly releasing a car carrying the potential for a fuel-fed fire.

Hare was inducted into the Alabama Lawyers Hall of Fame and the Inner Circle of Advocates, the top 100 plaintiff lawyers.

Perhaps his grandson, Francis, said it best: "My grandfather's greatest contribution to civil law may have been to help bring about broad acceptance of the belief that individuals and companies responsible for harming others should be held accountable.

"The law is at its finest," Hare added, "when it protects the weak.'"

Henry family
National brick industry leaders
Dallas County

Davis and Denson Henry run one of the top five brick companies in America, but their family's 65-year-old success story comes by the one thing that matters to the business even more than bricks.

It's all about the people.

In 2017, the Henry brothers honored their friend and employee Joe Polnitz, Jr., for his 50th anniversary with the company. Founder J. D. Henry (grandfather of Davis and Denson) hired Joe in 1967, just like he had hired Joe's dad years before. Denson Henry made the announcement at a company meeting, prompting cheers for Joe and his wife, Mary, who made a surprise appearance to join in the celebration. At the time of the Polnitz celebration, Henry Brick boasted three who had worked at least 40 years with the company, 12 who had logged at least 30 years, and 15 more who began over 20 years ago, including Davis and Denson Henry, who now lead the company in its latest era of remarkable success.

One of the top five brick producers in America, the Henry family has become well known far beyond the scope of their business. In 2015 Davis Henry was asked to testify before the congressional hearing on economic and trade issues. The Henry family has also become heavily involved in charitable causes, and active in government through organizations like the Business Council of Alabama.

"We really are like a family," explained Davis Henry. "We care about our people because that's what they are: our people. That's a big part of our success, because we are all in this together."

John Hanning, company Vice President and 32-year member of the Henry Brick company family, believes that Henry Brick has gone the extra mile for its workers when many other companies would not have. "When the 2008 crash hit, almost 80 percent of the brick market disappeared because most home building stopped," Hanning explained. "Henry Brick continued paying health insurance for employees who had been laid off, and we brought them back as soon as possible. We took care of our people."

For over a third of Alabama's 200-year history, Henry Brick has become a national success and a stable employer for its families...one brick at a time.

Rev. Chris Hodges
Church of the Highlands
Jefferson County

The first services were held in a high school, on February 4, 2001. Chris Hodges had moved to Alabama with the express mission of founding a church that proactively reached out to the needs of people, connecting them to God. He assembled a "Dream Team" of only 34 people who were small in number but large in their commitment to the mission of reaching people for God.

That first worship service, even in a high school, was an immediate success as 350 people attended. That, however, was only the beginning, as the church has grown to a multi-campus congregation with almost 50,000 people worshipping weekly.

Hodges has also focused considerable time and energy on helping other churches reach people for Jesus Christ. His church has launched other churches, and has also created programs to help unaffiliated churches grow in their own communities.

The Church of the Highlands and its network of churches have become one of the largest churches in America, and a leading authority in the field of growing new flocks of believers and reaching the lost.

Hodges, the author of multiple best-selling books, lives in Birmingham with his wife, Tammy.

Alton C. Hyche
Founder of Brookwood
Tuscaloosa County

In 2018, the newly finished highway, from the town of Brookwood to Interstate 20/59 at the Mercedes plant, was renamed the Alton C. Hyche Parkway.

Leaders in the state government, Tuscaloosa County officials, and just about everyone in the area of the new road understand that it would never have been built without the persistence of Hyche, who founded the town over 40 years ago. The road means safe travel for school buses and new businesses coming to town.

Serving as mayor for almost all of the town's existence, Hyche has led the transformation of the area into a growing town with new businesses arriving, over 900 business licenses issued annually, and the thriving 6A high school with state-of-the art cultural programs. The mayor, town council, community, and schools largely work in concert with each other, something that rarely happens without leadership at the top.

Jemison family
Leading developers
Jefferson County

Robert Jemison, Jr., was born into a family of achievers and developers. His father, Robert Jemison, Sr., was a leading businessman during the infancy of Birmingham, developing the historic area known as East Lake. Robert Sr.'s uncle, also named Robert Jemison, was a Confederate Senator and leader in the Civil War era.

Robert Jemison, Jr., followed his father's path into the realm of real estate development, and the fruits of his labor became some of the state's signature communities.

In the western part of town, he developed Ensley Heights and Central Park. He brought in a landscape architect from Boston to design the town of Corey (now known as Fairfield) as an industrial town. Redmont, also a Jemison creation, still boasts some of Birmingham's most stately and elegant homes, many with striking views of Birmingham from atop Red Mountain.

Perhaps his best known achievement was the development of Mountain Brook Estates. Now the City of Mountain Brook, the area is reputed to be the wealthiest zip code in America on a per capita basis. In many of his later developments, especially Mountain Brook, Jemison carefully preserved trees and natural areas whenever possible.

The Jemison descendants have continued Robert Jemison, Jr.'s devotion to preserving nature and using resources for charitable causes.

Devin Laney
CEO, Innovation Depot
Jefferson County

In the late 90s, Devin Laney saw a need in his college town, and created a website to meet that need. It was the early days of the internet, and Laney's website, for his fellow musicians playing near the University of Alabama, helped many performers connect with event planners and clubs for bookings.

Now, Laney spends his career helping others launch their dreams.

These days, Laney serves as the CEO of Innovation Depot, a business incubator and job creator in Birmingham. Originally founded in 1986, Innovation Depot was first named the Birmingham Business Assistance Network, and later the Entrepreneurial Center. Partnering with the UAB's Office for the Advancement of Developing Industries, the organizations purchased an old department store building in downtown Birmingham and renamed the operation Innovation Depot. In its first year, the Velocity Accelerator program created 55 jobs and raised over a million dollars in funding.

The Depot incubated over 100 startup companies, creating over 900 jobs and bringing a $1.4 billion impact from 2011 to 2016.

Harper Lee
Pulitzer Prize winning author
Monroe County

She authored the greatest American novel. She created a fictional character who still stands the ultimate standard for the legal profession. She inspired millions to write, fight for just causes, enter the world of theater, or enter the legal profession. She has been the subject of more books than many American presidents.

The great American novelist was a child in Monroeville, but she will always remain a citizen of the world.

Nelle Harper Lee grew up in Monroeville (Monroe County), the daughter of a prominent local attorney.

Her 1960 debut novel, *To Kill A Mockingbird*, became an instant classic. The following year, Lee received the Pulitzer Prize for her novel. *Mockingbird* was named the greatest novel of the 20th century, and earned innumerable awards and honors.

The major characters in *Mockingbird* have become a permanent part of American culture. People across America and beyond still name children (and even pets) after Scout, Atticus, or Dill. The name Boo Radley became a common euphemism for a creepy neighbor. Scout became a metaphor for the cheerfully guileless child whose wisdom extends far beyond her years. Atticus Finch became the metaphor for the lawyer who refuses to sacrifice integrity or courage at the altar of public approval.

To Kill A Mockingbird tells the story of a young girl nicknamed Scout, a tomboy and the daughter of a prominent local attorney. Most readers believe that Scout transparently represents Lee herself, although Harper's real-life sisters, Weezie and Doty, have always debated that. Scout's father, Atticus Finch, represents her father. A criminal trial with clear racial undertones becomes the centerpiece of the story, and one of the great courtroom dramas of American history even though the story is fictional. Lee actually did base the trial on a case her father undertook as an attorney, although the facts were changed.

Scout's friend, Dill, portrays her dear childhood friend and future author Truman Capote. Because of a turbulent home life, Capote was sent to Monroeville to live with cousins and hopefully enjoy a stable childhood. Fortunately for readers across the globe, his cousins were neighbors of the Lee family. The two children became fast friends, and in adulthood Lee accompanied Capote to Missouri to conduct research and interviews for his literary classic, *In Cold Blood*.

With occasional exceptions, Lee avoided the light of public attention and lived most of her years privately in a Manhattan apartment at 433 East 82nd Street. She occasionally made public appearances, like an annual event at her alma mater, the University of Alabama, for students who wrote essays about her. She appeared at the White House to accept the Presidential Medal of Freedom, the highest honor bestowed on a civilian, from President George W. Bush in 2007. In 2010 she visited again to accept the National Medal of Arts from President Barack Obama. She also appeared at an event in Eufala, as her sister Weezie (Louise) helped organize the event.

Until late in her life, Lee had no other published novels. Her unusual unwillingness to write another novel, combined with her love of privacy, left her as a mysterious figure and only added to her panache.

Late in her life, Lee's attorney Tonja B. Carter claimed to have found the original manuscript of *Go Set a Watchman*, which was published by Harper Collins in 2015. A number of controversies arose from the book's publication, but nothing tarnished the image, reputation, or greatness of Harper Lee or her signature work, *To Kill A Mockingbird*.

Alabama's greatest historian, Dr. Wayne Flynt (along with his wife, Dartie) became close friends with Nelle Harper Lee over the last thirty years of her life. The eulogy Dr. Flynt delivered at her funeral included the powerful and insightful explanation of the book's lasting value to society:

"That is why it is required reading in so many Irish, British, Canadian, Australian, New Zealand, Austrian, Dutch, Czech, and German schools, why it has been translated into some forty languages: because the story is a story of the human experience, not just the story of what happened in Maycomb, Alabama."

Almost 60 years after its publication, *To Kill A Mockingbird* still sells over a million copies a year.

Dr. Larry Lemak
Acclaimed surgeon
Jefferson County

As one of the world's premier surgeons, Dr. Larry Lemak somehow still manages to serve as a medical consultant and caring physician to athletic organizations across America. Lemak Health has become an elite orthopedic surgery center and sports medicine venue.

By the Numbers

4...Dr. Lemak has founded no less than four organizations, including Lemak Health, the National Center for Sports Safety, the Alabama Sports Foundation, and the American Sports Medicine Institute.

20,000...The National Center for Sports Safety has educated over 20,000 coaches in youth, recreational, and high school sports in ways to prevent and mitigate injuries to athletes.

250...The American Sports Medicine Institute has provided sports medicine training to over 250 orthopedic surgeons.

2,000...Dr. Lemak has provided medical care for over 2,000 professional football players.

1996...The Alabama Sports Hall of Fame inducted Dr. Lemak, both for his work in sports medicine, and influence in helping Birmingham obtain the 1996 Olympic soccer games.

Dave Mattingly
National reporter
Jefferson County

When Dave Mattingly enjoyed his family vacation on that cloudless Tuesday morning, it probably seemed like just another day.

That particular Tuesday morning was September 11, 2001, and millions of Americans relied on the expertise and experience of Mattingly, as he was one of the first reporters on the scene of the United Airlines Flight 93 crash. Mattingly cut short his vacation near Schwenksville, Pennsylvania, to quickly arrive at the crash site and begin revealing the tragic story to a shocked nation and world.

His reporting has won both Peabody and Emmy Awards. He has been among the first on the scene for national events, covering terrorist attacks, the *Gore v. Bush* case, tragedies in Haiti, the Columbine and Aurora shootings, Hurricane Katrina, and the 2008 presidential election, with one of the first major interviews with vice presidential nominee, Governor Sarah Palin.

An alumnus of the University of Alabama, Mattingly learned his craft at Birmingham's WVTM Channel 13 before becoming a national reporter at CNN for two decades. He then accepted an anchor position in his hometown of Louisville, Kentucky.

Dr. Forrest McDonald
Author, historian
Tuscaloosa County

The professor stood in front of the class to begin the new semester's opening lecture. The class covered American History from 1865 (the end of the Civil War) to the present time.

But this wasn't just any year, and this wasn't just any professor. The year 1987 marked the 200th anniversary of the U.S. Constitution, and the professor was chosen in this landmark year for the National Endowment for the Humanities Jefferson Lecture, which is the highest honor the federal government confers for distinguished intellectual achievement in the humanities.

Professor Forrest McDonald stood, twirling the unlit cigarette in his fingers. That was the year he quit smoking, but enjoyed holding a cigarette during lectures so he kept that small joy without actually smoking it. "First, we're going to cover the time between the end of the Civil War until the Spanish-American War at the turn of the 20th century," he began. He paused, for just a few seconds, for effect.

"Nothing happened," he said, sporting an impish grin. "Now, on to the Spanish-American War."

Forrest McDonald was an unconventional thinker, a brilliant writer, a relentless researcher, and riveting lecturer. He authored 20 books, most of which dealt with the foundation of the American republic or the careers of its founding fathers. He enjoyed sharing his vast knowledge of the inside scoop on both the historic and modern events that have defined America. While researching the life of utility baron Samuel Insull, he learned of fascinating and sometimes even scandalous political stories arising from Chicago and shared them with his students. Although an unabashed conservative, McDonald was respected by colleagues from both the political left and right.

Josiah Morris
Founder of Birmingham
Jefferson County

He started his business career as a 15-year-old employee at a mercantile company. It did not take long, however, for Josiah Morris to become his own man in the business world. As he acquired wealth, he opened his own banking business in Montgomery.

Then came the advice from a friend.

New and expanding railroads were becoming the future of Alabama, and the ability to transport coal effectively and affordably was a paramount concern. The chief engineer for the South and North Railroad, John Milner, was a personal friend of Morris. Milner suggested that Morris use his bank to finance the creation of a new industrial town in the area known as Jones Valley, an area that would soon become the intersection site for multiple railroads.

Morris founded the Elyton Land Company in 1870, and the new city was born. Based on the city's industrial purpose and future potential, Morris named it Birmingham, after the similarly situated city in England.

In the 21st century, Morris Avenue marks the center of Birmingham's downtown area, and the brick-paved streets remain a tribute to the era in which Josiah Morris created Alabama's largest metropolitan city.

April Mraz & Cherie Stine
Founders, Tech Candy
Shelby County

Celebrities carry them. National publications feature them. Retail stores across America sell them.

And it all happened because two fans of iPhones didn't like their cases.

But these weren't just any two people. April Mraz and Cherie Stine had already introduced the successful Stretchy Shapes, a boutique line of the highest-trending children's silicone bracelets launched at the New York Toy

Mardi Gras

in Mobile

According to the Encyclopedia of Alabama, Pierre Le Moyne d'Iberville "recorded the first observance of Mardi Gras in Mobile in his journal in 1699." The celebration is held each year on "Fat Tuesday," the last day and night before the season of Lent, the 40 days preceding Easter. The celebrations are known for being elaborate, yet family oriented parades and festivities are also a part of the city-wide observance.

A number of the parades feature local Mystical Societies, named as such because their membership rolls remained secretive. Over the centuries, more societies were created, including those representing members of other social classes and demographics.

One hero of the Mardis Gras tradition emerged at the end of the Civil War. At the end of the war and afterward, Union troops occupied Mobile, which had ceased its parades during the war. Undeterred by the hostile occupying troops, Joseph Stillwell Cain led a parade through Mobile dressed as an Indian chief. Inspired by his bold show of defiance, the people of Mobile resumed their annual Mardis Gras celebrations. Cain also influenced the date of the celebrations, which he helped change from New Year's Eve to Fat Tuesday.

Each year, on the Sunday before Fat Tuesday, Mobile hosts the popular Joe Cain Day parade.

A Mardi Gras King and Queen are elected each year, and some of the parades are followed by elaborate balls at different locations in the city. The festivities last for weeks leading up to Fat Tuesday, making it collectively the social event of the year. The Mardi Gras traditions and changes through the years are captured for posterity at the William and Emily Hearin Mobile Carnival Museum.

The Mardi Gras festival remains an important part of the city's identity, and one of the great national traditions originating in Alabama.

Fair in February 2010. The product quickly sold nationally in hundreds of stores, including Nordstrom and Hallmark, before selling internationally the next year.

When April and Cherie realized that neither of them liked the iPhone protective cases available on the market, they devoted their time and company resources to developing a product line that provided both style and protection. The protective cases were released and marketed under the name "Tech Candy," and proved so popular that April and Cherie have now expanded the product line to include a variety of Tech Candy tech accessories. Despite becoming a national company, Tech Candy continues operating in Shelby County.

Lycurgus Musgrove
Business titan and benefactor
Walker County

He became one of America's great eccentric millionaires in the roaring 1920s. His enormous generosity resulted in schools and churches for his beloved hometown. He died in poverty, with the many monuments to his charitable spirit still standing.

Lycurgus Breckinridge Musgrove grew up in Jasper (Walker County), a city created from land donated by his grandfather, Edward Musgrove. While he was raised in a prominent and prosperous family, Lycurgus (nicknamed "Colonel Musgrove") possessed a great mind for anticipating and developing businesses. Forming the Jasper Land Company with investors, he became wealthy as the first developer of coal mining in Walker County. His diverse business investments and famously strong networking resulted in a multi-state presence in Jasper, New York, and New Orleans, among other cities.

Musgrove enjoyed his own suite in Manhattan's luxurious Waldorf Astoria Hotel, as well as an ornate country cabin just north of Jasper, off of the road now known as highway 195. He famously took friends from one city to party with friends and associates from his other cities. At least once, Musgrove transported his personal cooks from Jasper to New York to prepare Alabama delicacies such as possum for his New York socialite friends.

In 1920, Musgrove ran for the U.S. Senate, challenging the incumbent, Oscar Underwood. As the Democratic Party's leader in that body, Underwood would, by most accounts, have a safe path to reelection. However, Underwood's opposition to prohibition and to the Ku Klux Klan made him a vulnerable candidate. Underwood held on to his seat by a narrow margin of victory, but Musgrove established himself as a force in politics, as with virtually everything else he did.

Musgrove managed to financially survive the stock market crash of 1929, but encountered financial ruin arising from a series of events that remains shrouded in mystery. According to legend, Queen Marie of Romania and her daughter were entertained in America by the president of the L & N Railroad. Musgrove, a nationally prominent businessman, was invited on the rolling party for the royals on L & N rail cars. A controversy erupted among the four of them, causing a bitter rivalry and/or jealousy from L & N President J. B. Hill toward Musgrove. Hill set out to ruin the Jasper native financially. Apparently, Hill succeeded, and Musgrove lived his final years in poverty.

Monuments to the Colonel's vast generosity remain, however, throughout Jasper. The site of Bevill State Community College and the longtime site of Jasper (formerly Walker) High School sit on land donated by Musgrove. So do the downtown Methodist and Presbyterian churches. Musgrove paid for the elegant marble exterior of the First United Methodist Church in Jasper.

As a monument to his mother, he paid for a striking, marble interior stained glass dome to be constructed in Kansas City and moved to the Methodist church in Jasper. His summer cottage ultimately became the Musgrove Country Club in Jasper.

Tena Payne
Founder, Earthborn Pottery
Jefferson County

The troubled teen didn't yet know it, but her life had been changed. As she watched the potter guide the clay, making something as unique as it was beautiful, she couldn't take her eyes off the spinning wheel...the muddy clay...the changing shape...the contentment and peace of its creator.

She would ask her teacher to loan her Homewood High School's new potter's wheel over the Christmas holidays. She would study, work, practice, and practice again on her new passion.

She would be troubled no more.

Decades later, Tena Payne provides pottery to restaurants and customers in Las Vegas, Manhattan, London and plenty of other exotic locations. The restaurants and resorts that use Earthborn pottery include the *Bellagio*, *Caesar's Palace*, and *Treasure Island* in Las Vegas, the *Lodge at Torrey Pines*, *Peche* in New Orleans, and the *Hot and Hot Fish Club* in Birmingham.

"Only God could direct a path like mine," Payne explained. "There have been so many turns. It took too many things happening to get me from troubled teen years to the success that we have had."

Tena located Earthborn in Leeds, where she has become one of the elite pottery makers in America. All because she realized her passion and seized an opportunity over the Christmas holiday break from school.

Christi Parsons
National reporter
Tuscaloosa County

Christi Parsons served as a longtime White House reporter for the *Chicago Tribune*, after covering Illinois state politics for that newspaper. She had the distinction of reporting on Barack Obama for a longer time than any other reporter, from the state Senate in Springfield to the White House.

In 2006, two years before Obama's election as president, Parsons moved to Washington to cover the expected Obama run for the presidency. She provided reports and developed campaign sources for the *Chicago Tribune* and all other newspapers owned by the *Trib's* parent company.

A native of Tuscaloosa, Parsons was an outstanding student at the University of Alabama, where she began her journalistic pursuits with the campus newspaper, *The Crimson White*. She furthered her education at the Yale Law School.

Jimmy Rane
Business titan, benefactor
Henry County

Jimmy Rane just might be one of the greatest role models Alabama has ever produced, and the reasons have little to do with his wealth.

While it's true that *Forbes* has listed him as the wealthiest Alabamian, his decisions on the path to success and the way he has spent his money make him one of America's great success stories.

Rane, a native of Abbeville (Henry County) was pursuing a law degree and starting a family when tragedy struck. His wife's parents tragically died in an automobile accident. According to *Forbes*, Rane helped mediate a disagreement over the estate and became involved in a business. Part of his father-in-law's estate included land and an old wood treatment business with equipment that wouldn't work. Rane decided to take on the herculean task of running a wood treatment business while building a law practice. As for the nonworking equipment, he asked his dad to co-sign for a loan to get the equipment working so he could start the business.

After he became an attorney, Rane worked day and night building both businesses, unaffected by the ebbs and flows of income with new startups.

Great Southern Wood has now become the largest wood treatment company in the entire world, with a presence on multiple continents and annual sales exceeding

Trivia

Which Alabama city was once the sock capital of the world?

Not too long ago, on the Planet Earth, one out of every eight socks was made in Fort Payne.

Unfortunately, trade agreements, combined with foreign sweatshop factories using child labor, sent most of the sock-producing jobs overseas.

But in the 21st century, Fort Payne's Gina Locklear has ignited the beginning of a comeback.

Gina and Emily Locklear grew up in the sock industry, as the children of the owners of Emi-G Knitting (named after the two girls). Gina Locklear now operates the company, producing two lines of socks: Zkano, an online brand, and Little River Sock Mill, sold in stores including Margaret O'Leary in Manhattan. Zkano socks bring all types of stripes and colors, while the Little River Sock Mill socks sport a more traditional look. Each brings a price of only $13 to $30 a pair.

As the founder of the two modern sock brands, Gina has created new products while upholding a family business and preserving the identity of her hometown.

a billion dollars each year.

Rane's work ethic made him legendary long before his company became an international powerhouse. Thankfully, the way he enjoys spending money has become a lesson in loyalty, love, and appreciation of traditions.

In years past, Abbeville had become typical of a wonderful small town that time had seemingly passed by. Jimmy Rane has kept the Great Southern Wood headquarters there. He has also changed both the look and image of the town, renovating much of the downtown area and making Abbeville a destination rather than a place one drives through only after taking a wrong turn.

Rane has also established a foundation that provides scholarships for deserving students, empowering many local youngsters to pursue their own dreams and to seize opportunities just as Jimmy Rane has.

Rane has served in countless civic capacities, but one of his favorite undertakings has been his service on the Auburn University Board of Trustees.

Rane has also proved as brilliant in marketing as he has been in building a business. His Yellow Wood ads raised public awareness of the company and elevated him to a jovial television star in his yellow hat and yellow western shirt. In one marketing campaign, the company announced that it would change its signature color from yellow, and built a series of ads promoting the change. The new color? As it turns out, the signature "yellow" was replaced by "yella," Therein lies the genius of Abbeville's favorite son and one of the state's great examples for us all.

Howell Raines
Pulitzer prize winner
Jefferson County

November 26, 1964, became historic for Birmingham and for football in Alabama. It was the day that the state's top rivalry became known as the "Iron Bowl." For the young Howell Raines, a Birmingham native and graduate of both Birmingham Southern and the University of Alabama, the game brought his first assignment as a reporter for the *Birmingham Post-Herald*. Other early jobs included stints with the *Tuscaloosa News*, *Birmingham News*, and WBRC-TV in Birmingham.

In his elite career, Raines reached the height of journalism, receiving the Pulitzer Prize for Feature Writing and rising to the position of executive editor of America's newspaper of record, The *New York Times*.

Raines was also an accomplished book author, writing well-received and acclaimed works such as *Whiskey Man* (1977), *My Soul is Rested: Movement Days in the Deep South Remembered* (1977), *Fly Fishing Through the Midlife Crisis* (1993) and *The One That Got Away: A Memoir* (2006).

Raines joined such elite talents as Ernest Hemingway and Rick Bragg as the rare talents who could write with the pace of a newspaper reporter but with the detailed eye of a novelist.

With the *New York Times*, Raines spent several years as the newspaper's Editorial Page editor, developing a reputation for acerbically demanding excellence and publicly calling out elected officials. Famed writer Bob Woodward once quoted then-President Bill Clinton complaining about members of Congress being afraid of what Howell Raines would write about them.

In his first year as executive editor, the *Times* won seven Pulitzer Prizes. Soon into his tenure, however, a national controversy over a rogue reporter who fabricated facts and sources caused an upheaval within the company. Though he wasn't involved, Raines was still the head guy, and ultimately the issue cost Raines his job. After his years with the *Times*, Raines has continued writing, including *The One That Got Away*, and resumed his journalism career as a columnist.

Sequoyah
Inventor, Cherokee alphabet
DeKalb County

His invention forever changed the lives of his fellow Cherokee tribesmen. Giant redwood trees are named after him. A sport utility vehicle bears his name, as does a U.S. postage stamp and a statue in the U.S. Capitol's Statuary Hall.

His name was Sequoyah, and he spent much of his adult life living in the area that is DeKalb County, Alabama. Born around 1776, he grew up learning the farming and blacksmith skills typical of men in the late 18th century. He served in the Creek Wars, and was honorably discharged after the Battle of Horseshoe Bend.

By his thirties, Sequoyah became determined to develop an alphabet for the Cherokee language. At one point, he became so enamored with the idea of developing the alphabet that he neglected home and farm duties. His wife burned all of his papers and notes.

Undeterred, Sequoyah finally developed the alphabet and presented it to the leadership of the Cherokee Nation. Before the Cherokee National Council in 1821, he presented the 86-character syllabary and proved that it could accurately represent the Cherokee language. In the following months, much of the Cherokee Nation became literate in their new alphabet, and a Cherokee newspaper was founded just a few years later.

Even missionaries recognized the opportunities presented by this new communication, and translated biblical passages and hymns into the language.

Many believe the giant Sierra redwood tree, Giant Sequoia, was named in his honor. The postage stamp bearing his likeness was unveiled in 1980.

Dr. Courtney Shropshire
Founder, Civitan International
Jefferson County

Dr. Courtney Shropshire missed the boat, and it changed his life.

As a highly respected doctor in Birmingham, Shropshire was unaccustomed to missing anything. He had studied at the Johns Hopkins School of Medicine, and then at the Mayo Clinic. He was a thorough and meticulous doctor who did not miss details or meetings.

He did, however, miss his and his wife's boarding time to embark on a trans-atlantic luxury cruise.

However frustrating that might have been for Dr. Shropshire, disappointment changed to gratitude when the ship on which they should have been passengers, the *Titanic*, struck an iceberg and sank.

Thousands died in the famous disaster, and from the evidence of the following years, Shropshire was inspired by his spared life to a renewed purpose of serving others and looking beyond one's self.

Shropshire had been a member of a local civic club, but he and others decided that the group focused too much energy on helping the businesses of the individual members rather than reaching out to help the less fortunate of society.

Shropshire, who saw that his own life had been providentially spared, propelled the group to action and became its leader. The group dropped the charter from the other civic group and formed their own organization. They named it the "Civitan" club, because of the group's focus on other citizens of the world rather than on themselves.

Dr. Shropshire not only founded the first Civitan club, but also became its first international president for two terms. He remains the only person to serve two terms as Civitan International President.

In 2017, Civitan International celebrated its 100th anniversary, and Dr. Shropshire's commitment to look beyond himself remains the gold standard of civic service.

Cliff Sims
Author, presidential aide
Coffee & Jefferson Counties

A native of Enterprise (Coffee County), Cliff Sims didn't even wait for his college graduation before founding one of the most important news sources in Alabama.

YellowhammerNews.com quickly became a premier source for keeping up with political developments in the state. The site also became a favorite of conservatives, based in no small part on the vast network of highly connected sources developed by the young Sims.

Sims also served as president of the College Republicans of the University of Alabama, and authored regular works for national publications while still a student.

After Donald J. Trump's victory in the 2016 presidential election, Sims was hired as Special Assistant to the President overseeing message strategy at the White House Communications Office. After navigating the stormy waters of the Trump White House, especially after clashes with Chief of Staff John F. Kelly, Sims ultimately returned to the private sector.

Sims followed his Washington years by returning to Alabama and authoring his memoir of his White House years, titled *Team of Vipers*, published by Thomas Dunne Books, an imprint of St. Martin's Press.

Scott Stantis
Political cartoonist
Jefferson County

Few Americans have their opinions seen by more people than Scott Stantis. Over 400 newspapers publish his political cartoons. His work has been featured in the *Chicago Tribune*, *Newsweek*, *U.S. News and World Report*, *The Birmingham News*, *The New York Daily News*, and *The Los Angeles Times*.

He was chosen as the lead cartoonist for the *Chicago Tribune* in 2009, ending a nine-year search to replace a local legend at the paper.

He is a native of California, but Birmingham was where the career of Stantis became national in scope. He had previously served as a cartoonist for *The Arizona Republic*, and *The Commercial Appeal* in Memphis. He also served as president of the Association of American Editorial Cartoonists (AAEC).

Dan Starnes
Founder, Starnes Publishing
Jefferson County

Some people might think newspapers are a dying breed.

Dan Starnes has proven them wrong.

For proof, look no further than Birmingham's Starnes, who founded a successful newspaper...and another...and another...growing his business to become Starnes Publishing, Starnes Digital, and Clearview Strategy Partners.

From his office in Homewood, Starnes directs the production of newspapers in a variety of communities, reporting local news, hiring local reporters, and featuring local advertisers. It's called "hyperlocal news," and it succeeds because people care about what their family members and neighbors are doing.

Starnes founded newspapers that have succeeded because he knows the internet spews 24/7 news from the Middle East or the petty politics of Washington. Instead, he focuses on the civic club's fundraiser, the new coach or preacher in town, or the scholarships won by local students.

Starnes has founded a variety of successful hyperlocal newspapers, including the *Homewood Star*, *Village Living*, the *Hoover Sun*, *280 Living*, the *Vestavia Voice*, *Cahaba Sun*, and *Iron City Ink*.

Working hard, producing quality journalism, featuring local people, and carrying local ads have vaulted him and his company to the top shelf of media in Alabama and have disproved fatalistic thoughts about the future of community newspapers.

Kathryn Stockett
Best-selling author
The University of Alabama

After studying creative writing at the University of Alabama, Kathryn Stockett moved to New York, working in publishing before pursuing her aspirations as a novelist. Her debut novel, *The Help*, immediately transformed her career and vaulted her into the upper realm of modern fiction authors.

By the Numbers

60...An amazing 60 literary agents rejected her manuscript of *The Help*, before agent Susan Ramer had the foresight to recognize the future classic.

10 million...*The Help* has sold over ten million copies, placing Stockett among the legendary authors produced by Alabama and its universities.

42...*The Help* has been translated into 42 different languages.

Julia Tutwiler
Educator, founder
Tuscaloosa & Sumter Counties

Libraries have been named after her because she remains one of the great educators in the history of Alabama.

Buildings at colleges and universities have been named after her, because she was a co-founder of one college and instrumental in the development of another.

A prison was named after her, as she became one of the great American crusaders for humane conditions for the incarcerated. She also fought for an end to convict leasing, which basically enslaved prisoners (mostly African-Americans) by leasing their services to private interests.

Julia Tutwiler was born in Tuscaloosa, raised as the daughter of an educator; her father served on the first faculty at the University of Alabama in 1831. He also founded the Greene Springs School for Boys in Hale County, and Julia had a front-row seat to establishing a new school. Her parents were ahead of their time, believing that women should have the same educational rights as men. Interestingly, her father was an anti-secessionist Whig during the Civil War.

Tutwiler served as president of the college now known as the University of West Alabama from 1881 to 1910. She was a co-founder of the school now known as the University of Montevallo. Using her skills as an educator, she crusaded against the insufferable treatment of prisoners and the mentally ill, educating the public and government officials about the true cost of abusive conditions to society.

In 1873, she traveled to Germany with her brother, studying and teaching there for two years. During that time, she authored a poem about her homeland, simply titled: "Alabama." That poem now serves as the state song of Alabama.

Kathryn Tucker Windham
Renowned author, storyteller
Dallas & Clarke Counties

In its first 200 years, Alabama has produced some of the world's great storytellers, and Kathryn Tucker Windham was unquestionably one of the greatest.

Born in Selma, she was raised in Thomasville (Clarke County) as the youngest child of a banker and a teacher. Her gift for communicating was apparent at an early age, as she authored movie reviews for the local newspaper by the age of 12.

After graduating from Huntingdon College, she worked in journalism and eventually became publicity director for the Alabama War Bond Committee during World War II. She worked as a reporter and freelance writer for a variety of publications, including the *Alabama Journal*, *Progressive Farmer* magazine, *The Birmingham News*, and the *Selma Times-Journal* over the next three decades.

Her most famous work, however, occurred beyond the realm of newspaper journalism. In the 1960s, during her years in Selma, she began writing books. She authored a cookbook, a compilation book titled *Alabama: One Big Front Porch*, and her famous series of ghost story books, beginning with her signature work, *13 Alabama Ghosts and Jeffrey*.

Windham was featured many times at the annual National Storytelling Festival in Tennessee, for years on Alabama Public Radio, and weekly for two years on National Public Radio.

She has been inducted into the Alabama Women's Hall of Fame, and the Alabama Newspaper Hall of Honor at Auburn University.

Byron York
National columnist
Jefferson County

One of America's leading opinion columnists, Byron York has also become a leading voice on national television, social media, and podcasts.

York has become a leading conservative voice of his generation. He has also become a leading voice from the right on television, primarily on the Fox News Network. He has joined columnists such as George F. Will and William F. Buckley as those who have succeeded grandly in both opinion columns and television.

For York, success in the media is nothing new; he grew up with it, as the son of legendary Birmingham newscaster Tom York.

Byron York has written for the Washington Examiner, The Wall Street Journal, the New York Post, and National Review.

York graduated from the University of Alabama, and earned a masters degree at the University of Chicago.

The Alabama Department of Archives and History

By: Georgia Ann Conner Hudson,
Communications Officer

For well over a century, the Alabama Department of Archives and History has been the home of Alabama history, collecting, preserving, and sharing the artifacts and records that tell the story of the state and its people. Located atop Goat Hill, directly across the street from the State Capitol, the stunning, Greek-Revival Style Archives building contains award-winning, Smithsonian-quality museum exhibits, a state-of-the-art research facility, and myriad activities and programs for all ages. The Archives serves the state of Alabama as its official government records repository, as a special collections library, and as Alabama's history museum. Opened in 2011 and 2014, the Museum of Alabama's completely re-designed museum exhibits have made the Archives a new destination for Alabamians and visitors from across the nation and the globe. A visit immerses guests in the story of Alabama from

Native American history to the Civil War, to the Civil Rights Movement, and beyond.

In 1901, Alabama created the first state-funded archival and historical agency in the U.S. The movement to create the Alabama Archives represented a convergence of cultural interests. The progressive movement, then spreading across the United States, reflected an interest in improved education. With the growth of schools, an increase in the number of professional historians, and the professionalization of historical training and education came an increasing need for a facility where Alabama's historical materials could be studied and accessed by the public. There was also a growing interest in preserving the materials that document the past. By the turn of the twentieth century, Alabama was more than eighty years old, yet there was no formal system in place for preserving its historical records and artifacts.

ALABAMA: THE BICENTENNIAL proudly joins Alabama Archives Director Steve Murray and the Friends of the Alabama Archives to help underprivileged fourth graders learn and experience the state's amazing history.

Thomas McAdory Owen, an attorney from Jefferson County, Alabama, advocated for the established of the Archives and served as its first director. In 1893, he married Marie Bankhead, daughter of U.S. Senator John Hollis Bankhead. Marie shared Tom's interest in history, and her family's political connections throughout the state helped advance his idea of creating a state archives. On February 27, 1901, Governor William J. Samford signed into law the bill establishing the Alabama Department of Archives and History. Just a few days later on March 2, Owen was named director.

The Archives' first office space was in the Senate cloak room at the State Capitol. Almost immediately, Owen began acquiring significant records and artifacts that documented Alabama's past. He envisioned the agency as a cultural institution with a broad mission, serving Alabama's citizenry not only as the state archives but also as the state history museum. He persuaded the legislature to allow use of the Senate Chamber as a public display space when the legislature was not in session. When the Capitol was expanded in 1906-07, the Archives gained new office and collections space in the new south wing, a room still referred to today as the "Old Archives Room."

During Owen's tenure, the Archives considerably increased its holdings to include significant Civil War-era collections, nineteenth- and early twentieth-century personal papers, nineteenth-century portraits, and Civil War flags. The passage of a law in 1915 stipulating that public officials transfer non-current records to the Archives assisted Owen in collecting Alabama state records from the previous century. With a growing collection of historical materials, Owen envisioned construction of a permanent building to house the Archives. In 1919, the legislature created a State Memorial Commission to plan for a state building that would memorialize those killed during World War I and also house the Archives. The Commission began purchasing land across the street from the Capitol. Owen died in 1920 and never saw his dream of an adequate home for the Archives become a reality.

After Owen's death, the Archives board of trustees chose his widow, Marie Bankhead Owen, to succeed him as director. She was the second woman to head a state agency in Alabama and served as director of the Archives for the next 35 years. One of Marie's most lasting contributions was her success in securing New Deal funding in the late 1930s to construct the War Memorial Building that would also serve as the Archives' permanent home. The building opened in 1940 to national acclaim.

The original construction included only the central portion of the current building. Expansions to the east in 1974 and the west in 2005 completed the architect's original intent for an H-shaped building. The walls of the central building are lined with richly veined marble quarried in Sylacauga. The interior is defined by ornate architectural elements, art deco light fixtures, and intricate carved reliefs representing various themes of Alabama's history.

After nearly a decade of research, design, and fundraising, the first two permanent exhibitions of the newly designed Museum of Alabama opened in 2011. The Land of Alabama introduces visitors to Alabama's diverse geology and the natural resources that helped shape the state's history. The First Alabamians tells the compelling story of fourteen thousand years of Native American history through original murals, a diorama, and the Museum's impressive artifact collections.

Almost immediately after the opening of these galleries, work began on what is now the centerpiece of the Museum of Alabama, the Alabama Voices exhibit. This Smithsonian-quality exhibit covers the dramatic unfolding of Alabama history from the dawn of the 1700s to the beginning of the 21st century. More than 800 artifacts, hundreds of images and documents, and twenty-two audiovisual programs tell the story of struggles over the land, the rise of a cotton economy, the Civil War, industrialization, world wars, civil rights, the race to the moon, and more. Voices taken from diaries, letters, speeches, songs, and other sources convey the experiences of Alabamians who lived through and shaped the history of these periods. Occupying nearly 11,000 square feet, Alabama Voices opened to wide acclaim in 2014 as an important new cultural and educational resource for the state.

Additional galleries include Alabama Treasures, an exhibit space that has been restored to its original appearance when the building first opened in 1940. It houses temporary and traveling exhibits utilizing some of the museum's original display cases. Throughout the year, various temporary exhibits are on display throughout the building featuring textiles, original records, artifacts, and other materials.

The Hands-On Gallery is a popular destination for children and families. Featuring crafts, touch-its, and educational activities based on different themes of Alabama history, this gallery helps young visitors connect with the past while building new memories with their families. The Hands-On Gallery also houses Grandma's Attic, where children can dress up in period costume and play with vintage toys and games.

In addition to the Museum of Alabama, the EBSCO Research Room allows visitors to delve deeper into Alabama's past and their own family history. Offering state-of-the-art research tools and access to original records from the Archives collection, the Research Room is a must-visit destination for anyone interested in genealogical and historical research. An expert staff is on hand to provide guidance. Free access is provided to many online resources such as Ancestry.com through the Research

Room's computers.

Throughout the year, the Archives offers numerous public programs such as lunchtime lectures, symposiums, workshops, film screenings, and family activities. The building has become a vibrant part of Montgomery's cultural landscape, attracting visitors from all walks of life.

While the Archives serves the entire state, its collections and museum exhibits also document the story of the City of Montgomery and the pivotal role that it played in both the Civil War and the Civil Rights Movement. Located just steps away from where many of these transformative events occurred, Alabama's Department of Archives and History's rich Civil War and Civil Rights collections place these turning points into the larger context of Alabama and national history.

Now in its second century of service to the state of Alabama, the Alabama Archives has become the thriving cultural institution that Thomas Owen envisioned in 1901, committed more than ever to its core mission of collecting, preserving, and sharing Alabama's history.

The Alabama Department of Archives and History and the Museum of Alabama are open Monday through Saturday, 8:30 to 4:30. The EBSCO Research Room is open Tuesday through Friday and the second Saturday of each of month from 8:30 to 4:30. Admission is always free.

Visit www.archives.alabama.gov for the latest information on exhibits and upcoming events.

Friends of the Alabama Archives

Alabama Department of Archives and History

Autos & Air Travel

Airbus, NASCAR, Talladega, NASA, Astronauts, Auto manufacturers, Aviators

Pictured on the previous page, Top left: the Tuskegee Airmen, trained in Macon County, became an important force in the war effort and in shattering old stereotypes. Top right: a souvenir program for the first racing weekend at the Talladega Superspeedway. Middle, left: (L-R) Alabama Gang members Neil Bonnett, Donnie Allison, and Bobby Allison. Middle, right: Huntsville has played a major role in the NASA moon landings, which have included many alumni from Auburn University. Bottom: (L-R) Honda and Mercedes have joined Hyundai, Toyota, Mazda, and Airbus to form one of the leading automotive and air manufacturing sectors in the world.

Brian France, son of Bill, Jr., has served as NASCAR's chairman since his own father's retirement in 2003. Like his father, Brian grew up learning the world of NASCAR from the bottom-up. His first real job was as a janitor at the Talladega Superspeedway.

Under Brian's leadership, the sport has continued growing, prospering, and entertaining fans throughout the world. *Time* magazine named him one of the "100 Most Influential People of the Century."

Even in its infancy as a sport, NASCAR became a darling of Alabamians, in no small part because so many of its champions hailed from the state. In NASCAR's first decade, some of its greatest champions were three brothers from DeKalb County, Alabama.

The France family
Founders of NASCAR and The Talladega Superspeedway

Seventy years ago, Bill France believed professional racers should drive the same types of cars as regular people. He founded NASCAR (the National Association for Stock Car Auto Racing) on February 21, 1948, and its bond with the people of Alabama has become a major part of its success.

Though a large man, "Big Bill" earned his nickname in more ways than one. William Henry Getty France was a man of big ideas and a huge vision for what his creation, NASCAR, could become. The idea of racing regular cars was brilliant, but it wasn't his only historic idea. The world-famous speedways in Daytona and Talladega originated in the creative mind of "Big Bill," as did the International Motor Sports Hall of Fame. France fully understood the sport from the bottom-up, largely because of his own journey from apprentice mechanic, to mechanic, to driver, to race car builder, to the creator of a racing series.

In 1934, Bill and wife Ann traveled toward Miami, where he hoped to find a job as an auto mechanic. During the trip, they spent a night in Daytona, liked it, and stayed there to build their lives and family.

Today, the seeds of success planted by "Big Bill" France have produced a harvest of worldwide success. An amazing 17 out of America's 20 biggest sporting events, in attendance, are NASCAR races. Over 150 countries broadcast its races. Over the last generation, NASCAR has become America's fastest growing sport. It's not uncommon to see, in any part of the United States, bumper stickers bearing only a number. Usually, that represents the car number of their favorite racer.

At Bill's retirement, NASCAR was a wonderful sport but still mostly popular in the Deep South. His son, Bill France, Jr., took the reins of NASCAR and transformed it into a global empire, reaching fans across the globe. The younger Bill France was much more than the son of NASCAR's owner; he was imminently qualified to grow the business. According to the *New York Times*, Bill, Jr., worked at race tracks, and "...he was a corner worker, flagman and chief steward. He dug post holes, parked cars, sold programs, repaired guard rails, worked in concession stands and took tickets."

The Flock brothers
Early NASCAR legends
DeKalb County

Tim, Bob, and Fonty Flock quickly became three of the top stock car racers in the sport. Tim was the biggest star, winning two Grand National Championships (1952 and 1955) and a whopping 40 NASCAR races.

Although he was named Driver of the Year in 1952, his signature season came in 1955, when in 39 starts he posted 18 victories and 32 top-five finishes.

Tim Flock remains the only driver in history to win at Daytona in each of the three NASCAR divisions, Grand National, Modified and Convertible.

His fame has extended far beyond his career, as he was named one of the 50 greatest drivers in NASCAR over 40 years after his last Grand National Championship. He was also inducted into the International Sports Hall of Fame in 1991 and the Alabama Sports Hall of Fame in 2006.

Bob Flock joined his brothers as one of the sport's early champions. Although his budding stardom was cut short by a serious racing accident in 1951, Bob still managed to win four different races in the top division of NASCAR. Due to health reasons arising from that accident, Bob retired from active racing in 1956.

Brother Fontell Flock was known as "Fonty" to racing fans, and for a time, it appeared that he might join brother Tim in the ranks of the great drivers. He won 19 different NASCAR events, but like brother Bob, his racing career ended prematurely. Fonty was seriously injured in an accident in 1957 at the Darlington Raceway.

The Flock brothers served as champions who played a foundation role for NASCAR, and for the role of the state of Alabama in the sport's journey to success.

The Talladega Superspeedway
Talladega County

In 1968, Big Bill France and others broke ground on the construction of a raceway, located just off of Interstate 20, on an abandoned airfield outside of Talladega. The site was a short drive from the major metropolitan cities of Birmingham and Atlanta. The interstate and central location made Talladega easily accessible for almost the entire Deep South, making it perhaps the perfect location.

Fifty years later, Alabama Governor Kay Ivey joined the current owners of the Talladega Superspeedway to announce a $50 million project to make the fan experience the greatest in all of American sports. It was only fitting that the track's 50th anniversary begat the $50 million project.

In the intervening years between the moment the first shovel hit the Talladega soil and the 2018 announced expansion, the Talladega Superspeedway has become the most exciting race track in all sports, providing more speed, thrills, photo-finishes, and even tragedy than any other venue.

And that is exactly how Big Bob envisioned it.

France wanted a track that was longer than the other NASCAR tracks, and steeper in its incline. As the *Encyclopedia of Alabama* described it:

"The banking in the turns at Talladega is 33 degrees, compared with 31 degrees at Daytona. The backstretch straightaway is 4,000 feet long. The 4,300-foot, curving frontstretch creates a slight fifth turn in front of the main grandstand, which is why the track is called a tri-oval."

The result was record-breaking speeds and an almost unimaginable non-stop excitement. Word quickly spread of the track's design and intended speed. One result, however, was not intended at all. Drivers became so concerned about the track, especially after the qualifying for the track's opening race weekend in 1969, that a group of NASCAR's leading drivers boycotted the race. Richard Petty, still known as "The King" in the racing world, led the boycott of the new Talladega track.

The race was successful anyway, and soon the NASCAR community was fully on board.

As wonderful as the races and fan support were for the growing support, the boycott was not the last controversy for the Talladega Superspeedway. Several accidents, including fatalities and one spectacularly dangerous crash, inspired public debate over the record speed of drivers at the Talladega track.

Largely because of Talladega, the era of "restrictor plates" began, in which the top racing speeds of the cars were limited. The result, in addition to somewhat safer driving, was actually more exciting for fans, with closer and more suspenseful finishes.

NASCAR might only use Talladega a few weekends each year, but the Superspeedway remains in almost constant use. Racing teams and their drivers routinely test cars there. Racing companies offer events for fans which give them an unforgettable on-track experience. Even Hollywood has a frequent presence there, with television ads and even movies filmed there.

The most famous movie based in Talladega was *Talladega Nights*, the comedy featuring the legendary combination of Will Ferrell and John C. Reilly, along with some of Hollywood's biggest stars such as Gary Cole, Michael Clarke Duncan, Sacha Baron Cohen, Molly Shannon, Jack McBrayer, and Rob Riggle.

The part of Texas Ranger Bobby, son of Ferrell's character Ricky Bobby, is played by Chilton County native Grayson Russell.

Even with the new improvements to the Talladega Superspeedway, some things will not change. The track will

still feature, fifty years later, the same thrilling fast-paced action and the best fans in all of racing in Talladega, Alabama.

The Alabama Gang
Hueytown's NASCAR champions

In the 1960s, a second invasion of Alabama brothers produced great wins and championships, as the Flock brothers from Ft. Payne had done a decade earlier.

These two brothers, based in Hueytown, made their mark in the sport's history and then shepherded a great legacy of drivers who collectively became known as the "Alabama Gang."

Bobby Allison was the first and still greatest driver in the Alabama Gang. Amazingly, Bobby met his future wife, Judy, after a race in which his car hit the wall and burst into flames.

The story of his connection to Hueytown is almost as unlikely. A native of Miami, Allison and his brother ***Donnie Allison*** ended up in the Birmingham area, and it might have been because of a stop at a gas station. The brothers and two friends ventured to Alabama because they had heard it was a good area for racing. Driving by a gas station, the guys noticed a '34 Chevy modified with a Cadillac engine. They stopped, spoke to the owner about his car and local racing, and learned that a race was scheduled that night in the Birmingham suburb of Midfield. Bobby finished in fifth place that night, but earned more than the races in Florida paid, and the rest, as they say, is history.

Born Robert Arthur Allison, Bobby launched a spectacular racing career from Hueytown. He was named one of NASCAR's 50 greatest drivers, and that barely makes the list of his own 50 greatest honors and awards. He was inducted into the NASCAR Hall of Fame (2011) and the Alabama Sports Hall of Fame (1984). He finished either first or second in the Winston Cup six different times, winning the title in 1983. He may have been the most diverse driver in the sport's history, winning 717 races in different divisions, including NASCAR, Busch, ARCA, IROC, USAC, Indy, late models, modifieds, dirt and ice.

In one of racing's greatest family moments, Bobby won the 1988 Daytona 500, and the second-place driver was his son, Davey.

Donnie Allison proved, during his rookie year of racing, that he was much more than merely Bobby's brother

Donnie won the NASCAR Rookie of the Year award in 1967, as well as the 1970 Indianapolis Rookie of the Year, and Sportsman Most Popular Driver in 1970. He won an impressive ten Winston Cup races, nine super speedway wins, and 15 super speedway pole positions.

Donnie became a hall of famer in his own right, being inducted into the Alabama Sports Hall of Fame (1999), the Talladega-Texaco Walk of Fame, Alabama Racing Pioneers Old Timers Club, and is listed in the *Encyclopedia of Auto Racing Greats*.

The next generation of Allison racers began early, as ***Davey Allison*** drove in his first race just a few months after high school graduation then won his first race two weeks after that. Winning became a regular event for young Davey, who triumphed in 45 short-course races in his first five years.

Fittingly, he won his first major race at Talladega in 1983, in an ARCA 500K race. He was the ARCA Rookie of the Year the next year, and became one of the most popular drivers in all of racing. He kept winning at an elite pace, with 19 Winston Cup victories, 66 finishes in the top-five, along with 93 in the top-ten.

Tragically, Davey Allison passed away from injuries arising from a helicopter accident at the Talladega Superspeedway infield in 1993.

Bobby Allison's youngest son, ***Clifford Allison***, traveled an unusual journey into racing. He briefly worked in a Kentucky coal mine before returning to his family's home of Hueytown and embarking on his own racing career.

After beginning his career as a crew chief, Clifford became a driver like his father, uncle, and brother. Like them, he was also an excellent driver, doing well on the ARCA and NASCAR Busch Series circuits. In August of 1992, during a practice run at the Michigan International Speedway, Clifford sustained fatal injuries from a crash. He passed away only 11 months before his brother Davey's fatal helicopter crash. His last race was, appropriately, at the Talladega Superspeedway.

Hut Stricklin was a championship racer who competed on virtually every level of stock car racing. A native of Calera (Shelby County), Waymond Lane Stricklin, Jr., was a member of both the Alabama Gang and the Allison family. Hut married Pam Allison Stricklin, Donnie's daughter, who was introduced to Hut by her cousin, Davey Allison.

Hut wasted no time winning a championship, capturing the 1987 NASCAR Dash Series title at the age of 26.

When Bobby and Donnie Allison returned to Florida from their first Alabama visit, they quickly found their friend ***Charles "Red" Farmer*** and told him all about the virtual gold mine of racing in Alabama. Red was convinced by his friends; when Bobby and Donnie Allison made the move to Hueytown, he joined them.

Red fit in well in his new home of Alabama, and it didn't hurt that he was also a hall-of-fame driver. He won almost 800 feature races, and has won NASCAR national championships in three different decades (the 50s, 60s, and 70s).

The Allisons weren't the only ones who considered Red Farmer a great guy. In several different years, he was voted the most popular driver in NASCAR by his peers.

In 1990, Red Farmer was inducted into the Alabama Sports Hall of Fame.

Neil Bonnett was a native of Hueytown, and he was a star.

But he wasn't just a star driver, although that was how he became famous. Bonnett became an excellent television broadcaster, as well as an accomplished hunter and fisherman.

Bonnett drove in his first race in 1974, and captured his first checkered flag for victory only three weeks later. His career was sixteen years old when an accident forced him out of racing, at least temporarily, in 1990. During his rehabilitation, Bonnett transitioned from one of racing's most popular drivers to one of television's most popular sports commentators. He also hosted a weekly show titled *Winners* on the TNN cable station.

In 1993, Bonnett's doctors cleared him to resume racing, but tragically, he was killed less than a year later in a practice run at the Daytona International Speedway.

Bonnett posted 18 Winston Cup races and was inducted into the International Motorsports Hall of Fame and the Alabama Sports Hall of Fame.

Mercedes Changed Everything

Everything changed in 1993.

Alabama's reputation, economy, and future began its transition on one day.

Amazingly, that was only the beginning of the journey that has vaulted Mercedes and Alabama to an internationally recognized team.

In April of that historic year, Mercedes Benz U.S. International had announced its plans to locate its first major manufacturing plant in the United States. The company identified hundreds of potential sites in 35 states, and the battle to recruit a game-changing project began.

Billy Joe Camp
Leading Mercedes recruiter
Montgomery County

Governor Jim Folsom, Jr., asked Alabama Secretary of State Billy Joe Camp to resign his office to lead the Alabama Development Office. This was an extraordinary request, first suggested by Barber Companies executive Don Erwin. But the governor was persuasive, and Camp became the project's organizer and catalyst.

The recruiting effort had to clear many hurdles, the tallest one being the state's historic reputation. Making matters worse was the past experience of a Mercedes board member who was held as a prisoner of war in Alabama (during World War II) and held a less-than-flattering image of the Alabamians he had encountered.

Camp understood the problem, and held Alabama's first reception for the Mercedes executives at the opulent North River Yacht Club in Tuscaloosa. The second event was a dinner at a physician's home in Birmingham. As a surprise guest at an Atlanta reception, Camp brought Alabama football coach Gene Stallings, who had just won the national championship in January.

Elmer Harris
President, Alabama Power Co.
Chilton and Jefferson Counties

Another powerful weapon in the battle for Mercedes was Alabama Power Company President Elmer Harris. A native of Chilton County, Harris earned two degrees from Auburn (including a MBA). During his time in the United States Air Force, he studied at United States Air Force Flight School in 1964, Air Command and Staff College at Maxwell Air Force Base in 1970 and Air War College in 1985.

In September of 1993, the time had come for the announcement, and the Alabama team remained cautiously optimistic.

Then came the bad news.

The *Washington Post* reported, as a fact, that North Carolina had been chosen as the site. Thankfully, this turned out to be false reporting, but at the time the deeply disappointed Alabama officials could only hope the newspaper was wrong.

Mercedes officials fully understood the historical import of this decision, and spared no expense to maintain the announcement's drama until the final moment.

To prepare for the announcement, 18-wheelers carrying Mercedes vehicles left New Jersey, headed for the announcement site. The plan was such a closely held secret, that even the truck drivers didn't know where they were headed. In those days before ubiquitous cell phones, they had to stop every 100 miles to receive directions for their next 100 miles.

When Mercedes announced the winning location, the world watched as Alabama won a recruiting battle unmatched in its history. The efforts by Governor Jim Folsom, Jr., Billy Joe Camp, and the elite team that represented the state has become legendary.

Nothing was ever the same after that, in the realm of economic development and the image of the state. Some cynics criticized the massive tax breaks and deferments offered as incentives to Mercedes, but the impact of that 1993 decision on the state cannot be fully quantified.

In 2015, Mercedes announced another billion-dollar expansion of the plant, including a major new battery plant nearby in Woodstock.

Jason Hoff
CEO and President
Mercedes-Benz US International

Jason Hoff, CEO and President of Mercedes-Benz U.S. International, has led the plant to unprecedented growth, achieving a fifty-percent increase in production since taking over in 2013. He had previously served in various leadership roles from 1994 to 2010, helping vault the Vance plant to one of the world's best. Hoff then worked in the company's headquarters in Germany for three years before being tapped to lead the Alabama operation.

The Mercedes progress since that 1993 day can be seen...by the numbers.

By the Numbers

5.8 billion...That's the total investment of Mercedes in Alabama, at least so far, once the currently undertaken expansion has been completed.

1.5 billion...That's the annual impact of the Mercedes plant on the state of Alabama. That will only grow with the second campus that was first announced in 2017.

4,706,500...That's the total number of square feet of the massive Mercedes campus in Vance (also 966 acres).

3,700...The Mercedes Plant employs over 3,700 team members in Vance.

4...Four different vehicles are produced at the Mercedes plant in Vance, including GLE Sport Utility Vehicle (SUV), GLS-Class Luxury SUV, C-Class Sedan, and the GLE Coupe.

Honda

Honda has become the engine of success in East Alabama.

Honda America's impact on East Alabama has been nothing short of enormous, but its decision to locate its plant in Lincoln composed only the first chapter of a splendid story of success.

Since automobile production began on November 14, 2001, Honda Manufacturing of Alabama has made a staggering impact on the state, its economy, and its families.

By 2008, Honda announced it was moving production of the Ridgeline from Canada to Alabama. In the years that followed, the Accord V-6 sedan, the Acura MDX, and the Honda Odyssey followed the same path and are now produced in Lincoln.

In 2018, the next chapter was unveiled to the world. On December 6, over 1,500 employees of Honda Manufacturing of Alabama celebrated the beginning of mass production of the all-new 2019 Honda Passport SUV.

The Passport will be produced exclusively in Alabama.

They say numbers do not lie, and the numbers arising from the Honda Manufacturing of Alabama are pretty impressive:

By the Numbers

6.8 billion...In 2014, the state of Alabama honored Honda for producing a $6.8 billion impact on the state's economy and creating 43,000 jobs (counting subcontractors and spin-off businesses) in Alabama.

67...Honda workers average 67 percent higher pay than the average Alabama worker.

4,500...That's the number of associates employed at the Lincoln plant of Honda Manufacturing of Alabama.

340,000...That's the whopping total of vehicles and V6 engines produced by the Honda plant each year.

1,350...The acreage of the Honda plant totals 1,350, situated right near Interstate 20 for convenience for employees, shipping finished products, and access by subcontractors.

$11 million...Alabama charities and nonprofits have received over $11 million from Honda Manufacturing of Alabama. That's one reason why the Honda impact on the state of Alabama extends far beyond capital investment, the number of jobs created, or the number of subcontractors relocating or expanding to Alabama.

Hyundai Motor Manufacturing Alabama employees sign the first Hyundai Santa Fe produced at the plant in 2007.

Massive Hyundai plant keeps adding more jobs

On April 2, 2002, Hyundai Motor Company made the announcement that Governor Don Siegelman and his team had so zealously pursued. Montgomery, Alabama, had been chosen as the site for the first Hyundai production facility in the United States.

Ten days later, Hyundai Motor Manufacturing Alabama was incorporated.

On May 20, 2005, Chung Mong-koo, chairman and chief executive officer of Hyundai Kia Automotive Group joined former President George H. W. Bush and Alabama Governor Bob Riley to cut the ribbon for the newly opened Hyundai plant.

According to Luther Strange, a former U.S. Senator who was then an attorney involved in negotiations between Hyundai and the state, the timing could not have been better for working families in Alabama. Strange explained that, around the same time Hyundai was successfully recruited, "Hyundai and all of the automotive manufacturers and suppliers came at a critical time, when the Russell Corporation and the old textile industry were dying out and moving jobs overseas." Strange added that "The good news was that the people who were displaced in the old textile industries were retrained and recruited for jobs in the automotive manufacturing sector."

Since then, the metropolitan Montgomery area has undergone countless changes, in no small part because of the colossal economic impact of the Hyundai plant and the subcontracting companies locating or expanding in the area.

The numbers tell a compelling narrative of success.

By the Numbers

398,851...The plant's record number of vehicles produced by the Montgomery plant during 2014.

3,000...The Montgomery plant employs over 3,000 team members.

7,000...That's the total number of jobs created by Alabama-based suppliers and subcontractors.

$1.8 billion...Hyundai has invested just south of two billion in its Montgomery plant.

$800 million...That's the amount of investment by suppliers. One example is the location of the Korean company, Hanil E Hwa in Selma, which located there after a relentless effort by the local Economic Development Authority. The company soon became one of the largest employers in Dallas County.

Airbus
The sky is the limit

As the state's bicentennial year began, Airbus and Alabama scored another victory together.

On the 16th of January, 2019, CEO and Chairman for Airbus Americas, Jeff Knittel, joined Governor Kay Ivey and other officials to break ground on another massive new project for Airbus in the City of Mobile.

The A220 Final Assembly Line announcement meant hundreds of new jobs, many additional airplanes produced, and the overall Airbus investment in Mobile passing $1 billion. The new assembly line's location was set at just a few feet from the existing A320 Final Assembly Line, which began operations in March of 2015. The company's website explained the Airbus decision to locate the A320 line in Mobile: "We have had an exceptionally positive experience in Mobile over the years–the people, business community, local government and community have all been welcoming and supportive of our activities here."

"Together we've already put Mobile on the map in the world of global aviation, and together we are making a new mark for the future," explained Knittel.

"With the addition of the new A220, Mobile is poised to do something that no one could have dreamed about. With the production of the A320 and A220, Mobile will become the fourth largest commercial aviation site in the world," Mayor Sandy Stimpson said.

Airbus first landed in Mobile in 2007, when it located its Airbus Engineering Center near the present location of the assembly lines. In its first ten years, the center paid over $180 million in salaries and donated over half a million to local charities.

The arrival of Airbus meant the arrival of subcontractors and associated businesses. The economy and growth in Mobile was changed for the better. As Mayor Stimpson explained, the assembly lines have placed Mobile among the world's elite cities of commercial aviation.

With more than 5,000 employees, Airbus Americas is the US-based operation of Airbus, encompassing the regional corporate offices, engineering centers, training facilities, MROs and spare parts distribution centers, as well as manufacturing facilities producing commercial aircraft, helicopters and satellites, according to the company's website.

Pictured (above) Workers pose in front of the very first plane to come off the production line at the Airbus Alabama facility in Mobile in February 2016.

Photo and accompanying caption courtesy of the Encyclopedia of Alabama, which obtained the photo from the Alabama Department of Commerce.

Alabama Governor Kay Ivey (3rd from left) Huntsville Mayor Tommy Battle (inside right) and Commerce Secretary Greg Canfield welcome officials from Toyota and Mazda to Huntsville.

Even before the tenth day of January, 2018, Huntsville enjoyed one of the world's most sophisticated economies. NASA and related government contractors, the high-tech industry, and the Redstone Arsenal combined to make Huntsville a mecca for scientists, engineers, and those working on projects and ideas not yet understood by the public.

But on that January day, Huntsville's future became even brighter when officials announced that the massive Toyota-Mazda jointly operated plant would be constructed in the metropolitan Huntsville area. Alabama Governor Kay Ivey, Huntsville Mayor Tommy Battle, and Alabama Secretary of Commerce Greg Canfield welcomed officials from Toyota and Mazda for the historic press conference.

As Alabama celebrates its bicentennial, Huntsville and surrounding areas have already begun planning for the infusion of new jobs, workers, subcontracting companies, and the new and expanding businesses that accompany them.

Even before the plant begins producing vehicles, the numbers reveal a powerful story that awaits Huntsville:

By the Numbers

$1.6 billion...The combined investment by Toyota and Mazda in the new joint operation.

300,000...The number of vehicles produced each year by the plant (each company will produce 150,000).

4,000...Over four thousand jobs will be created by the Huntsville plant, although the supplier companies expanding or relocating to Huntsville will make that number much higher.

$50,000...That's the average projected salary of workers at the Huntsville plant.

Dr. Deborah Edwards Barnhart
CEO, US Space & Rocket Center
Madison County

When the U.S. Space and Rocket Center chose its current leader, it was fittingly someone who had spent her entire life soaring to new heights.

Dr. Deborah Edwards Barnhart has excelled at an elite level in the classroom, in the United States Navy, and in the corporate world. She holds degrees from the Massachusetts Institute of Technology, Vanderbilt University, the University of Maryland, and the University of Alabama at Huntsville. In the U.S. Navy, Edwards commanded five different units during 26 years, ultimately rising to the level of Captain. She became a pioneer when she was one of the initial ten women assigned to duty aboard naval ships.

In the corporate world, Edwards rose to the level of vice president for three different companies (Honeywell International, McDonnell Douglas, now Boeing, and United Technologies Aerospace).

Among her seemingly countless other honors and awards, Edwards received NASA's Distinguished Public Service Medal, the highest form of recognition awarded by NASA to a non-government individual.

Edwards now serves as the Chief Executive Officer and Executive Director of the U.S. Space & Rocket Center in Huntsville.

Nancy Jan Davis
Astronaut
Madison County

Nancy Jan Davis grew up in Huntsville, becoming one of her hometown's most accomplished astronauts. The 1971 graduate of Huntsville High School put up some incredible numbers:

By the Numbers

11 million...Davis has traveled over 11 million miles in outer space.

445...She has orbited the earth 445 times.

673...Davis has spent a total of 673 hours in space.

4...She earned four degrees, including two bachelor's degrees (one from Auburn University and one from Georgia Tech) and then a master's and doctorate from the University of Alabama in Huntsville.

3...Her 1992 space mission aboard the *Endeavour* included three links to Alabama, with Davis, fellow astronaut Mae Jemison, and the Spacelab that was developed in Huntsville at the Marshall Space Flight Center.

Henry Hartsfield
Astronaut
Jefferson County

Henry Hartsfield, the astronaut, graduated from Birmingham's West End High School. He had the unusual distinction of flying on both of the space shuttles that later crashed, the *Challenger* and the *Columbia*.

A proud alumnus of Auburn University, Hartsfield joined fellow Auburn graduate Ken Mattingly for their most high-profile mission aboard the *Columbia*.

By the Numbers

3...Hartsfield flew missions on three different space shuttles, the *Challenger*, the *Columbia*, and the *Discovery*.

483...Hartsfield spent a total of 483 hours in outer space.

112...On his first space flight, on the *Columbia* in 1982,

Hartsfield orbited the Earth 112 times.

500,000....When Hartsfield and fellow astronaut (and fellow Auburn alumnus) Ken Mattingly returned to Earth, over half a million people were waiting at the site, including President Ronald Reagan and First Lady Nancy Reagan.

Mae Jemison
Astronaut, doctor
Morgan and Madison Counties

Mae Jemison, the engineer, astronaut, doctor, and Peace Corps volunteer, was born in Decatur.

An outstanding student, Jemison always wanted to venture to the next frontier. After earning a degree in chemical engineering from Stanford University, she entered medical school at Cornell University. Even during med school, she spent time helping at a refugee camp inThailand.

Then, it was time for another frontier, and Jemison served as a physician for the Peace Corps in Sierra Leone and Liberia.

Finally, it was time for the ultimate frontier, outer space. Jemison became the first African American astronaut and space traveler on September 12, 1992. She traveled on the *Endeavour,* along with fellow Alabama native Jan Davis, conducting experiments on weightlessness and motion sickness. They worked in the NASA Spacelab, which was developed in Huntsville at the Marshall Space Flight Center. She spent a total of just over 190 hours in space.

Schools have been named after her, including Mae Jemison High School in Huntsville, and also an elementary school in Detroit, Michigan.

Ken Mattingly
Astronaut
Auburn University

When astronaut Ken Mattingly and fellow astronaut Henry Hartsfield flew the *Columbia* space mission in 1982, it marked the first time that two alumni of the same college served as astronauts on the same flight. The "A" and the "U" on the logo may officially stand for Auburn University, but it could also represent Astronaut University, because the school has produced so many astronauts.

By the Numbers

1...At Auburn, Mattingly was the top leader on campus, serving as president of the school's Student Government Association, and as a member of Delta Tau Delta fraternity.

6...Mattingly served his country in six different capacities, as (a) naval officer; (b) aviator; (c) aeronautical engineer; (d) test pilot; (e) Rear Admiral in the United States Navy; and (f) astronaut aboard space shuttle flights and a moon landing.

3...The 1982 *Columbia* mission actually involved three Auburn alumni, including then-Kennedy Space Center Director, Dick Smith.

800...At the time of the *Columbia* mission, over 800 NASA employees had been educated at Auburn.

Kathryn Thornton
Astronaut, scientist
Montgomery County

Montgomery native and Auburn graduate Kathryn Thornton became one of America's premier scientists of the late 20th and early 21st centuries.

By the Numbers

970...The number of hours Thornton spent in outer space.

17 (out of 5,000)...In 1984, Thornton was one of just 17 new astronauts that NASA chose from among over 5,000 candidates.

007...Thornton wasn't exactly a spy like the fictional 007 agent James Bond, but her first space mission was to deploy an American spy satellite designed to listen in on Soviet military communications.

21...During her career, Thornton set a record for the most

Barber family generosity brings speedway and museum to Leeds

Before he ran the largest dairy company in Alabama, George Barber, Jr., was a racer.

Sure, he also sold real estate before taking over Barber Dairies, but his heart always remained on the racing track. George's dad, George Barber, Sr., founded the company in the 1930s and built it into a dominant commercial force in the State of Alabama. After running the company for years after his dad's passing, George, Jr., accepted an offer to purchase the company.

It was time, once again, to chase his dream of racing.

The Barber Motorsports Park sits on 880 acres in Leeds, just on the outskirts of Birmingham. The park was built to be powerful and imposing, but also sophisticated.

According to the park's website, "The Park, which opened in 2003, has a 17-turn, 2.38-mile (3.83 km) road course, designed by Alan Wilson, viewable from several naturally wooded or grass-covered banks."

The park also features the museum, which houses the world's largest motorcycle collection. The nonprofit park and museum complex is considered to be the largest philanthropic project by one person in Alabama's two-century history.

The Barber family has continued its longstanding history of generosity to charities in Birmingham, and statewide.

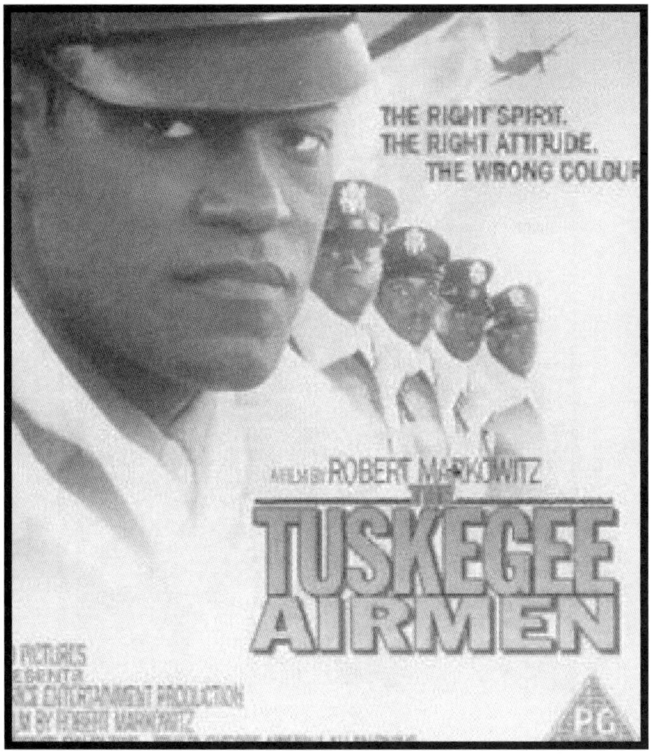

extravehicular activity ("spacewalk") hours by a female astronaut.

1...She was truly recognized as a woman at the top of her profession when the American Legion Auxiliary presented Thornton with the Woman of the Year award (1992) for her accomplishments as "one of America's preeminent scientists."

The Tuskegee Airmen
American heroes
Macon County

In many ways, the Tuskegee Airmen helped change the way the American armed forces establishment viewed African Americans.

One collateral by-product of World War II was the integration of women and minorities into the mainstream American workforce, especially with jobs requiring highly skilled workers.

That change was especially pronounced in the United States military, where the leaders had neither the time nor the manpower to exclude qualified and capable people. In 1940, as America prepared for war, Tuskegee became the home of an important facility for the training of African-American pilots. The many pilots produced in Tuskegee made a substantial impact on the success of the air wars, especially in the European arena.

The Tuskegee Airmen included "the 99th, 100th, 301st, and 302nd Fighter Squadrons that were assigned to the 332nd Fighter Group during World War II, which escorted American B-17 and B-24 bombers over Nazi targets in central Europe, its pilots flying red-tailed P-51 Mustangs," according to an official history of the group.

One of the outstanding movies of 1995, *The Tuskegee Airmen*, inspired a renewed public awareness of this outstanding group of American heroes. The movie starred Laurence Fishburne, and painted a vivid portrait of how the war effort caused many to reconsider past prejudices. After Fishburne's character flippantly ordered the planes' tails painted red, the issue of the red tails became the subject of public debate. According to Staff Sergeant James Sheppard, the "red tail" nickname came when "the 332nd Fighter Group painted the tails of their P-47's red."

Released in 2012, the movie *Red Tails* also told the story of the Tuskegee Airmen. Starring Cuba Gooding, Jr., and Terrence Howard, the movie also achieved acclaim and commercial success. Gooding starred in both movies about the airmen.

Although not an Alabamian, Willa Beatrice Brown should probably qualify for honorary citizenship. After becoming the first African-American female licensed as a private pilot in America, she founded the National Airmen's Association of America, and opened the Coffey School of Aeronautics with her husband.

The government chose the Coffey School to train African-American pilots for the new program and send over 200 pilots to the facility in Alabama.

When their country needed them, the Tuskegee Airmen provided badly needed aviators for the United States and helped bridge the gap of race relations within the armed forces.

Dr. Werner Von Braun
Rocket scientist
Madison County

He became one of the world's most famous scientists. Walt Disney asked him to introduce videos about space travel. Huntsville's civic center is named after him.

He was Dr. Werner Von Braun, and his work was instrumental in America's space program and mankind's ability to land on the moon.

Von Braun was raised in Germany, from a family of nobility descended from some of history's most famous monarchs. He became fascinated with physics and established himself as an expert on rocket science. His native nation of Germany, seeking to regain its status as a world power, was restricted by the Treaty of Versailles in developing conventional weapons. Signed in 1919, that treaty pre-dated the then-modern science of rockets and did not mention them. That allowed Germany to pursue the science of rocket weaponry. Like most other German scientists, he joined the Nazi Party because the failure to do so would have ended his career. He was quoted as describing Adolf Hitler as "a pompous fool with a Charlie Chaplin moustache."

At the end of the war, Von Braun and other German scientists were brought to the United States as part of Operation Paperclip, to give America a scientific advantage in the Cold War. His work influenced all major rocket and space exploration projects in his time, and in all projects afterward.

When the NASA space agency was created, President Eisenhower appointed Von Braun as the first director of the Marshall Space Flight Center in Huntsville.

James Voss
Astronaut
Walker and Lee Counties

Born in Cordova and raised by his grandparents in Opelika, James Voss became a record-setting astronaut in the 20th and 21st centuries. While in college at Auburn University, Voss led an unusually busy life for a student, becoming a second lieutenant in the United States Army and a member of the Auburn wrestling team.

By the Numbers

1...Voss set the record for the longest spacewalk, an eight hour and 56 minute walk from the International Space Station.

1...Voss was born in Cordova just one year before the town's most famous athlete, Major League Baseball pitcher Doyle Alexander.

5...Voss served as an astronaut on five different space shuttle flights: flying aboard the Atlantis (1991, 2000), Discovery (1992, 2001), and Endeavour (1995).

Tom Richardson

and the Bermuda Triangle mystery of the disappearing Flight 19

One of the greatest mysteries in aviation history helped give rise to the legend of the Bermuda Triangle. However, an Alabamian in the rescue effort believed it wasn't such a mystery. On December 5, 1945, five TBM Avenger torpedo bombers departed for a routine, three-hour flight from Ft. Lauderdale, Florida. The group was known as "Flight 19" because it was the 19th such exercise that day.

For reasons still unknown, the planes simply disappeared and were never found. Over 300 boats and aircraft were sent looking for the planes and crew, but they were never found.

Tom Richardson left his aeronautical engineering studies to enlist in the war effort. He became a flight instructor, and was the duty officer at the Fort Lauderdale Naval Air Station on that fateful day. He was deeply involved in the rescue effort, and he believed that the disappearance wasn't quite the mystery that others claimed. "The weather reports weren't worth the paper they were written on," he explained to the *Daily Home* newspaper in 2007. "The weather turned miserable that day. They should have never flown."

The disappearance came about a month before his service ended, and Richardson spent the remainder of his time in the Navy flying search-and-rescue flights, hoping in vain to discover evidence of his colleagues.

Conspiracy theorists went on to make good money off of this mystery. Richardson went on to become a business leader in Talladega, serving as CEO of Kockums (formerly known as Soderhamm) forestry products factory. He also became an accomplished artist, and a leader in the Talladega community, including the First United Methodist Church.

Trivia

Which Alabama city is the peanut capital of the world?

Each year, over 120,000 people gather in the world's peanut capital of Dothan for the National Peanut Festival. Alabama's peanut industry helps feed America, and the size and scope of the annual peanut harvest show that the state stands tall as a leading producer of the favorite national snack.

Alabama's history with the peanut extends beyond its crop, as George Washington Carver became globally famous for his innovative research on uses for the peanut, from peanut butter to soaps to oils to a multitude of other uses.

The best way to understand the impact of the peanut industry in Alabama just might be to examine it...by the numbers:

By the Numbers

400 million...That's how many pounds of peanuts are harvested annually in Alabama.

200,000...Over 200,000 acres of Alabama land are devoted to the state's peanut crop.

$100 million...That's the economic impact of the peanut industry each year.

120,000 people...The National Peanut Festival in Dothan is enjoyed by at least 120,000 people each year, including many tourists.

2...A second peanut event, in addition to the National Peanut Festival, was established in Alabama, with the world's largest peanut boil in Crenshaw County

Trivia

Which Alabamian invented the portable hearing aid?

Born in Montrose, Miller Reese Hutchinson grew up in nearby Mobile, attending Spring Hill College before earning a doctorate at Alabama Polytechnic Institute at Auburn (now Auburn University). By age 16, Hutchinson had already earned his first scientific patent.

His early devotion to developing a portable hearing aid came from the suffering of a childhood friend, Lyman Gould, who suffered from hearing loss.

Hutchinson gained fame for supplying a portable hearing aid to Queen Alexandria, consort of Edward VII of England. Hutchinson was an invited guest to the coronation of King Edward.

Not bad for a kid from Montrose.

But the story did not end there. Hutchinson invented many more items, and became a valued assistant to inventor Thomas Edison. Edison called his assistants the "Muckers," and bragged that Hutchinson was the "best Mucker of them all."

President John F. Kennedy (left) visits with Huntsville's Dr. Werner von Braun (right) during Kennedy's visit to Alabama in May of 1963.

Alabama native Mae Jemison, an astronaut, doctor, and Peace Corps volunteer, floats on a spacecraft. A high school in Alabama and an elementary school in Michigan have been named after her.

The crew of the1995 *Columbia* mission, with Alabama native Kathryn Thornton (top right) as payload com-

Astronaut Jan Davis, a Huntsville native, is pictured on the flight deck of the Space Shuttle *Discovery*.

ARTISTS

Actors, Composers, Dancers, Musicians, Sculptors, Painters, Poets, Photographers

Alabama
Country music's greatest group
DeKalb County

Some time during the late 1950s, in a church in DeKalb County, two young cousins sang a duet during the Sunday morning worship service. Only the age for the first grade, maybe younger, the boys probably impressed the congregation for being bold enough to sing, and maybe even for having some talent. Randy Owen and Teddy Gentry were raised in the Lookout Mountain area, and were seemingly born to perform. From that moment, the love of music and the joy of family would converge to change the face of country music and set records for success that might never be broken.

Owen and Gentry had another cousin, Jeff Cook, who had become a successful young radio DJ in the DeKalb County area as well as a highly skilled guitarist. The cousins sacrificed much in the early years, enduring the seemingly endless travel, awful hours, paucity of income, and setbacks that often accompany young musicians and artists.

Despite other issues, the cousins were blessed with plenty of talent, confidence in the quality of their music, the ability to put on an entertaining performance, and the strength that can arise from only family or the closest of friends. They borrowed money, they saved their pennies, and they wrote their own music. They called their band *Young Country*, then *Wild Country*, and finally *Alabama*. They went through half-a-dozen drummers before finding Mark Herndon. And then they left to spend a summer in Myrtle Beach, South Carolina, at a bar called *The Bowery*. Ultimately they were given a chance by a couple of smaller recording labels and then by RCA, and the result changed not only their lives but country music itself.

Alabama began an almost unimaginable streak of 21 released songs in a row that hit number one on the charts. They added six more over the next couple of years for 27, total. Their first signature hit, "My Home's in Alabama," celebrated both their hearts and their heritage. So many other hits have become staples of music heard at gatherings and on cell phones, and "Dixieland Delight" can be heard anywhere from birthday parties to 100,000 people singing all the words in a football stadium.

Before *Alabama*, most country music recordings were made by individuals rather than groups. The cousins from DeKalb County changed that quickly, becoming one of the most highly honored acts in the history of American music: 73 million albums sold, eight different Entertainer of the Year awards, two Grammys, the Artist of the Decade Award, 21 Gold, Platinum, and Multi-Platinum records, and the RIAA Country Group of the Century.

The group's website recounts one of Gentry's favorite stories: "I was in Nashville," he says, "walking by this club full of young people--I'm talking 18 or 20. The band started playing "Dixieland Delight" and everybody in the place started singing and sang all the way through. I had to smile at the longevity of the songs. Maybe some of those kids didn't even know who *Alabama* was, but they knew the music, and so I think that's a tribute to the fact that we spent a career putting out good songs that stand the test of time."

Yes, their music is timeless, and so is their impact on country music and the state of Alabama.

Pictured on the previous page: ***Top, left;*** *This portrait of The Commodores hangs in the Alabama Music Hall of Fame.* ***Top, right;*** *Nall stands as one of the world's premier artists. His work has been exhibited and acquired around the globe.* ***Middle, left;*** *The Thrasher Brothers, from Cleburne County, have performed in gospel, country, and even opera productions.* ***Middle, left;*** *Tallulah Bankhead stars as Catwoman in the 1960s series Batman. She became the most famous member of a family that included two U.S. Senators and a U.S. Speaker of the House.* ***Bottom, left;*** *the photo "Coleman's Cafe" in Greensboro was taken by the great William Christenberry.* ***Bottom, right;*** *Octavia Spencer has become one of America's great modern movie stars.*

Alabama Shakes
Grammy-winning musical group
Limestone County

The story of *Alabama Shakes* might seem like the plot of a major movie or great American novel, but the Limestone County natives have earned their enormous success through challenging and painful circumstances.

The seeds of the future band were planted by Jamie Howard, a young girl who passed away from retinal cancer at the age of 13. After the cancer had blinded her, she sweetly looked beyond her own suffering and spent much of her time teaching her younger sister, Brittany, to write poetry and play the piano. The children grew up in a junkyard, owned by their family, and played on stacks of cars and in the type of things typically found in a junkyard. Their house burned down because of a lightning strike, and combined with the death of Jamie, the events gave little sister Britanny a perspective and wisdom far beyond her years.

Years later, Brittany told NPR that she attended a band concert at her school when she was 11 or 12 years old, and decided that night that she wanted to start a band. One of the performers that night, Heath Fogg, would become the guitarist for the band they would form together, *Alabama Shakes*. Along with drummer Steve Johnson and bass player Zac Cockrell, they would take the American musical scene by storm and become one of the most recognizable groups from any genre.

Howard began hosting jam sessions at the home that had belonged to her late great-grandparents, and invited Fogg (whom she had heard play at parties), Cockrell (with whom she had a class at East Limestone High School), and Johnson, who had been invited by Cockrell.

Their first smash-hit single, "Hold On," became the number one song in America in 2012. They have since had an album also reach number one, won multiple Grammys and other music industry awards, released more hit songs and albums, and toured nationally and internationally.

Lucas Black
Television and movie star
Lawrence County

"Do you know where Mickey Wiggins' store is?"

That question launched the career of a leading young Hollywood actor, Alabama's own Lucas Black.

Cullman served as the unlikely site for movie auditions. The producers of an upcoming Kevin Costner film were searching for ten authentically Southern children, and interviewed roughly 10,000 in their search.

After standing in a lengthy line with his mom, Lucas Black, a ten-year-old from Speake (Lawrence County), finally had his turn with the casting staff. He delivered his rehearsed lines, and then answered some of their questions.

They asked young Lucas where he lived, and that was when he replied by asking them if they knew where Mickey Wiggins' store was. That seized their attention, and an acting career had been launched.

Black has become a star both in the movies and on television. His character in the *NCIS* series has won both acclaim and a large following. On the big screen, he portrayed characters in *War*, *Crazy in Alabama*, *42*, *Slingblade*, *Fast and Furious*, *Ghosts of Mississippi*, and many other major motion pictures.

Black has always embraced his Alabama heritage, and has reportedly even turned down roles that required him to conceal his Southern accent.

tWitch (Stephen Boss)
Television and YouTube star
Montgomery County

He may be a rising star in the Los Angeles scene, but for Montgomery native Stephen Boss, life will always include his Southern hospitality.

"Southern hospitality is a real thing," he explained to medium.com. "So, for me, what helps me draw the parallels is that even though we're in the big city, these are still all my folks. When I'm walking around, I say hello to folks [and] when I step into an elevator I say hello to folks."

Boss, who often goes by the nickname "tWitch," got his first shot at television stardom with his role on *So You Think You Can Dance*. That, along with a variety of dancing and movie roles, has made him a rising star in the world of Hollywood. In 2014, he became a nationally recognizable personality as the DJ on *The Ellen DeGeneres Show*. His gregarious personality and banter with the host have raised his profile, and his career grew. In May of 2018, he starred in a YouTube spinoff show, *tWitch, Please...Help Me Dance*; its first episode received over 3.5 million views.

Pat Buttram
Television and movie star
Winston County

It all started in Chicago. During a live performance of the WLS National Barn Dance radio program, aired from the 1933 World's Fair, members of the audience were interviewed. One of those people was a tourist from Nauvoo, Alabama, named Pat Buttram.

Buttram's folksy charisma was not lost on the show's producers, who hired him and dubbed him "The Winston County Flash." After performing with the show for 13 years, Buttram began a career in Hollywood that made him a national presence in movie theaters and on television sets.

Born in Addison (Winston County) in 1915, Maxwell Emmett "Pat" Buttram was the son of a Methodist minister, and aspired to the same path in life as his father. The Buttrams moved to Nauvoo for his dad to assume the ministry of the Methodist church there, and Pat ultimately graduated from Mortimer Jordan High School. He entered the prestigious Birmingham Southern College, still planning on a life of ministry until that fateful day in Chicago.

Buttram's first roles in Hollywood served as a great launching pad for his future career. After serving in a sidekick role in the *Roy Rogers* series, Buttram landed a role as the sidekick for Gene Autrey, whom he already knew from the Barn Dance production.

After continuing his successful ascent up the Hollywood ladder, Buttram received the role of a lifetime when he successfully pursued the role of "Mr. Haney" on the legendary *Green Acres* television series. The Haney character was a local conman, always trying to sell products and services to the show's main character, Oliver Wendell Douglas. After *Green Acres*, Buttram became one of the favorite actors used for voice roles in Disney movies, including *The Aristocats* (1970), *Robin Hood* (1973), and *The Rescuers* (1977).

Buttram was honored with stars on the Hollywood Walk of Fame and the Alabama Walk of Fame. He played roles in over 40 movies.

Wes Chapman
Globally famous ballet instructor
Bullock & Jefferson Counties

"You can imagine how that went."

That was the understated description, given by Wes Chapman, of how his football coach-father first reacted when Wes began ballet lessons during his elementary school years. Chapman described the reaction to *Iron City Ink*, but then quickly added that his dad became his biggest fan.

Coach Chapman might have become his son's biggest fan, but he certainly wasn't the only one. Just one year out of high school, Wes Chapman was hired by the world's premier ballet personality, Mikhail Baryshnikov, to perform with the American Ballet Theatre in New York. He later performed with the Bavarian National Ballet in Germany, before returning to America.

Originally from Union Springs, Chapman performed in his high school, the Alabama School of Fine Arts, where he returned in 2015 as the chair of its dance department.

For Chapman, the opportunity to challenge and inspire students toward the fulfillment he received from the performing arts was well worth the opportunity.

Dr. Mattie Moss Clark
Musical innovator, educator
Dallas County

She started out small, as the seventh of nine children in her family's Selma home.

That was about the last thing that was ever small about Dr. Mattie Moss Clark, who became a giant of American music and education.

Her gift of musical talent became apparent even during her childhood, as Clark was playing the piano by age six and playing for church services by age 12. After studying classical music at Selma University, Clark continued traveling with her mom to play at church services. After moving to Detroit to be near her sister, Sybil Burke, Clark soon became Music Minister of the Greater Love Tabernacle

Church of God in Christ.

Soon thereafter, her musical career blossomed, as described by the Church of God in Christ biography of her:

In 1958, she recorded "Going to Heaven to Meet the King," with the Southwest Michigan State Choir, becoming the first person to commit the sounds of a choir to record. She is credited as the first person to separate vocal parts into soprano, alto and tenor. She received three gold albums with the Southwest Michigan State Choir, and went on to write and arrange hundreds of songs and record over 50 albums.

Clark founded the Clark Conservatory in Detroit in 1979, while tirelessly serving both her church and community by lending her talents and time to causes and events.

So that seventh-born Selma girl rose to stir the hearts and souls of people across America and beyond by using her three-part harmony and her immense talent to serve a cause greater than herself.

Nat King Cole
Chart-topping musician
Montgomery County

Born in Montgomery, Nat King Cole became a star in a band, as a solo performer, in records, on television, and in the movies. Any venture involving music and Nat King Cole, it seemed, turned out successful.

Ironically, the preacher's kid who would become famous as a jazz singer started out as a classical piano player. By then, Cole and his family had moved to Chicago. His career with classical piano ended during his teenage years when he discovered the great jazz musician Earl Hines.

Cole formed a group called the *King Cole Trio*, touring and ultimately making the charts with singles such as "That Ain't Right" and "Straighten Up and Fly Right" (honoring one of his dad's sermons).

In the 1950s, Cole became a solo act, and the success continued with a number of chart-topping hits, including the classic "Unforgettable." He had truly become a star.

Cole made history in 1956, becoming the host of a television variety show, *The Nat King Cole Show*. As the first African-American to host a nationally televised series, Cole also became the first black man whom many white families welcomed into their homes in any capacity. Although the show lasted less than two years, history had been made.

Cole played a number of roles in movies, often playing himself. He also played fellow Alabama native W.C. Handy in a movie, and appeared on some of the era's most popular television shows such as *The Ed Sullivan Show* and *The Garry Moore Show*.

Cole passed away in 1965 from lung cancer. His music, and the legacy of his life, have continued to the delight of his countless fans. Part of that legacy has included the career of his daugthter, Natalie, who became a star in the music world.

Chip Cooper
Internationally known photographer
Tuscaloosa County

"You are a very great American photographer plus Georgia O'Keeffe rolled into one. O'Keeffe, because you have her eye. You paint with film."

–Harper Lee, author of *To Kill a Mockingbird*
Speaking of Chip Cooper's photography

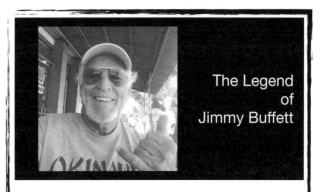

The Legend of Jimmy Buffett

As a freshman at Auburn University, Jimmy Buffett saw something that changed his life and brought joy to millions.

Johnny Youngblood, a fellow freshman and pledge brother in Sigma Pi social fraternity, used his guitar skills as a way to meet girls. Buffett followed his friend's lead and the path of life took a tropical turn.

Raised in Mobile, James William Buffett's life of celebrating through music began, fittingly, on Christmas Day of 1946. Buffett graduated from McGill-Toolen High School in Mobile, and began his college education at Auburn before his newfound musical interest trumped everything, especially his grades.

Officially, his education included Pearl River Junior College and later a degree in history from the University of Southern Mississippi, but according to the *Encyclopedia of Alabama*, the most important part of his education might have been his time in the hippie counterculture in New Orleans. A peptic ulcer prevented his military service during the Vietnam War.

Buffett moved to Key West, Florida, where he developed the tropical caricature that has become his personal trademark. The list of Buffett classics is seemingly endless, and his signature song, "Margaritaville," became a national hit in 1977.

Despite the beach bum persona, Jimmy Buffett has established himself as a highly accomplished author and businessman. He has written several successful books, reaching the unusual distinction of making the *New York Times* best-seller lists with both fiction and non-fiction works. Two different restaurant chains have been named after famous Buffett songs, including "Margaritaville" and "Cheeseburger In Paradise."

Buffett's career, however, has always been about much more than making money. His focus remains on his fans, just as his career has been built on engaging with concert audiences. He works tirelessly for disaster victims, especially from hurricanes, with benefit concerts and fundraising appearances.

Harper Lee's opinion, that Chip Cooper paints with film, is shared by many. Cooper has become one of the Deep South's most accomplished photographers. His work has been featured in the U.S. Capitol Gallery, in multiple foreign countries, in the pages of countless publications such as the *New York Times* and *USA Today*. He and his art have been profiled on the airwaves as part of national broadcasts.

Chip Cooper has been honored with more awards and commendations than even he could probably remember, and he has done it all while still based in Tuscaloosa, Alabama. After starting his career as a stringer for the *Birmingham News*, Cooper spent three years as a photographer for Bryce Hospital before becoming the Director of Photography for the University of Alabama in 1976. He served in that position for 24 years.

The career of Chip Cooper has begat profound and provocative work, but the way it started can only be explained by either providence or serendipity. As a student at the University of Alabama, he took a class in Studio Art, which consisted of students drawing different objects placed in the middle of a room. According to Cooper, the other students in the class were experienced at sketching, and he was basically drawing stick figures. A fellow student kidded him about his poor drawing and said "Hey Cooper, why don't you just take a photo of it instead."

Misunderstanding the remark as serious advice, Chip Cooper did exactly that, and realized that the 35-millimeter camera empowered him to see things as he had never seen them before.

However that historic advice was meant, it resulted in artistry that has benefitted the people of Alabama and lovers of art across the globe.

The Commodores
Grammy-winning musical act
Macon County

As the legend goes, five students from the Tuskegee Institute pulled out a dictionary, and one of them, William King, put his finger on a word without looking.

The group had agreed that whichever word his finger landed on would become the name of their new musical group. The winning word was "commodore," and the band went on to become one of the biggest acts of the 1970s and 1980s.

Years later, King joked that the group was lucky that his finger landed on that word, because they could have become the "commodes."

Dictionary luck notwithstanding, the Tuskegee students made their own luck as *The Commodores* with a combination of funky music and romantic ballads. Hits like "Brick House," "Easy," and "Three Times A Lady" made the group a consistent presence in the top five of Billboard charts for years.

Until Lionel Ritchie left to launch a solo career in 1982, the band was at the top of their game. Even after Ritchie's departure, the group won a Grammy for its 1986 hit, "Nightshift."

As for Ritchie, he became one of the most successful solo acts of all-time, with over 90 million records sold.

Courteney Cox
Television and movie star
Jefferson County

Courteney Cox became one of America's favorite television stars. Her iconic role as "Monica" in the 1990s sitcom *Friends*, made her an international star. Each week, millions of viewers followed the adventures of the single young people in Manhattan. After *Friends*, Cox continued her television and movie success in projects such as *Ace Ventura*: *Pet Detective* (1994), *Scream* and *Scream 2* (1996 and 1998), *Commandments* (1997) and *Cougar Town*.

Surprisingly, acting did not serve as her first career choice. The Mountain Brook native had actually studied architecture at Mount Vernon College for one year, but decided to move to New York to pursue a career in modeling. Her timeless beauty and authentic personality made television an almost inevitable path, and she landed her first television role in *Family Ties*, as the girlfriend of the Alex P. Keaton character portrayed by Michael J. Fox.

Tillman Crane
Internationally known photographer
Morgan County

One of modern America's premier photographers and photography teachers, Tillman Crane has built a career and a legacy by seeing and portraying the world in vividly original images. The Decatur native has contributed to the world of art in ways that can be seen, and appreciated, when viewed by the numbers.

By the Numbers

5...Crane has taught photography in at least five different countries: China, Mexico, Scotland, England and throughout the U.S.

4...Crane has published four photography books, including: Tillman Crane/Structure (2001), Touchstones (2005), Odin Stone (2008) and A Walk Along the Jordan (2009).

6...His works have been featured in major collections in six different nations: U.S., China, England, Ireland, Italy and Scotland.

1...One statement by Crane about his fascination with light says it all, as revealed on his website:
"Regardless of the subject - stone, tree, building, machine, or object - it is the light that I am really trying to capture."

William Christenberry
Painter and photographer
Tuscaloosa County

The Washington Post described him as "one of the most respected and influential artists of the modern South."

William Christenberry was inspired by the landscapes and ordinary but powerful images of his beloved Deep South. A native of Tuscaloosa, he spent many summers in nearby Hale County, developing a deep appreciation of rural architecture and images. In his early years, he aspired to paint impressionist art, and in that season of life saw photographs as merely depicting images.

As the years progressed, he increasingly saw photographs as art, and began to develop his own photography art.

Christenberry left a legacy of indelible and powerful depictions of his homeland.

Douglas Edwards
The first television news anchor
Pike County

The first television news anchor in history got his start announcing the organ music from the Methodist Church in Troy.

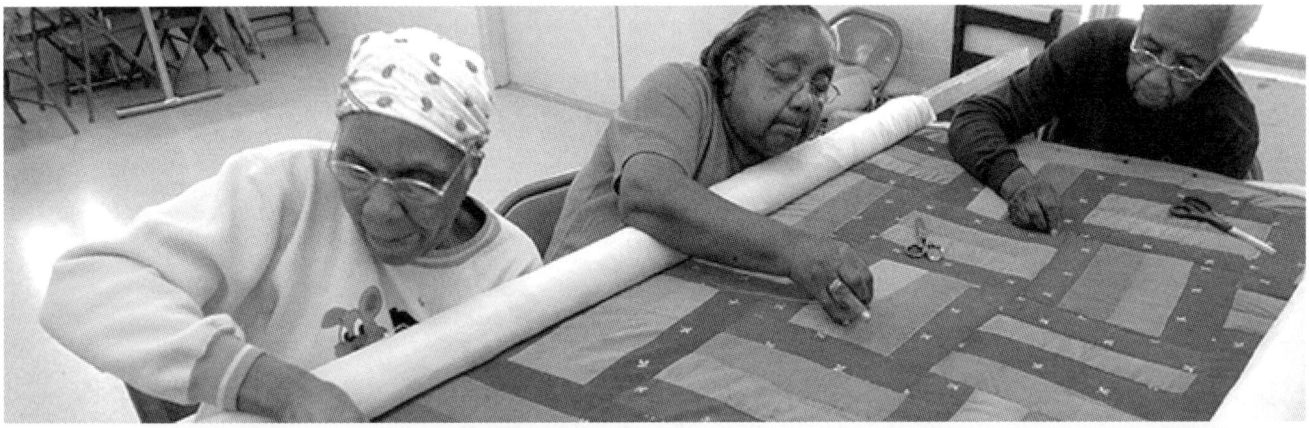

The quilt makers of Gee's Bend

Artists are usually not typical people, and the quiltmakers at Gee's Bend are certainly not typical artists, if there is such a thing.

The community of Gee's Bend in Wilcox County sports a population of roughly 700. Most are descended from slaves of the Pettway plantation. Pettway remains a prominent last name in the African-American community in Wilcox County, and also up in Dallas County and on into Prattville (Autaga County).

The Alabama River surrounds Gee's Bend on three sides, running much wider there than it does under the famous Edmund Pettus Bridge. But it's not the culture or the geography that has made the people of Gee's Bend known across America.

Gee's Bend has become the most well-known of the communities producing exotic and colorful quilts, but other Wilcox County communities such as Alberta and Rehoboth have contributed equally to the art that represents the culture and the area.

While many of the quilts are composed to follow patterns, a great many more are works of highly individualized, even idiosyncratic expression.

While the Troy Methodist organ assignment might not have seemed like a stepping stone to history, the joy of broadcasting helped stir the imagination of the then-15-year-old Douglas Edwards.

In 1947, the CBS network started the first ever televised daily newscast, and Douglas Edwards was chosen for the historic job. After a year, thanks to the popularity of Edwards, the show was re-titled *Douglas Edwards with the News*, and he held the job for 14 years before Walter Cronkite succeeded the one who started it all.

"Doug was the inventor of television news anchoring," explained Dan Rather, who later succeeded Cronkite as the face of CBS News.

Edwards was born in New Mexico, and his family moved to Troy during his early teenage years. He studied at the University of Alabama and Emory University, and later took classes at the Georgia Evening College. Originally intending to study medicine, Edwards found the lure of broadcasting irresistible.

He entered the world of radio, working at WAGF in Dothan, WSB in Atlanta, and then WXYZ in Detroit before joining CBS in 1942. He rose to the top quickly, anchoring nightly news reports for CBS before being assigned to Europe under the legendary Edmund R. Murrow, in the waning months of World War II.

After returning to America, Edwards was chosen to anchor the twice-weekly *CBS News Roundup*, making him the first major radio journalist to broadcast regularly on television. When CBS offered him the daily news anchor job, he was at first reluctant to accept, since television was considered beneath the high standards of radio journalism at that time. Thankfully, CBS President Frank Stanton persuaded him of television's bright future, and the path to history had been cleared.

Edwards won a Peabody Award, multiple Emmy nominations, and countless other journalism and broadcasting awards.

Despite the accomplishments and place in history, the next act of Douglas Edwards' career might have been his most impressive. With a dynamic news team now at competitor NBC, the ratings for the CBS daily newscast were beginning to slip, despite the high approval ratings of Edwards. Also, the corporate politics to choose his ultimate successor had reached critical mass. In 1962, CBS News announced that its popular number-two guy in broadcasting, Walter Cronkite, would succeed Edwards as the nightly news anchor. Edwards had done nothing wrong, but in the cutthroat world of national broadcasting, the only factor that counted was the latest ratings.

Setting aside the presumably painful and embarrassing

experience, Edwards was literally the first to congratulate Cronkite on his promotion and tell him that there were no residual hard feelings. Cronkite famously described the moment as "the classiest damn thing I ever saw."

From the Troy Methodist Church, to the battlefields of Europe, to national broadcasting history, to a historically gracious departure, Douglas Edwards made Alabama proud at each step on a unique and historic path.

The Erwin brothers
Movie producers
Shelby County

Their careers began with fun, frolic, and football. Now, they produce faith-filled feature films.

The results speak for themselves. Jon and Andy Erwin, Alabama natives, have produced hit movies that entertain audiences and provide spiritual insight.

Their film, *I Can Only Imagine*, cleared $85 million in ticket sales nationally. Starring Hollywood legend Dennis Quaid, the movie tells the powerful story behind the hit Christian song by the same title.

Before that, their most recent production also told a true story. *Woodlawn* gave the riveting account of how a high school football team found unity, purpose, and meaning through a spiritual awakening. That team included Tony Nathan, a high school All-American who later played at Alabama and in the NFL.

In the actual event, the pastor who shared his faith and challenged the team was none other than the Erwin brothers' father. Hank Erwin, the inspiration for the hit movie, has served as a minister, Alabama State Senator, and talk show host.

The tradition of serving others goes back even further, as their grandfather received the Congressional Medal of Honor for risking his own life to save his entire crew aboard an air mission over Japan during World War II.

No matter how acclaimed or profitable their films become, they will remain the same brothers who grew up wanting to make movies and got their start pulling cable for ESPN as teenagers.

Maybe that's the secret of their success.

Fannie Flagg
Author, actress, comedian
Shelby County

One of America's greatest modern creative talents, Fannie Flagg, has entertained millions as a screenwriter, actress, television personality and best-selling author.

Her most famous work, *Fried Green Tomatoes at the Whistle Stop Cafe*, was originally the book that spent 36 weeks on the *New York Times* best seller list. It later became both a major motion picture and Broadway play.

Raised in the Birmingham area, she was born and raised Patricia Neal. She entered the Miss Alabama pageant during her teenage years, winning a scholarship to a local acting school. She had begun writing at the age of ten, under the encouragement of her parents who saw that she was clearly a talented young girl.

After beginning her career on Birmingham's WBRC Channel 6 *Morning Show*, she moved to New York and launched her writing and acting careers. After she joined an actors guild (Actors' Equity) she learned that she could not use her real name because it was too close to another actress' name. Faced with the need to choose a stage name, she followed the advice of her grandfather, who recalled that the name "Fannie" was successfully used by several comediennes in the Vaudeville era.

Flagg's energy and dynamic personality brought her appearances on many of the top television shows, from dramas to celebrity game shows. She has performed prominent roles in a number of successful Broadway productions. Her books, and the movies in which she starred, have been consistently successful through the decades, including her role in the movie adaptation of the Mark Childress classic, *Crazy In Alabama*. She has been nominated for two Academy Awards and won the Harper Lee Award for her writing.

Although a talented writer, Flagg suffered from a lack of confidence in her younger days because of a serious problem with spelling words correctly. A school teacher watched one of her *Match Game* show appearances, in which Flagg misspelled several words. The teacher detected a pattern in the misspellings, wrote a note to Flagg explaining the term "dyslexia," and Flagg was suddenly made aware of the reason for her spelling problem, and began to address it.

Thankfully, the teacher watched television that day, and Fannie Flagg overcame her confidence problem to become one of America's greatest modern entertainers.

The Ghigna family
Artists, authors
Jefferson County

Few families have produced as many contributions to the art of Alabama as the Ghigna family of Homewood. Charles Ghigna, known as "Father Goose," has authored over 100 children books. The ACT and SAT college entrance tests have used his writing for their reading comprehension sections. He has composed over 5,000 poems, and has been an official nominee for the Pulitzer Prize.

He has taught creative writing at Samford University and the Alabama School of Fine Arts.

Debra Ghigna, like her husband, has carved out a career as an accomplished author of children's books. She has composed and published poems, and has also contributed writing to her husband's children's books.

Chip Ghigna, the son of Debra and Charles, chose another realm for his artistic creativity. His paintings appear in both galleries and private collections in the United States and France, where he frequently exhibits his works. Chip's paintings have been featured by both the *Birmingham News* and the *Leeds Tribune*.

Vern Gosdin
Star vocalist
Randolph County

They called him "the voice," decades before the television show by that same name hit the airwaves. Vern Gosdin grew up on a farm in Woodland, and has been named the most famous person ever produced by Randolph County.

The *Chicago Tribune* described him as having ..."an ability to blend in with his backup harmony that is arguably the best of any solo singer in the business."

Despite the golden voice, Gosdin traveled an improbably difficult road to success. His debut came in Birmingham, singing with two of his brothers on a gospel radio show. He ultimately formed a group with one of his brothers, performing for several years before leaving the business.

He left the world of music, starting a glass company in Atlanta. Then the opportunity to record a duet with fellow Alabamian Emmylou Harris brought him back to his calling, this time permanently.

Gosdin has boldly written about the trials of his own life, often helping him connect with his fans in ways to which other musicians could only aspire.

W.C. Handy
Jazz music legend
Lauderdale County

"He looked like a preacher or a professor, but despite his dignified appearance, William Christopher Handy was Memphis music's first international star, its first great songwriter and its first major music mogul."
-Memphis Music Hall of Fame

He was born the son of former slaves in Florence (Lauderdale County). His uncle, also a former slave, taught him the joy of making music, and by the age of 19, W.C. Handy was teaching music. He became a talented cornet player, even performing with a group at the 1893 World's Fair in Chicago. He traveled extensively as a rising young musician, performing as far away as Cuba.

Handy didn't just look like a professor; he lived as a lifelong learner, always on the lookout for new information and better ways to create music. He heard a musician pick at a guitar string with a knife, making a funny sound that the fellow had picked up from Hawaiian music. Handy incorporated it as part of his own blues sound.

Handy was also smart enough not to make the same mistakes twice. A manager had taken advantage of Handy, offering him only $50 for the rights to his song "Memphis Blues" because Handy was in debt. When Handy wrote "St. Louis Blues" in 1912, he had an investor lined up to get the song on the market. Before the public had record players, "St. Louis Blues" sold over a million copies in sheet music form, and Handy became a wealthy man.

The two songs made him famous, and Handy became one of the great ambassadors for the Blues music industry, which his music had largely created.

The W. C. Handy Museum was established in Florence, and Memphis honored him with the Handy Park and the Handy Theater. After his passing, the U.S. Postal Service honored Handy with a commemorative stamp.

Emmylou Harris
Star musician and vocalist
Jefferson County

Born and raised in Birmingham, Emmylou Harris became one of the most diverse and talented folk and country singers of modern times.

She performed with many of America's great musical legends such as Bob Dylan, Dolly Parton, Linda Ronstadt, Gram Parsons, and Neil Young.

Beginning her career in New York City's Greenwich Village, she expanded the scope of her reputation and became a beloved fixture in musical scenes across America, such as Nashville, Los Angeles, and Washington, D.C.

Even without a signature, number one hit, she carved a place in musical history with her creativity, her popularity in the 1960s and 1970s, and the number of the great stars of the day who enjoyed singing with her.

Ty Herndon
Country music star
Choctaw County

If you ever drive southward on Alabama Highway 17, you won't stray far from the Mississippi state line. If you keep heading down through Sumter County, you'll eventually find yourself in Butler, Alabama, the county seat of Choctaw County. Butler might be a small town, but it has produced three major league baseball players, two NFL football players, and some of the finest catfish that has ever been fried.

Butler also produced a young kid who could sing. Really sing. His name is Ty Herndon, and by the time he was 17-years-old, he had already been a finalist in the first season of the television hit show Star Search, and a regular cast member at OPRYLAND, USA.

Herndon left Nashville and made his way to Texas, where he hit the roads as an entertainer at honky-tonk bars. Despite playing in many small venues, his talent once again emerged, and he was named Entertainer of the Year in Texas. The big record companies came calling, and Ty Herndon soon recorded a smash-hit album and his first number-one hit song, "What Matters Most."

His first album, also titled What Matters Most, had the biggest first-week shipment in the history of Epic Records' Nashville, according to his website, tyherndon.com.

In a seven-year span, Herndon recorded three different number-one hits, seventeen released songs, and multiple top-ten hits.

Herndon not only records popular and meaningful songs, but also lends his talents and time to causes he holds dear, such as acceptance of alternative lifestyles.

In 2006, the American Idol television show received over 63 million calls supporting Hoover's own Taylor Hicks to win its internationally televised competition. At that time, the show had become one of the biggest on television, and launched a genre of entertainment shows copying its format.

Hicks, who entertained audiences with his blues music, New Orleans-style voice and harmonica playing, won the competition and became the American Idol for that year. He performed across America and beyond. His face graced the cover of People magazine. He signed a recording contract with a major company, and he quickly achieved everything to which musicians could aspire.

And it all began because of a hurricane.

After high school, Hicks studied journalism at Auburn University for three years, but never graduated. He wanted to sing, play his harmonica, and compose music. He had picked up his first harmonica at a flea market in nearby Bessemer, Alabama. Music, as he would admit years later, helped soothe the pain of a childhood dominated by his parents' divorce.

Hicks found himself drawn to the music of Ray Charles and other blues legends. As a teenager, he sneaked out to play blues music in restaurants and bars, and got away with it until his father and stepmother dined at a Mexican restaurant one evening and realized who was singing and playing the harmonica. "Well, there's Taylor," his dad deadpanned.

And then came Hurricane Katrina.

When the massive storm began to strike America's mainland, Hicks was in New Orleans for a friend's wedding. His flight home was canceled, and the airline instead gave him a voucher for a free flight. Hicks booked a flight to him a voucher for a free flight. Hicks booked a flight to Las Vegas, and made his way to the audition for *American Idol* in that city. At his audition, the show's designated curmudgeon, Simon Cowell, told Hicks he would never make the finals. Hicks' first performance on the show inspired a rare apology from Cowell, and the career of Taylor Hicks sped toward the history books.

The first album by Hicks after *American Idol*, titled *Taylor Hicks,* reached number two on the charts, and he has enjoyed a variety of successes, including well-received performances on Broadway.

Despite the fame and international notoriety, Hicks remains, above all, both a musician and a son of Alabama. He gives generously of his time and talents to help charitable causes throughout the state.

Jahman Hill
Author, award-winning poet
The University of Alabama

It's nothing unusual for a college student to write poetry in an inspired moment. It is unusual, however, for that student to become an internationally recognized poet and published author.

Jahman Hill grew up in Rochester, New York, but became a successful poet during his years at the University of Alabama, where he pursues graduate studies. As a spoken-word poet, he finished third in the world in the 2018 Individual World Poetry Slam, held in San Diego that year. His book of poetry, *Made From My Mother's Ceilings*, has earned him speaking engagements across America. He remains a popular speaker locally, including frequent events at the Birmingham Public Library.

Polly Holliday
Television and movie star
Walker & Talladega Counties

"Kiss my grits!" Those words have become commonplace in America, thanks to a sassy-mouthed waitress, Flo, played by Jasper's own Polly Holliday.

During her childhood, the Holliday family moved to Sylacauga, where one of her brother's friends was future megastar Jim Nabors. After moving to New York, Polly worked in a number of productions including *All the President's Men* with her friend Dustin Hoffman.

Her big break, however, came as the character named Flo in the sitcom *Alice*. Flo and her trademark phrase proved so popular that she was given a spin-off series, aptly titled *Flo*.

Holliday's other television and movie credits include *The Golden Girls*, *Private Benjamin*, *Mrs. Doubtfire*, *The Parent Trap* and *Gremlins*.

Jason Isbell & The 400 Unit
Grammy Award-winning group

Grammy-Award-winning act *Jason Isbell and The 400 Unit* has become the latest success story from the Muscle Shoals music scene, achieving national success for the guys from the Quad Cities.

Raised in rural Lauderdale County, Isbell was taught to love and play music by his grandfather. He played with local bands and developed the reputation as a talented artist, attracting the attention of several leading musicians who mentored him. One was David Hood, the Muscle Shoals music legend and father of *Drive-By Truckers* co-founder Patterson Hood. Isbell eventually joined the band before establishing a solo career in 2007.

Bassist Jimbo Hart is a son of Muscle Shoals, being born and raised in the recording mecca. He has played with a variety of top-shelf artists.

Drummer Chad Gamble hails from Tuscumbia, and got his start in the University of Alabama band scene, along with his brother, keyboardist Al Gamble of *St. Paul & the Broken Bones*. The *Gamble Brothers* have been recognized for their accomplishments by the Alabama Music Hall of Fame.

Derry deBorja is the non-Alabama native, but has fit in perfectly with the band as its accomplished keyboardist, after his touring with the group *Sun Volt*.

Interestingly, the band's name, *the 400 Unit*, comes from the psychiatric unit at Florence's Eliza Coffee Memorial Hospital.

Sonny James
Country music legend
Marion County

The journey of Sonny James took him and his music from Hackleburg to South Korea to Nashville, Tennessee, to the moon, and back to Nashville.

The musical life of Jimmie Hugh Loden began at age three, when he received his first musical instrument, a mandolin, which was hand-made by his father from a molasses bucket. By his teenage years, he was winning fiddling contests and traveling with his family as a musical group.

In his later teenage years, James began performing as a solo act or with others outside his family.

Then, Uncle Sam called. Sonny James was drafted to serve in the Korean War, and was stationed in the infamous Inchon area. He served in the 252nd Truck Company from Hamilton, Alabama. But James did something else in Korea as well. During his down time, especially late at night, he composed songs, refining his talent as a writer and preparing for a future after the war.

After his return home, James continued gradually building his brand as an outstanding vocalist, musician, and songwriter.

From 1953 to 1983, the Southern gentleman had a total of 72 chart hits. At one point, James saw 21 out of 25 singles hit number one. Between 1960 and 1979 he spent more weeks at number one (57) than any other country music artist.

In 1971, James made a cassette tape of his music for the crew of the Apollo 14, so his musical journey literally made it to the moon and back.

Sonny James was known as the "Southern Gentleman" of country music, and the people of Hackleburg remain proud to call him one of their own.

Jamey Johnson
Star vocalist and songwriter
Coffee & Montgomery Counties

Jamey Johnson has soared to the top of the country music world, but has remained well grounded without ever losing sight of his family, his friends, his homeland, his background, or his people.

Born in Enterprise (Coffee County), Johnson grew up mostly in Montgomery and graduated from Jefferson Davis High School. He played and sang gospel music in churches as a youngster, and was known to even sneak out and play tribute music at the tombstone of the great Hank Williams. According to *broadwayworld.com*, he has understood musical theory since his junior high years.

After serving in the Marine Reserves, he rocketed to country music stardom as both a songwriter and performer. One of his first recognitions as a songwriter came in 2005 when he co-wrote "Honky Tonk Badonkadonk" which was recorded by Trace Adkins. His song "Give It Away", co-written with George Strait, received a Song of the Year award in 2007. "In Color" earned him another Song of the Year in 2009. Johnson was honored with five Grammy Award nominations within a two-year span, 2009 and 2010.

Funny Maine
Comedian and YouTube star
Jefferson County

When Funny Maine posts any type of YouTube video, there are pretty much two guarantees: the video will be really funny, and hundreds of thousands of people will find it and enjoy it.

A Birmingham native and graduate of Jackson-Olin High School, Jermaine "Funny Maine" Johnson was a self-described class clown. After his first stand-up comedy performance at UAB, he walked away to a standing ovation. He had become a comedian with a nice local following.

And then came the videos.

As he explained during a guest appearance on the *Rick & Bubba Show*, some of his YouTube videos receive millions of hits in a given week. His videos are typically titled, "How Alabama fans watched... " with the week number or championship game name completing the title. In each video, Funny Maine watches the television, sporting various types of Alabama jerseys or t-shirts. The camera is positioned to give the perspective of the television looking back at him.

He seemingly lives and dies with each Crimson Tide football game. He fusses incredulously about officiating, and he even laughs when rivals lose. His glee at the 2018 Purdue thrashing of the Ohio State University Buckeyes was one of his most popular comedic rants.

No matter what happens in the world of college football that week, Funny Maine is funny, but he also remains positive and clean. Funny Maine was reminded of his responsibility one Sunday morning, as his dad, a paastor, cited one of his son's videos from the pulpit during a sermon. The congregation laughed, and Funny Maine was once again glad that he keeps all of his material clean.

But that's how he would do it anyway.

Funny Maine has become the future of entertainment in Alabama, and has become a great lesson in how audiences will find and enjoy outstanding talent.

Dean Jones
Movie star
Morgan County

Before graduating high school in Decatur, Dean Jones already had his own radio show, *Dean Jones Sings*.

The golden voice and likable personality helped make Dean Jones one of America's leading actors for decades. From his first days on the Broadway stage to his later years in Disney movies, Jones played a variety of character types with considerable skill.

Even during his early years, beginning with his Broadway debut in 1960, Jones landed roles alongside stage and film legends such as Jane Fonda, Elvis Presley, Frank Sinatra, and Glenn Ford.

In 1968, Disney cast Jones in its classic, *The Love Bug*, along with the sequel *Herbie Goes to Monte Carlo* and subsequent television spin-offs. Jones successfully starred in a variety of Disney productions, but the *Herbie* movies became the signature films of his illustrious career.

In the mid-1970s, Jones became a born-again Christian and performed in a number of Christian productions throughout the rest of his life. He passed away in 2015.

Creator
of things old and new

Cullman's Ben Johnson creates traditional art and daily creativity on social media

As a traditional artist, Ben Johnson's paintings have been featured in a variety of exhibits and galleries. He has twice received the high honor of featured artist at Alabama's inauguration festivities.

And then there's social media. Johnson gives thousands of followers a daily dose of creativity with Facebook posts that are typically entertaining and comically irreverent. Many posts inspire hundreds of comments, making it one of the state's great interactive Facebook pages. The combination of traditional and new has made him emblematic of a new age at the dawn of Alabama's third century.

Bruce Larsen
World famous sculptor
Baldwin County

His sculptures sit in the homes of the world's elite, the sets of Hollywood films, and of course in his home state of Alabama. The world-famous sculptor from Fairhope has become one of the best known sculptors by taking seemingly unrelated items and creating powerful and compelling images of everyone from world leaders to Olympic gymnasts in action.

Larsen created his first sculpture, a centipede, out of clothes hangers and other items when he was only ten years old. Since then, the world has benefitted from his exceptional creativity and boldly expressive work.

In 2017, Larsen was inducted as part of the inaugural class of the Alabama Center for the Arts Hall of Fame.

George "Goober" Lindsey
Television and movie star
Walker County

Long before he was "Goober," George Lindsey was the life of the party at home and school. Growing up in Jasper (Walker County), Lindsey excelled at sports, but his life changed one day when he saw a production of *Oklahoma!* in nearby Birmingham and knew that he wanted to become an entertainer.

But first came college, and after beginning his education at Walker College (now Bevill State), Lindsey earned a football scholarship to Florence State Teachers College (now the University of North Alabama) where he played quarterback and performed in local theater productions. He began his teaching career, but the stage called, and he left Alabama to chase his dreams in New York City.

Ultimately, Lindsey made his way to the Broadway stage, landing a role in *All American*, and the off-Broadway production of *Wonderful Town*. After concluding his tour with *Wonderful Town*, he headed to Hollywood, landing bit roles on shows such as *The Rifleman* and *Twilight Zone*.

Then came Goober.

Goober became a household name in America because of Lindsey's portrayal of the lovable character. Even after *The Andy Griffith Show* ended its historic run, Lindsey portrayed Goober on the spin-off series *Mayberry RFD* and later on the variety show *Hee Haw*. Lindsey also played roles in various Disney movies.

Despite Hollywood fame and innumerable entertainment opportunities, Lindsey remained loyal to his home state and his hometown of Jasper. He frequently made charitable appearances, raised over a million dollars for Special Olympics, and established the George Lindsey/University of North Alabama Television and Film Festival at his alma mater.

In 2012, at the age of 83, Lindsey passed away. He was buried at the Oak Hill cemetery in his beloved hometown of Jasper.

Little Big Town
Award-winning musical group
Samford University

It all began at Samford University.

Kimberly Schlapman (then Kimberly Rodes) and Karen Fairchild met while both were students at Samford University. They became friends and sang together. Karen moved to Nashville, and Kimberly made her way there less than a year later.

Jimi Westbrook joined the girls, followed by Phillip Sweet, and the group called *Little Big Town* found its trademark four-part harmony.

Little Big Town has been honored as the New Group of the Year, and for Vocal Group of the Year, Vocal Event of the Year, and multiple times for Single of the Year.

Daniel Moore
Renowned sports artist
Jefferson County

One request changed his life and begat the career of a great artist.

Daniel Moore, a native of Hoover (Jefferson County), was working as a young staff artist at the Alabama Power Company. Someone asked him to compose an illustration of a runner for the cover of a running magazine. After doing it, and liking it, Moore requested permission to create a poster from the image. The poster sold well, and a friend suggested that he try painting an image of a football game.

As a University of Alabama football fan, Moore chose the famous goal line stand that preserved the 1978 national championship for his Crimson Tide football team. The popularity and sales exceeded his hopes, and Moore suddenly had the income to start his own business, New Life Productions.

Since then, Moore has become a nationally celebrated artist, commissioned by the U.S. Postal Service to create illustrations for a stamp series on famous coaches. Other organizations that have commissioned his work include the Super Bowl, the National Football League, the National Basketball Association, the PGA of America, and Major League Baseball.

Thousands of collectors remain ready to purchase each of his new prints, and his works adorn the walls of homes and offices of his fellow Alabama fans across the state and beyond.

Moore was named the national Sports Artist of the Year by the United States Sports Academy in 2005.

The Muscle Shoals scene
Hub of American creativity
Colbert County

The Rolling Stones came to Muscle Shoals to record three songs. If you were to stop by the Muscle Shoals Sound Studio at 3614 Jackson Highway in Sheffield, between the late 60s and the mid-80s, you might see them, or Cher, or Paul Simon, or *Lynyrd Skynyrd* (the original band), or Steve Windwood, or the *Oak Ridge Boys*, or *Dr. Hook*, or just about anyone who wanted that soulful blend created by the studio band.

But this wasn't just any studio band. *The Muscle Shoals Rhythm Section* founded the studio, and they were some of the world's best.

The MSRS band that established the studio consisted of Barry Beckett (keyboards), Roger Hawkins (drums), David Hood (bass), and Jimmy Johnson (guitar).

Jerry Wexler, a legendary music executive and vice president of Atlantic Records, contributed financially to help the group obtain state-of-the art equipment because he wanted the band to be available for his company's musicians. The studio moved to a new riverfront location, still in Sheffield, in 1978.

As late as 2010, the *Black Keys* recorded their Grammy winning album "Brothers" at the historic studio. In 2013, the studio was purchased by the Muscle Shoals Music Foundation, headed by Judy Hood, wife of MSRS original member David Hood.

Jim Nabors
Television star and vocalist
Talladega County

In the 1960s, he became one of the most recognizable faces on television. He was blessed with a baritone voice that was unforgettable.

Jim Nabors grew up in Sylacauga, the town that in many ways was built by marble. Jim Nabors enjoyed a career of international fame, television shows, and an intensely private personal life based in his second hometown in Hawaii.

For Nabors, the big break in his career came when he performed one night at a California night club. Fortuitously for Nabors, his audience included Andy Griffith. Soon afterward, Nabors was cast for a one-time role as Gomer Pyle in the hit television series, *The Andy Griffith Show*. The character proved popular, and the Gomer character became a regular.

Ultimately, his popularity inspired a spin-off series, *Gomer Pyle, USMC*, in which Nabors' character Gomer joined the U.S. Marine Corps.

For most actors, an iconic role defines their careers and sometime entraps them into certain types of roles. For Nabors, the golden voice made him a highly coveted performer on any stage.

For over three decades, Nabors helped kick off the Indianapolis 500 race by singing "Back Home Again in Indiana" with the Purdue University band each year.

For his role as Gomer Pyle and his altruistic representation of the United States Marine Corps, Nabors was named as an honorary Sergeant of the United States Marine Corps. Fewer than 100 people have been awarded that honor, which by law can only be bestowed by the Commandant of the Marine Corps.

A 1974 session at Muscle Shoals Sound Studios in Sheffield, Alabama, during which Donnie Fritts recorded Prone to Lean for Atlantic Records. From left, front row: John Prine, Donnie Fritts, Jerry Wexler, Jerry Masters, Steve Melton, Tom Roadie, Mike O'Rear; from left, standing: David Hood, Jimmy Johnson, unidentified, Eddie Hinton, Tony Joe White, Mike Utley, Kris Kristofferson, Roger Hawkins, Barry Beckett, Sammy Creason, Pete Carr, Dan Penn, Billy Sharp, Laura Struzick, Carol Little, and Diane Butler.

Nall
World renowned artist
Pike and Marshall Counties

One of the world's elite artists, his works have been purchased, admired, and commissioned by the Beaux Arts Museum of Nice, Italy, the Boston Museum of Fine Arts, His Serene Highness Prince Albert of Monaco, and Fondazione Festival Pucciniano.

His porcelain patterns have been exhibited at international porcelain fairs at the Caroussel du Louvre in Paris, in Stuttgart, Germany, in the Chateau do Bagatelle in Neully, at Podium boutique in Moscow, and in New York's "Arts and Crafts Museum."

His masterpiece "Jesus talks with the women of Jerusalem" was publicly unveiled at the twelfth-century Cathedral of Saint-Paul de Vence, France.

He began, however, as a kid in Troy, Alabama (Pike County), before moving to Arab, Alabama, where he graduated high school.

Nall studied at the University of Alabama, and then pursued his life's journey as an artist at the Ecole des Beaux-Arts in Paris. He distinguished himself, even among the most talented Parisian students. As described on Nall's website, he was mentored by Salvador Dali, who famously encouraged the young Nall to "Draw from life, draw, again and again..."

Nall's vast talents and global fame have never kept him far from his home state of Alabama. He has spent time as an artist in residence at his alma mater, the University of Alabama, and later at Troy University. He currently lives in Fairhope, where he has constructed a studio at which he mentors aspiring artists.

Fred Nall Hollis was named Alabama's Distinguished Artist of the Year by the Alabama State Council on the Arts in 2007. That same year, he helped establish an artists exchange between the Tuscan region of Italy and the state of Alabama.

In recent years, Nall has provided art and selected the works of Alabama artists for exhibit in the properties of the Retirement Systems of Alabama, including the Grand Hotel in Point Clear, the renovated Battle House Hotel in Mobile, the Ross Bridge Resort in Birmingham, and the Mariott Shoals Hotel and Spa in the Florence/Muscle Shoals area.

Dan Penn
Singer and songwriter
Lamar County

Growing up in Vernon, Dan Penn resolved to chase his dreams of writing and performing great music.

While still in his teens, he moved to Colbert County, to become part of the emerging Muscle Shoals music scene. He quickly became the lead singer in the *Mark V Combo*, and spent the next several years as a successful in-house songwriter for FAME Studios.

Penn made the people of Lamar County proud, authoring many chart-topping hits such as "Cry Like a Baby" (a #2 hit for the *The Box Tops* in 1968), "Out of Left Field," (recorded by Percy Sledge and Hank Williams, Jr.), "I Hate You," (recorded by Ronnie Milsap, Bobby Blue Bland, and Jerry Lee Lewis) and "Hillbilly Heart," (a top-five hit recorded by Johnny Rodriguez).

Sam Phillips
The founder of Rock and Roll
Lauderdale County

Sam Phillips, of Florence, Alabama, changed music forever.

Phillips has been called the founder of Rock and Roll. He produced history's first Rock and Roll record. He founded Sun Records, and his Sun studio became hallowed ground for musicians and fans alike.

His early years included work as a DJ at WLAY-AM in

Muscle Shoals, learning much about the "black" musical sound because of WLAY's "open" format of playing music by both black and white musicians. He moved to Memphis and started working for radio stations there. He had learned much about the process of producing records during his radio years, and decided to launch his own recording studio and record label.

He founded Sun Records, and sought out new talent from the Memphis area and beyond. He paid the bills by letting average people pay him to create a record from their playing and singing in his studio.

The 1950s began with a bang, as Phillips recorded what many believe was the first rock and roll record: "Rocket 88" by Jackie Brenston and his *Delta Cats*. That band was led by a 19-year-old future star named Ike Turner.

As the decade progressed, Phillips was developing and promoting the new sounds of the region and era. Then came the fateful day in 1954. A teenager visited the studio and asked to record a song for his mom.

The kid's name was Elvis Presley.

As he listened to the kid record the song, Phillips heard much more than a thoughtful gift for a mother. He heard the future.

Seemingly overnight, Phillips had promoted Elvis into a star. Needing funds for his recording company, Phillips sold the rights to Presley's music to RCA records for a mere $35,000. While that might seem like the worst deal since the Louisiana Purchase, Phillips used the money to launch a great many stars and hits, while RCA had the resources to develop Presley's international fame.

The 1954 visit to the Sun studio remains iconic in American history. The studio remains a tourist attraction and musicians from around the world record music there just to become part of its history.

Wilson Pickett
Legendary musician
Autauga County

The unique music of Wilson Pickett, a legend of the 1960s and 1970s, arose from an equally unique life that included a beautiful reunion with his home state of Alabama.

His early life in Alabama, however, didn't start out so beautifully.

Born in Prattville (Autauga County), Pickett was raised by a physically abusive mother and grandfather. He fled to Detroit to escape the abuse, although he carried with him a love and understanding of the singing he heard on the farmland of Autauga County.

Once in Detroit, he began singing gospel music but desired a path to the world of secular music. Ultimately, his distinctive voice, rhythms, and energy caught the attention of producers and the music world, and specifically producer Jerry Wexler.

The result was a career that included timeless hits like "In the Midnight Hour." In 1966, Wexler wanted to take Pickett to the FAME Studios in Muscle Shoals, to record with rising star producer Rick Hall and the *Muscle Shoals Rhythm Section*. Pickett, wary of his home state's issues with race relations, didn't want to return. He was surprised to learn that Hall and the *Muscle Shoals Rhythm Section* were white, and that didn't help. Despite his concerns, he made the trip to Muscle Shoals out of respect for Wexler.

To his great surprise, the creative energy and compatibility between Pickett and the Muscle Shoals people resulted in such hits as "Mustang Sally" and "Land of a Thousand Dances." Given the hardships of his childhood, the return to his homeland of Alabama and the resulting success were surely redemptive and joyful.

Even after his days of producing new albums and singles, Pickett remained a popular touring musician, engaging audiences with his signature energy. He passed away in 2006 from a heart attack.

Wilson Pickett was inducted into the Rock and Roll Hall of Fame in 1991.

Curly Putman
Greatest country music songwriter
Jackson County

Many believe Curly Putman was the greatest songwriter in country music history.

A native of Princeton (Jackson County), Putman wrote a multitude of country music's greatest chart-topping hits, but he also authored songs that transcended any genre or style.

"Green, Green Grass of Home," according to the *Encyclopedia of Alabama*, "has since been recorded more than 400 times – in virtually every language in the world."

"He Stopped Loving Her Today" became the signature hit of the legendary George Jones, and is considered by some to be the greatest country song ever recorded.

Putman's ability to compose popular songs was matched by his clever creation of titles, adding to the success of his music. One example was his hit song performed by *The Statler Brothers:* "You Can Have Your Kate and Edith Too."

He won a whopping total of 36 BMI Awards during his unmatched career.

Putman was inducted into the Alabama Music Hall of Fame and the Nashville Songwriters Association International Songwriters Hall of Fame.

Billy Reid
International clothier
Lauderdale County

His designer coats have appeared in two James Bond movies. His clothes have been worn by top celebrities. He has been featured and honored by *Vogue, GQ, New York Magazine,* the Perry Ellis awards, and the Council of Fashion Designers of America.

His stores can be found in New York, Chicago, New Orleans, Atlanta, Houston, Dallas, Charleston, and Washington, D.C.

One of the world's great fashion moguls, Billy Reid, has become known across the globe for his distinctively elegant but practical designs.

And it all happens in Florence, Alabama.

That's where Billy Reid's company keeps its headquarters. "When we began opening our shops, our budget was limited," Reid remarked to *GQ* magazine. "We wanted them to feel as if you were walking into our home as a welcomed guest."

His love of hosting customers remains as timeless as his clothing. That came from his mom, who operated a women's clothing store in an old farmhouse in Louisiana. As for the timeless clothing, Reid explained his philosophy on his website: "I am traditionalist at heart. I start with classic American clothing, and take it in a modern direction... that still stays true to the traditional. I think through every button, every thread, every stitch. Some people on our team call it considered clothing for the modern soul. I just call it good clothing, made with integrity so you can look and feel your best, no matter when and where you wear it. My name is on everything we make, and I take pride in that. I hope you will, too."

And for that, Alabamians, well dressed people anywhere, and James Bond will remain grateful.

Robin Roberts
National television host
Macon County

Born in Tuskegee, Robin Roberts understood the idea of making history. Her father was one of the famed Tuskegee Airmen. The Roberts family later moved to Mississippi, where Robin became a star athlete and equally accomplished student.

She climbed the career ladder quickly, landing a job at ESPN, the sports network. She also served as an occasional reporter on ABC's morning program *Good Morning America*. Ultimately, she was named co-host of the morning show, where she and fellow host George Stephanopoulos elevated the show to the top morning program on American television, displacing longtime morning leader *The Today Show* from NBC.

After battling and defeating breast cancer, Roberts learned that she had contracted a rare blood disease from her previous chemotherapy treatments. She announced that she would need a bone marrow transplant, and the national bone marrow donation registry, *BeTheMatch*, reported an 1,800 percent spike in donors nationwide.

Roberts has continued to soar as a broadcaster and journalist, while using her personal journey to inform, challenge, and inspire her audiences.

Rick & Bubba
Radio hosts and celebrities
Etowah and Jefferson Counties

Not many radio careers have begun by reading Shakespeare, on the radio, in a good-old-boy style.

It began in Gadsden (Etowah County), when radio host Rick Burgess got his producer, Bill "Bubba" Bussey, to read redneck-Shakespeare for a segment they called *Good Ole Boy Theater*.

This was their first moment of skyrocketing audience ratings, but it was only the beginning for the duo who first met in college. After school, Bussey worked as a producer at the Gadsden radio station, and recommended his old friend Burgess for a job as local morning show host. After the *Good Ole Boy Theater*, Bussey joined his friend on the air, where the two dubbed themselves "the two sexiest fat men alive," becoming national celebrities.

Now working from Birmingham, Rick and Bubba entertain listeners in 17 states and online who enjoy *The Rick & Bubba Show* each morning. Their first book reached the *New York Times* best-seller list, as have multiple books since then. Their "best of" CDs, released each year, always become big sellers, as do just about everything else they become involved with.

Both Rick and Bubba are funny, creative, talented, and original, but their success originates from something else. They also provide famously clean, family-friendly entertainment that conspicuously avoids the divisive strife and depravity that plague almost every format on radio.

They also engage with their audience daily, from the seemingly endless public appearances to their own personal issues, including the Burgess family's tragic loss of their little boy, just a toddler, in 2008. They wanted his passing and their public journey to help others dealing with grief. Unlike many other public personalities, Burgess and Bussey want their audiences to know them. So, each morning, massive audiences tune in to spend quality time with people who are like family.

Only much funnier. And as they'll probably tell you, much sexier too.

International fashion designer and retailer Billy Reid keeps his headquarters in Florence.

Grayson Russell
Movie star
Chilton County

He was just a kid at Clanton Middle School, and then Chilton County High School, where he graduated in 2016. That's nothing unusual, except for the movie star thing.

And it all started with Rice Krispies.

At the age of five, Grayson Russell entered a contest, singing the Rice Krispies jingle on a video, winning a year's supply of the cereal. Then a family friend, who happened to be car dealer Mark McKinnon, used Grayson in his dealership's television ads.

Then came the audition.

Grayson's parents wanted to introduce him to the audition process, so for the experience, they took him to audition for a role in the upcoming Will Ferrell film *Talladega Nights*. Grayson won the role, and stole the scene at the family dinner table with the hilarious rant against his grandfather.

Grayson also played a role in each of the *Diary of a Wimpy Kid* movies, as well as a variety of other parts.

Ray Sawyer
Musician famous as "Dr. Hook"
Mobile County

Ray Sawyer, famous as "Dr. Hook," became one of music's biggest stars in the 1970s and 1980s. The native of Chickasaw (Mobile County), produced songs still played on radio stations and downloaded onto iPods.

There was, however, one thing in life that he attempted but failed.

He tried to leave his musical career, and it almost killed him.

As he explained in the *The Encyclopedia of Folk, Country and Western Music*, he had tired of playing clubs and decided to drive to Oregon and become a logger. He had already purchased his plaid shirt and looked the part. On the drive westward, he was involved in a serious automobile accident, resulting in the loss of an eye. He hurried back to the world of music, now wearing an eye patch that caused him to resemble the fictional "Captain Hook" from *Peter Pan*. The band marketed his look and chose the name *Dr. Hook and The Medicine Show*, later shortened to simply *Dr. Hook*.

The band turned out hits that became classics, such as "The Cover of Rolling Stone." That song, fittingly, landed the band on the cover of *Rolling Stone* magazine. Other hits include "When You're in Love With a Beautiful Woman", "Sexy Eyes," and "Baby Makes Her Bluejeans Talk."

Even after leaving *Dr. Hook*, Sawyer toured as a solo act until passing away on December 31, 2018, at the age of 81, after a brief illness.

Tommy Shaw
Rock music star
Montgomery County

A grandfather sat on his front porch in Montgomery, Alabama, some time around 1958, and offered a nickel to one of his grandchildren. The only condition was that the youngster, five-year-old Tommy, sing for the nickel.

Tommy Shaw, known as one of the world's great guitarists and composers, jokes that it was his first paying gig.

It certainly wasn't the last paid performance by Shaw, who has sold millions of albums and concert tickets in his years with rock bands *STYX, Damn Yankees*, and in his solo career.

After the performance for his grandfather, and after receiving a guitar from his parents as a ten-year-old, Shaw believed that a musical career would become his future.

He played with some local bands in Montgomery, and then had the opportunity to audition for *STYX* after one of the band's original guitarists left the group. *STYX* began their touring career by opening for the rock band *Bad Company*, but often proved more popular with the crowds than the featured act. Shaw wrote several of the group's biggest hits, such as "Too Much Time On My Hands."

After *STYX* became an internationally best-selling band, the group split in the mid-eighties over creative differences. Shaw's second major band, *Damn Yankees*, was born out of his friendship with musical legend Ted Nugent. Shaw's subsequent solo career, reunion tour with *STYX*, charitable work for victims of the September 11th attacks, and continued work composing new music have kept him relevant and important in the world of rock music, and for the greater global good.

Percy Sledge
Legendary vocalist
Colbert County

Sometimes, history is made in the most unlikely ways.

Percy Sledge was a young orderly at the Colbert County Hospital. A native of Leighton, Sledge grew up working in cotton fields, dreaming of becoming a professional singer.

Beyond his personality, his voice also connected him with people, namely the crowds when he sang in bars and at college parties. During one performance, at a University of Mississippi fraternity party, Sledge sang a song he had composed about a girl who had left him for another guy. A young music producer and college student, told Sledge that if he ever wanted to cut a record, to come by.

The result was a song birthed by Sledge in the cotton fields, refined by fellow band members, and ultimately produced in Muscle Shoals to become one of the great American classics.

"When a Man Loves a Woman" was named by *Rolling Stone* as one of the greatest songs in American history. The song has been released by other artists, covered by countless musicians and bands, and became the title of a major motion picture in 1994 starring Meg Ryan and Andy Garcia.

Sledge performed other songs that became hits, but his signature work, "When a Man Loves a Woman," remains one of the greatest soul songs and one of those timeless classics that is performed and enjoyed far beyond Percy Sledge's native Colbert County, Alabama.

The Speer Family
Gospel music legends
Montgomery County

The Speer Family legacy just might stand unmatched in the history of American music. They not only entertained, enlightened, and inspired fans of gospel music, they did it for over 77 years.

In 1921, the *Speer Family* began performing as a four-member group of George Thomas Speer, his wife Lena Brock Speer, his youngest sister Pearl Speer Claborn and his brother-in-law Logan Claborn. A few years later, it was just George and Lena until their children Mary Tom and Ben joined the band.

By the 1940s, they were performing regularly on WSFA in Montgomery. By the late sixties, the original Mr. and Mrs. Speer had passed away, but the group continued singing and expanding. In 1979, an amazing 58 years after the group was founded, they scored their first number-one hit with "What Sins Are You Talking About."

They had additional number-one hits, and the group announced its retirement in 1998, an amazing 77 years after they began honoring their God in song.

Octavia Spencer
Oscar-winning movie star
Montgomery County

One of Alabama's brightest stars got her start, fittingly, right home in Alabama.

Octavia Spencer grew up in Montgomery, wanting to become an actress. She didn't think it was a realistic career path, so she just enjoyed acting in local productions.

Then the movie *A Time to Kill* was filmed in Alabama, and she tried out for a bit part. She got the job, and her acting career began. Spencer continued getting small parts, entertaining audiences and building her resume as a supporting actress in comedies.

Then came *The Help*. Her friend, actor and director Tate Taylor, is a fellow Southerner who grew up in Mississippi and was educated at Ole Miss. He also happened to be a pre-school classmate of author Kathryn Stockett, who authored *The Help*. Stockett chose Taylor to direct the movie version of her book, and Taylor was convinced that Octavia would be perfect for the role of Minny the maid.

Octavia became one of the world's top actresses almost immediately, winning an Academy Award, a Golden Globe Award, and a BAFTA Award for her performance.

Soon afterward, she won another Oscar nomination, portraying computer programmer Dorothy Vaughan in *Hidden Figures*, a film telling the story of three African American women who worked at NASA in the space program's infancy.

St. Paul and the Broken Bones
Award-winning musical group

This Alabama-based band has opened for *The Rolling Stones*, and has played to a sold-out Carnegie Hall. They have been profiled in the pages of *Rolling Stone* magazine.

St. Paul and the Broken Bones has become known for creating superb music while delivering some of the most entertaining live performances in America. Their on-stage energy has been described as almost evangelical, which is fitting, as lead singer Paul Janeway once aspired to become an evangelist.

Janeway has assembled a talented band that includes keyboardist Al Gamble, a Tuscumbia native who has already been recognized by the Alabama Music Hall of Fame as a Music Achiever. Guitarist Browan Lollar grew up in Muscle Shoals and formerly played with Jason Isbell. Bassist Jesse Phillips lives in Birmingham, making his way in life to the Magic City through British Columbia, Montana, and New Orleans. Trumpeteer Allen Branstetter hails from Jasper, and his fellow brass musician, Ben Griner, plays the trombone and lives in Birmingham. Drummer Andrew Lee lives in the Southside area of Birmingham, and honed his skills with his high school marching band.

Jimmie Lee Sudduth
Nationally known folk artist
Fayette County

He began his career by drawing pictures in the dirt with a stick. During his 93 years on this planet, Fayette County's Jimmy Lee Sudduth became one of America's leading folk artists.

During his career, he painted with everything from acrylics to mud. He claimed he could use the mud from his land, along with rocks and dirt, to create 36 different colors. For his canvas, he might have used a roof shingle, floor tile, or some other piece of material. His talents went beyond painting, as his early works of art included dolls that he carved from wood.

Sudduth's works have been collected and exhibited across America and beyond.

Channing Tatum
Movie star
Cullman and Elmore Counties

He was born in Cullman County, and was eventually discovered by a talent agent in Miami. In between those times, he also lived in Wetumpka, Mississippi, Tampa, and Glenville, West Virginia.

Tatum first became a dancer, and then a model representing Armani and Abercrombie & Fitch, among others. Finally, the acting jobs began, and he never looked back. Tatum made it to the big screen in movies including *G.I. Joe: The Rise of Cobra*, *Haywire*, *The Vow* with Rachel McAdams, and *21 Jump Street*.

The Temptations
Motown music legends
Jefferson and Bullock Counties

Even if you've never heard of *The Primes*, *The Distants*, or *Otis Williams & the Siberians*, you might have heard of the group that drew from each of them and became the signature group of the Motown music era, *The Temptations*.

Trivia

Which music star was once a college football player?

May 11, 2003, was proclaimed "Ruben Studdard Day" by Alabama Governor Bob Riley. The day of celebration honored Studdard's victory in the *American Idol* television show.

A former college football player at Alabama A & M University, Studdard burst on the national stage with his powerful performances on the *American Idol* show. In the show's final round, he faced an opponent, Clay Aiken, who also became a star after the competition. The margin of victory was only 130,000 out of over 24 million votes cast.

Throughout his *American Idol* appearances and afterward, Studdard has frequently worn a shirt sporting the numbers "205," honoring his hometown area code and reminding the world that he is a proud Alabamian.

Studdard's first solo album went platinum, and his career has continued to soar as one of America's best and most likable performers.

The seeds of the band were planted in the late 1940s, in Ensley, Alabama, when Eddie Kendricks and Kell Osborne sang in the same church choir. Kendricks was originally from Union Springs (Bullock County), but lived in Birmingham during high school and made the historic connection with Osborne.

The legendary Motown sound relied heavily on the people and sounds from Alabama; *The Temptations* may have been the state's strongest influence in that era. Kendricks and Paul Williams had originally formed a doo-wop band in Birmingham years earlier before heading to Detroit along with Osborne to find fame and fortune. Melvin Franklin of the original group hailed from Montgomery.

Kendrick's smooth voice and star-persona played well with fans, and his voice remains a part of history through hits like "The Way You Do the Things You Do," "Just My Imagination," and "Get Ready." Every new generation since has known, loved, and sung their music.

The Motown sound might be named after Detroit, but *The Temptations* and the guys from Alabama helped shape the classic sounds of an era.

Toni Tennille
Pop music star
Montgomery County

She was a Tiger, a Knight, a Beach Girl, a Dragon, and then a star. Cathryn Antoinette 'Toni' Tennille was born and raised in Montgomery, and during her youth she always enjoyed music with her three sisters. When the time for college arrived, she became an Auburn University Tiger. During her Auburn years, she became part of the performing group on campus called the *Auburn Knights*.

After school, she performed with a group in California and met Daryl Dragon, a brilliant young musician who played keyboard for *The Beach Boys*. They began dating, and Daryl recommended Toni to the group as a back up singer. She became the one "Beach Girl" during their concerts.

When not touring with *The Beach Boys*, Daryl and Toni played and sang in local clubs together, using his last name and calling themselves *The Dragons*. Aspiring for more than just playing local clubs, the two paid to cut their own record; local stations in California liked it and gave it air time. Soon they had renamed themselves *The Captain & Tennille* and they launched toward stardom. Top hits followed, such as their #1 debut "Love Will Keep Us Together." The couple became some of American music's top stars, cranking out hit records and growing in popularity. The ABC network, wanting to capitalize on their popularity, asked them to host a weekly television show on ABC. In its first season, the show did well. Toni enjoyed it but Daryl didn't, so they turned down ABC's offer for a second season.

Although the couple divorced in 2014, after decades of marriage, their first song was prophetic in that love really did keep them together. Toni was at Daryl's side when he passed away in January of 2019.

The Thrasher Brothers
Award-winning musical group
Cleburne County

What does gospel music have in common with country music, Willie Nelson, the Middle East, a popular television series, Hank Williams, Jr., the opera, and Cleburne County, Alabama?

The answer, of course, is *The Thrasher Brothers*, the band with elite talent that extends from gospel to country to opera.

The brothers, proudly from Cleburne County, have performed on virtually every music show on national television. For a while, they even hosted their own show, bringing in an average of eight million viewers per week.

They have toured the world, including the Middle East, enlarging their fan base with each performance. They have performed with such music icons as *Alabama*, Willie Nelson, and Hank Williams, Jr. They have even performed with the *Birmingham Civic Opera*.

The proof of their greatness lies in the number of their fans, but also in the awards and honors bestowed on the boys from Cleburne County. *The Thrasher Brothers* have won five Grammys and a Dove Award, among countless honors, for their gospel music performances.

They were inducted into the Alabama Music Hall of Fame in 2005.

Samuel Ullman
Renowned poet
Jefferson County

General Douglas MacArthur, one of the great American legends, kept a favorite poem posted in his office. As the leader of the American forces occupying post-war Japan, he exercised enormous influence in that country. When the general spoke publicly, which was often, he typically quoted the poem as well.

That poem was titled "Youth," and its author was an Alabamian named Samuel Ullman. Ullman had retired from a career that included service as a member of the first Birmingham City Board of Education, and as lay rabbi for Temple Emanu-El. In his retirement years, he enjoyed writing, especially essays and poetry.

Because he passed away in 1924, he never had the opportunity to learn of how popular his poem became, especially in 1940s Japan.

Decades later, a visiting Japanese businessman wanted to see the home where Ullman had composed his poetry in retirement. After seeing the home in disrepair, he began an organized effort to turn the home into a museum. In 1994, the Ullman Museum opened, under the ownership of the University of Alabama at Birmingham.

Sela Ward
Television and movie star
The University of Alabama

She was an Alabama Crimson Tide cheerleader, homecoming queen, and a member of Chi Omega sorority. She began her career as a model, but her magnetic personality and impish smile made her destined for the big screen.

Sela Ward has won multiple Emmy Awards for her performances, including her breakthrough role in the series, *Sisters*. Her movie credits are lengthy but include such box office hits as *The Man Who Loved Women* (1983), *Nothing in Common* (1986), *Hello Again* (1987), *The Fugitive* (1993), *My Fellow Americans* (1996), *The Day After Tomorrow* (2004), *The Guardian* (2006), *The Stepfather* (2009), and *Independence Day: Resurgence* (2016).

Ward most recently became the co-star of the new CBS drama series *FBI*.

Hank Williams & Hank Williams, Jr.
Country music legends
Butler and Cullman Counties

They might be the most famous and successful father-son combo in the history of country music.

Hank Williams, Sr., was the shooting star of country music, shining so brightly but leaving this world too quickly, passing away at the astonishingly young age of 29.

Having grown up in Georgiana, Williams moved to Montgomery and soon landed a job entertaining audiences on WSFA. His talent kept taking him to higher levels of the industry at a rapid pace, and only his health slowed him down. An issue with his back caused serious pain, and propelled him to drug and alcohol use. He was fired from various jobs, including one with the *Grand Ole Opry* in Nashville, because of issues arising from his substance abuse.

Meanwhile, his elite talent and creativity practically vaulted him onto the national stage. He recorded some of the most popular songs in country music history, such as "Your Cheatin' Heart," and "Hey, Good Lookin'."

Hank's music was labeled as country, but much of it transcended one kind of style. Performers in rock and roll, such as Elvis Presley and *The Rolling Stones* considered him important influences on their career.

Hank Williams, Jr., grew up in the northern part of the state, but remained in the shadow of his magnificent father. Unlike so many who try and fail to reach success in the shadow of another, Hank, Jr., became a country music legend in his own right.

Like his father, Hank reflected the styles, temperament, and culture of his times. Hank, Jr., came along in the 1970s and 1980s; his hair length, clothing, beard, and language all arose from that era.

Hank, Jr., produced one hit song after another, cultivating his own massive following. His music spoke to the rugged independence of his fans, and quite possibly his own independence from the legacy of his father. Songs like "A Country Boy Can Survive," and "If Heaven Ain't A Lot Like Dixie," provided plenty of insight into Hank, Jr., and his fans.

Many years after his string of top hits had ended, ABC brought him in to sing the theme song for its iconic program, *Monday Night Football*. The theme song was a reprise of his classic hit, "All My Rowdy Friends Are Comin' Over Tonight." *The Monday Night Football* success for Williams started a trend, as many sports programs and reality shows now begin with celebrities singing theme songs.

Tammy Wynette

Country music legend
Marion County

As the legendary story goes, Tammy Wynette, the first lady of country music, was signing autographs after a concert when the next person in line happened to be her ex-husband, Euple Byrd. She and Euple had lived, with three children, in a cabin without running water. The last thing he had said to her, ridiculing her musical ambitions, was, "Dream on, baby."

Those were the words she wrote with her autograph.

That moment speaks volumes about the difficult journey of Virginia Wynette Pugh (later Tammy Wynette), from her difficult childhood and early life to the fame that ultimately awaited her. Her music reflected much of that pain. While working as a hair dresser in Midfield, Alabama, she managed to get an appearance on *The Country Boy Eddie Show*, on Birmingham's WBRC-TV, Channel 6. The rest, as they say, is history. Birmingham had become her adult home, but Wynette was mostly from Red Bay, Alabama, during her childhood. Her signature song, "Stand by Your Man," remains one of country music's iconic classics.

Wynette was known as the "First Lady of Country Music," in part because of her iconic hit "Stand by Your Man," and also because her life spoke to the culture of rural America, especially in the Deep South.

Tammy Wynette was inducted into the Alabama Music Hall of Fame in 1993.

Jon of Art

Lowndes County native makes statewide name for himself in the realm of contemporary art

You might see the visual artistry of Jon Osborne at art festivals or in homes. You also might see his work proudly displayed in art galleries such as the Grand Bohemian.

Jon of Art's work stands on the cutting edge of modern visual art, and has made him one of the bright young creative talents in the state of Alabama.

Michael Papajohn

The movie star you don't yet know

He graduated from Vestavia Hills High School, and then played college baseball at LSU. Michael Papajohn has become one of Hollywood's top stuntmen, taking the hits for such stars as Dennis Quaid and Adam Sandler, among many others. He has also acted in many roles, including the carjacker in the Spiderman movie.

One of the funniest moments came from an injury, as explained on his website, *MichaelPapajohn.com:* "While filming Charlie's Angels (2000), Michael was kicked in the jaw with a stiletto boot. He found himself in an emergency room, insisting that he was not the victim of domestic violence. The spousal abuse representatives had a hard time believing that he had been kicked by Cameron Diaz."

Trivia

Which Alabama restaurant was named after a 19th century club?

One of America's greatest chefs, Chris Hastings ,founded the Hot and Hot Fish Club in 1995. Hastings was imminently qualified after years of experience, and training under legends such as Frank Stitt.

Chris and wife Idie named the restaurant after an epicurean club in South Carolina, to which one of his ancestors belonged.

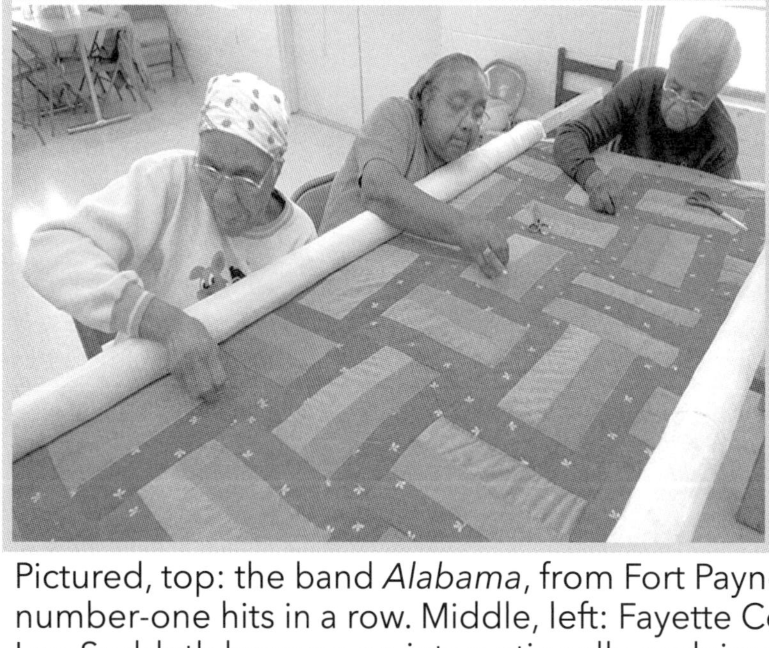

Pictured, top: the band *Alabama*, from Fort Payne, produced 21 number-one hits in a row. Middle, left: Fayette County's own Jimmy Lee Sudduth became an internationally acclaimed folk artist. Middle, right: Alabama Shakes, from Limestone County, has become one of the biggest acts in American music. Bottom, left: the ladies of Gee's Bend in Wilcox County have made their quilts a top item for collections and exhibitions. Bottom, right: music legend Hank Williams and his toddler son, Hank Williams, Jr., enjoy a moment together.

AMERICAN LEADERS

Alabamians guiding our state and nation

THIS CAMPAIGN POSTER was produced for the 1924 presidential campaign of Senator Oscar Underwood of Alabama. Underwood became the Democratic leader in the House, and then later that party's leader in the Senate. Photo courtesy of the *Encyclopedia of Alabama.*

Alabama Government Leaders

Governor
Kay Ivey
Wilcox County

Lieutenant Governor
Will Ainsworth
Marshall County

Speaker of the House
Mac McCutcheon
Madison County

Attorney General
Steve Marshall
Marshall County

Secretary of State
John H. Merrill
Cleburne and Tuscaloosa Counties

State Treasurer
John McMillan
Baldwin County

State Auditor
Jim Zeigler
Talladega County

Commissioner of Agriculture
Rick Pate
Lowndes County

Senate Majority Leader
Greg Reed
Walker County

Alabama Supreme Court

Tom Parker
Chief Justice

Mike Bolin
Associate Justice

Tommy Bryan
Associate Justice

Brady E. Mendheim Jr.
Associate Justice

James L. Mitchell
Associate Justice

William B "Will" Sellers
Associate Justice

Greg Shaw
Associate Justice

Sarah Hicks Stewart
Associate Justice

Kelli Wise
Associate Justice

Alabama in Washington

Richard C. Shelby
United States Senator
Tuscaloosa & Jefferson Counties

He has been called the most powerful United States Senator ever produced by Alabama, which speaks volumes, given the influential and powerful leaders produced by the state.

In each of the most critical areas of national life, Senator Richard C. Shelby has become a national leader. In the realm of national security, he has served as Chairman of the Senate Intelligence Committee, protecting our country's most closely guarded secrets and our spy agencies in the fight against terrorism and tyrannical regimes. For our nation's economy, Shelby has served as Chairman of the Banking Committee, strongly influencing the monetary policies and financial industry regulations that affect us all. In the sometimes murky world of government ethics, he authored the Shelby Amendment to clean up the ways in which lobbyists could spend money entertaining elected officials and their staffs.

Countless families have benefited because Senator Shelby authored and passed the law making it illegal to flee across state lines to avoid paying child support.

Most visibly to Alabamians, Shelby has served as Chairman of the Senate Appropriations Committee. Massive quantities of federal road improvements, new academic buildings, and new research centers testify to his success and power as chairman. When the state of Alabama recruits major industry, its leaders inevitably ask Shelby to help with the recruitment, as he has become an institution in the national government. Before chairing the Appropriations Committee, he served as Chair of the Senate Rules Committee, giving him vast influence over the Senate's entire legislative agenda.

Raised in Birmingham's Hueytown area, Shelby starred as a football defensive lineman, but injured his knee in the state's all-star game and was unable to pursue a college football career. Redirecting that competitive energy, Shelby became a powerful student leader at the University of Alabama, forging lasting relationships with future leaders such as Student Government President Walter Flowers. Along with academic work and student leadership, he found time to start a student laundry business, developing his business talents at a young age.

After launching a successful law practice in Tuscaloosa, he handily defeated a strong opponent for the Alabama State Senate in 1970. Eight years later, he ran successfully for the U.S. Congress, replacing his former law partner and close friend, Flowers. He was elected to the U.S. Senate in 1986, defying overwhelming odds to win the closest Senate race in America that year.

Shelby's vast success extends far beyond politics. His rare ability to see and seize opportunities has enabled him to build both a law practice and title company into highly successful businesses. That same foresight has propelled him to successfully leading the U.S. Senate in America's banking, intelligence, and national security. Thankfully, his talents leave a legacy of historic improvements in roads, schools, and jobs for the state of Alabama.

Richard Shelby, Alabama's longest serving U.S. Senator, has also become perhaps its most powerful member of Congress in the state's 200-year history. Shelby has led the Senate in the areas of national security, appropriations, and banking at various times in his illustrious career.

Trivia

Which Alabama industry is older than the United States of America?

Before the United States of America was formed, when its land hosted British colonies, the City of Mobile had already become well known for its outstanding seafood. Dishes like the shrimp jambalaya had become known far beyond the Deep South.

By the nineteenth century, Alabama had become a state, and its legendary shrimp was transported by rail, and on ice, throughout the young country.

Today, the state's reputation for seafood stands taller than ever, featured in some of the world's elite restaurants.

In the twentieth century, the freshwater fish industry became nationally known as well, especially

Alabama's oldest commercial crop remains a for catfish. Catfish farms became prominent in the state's Black Belt region, and many of those farms have expanded the scope of their work to include shrimp as well, a staple of delicious dining for our own families, and for fish lovers anywhere.

Doug Jones
U. S. Senator
Jefferson County

He skipped classes in law school, because he was headed to Birmingham.

No, it wasn't to catch a party or a ball game. Doug Jones was headed to the courthouse, to see the young Alabama Attorney General in action, in the trial of a lifetime. Bill Baxley was trying the criminal case against defendants in the gruesome bombing of the 16th Street Baptist Church in Birmingham.

Along with Bloody Sunday in Selma, the bombing stood as a signature event of the Civil Rights era in America.

Jones was raised as the son of a steel worker and homemaker from Birmingham's industrial Fairfield area. He was raised to identify with society's working people. After college at the University of Alabama and law school at Samford's Cumberland School of Law, he worked for U.S. Senator Howell Heflin. Ironically, Heflin became the last Alabama Democrat to serve in the Senate for over 20 years, until Jones himself won the same Senate seat.

In 1997, President Clinton appointed him as the U.S. Attorney for the Northern District of Alabama. When the opportunity arose, Jones seized the chance to re-try the 16th Street Baptist Church bombing cases that he had skipped law school classes to watch.

The ghosts of an era's sordid past had re-emerged, and the cases seized the nation's headlines. Jones relentlessly pursued guilty verdicts against the men whom he absolutely believed conducted the bombing. The jury returned guilty verdicts, and Jones became a national hero, and not just to his own Democrats and liberals. He became a public face of justice, earning the respect of people despite political differences. In 2017, Senator Jeff Sessions resigned his seat to become the Attorney General of the United States. Jones entered the race, but began as a prohibitive underdog. However, intra-party strife during the Republican primary election, along with scandalous accusations against their eventual nominee, Roy Moore, gave him a chance in the minds of the voters.

Jones ran the campaign as zealously as he had tried the 16th Street Baptist Church bombing cases, and he got the same result. The December 2017 election stood alone as the only political race in the nation. The nation's eyes, and its media, covered the race like a presidential election. Even national columnists including George F. Will came to Birmingham just to get the lay of the land politically.

On a suspense-filled night, Jones won the race and gave a conciliatory speech on national television. The kid from Fairfield had become a United States Senator. Interestingly, his ascent to the Senate meant that both Alabama Senators grew up as sons of blue-collar workers from the same area, Richard Shelby from Hueytown and Jones from Fairfield.

United States Senator Doug Jones was elected in 2017. The former prosecutor became famous for his pursuit of justice in the then-dormant cases of the 16th Street Baptist Church bombing.

Most thought the 16th Street Baptist Church murderers would never face justice. Most thought a Democrat could not be elected to the U.S. Senate in modern times. Jones has spent a career defying prevailing wisdom and the predictions of experts. He has built a career with the same indomitable spirit that has made his home state great for the past 200 years.

Trivia

Which Alabama leader had a city, county, and river named after him?

Few leaders in world history have enjoyed the power, the panache, and the mystique after death that still accompany the name of Chief Tuskaloosa. Thankfully, we have a vivid image of him from an artful description in the diary of the Spaniard Rodrigo Ranjel on the 10th of October, 1540.

"SUNDAY, October 10, the Governor entered the village of Tascaluça, which is called Athahachi, a recent village. And the chief was on a kind of balcony on a mound at one side of the square, his head covered by a kind of coif like the almaizal, so that his headdress was like a Moor's which gave him an aspect of authority; be also wore a pelote or mantle of feathers down to his feet, very imposing; he was seated on some high cushions, and many of the principal men among his Indians were with him. He was as tall as that Tony [Antonico] of the Emperor, our lord's guard, and well proportioned, a fine and comely figure of a man. He had a son, a young man as tall as himself but more slender. Before this chief there stood always an Indian of graceful mien holding a parasol on a handle something like a round and very large fly fan, with a cross similar to that of the Knights of the Order of St. John of Rhodes, in the middle of a black field, and the cross was white. And although the Governor entered the plaza and alighted from his horse and went up to him, he did not rise, but remained passive in perfect composure and as if he had been a king."

Robert Aderholt
U.S. House of Representatives
Winston County

As the son of a Winston County judge, Robert Aderholt grew up watching his dad resolving disputes and taking the responsibility to make difficult decisions. He also saw his father, Circuit Judge Bobby Aderholt, helping people, whether it involved child custody issues, painful divorces, or people who had been wronged.

Aderholt has taken the family mantle of public service, and he has become one of the most powerful members of Congress. As one of the highest ranking members of the prestigious House Committee on Appropriations, Aderholt exercises considerable influence over billions of dollars each year. Other congressmen, local officials from across America, and even the White House seek his help and expertise.

Throughout his two decades as a congressman, Robert Aderholt has spent his time, considerable energy, and superior networking to change America for the better. His priorities have included roads, water supply facilities, schools, colleges, law enforcement, the military, and our national security agencies.

In addition to his work on the appropriations committee, Aderholt has built a reputation as always remaining attentive to the needs of his district's people, especially in matters like social security benefits and help in dealing with the federal government.

Before entering Congress, Aderholt graduated from Birmingham Southern College and then Samford University's Cumberland School of Law. Following in his dad's footsteps, Aderholt served as a municipal judge in his hometown of Haleyville before becoming an aide to Governor Fob James. He also served as a delegate to the 1992 Republican National Convention.

Mo Brooks
U.S. House of Representatives
Madison County

Growing up, Mo Brooks was a baseball star for Grissom High School, and was named to Huntsville's All-City team. He still enjoys the game, and has always been an exceptional athlete.

Ironically, the hero of his high school baseball team became a hero, once again, on a baseball field in a deadly encounter.

In 2017, he was practicing with the Republican team for a charity baseball game, when a shooter opened fire on the practice. Brooks quickly helped render medical assistance to a wounded staffer, and then to Congressman Steve Scalise, who had been seriously wounded.

Morris Jackson Brooks, Jr., has served in the Congress since his election in 2010, becoming known as a zealous guardian for personal liberties and against government intrusion beyond its constitutionally permissible limits. Many conservatives, as well as libertarians, consider Brooks as one of the outstanding members of Congress and a champion of the Tenth Amendment.

Brooks met his wife, while they were students at Duke University. Mo Brooks graduated from Duke with honors in three years with a double major before entering the University of Alabama School of Law. He served as a prosecutor, judicial law clerk, and attorney before entering the political arena. Before his election to Congress, Brooks served as Madison County District Attorney, a Madison County Commissioner, and as a member of the Alabama House of Representatives.

Bradley Byrne
U.S. House of Representatives
Mobile County

Bradley Byrne has spent his career as a problem solver, in the world of education, as an attorney, and as a United States Congressman.

After graduating from Duke University and the University of Alabama School of Law, Byrne became a prominent attorney. He was elected to the Alabama State Board of Education, and later to the Alabama Senate.

He left the Alabama Senate to serve as the chancellor of the state's two-year college system, and found a variety of serious problems awaiting his skill set and urgent attention. While most of the institutions did outstanding work in educating our state's students, corruption was found in several circumstances, and in some cases it was systemic. Byrne made tough decisions and tough enemies, but persevered in his work to make the two-year college system elite, efficient, and ethical.

After making the 2010 runoff in the Republican gubernatorial primary, Byrne returned to his roots and practiced law for two additional years before running successfully for the U.S. Congress in 2013.

In Congress, Byrne serves on the Armed Services Committee, the House Education and Workforce Committee, the House Rules Committee, and the prestigious Republican Study Committee.

Gary Palmer
U.S. House of Representatives
Jefferson County

Gary Palmer spends much of his energy working to solve America's issues, but that's nothing new. He began doing that many years before he was elected to the U.S. Congress in 2014.

Before his successful 2014 campaign, Palmer founded and served as leader of the Alabama Policy Institute, an organization that developes and evaluates policy proposals through exhaustive research and consultations with experts. The institute has served as a leading resource for legislators, government officials, candidates, and the general public for help in understanding and evaluating issues and proposals.

Tackling tough issues was nothing new for Palmer, who spent his college years as a walk-on football player at the University of Alabama under legendary coach Paul "Bear" Bryant.

In Congress, Palmer was quickly recognized as one of its most thoughtful members. Even during the revised health care debate of the early Trump administration years, the congressional leadership relied extensively on Palmer for public policy guidance during the negotiations and public debate.

Many issues, especially ones like the health care debate, present an uphill battle without great odds for success. For Palmer, that just means that it's time to work harder and make sure that the facts and research are available to all. That led to his latest honor, in November of 2018, of becoming part of the House leadership as Chair of the House Republican Policy Committee.

Notwithstanding his growing national role, Palmer has continued zealously taking care of his people in Alabama, holding frequent town meetings across his district and remaining accessible to the people he was sent to Washington to represent.

Martha Roby
U.S. House of Representatives
Montgomery County

History, some say, is made from the ground upward. That's certainly how Martha Roby has built her career in the U.S. Congress.

She started on the Montgomery City Council, pushing for changes that would benefit her constituents, such as a tax holiday for back-to-school shopping. She built a network of people who were impressed by her good work, and after several years on the council, she looked to expand the scope of her public service and ran for Congress.

The halls of Congress might seem a surprising destination for someone who studied performing arts at New York University, but Roby grew up as part of a family in public service. Her father, Judge Joel Fredrick Dubina, serves as a senior judge on the U.S. Eleventh Circuit Court of Appeals. That made her next destination, Samford's Cumberland School of Law, a logical one.

Once she was elected to Congress, Roby wasted no time in securing a big achievement. She sits on the prestigious House Appropriations Committee, serving on three of its subcommittees. That places her squarely in the center of decisions on how the American government spends the tax dollars of its citizens.

Much of the federal government's most productive work occurs in Alabama's 2nd congressional district. That level of responsibility presents the perfect match for the skill set of Roby, who has remained a presence back home in her district, listening to her constituents and working for good government just like she did on the Montgomery City Council.

Mike Rogers
U.S. House of Representatives
Calhoun County

He just might be the most famous person from Blue Mountain, Alabama.

As an exceptionally hard worker, U.S. Congressman Mike Rogers learned his work ethic from his parents while growing up in Calhoun County. His mother worked in a local textile mill, and his father was a fireman.

A graduate of Saks High School, Rogers continued his education at Jacksonville State University. He became a leader in his community, and was elected to the Alabama House of Representatives.

Rogers ultimately ran for a seat in Congress in 2002 to replace Bob Riley, who had just been elected governor. Rogers won the seat, and quickly became an effective member of Congress, continuing the tradition in the 3rd district of Riley, Glen Browder, and Bill Nichols before him.

In his almost two decades of service, Rogers has built reputation as an authority on national security issues and a zealous advocate of his constituents. He serves on the Homeland Security Committee, where he works to protect and support the Anniston Army Depot and the Maxwell-Gunter Air Force Base in Montgomery.

Terri Sewell
U.S. House of Representatives
Dallas County

Terri Sewell, it seems, has always emerged as first in her class.

In her hometown of Selma, she graduated as the first African American valedictorian of Selma High School. That, as it turned out, was only the beginning.

Her education was second to none, as she graduated from Princeton University, the Harvard Law School, and Oxford University. As a Princeton freshman, she was assigned an upperclassman "big sister," Michelle Robinson, who became a lifelong friend and ultimately Michelle Robinson Obama. At Harvard, Sewell was a classmate of Michelle's future husband, Barack Obama, making her one of the few who knew each of the Obamas before they met each other.

Growing up in Selma, Sewell enjoyed a front-row seat to history and victories over systemic inequities in society. Her parents, highly respected educators in Selma, made sure that she learned both her academic lessons and those lessons taught by the history that surrounded them. The Sewell family counted historic figures, including Amelia Boynton, among their personal friends.

After successfully practicing law in Birmingham, Sewell sought election to the U.S. Congress in 2010, and of course she won. She became an officer of her freshman class, and has since skyrocketed into the leadership of both her party and of the House of Representatives.

Sewell serves as chairwoman of the House Intelligence Committee Subcommittee on Defense Intelligence and Warfighter Support.

She also serves as deputy whip of the House, and sits on the prestigious House Ways and Means Committee.

Kay Ivey
Governor of Alabama
Wilcox County

It wasn't exactly a typical beginning.

When Kay Ivey raised her right hand in the air and took the oath of office as Governor of Alabama, there was no parade, band, or multitude of people lining Dexter Avenue to hear her speak. Instead, she assumed the highest office in the land as her state suffered from strife and public distrust of Alabama's institutions. She was replacing a governor during a term, rather than after an election.

Since that day in 2017, under her leadership, the state has sped on a path of prosperity, with new and expanding businesses, high employment, and public confidence all soaring to great heights. About the only thing going down, it seems, has been the unemployment rate.

History just might record the signature accomplishment of her administration as the announcement, in January of 2018, that Huntsville had been chosen as the site for the $1.6 billion construction of the jointly operated Toyota and Mazda plant. Cities from across America competed vigorously for the plant, which will quickly employ 4,000 workers but will bring in exponentially more jobs in the form of contractors and support personnel.

Ivey may have had only three hours preparation to become governor on that fateful day, but she began walking that path decades ago. As a representative to the American Legion's Girls State, she met Alabama's first female governor, Lurleen Wallace. Ivey was not only aspired to a career in public service for herself, but has consistently supported Girls State as a way to challenge and instill a love of public service in future generations.

Ivey has become one of the most popular governors in America, even as she zealously continues her pursuit of new industry for the state. As a candidate for a full term as governor in 2018, she won both the Republican primary and the general elections by landslide margins over strong and likable candidates.

As the state begins its bicentennial celebration, the prosperity and public confidence serve as an excellent launching pad to the new century.

Oscar W. Adams, Jr.
Supreme Court Justice, pioneer
Jefferson County

Oscar W. Adams, Jr., led a life of firsts, clearing a pathway for future Alabamians by becoming the first African-American justice of the Alabama Supreme Court, and the first African-American elected to statewide office.

He was not, however, the first highly accomplished person in his family. His father, Oscar Adams, Sr., was the publisher of *The Birmingham Reporter* newspaper. His great-grandfather was a state legislator during the Reconstruction era, representing Marengo County of the Black Belt.

After graduating from Birmingham's Parker High School and then Talladega College, Adams pursued a legal education from the prestigious Howard University School of Law in Washington, D.C. Adams practiced law for decades in his hometown of Birmingham, handling landmark cases and representing an impressive array of clients including the Rev. Dr. Martin Luther King, Jr., the Southern Christian Leadership Conference, Fred Shuttlesworth's Alabama Christian Movement for Human Rights, and the National Association for the Advancement of Colored People.

Adams practiced law with James Baker, and later with U.W. Clemon, (a future U.S. District Judge for the Northern District of Alabama) forming the state's first African American law firm. The youngest attorney at that firm, Oscar W. Adams, III, still practices law in Birmingham.

In 1980, Adams was appointed to the Alabama Supreme Court by Governor Forrest "Fob" James, breaking an important racial barrier in the state. Two years later, Adams was elected statewide to a full term, breaking another barrier and cementing his already important place in Alabama history.

Perhaps most importantly, Oscar Adams, Jr., did not just become a man of great stature when he was appointed to the Alabama Supreme Court. That had happened long ago, as Adams had carved his role in the state's history long before that. Instead, the appointment to the court meant that an accomplished and prominent attorney would no longer be disqualified from consideration based on his or her race.

James "Jim" Allen
United States Senator
Etowah County

Senator Jim Allen was one of the most able and brilliant public servants in the history of Alabama. In the 65 years between his birth in Etowah County, and his passing in Baldwin County, Senator Allen became, in the words of his adversary Senator Ted Kennedy, "Perhaps the greatest parliamentarian ever to sit in the United States Senate."

Raised in Gadsden, Allen was educated in both his hometown and at the University of Alabama. He quickly became a promising young leader, elected to the Alabama House of Representatives in his 20s before leaving to serve in World War II. Allen served in the U.S. Navy, seeing action in the vitally important Leyte and Okinawa campaigns.

After the war, Allen became one of only three people to serve multiple terms as Alabama's Lieutenant Governor before running a successful campaign to succeed the retiring legend Lister Hill in the United States Senate.

Because the Alabama Senate uses the same parliamentary rules as the U.S. Senate, Allen brought his experience and intellect to the national legislature and of course made an immediate impact. Senator Kennedy's remark about Allen was typical of the reverence that national leaders held for Allen. Upon his passing, the *New York Times* reported "Senator Sam Ervin once said that if he had 'to stand with one man at Armageddon and battle for the Lord,' he hoped that man would be James Browning Allen of Alabama."

Almost a decade after his first wife passed away, Allen married Maryon Pittman Mullins, a journalist whom he met when she interviewed him for an article. After Allen's passing, Maryon succeeded her late husband as a United States Senator for the remainder of his term.

Richard Arrington
Mayor of Birmingham, scientist
Jefferson and Sumter Counties

A man of unquestioned intellect and networking skills, Richard Arrington became the mayor of Birmingham in the season of time the city needed him most.

Arrington's childhood and formative years could have come straight out of a great American novel. Fittingly, he was born on the anniversary of Yorktown Day (October 19) in 1934, the son of a sharecropper, in the Black Belt's college town of Livingston (Sumter County). Seeking to better provide for their young family, his parents, Richard Sr. and Mary, moved Richard Jr. and his brother James to Fairfield, a suburb of Birmingham. Richard Sr. took a job with the Tennessee Coal, Iron, and Railroad Company, and worked a second job as a brick mason.

Although he became a nationally prominent mayor and the face of a growing city, Arrington spent his career in the world of academia until public service called.

After graduating from Fairfield High School, Arrington chose a path that was rare for working class teenagers, and especially rare for aspiring politicians. He successfully pursued a degree in Biology from Birmingham's Miles College, where he served as president of Alpha Phi Alpha fraternity. That was followed by a master's degree in Zoology from the University of Detroit, and a doctorate in Biology at the University of Oklahoma, where he received the prestigious Ortenburger Award for his exemplary microbiology research.

Arrington may have studied in far away lands, but his heart remained in Birmingham. He returned to his hometown as Dr. Arrington, and became an academic dean at Miles College. In 1971, he successfully sought election to the Birmingham City Council and was reelected to that position.

By the late 1970s, Birmingham had not outgrown its well-earned national reputation for racial strife. An African-American boycott of Birmingham businesses, arising from racial strife and problems between citizens and law enforcement, had become another bad mark on the city's historical ledger.

It was in 1979 that Birmingham, needing a figure of unity, encountered the steady hand of Arrington's leadership.

Arrington was elected five times as the city's leader, and according to the *Encyclopedia of Alabama*, "his impact on the Birmingham economy was extraordinary in his 20 years as mayor." After retiring as mayor in 1999, Arrington returned to his original love, the academic world, where he has taught biology at both Miles College and the University of Alabama at Birmingham.

The Bankhead family
Two Senators, two Congressmen
a Speaker of the House,
Two archivists,
and a movie star
Walker County

They have been called the most important family in Alabama's history. Their collective impact extended far beyond the state, to national and even international influence.

John Hollis Bankhead became the patriarch of the family. Although not famous or powerful, his parents did have some measure of wealth, as John was born in 1842 on a plantation near Moscow, Alabama, on land that has become part of Sulligent (Lamar County).

At various times, John Bankhead was a soldier, farmer, coal mine operator, or prison warden, aside from his political activities.

Once in the U.S. Congress, Bankhead spent a total of 33 years as a member of either the House or Senate. He spent an extraordinary quantity of time on improving America's roads, and the Bankhead Highway extends from Washington, D.C., to California...right through Jasper, Alabama, of course. He also devoted time to issues like prison conditions, and (along with his sons) purchased a coal company at the time in which it became enormously profitable to do so in Walker County.

His son, William Brockman Bankhead, became America's Speaker of the House and a close ally of President Franklin Roosevelt. In college, the future speaker was a member of the first football team at the University of Alabama, in 1892.

When Speaker Bankhead passed away in 1940, President Roosevelt came to Jasper's First United Methodist Church for the funeral, on a train accompanied by his cabinet members, 63 members of the House of Representatives, 30 Senators (including Harry Truman) and many other dignitaries. Because the president was unable to walk the beautiful marble stairs leading to the church's front doors, and because the public was kept unaware of their leader's physical limitations (polio), the Alabama National Guard was put into action. Troops were sent to quickly build a ramp from the street, over the steps, to the church's front door. Roosevelt waved to adoring Americans as his car drove to the church, but the ramp allowed him to leave and return to the car outside the light of public scrutiny.

The public, as always, never saw that the president could not walk under his own power.

William Bankhead's older brother, John Hollis Bankhead, II, served in the U.S. Senate for 15 years. Before that, he practiced law, operated the family's coal company, and served in the Alabama House of Representatives. In the Senate, he worked especially hard to help farmers whose economic security had been devastated by the Great Depression. Bankhead worked to remedy the problem of excess cotton production, and for government limitation on growing other crops by paying farmers not to grow them.

His son, Walter Will Bankhead, inherited much of the grandfather's legendary business acumen, developing an elite law practice and serving as the lead businessman for the family's varied interests. He served in the Congress as well, but only for a few months after his uncle William's passing, until a special election was held.

Normally, two senators, a Speaker of the House, and a national highway system bearing the family name would be the highlights of any family's time in the national spotlight.

Not so.

Enter the one and only Tallulah.

Tallulah Bankhead was the one family member so famous that people often used her first name only. Even the off-Broadway musical about her life was simply named *Tallulah*.

Her mother died during childbirth, and sadly, she was christened at church on the day of her own mother's funeral. If that moment seems unconventional, it was also a metaphor one of the least conventional celebrities ever produced by Alabama. Tallulah's outsized and outspoken personality would define her legacy.

She auditioned as part of a contest for a screen test, and won. Hesitantly, her father let her go to New York and give the screen test a shot. Although she was young, un-

Bankhead family patriarch and U.S. Senator John Hollis Bankhead (center) visits with his granddaughters Talulah (left) and Eugenia (right) in Washington D.C. The occasion was a 1917 reunion of Confederate soldiers (photo courtesy of the *Encyclopedia of Alabama*).

known, and hungry to succeed, she was still a Bankhead, so her father put her up at the famous and luxurious and legendary Algonquin Hotel.

Tallulah saw a measure of success on the stage and in the early movie industry. She landed a prominent role in a London musical, and as always, she became famous in London simply as Tallulah.

For years, she starred in mostly smaller productions, and got her biggest role in *The Little Foxes*, for which she was named Actress of the Year. Movie executives wanted her to play the Scarlet O'Hara role in *Gone With The Wind*, but at age 34, they thought she was a little too far on the senior side for the role as written.

In 1950, she started her biggest role, as the emcee of the appropriately titled radio program titled *The Big Show*.

Tallulah attracted millions of listeners, and capitalized on her expanded fame by releasing her autobiography that spent a whopping 26 weeks on the *New York Times* bestseller list and sold over 10 million copies.

Tallulah passed away in 1968 of conditions arising from her long-time smoking habit. In addition to the off-Broadway production bearing her name, a festival is held in her honor in her hometown of Jasper each year.

Marie Bankhead Owen became a big name in her own right, as a prominent columnist and writer for various publications in the Deep South and beyond. She helped her husband, Thomas McAdory Owen, lead the effort that ultimately resulted in the creations of the Alabama Department of Archives and History, the first of its kind in America. Fittingly, Owen was named the state's first archivist. After his passing, Marie took over the position and became only the second woman in Alabama history to head a state agency.

Her legacy includes the building that still houses the state archives collection, and her successful efforts to prevent other agencies from taking over the beautiful Montgomery building.

Tommy Battle
Mayor of Huntsville
Jefferson and Madison Counties

Many elected leaders talk about jobs, but for Huntsville Mayor Tommy Battle, jobs have served as the focus of his entire career.

During his years at Birmingham's Berry High School, Battle began a series of jobs to pay for his college education, including the shipyards in Mobile and coke ovens in Birmingham. He not only learned the value of hard work, but the dignity of vigorously working to pay expenses. That work, and the resulting work ethic, paid off for Battle at the University of Alabama as he became a championship debater, chairman of the College Republicans, and ultimately chairman of the state's College Republicans.

Moving to Huntsville in 1980, Battle continued his interest in good government, and ran successfully for the Huntsville City Council just four years later while also operating multiple small businesses. Once again, the value of jobs had become a central theme of his career.

Elected mayor of Huntsville, Battle's years as mayor have been defined by...you guessed it...jobs. The Huntsville area has produced 24,000 new jobs, $500 million in new road construction, and $250 million in new schools during the Battle administration. Battle and his entire family have become pillars of the Huntsville community, including his wife Eula, son Drew, daughter-in-law Lauren, and grandson George.

Bert Bank
War hero, senator, media pioneer
Tuscaloosa County

If anyone marched to the beat of his own drummer, it was the patriot, soldier, broadcaster, senator, and mentor named Bert Bank.

As a young man, Bank marched to a place more horrible than most could even imagine. As a prisoner of war during World War II, he was part of the infamous Bataan Death March, in which the Japanese transported 76,000 American and Filipino soldiers close to 70 miles under brutal conditions. The march was described by *eyewitnesstohistory.com:*

"Japanese butchery, disease, exposure to the blazing sun, lack of food, and lack of water took the lives of approximately 5,200 Americans along the way. Many prisoners were bayoneted, shot, beheaded or just left to die on the side of the road."

The soldiers who survived the march didn't fare much better, as they were subjected to torture, food deprivation, and many of the same atrocities imposed during the march. When Bank returned to his hometown of Tuscaloosa at the end of the war, he weighed around 100 pounds, and was barely recognizable.

That march might have caused unspeakable trauma and pain, but it was not the march that defined the life and career of Bert Bank. Bank marched right into the world of broadcasting, acquiring and running WTBC-AM and WUOA-FM in Tuscaloosa. For the next five decades, Bank gave first and second chances to aspiring broadcasters and launched many prominent careers, including the legendary James Spann. He also hired a black disc jockey, breaking the color barrier in the local radio market.

In 1953, Bank had the foresight to create the radio

broadcasting network for the University of Alabama football games. Five years later, his old friend Paul "Bear" Bryant became the coach, and the broadcasting rights to Alabama football became a premium. Bryant was not the only Crimson Tide coach to befriend Bank, as he had the unique distinction of being on a first-name basis with every Alabama head coach from Wallace Wade (in the 1920s) to Nick Saban. Two decades after establishing the football network, Bank once again showed keen foresight, setting up a network with Alabama basketball, and his business genius was once again confirmed with Bama hoops reaching success at a national level.

Bank then marched into the political arena, and once again achieved success. The voters of Tuscaloosa County and surrounding areas elected him twice to the Alabama House of Representatives (1966 and 1970) and once to the Alabama Senate (1974).

In all seasons of his remarkable life, Bert Bank marched as a leader, survivor, winner, overcomer, and an inspiration for all.

Bill Baxley
Attorney General, Lt. Governor
Trial lawyer
Houston & Jefferson Counties

Even from his early years, Bill Baxley's capacity for outstanding achievement as a leader and communicator were obvious. After growing up in Dothan (Houston County), Baxley entered the University of Alabama, where he served as president of the prestigious Cotillion Club. Professor Anabel Hagood, winner of multiple national championships as the university debate team coach, declared that Baxley was the best public speaker she ever taught.

After graduating from the university and then its law school, Baxley began his rapid ascent to the highest levels of state government. After serving as District Attorney in Houston and Henry counties, Baxley was elected Alabama's Attorney General at age 28.

Baxley reopened the 16th Street Baptist Church bombing case and successfully prosecuted Robert Chambliss in 1977. He served two terms as attorney general and one term as lieutenant governor before winning the nomination of the Democratic Party for governor in 1986. A dispute over crossover voting between the primary and runoff elections of the two parties gave rise to a venomous dispute and lengthy court battle. After Baxley was declared the party's nominee, a public backlash against party leadership resulted in the first elected Republican governor since the post-Civil War Reconstruction years, Guy Hunt of Holly Pond (Cullman County).

Despite his enormous political gifts, Baxley returned to his first professional love, trying cases in Alabama courtrooms. As a founding partner of Baxley, Dillard, McKnight, James & McElroy, Baxley has become a legendary courtroom lawyer. He is often approached by aspiring leaders and lawyers alike, giving wise counsel in the political and legal worlds.

Jere Beasley
Lt. Governor, trial lawyer
Barbour & Montgomery Counties

He was called America's most successful trial lawyer by a 2003 book about the nation's legal system. The solo law practice Jere Locke Beasley founded has become one of America's most prominent law firms, with attorneys practicing across the country. His firm, now known as Beasley, Allen, Crow, Methvin, Portis & Miles, holds the American record for the largest verdict/settlement in five different categories, including an eleven billion dollar verdict on behalf of the state of Alabama against Exxon for fraudulent practices involving oil leases.

The national law firm might have become Beasley's grandest success, but it was by no means his first.

Beasley was raised in Clayton, a small town in rural Barbour County, Alabama, where his parents operated a grocery store. After graduating from Auburn University, Beasley enrolled in the University of Alabama School of Law, where he graduated in 1962.

In 1970, Beasley was elected Alabama Lieutenant Governor, and re-elected in 1974. During his first term, he actually served as acting governor for 32 days after Governor George C. Wallace was wounded during an assassination attempt while campaigning for the presidency in Maryland. Wallace required lengthy hospitalization before returning to the state, necessitating Beasley's role as acting governor.

Determined to handle his duties with class and dignity, Beasley remained in his own lieutenant governor's office to discharge the duties of governor, and called for a statewide day of prayer for Wallace's recovery as one of his first official acts in office.

Beasley and his firm are routinely named on lists of America's best lawyers, and have seen their work and their cases profiled in national media such as *Time Magazine, Business Week, Fortune Magazine, Forbes.com, Wall Street Journal, Los Angeles Times, USA Today, U.S. News & World Report, New York Times, 60 Minutes*, and many others.

Dr. Regina Benjamin
U.S. Surgeon General
Mobile County

In these days of divided government, an unusual event happened when the United States Senate voted unanimously to confirm America's Surgeon General in 2009.

But anyone who knows Regina Benjamin, a native of Mobile, would not have been surprised. Since her graduation from the University of Alabama School of Medicine at UAB (1984), she has spent her life tirelessly and selflessly serving the less fortunate in society.

After medical school, Dr. Regina Benjamin founded the Bayou La Batre Rural Health Clinic, offering medical care for whatever payment the patients could afford. The small fishing village, made famous in the movie *Forrest Gump*, badly needed the medical clinic, as many found quality medical care inaccessible because of insufficient income or insurance. Somehow, while operating the clinic, Dr. Benjamin managed to earn an MBA degree from Tulane University, using her master's degree in business to more effectively operate the clinic.

Dr. Benjamin's life's journey of caring for others was born in Mobile, where she was raised by a single mother. The spiritual faith that propelled her to public service was also inspired by her grandmother, a devout follower of the Catholic faith who held Mass services in her home.

Dr. Benjamin's intellect and dedication to others did not go unnoticed. Rising quickly in the medical community, she became the first African American female to become president of a state medical association (in Alabama) and to sit on the Board of Trustees of the American Medical Association.

In 2009, President Barack Obama nominated Dr. Benjamin as America's Surgeon General, and the U.S. Senate gave their unusual unanimous approval. After serving her country, she returned to her first love, the clinic she founded in Bayou La Batre.

Even before becoming the Surgeon General, she received a papal cross from Pope Benedict XVI for her outstanding service.

The John D. and Catherine T. MacArthur Foundation chose her as one of 25 recipients of a "Genius Award" in 2008.

Dr. Benjamin received honorary doctorates from Dartmouth College and the University at Albany-State University of New York.

Dr. Robert Bentley
Governor of Alabama
Tuscaloosa & Shelby Counties

In 2010, Robert Bentley was elected to serve as Alabama's 53rd governor. As the numbers reveal, his career mostly centered around service to others.

By the Numbers

1...A native of Columbiana, Bentley was the top leader, student body president, at Shelby County High School.

3...In only three years, Bentley graduated from the University of Alabama, majoring in chemistry and biology.

1...Bentley joined the United States Air Force in 1969, and again rose to the top in leadership. He was appointed commander of the hospital base at Pope Air Force Base, in Fayetteville, North Carolina.

8...For eight years, Bentley served in the Alabama House of Representatives, focusing much of his time and considerable expertise on medical issues such as the Alabama Medical Education Consortium (providing medical school admission for primary-care specialists), and the Rural Medical Scholars program.

2...The number two was meaningful, because Bentley was reelected for a second term as governor, and the city's third largest city received news that would ultimately transform its economy. Airbus announced the first of its Mobile assembly lines, bringing a host of jobs, outside contractors, and economic spin-off benefits.

2...With almost two years remaining in his second term, Bentley resigned over issues arising from staff relations and campaign finance, either of which could have become dispositive of his term had he remained in office.

Tom Bevill
Congressman, soldier, attorney
Walker County

It began on the beaches of Normandy, on D-Day, the most important invasion in the history of the world. Tom Bevill's service to America took him on a journey from wartime France, to the halls of the United States Congress, where he worked tirelessly to make his nation, and his beloved Alabama, better than it was when he arrived.

Maybe the sea-based invasion of Normandy and the land-battles against Nazi Germany in France inspired Bevill's emphasis on transportation. Maybe it was the difficult geography of his beloved Walker County, where he came from Townley, later practicing law in Jasper. Whatever the reasons, Bevill became an expert on the appropriations process, empowering Alabama for growth in both transportation and education by steering massive amounts of federal funds to the state, earning Bevill the moniker, "The King of Pork." Bevill served as an important sub-committee chairman on the House Appropriations Committee for decades.

Bevill loved to speak of his hometown of Townley, once a thriving community that sported a hotel and two movie theaters, as he liked to recall.

He also admired fellow Walker County native and U.S. Speaker William B. Bankhead, and in many ways modeled his career after him. He never forgot a personal thanks received from legendary FBI Director J. Edgar Hoover, which taught him much about how expressed gratitude is remembered. Most of all, Bevill loved to speak of his family and his fellow Alabamians, investing his years in the Congress working on projects that would make their lives easier. Funding for the development of NASA's Marshall Space Flight Center, the Tennessee-Tombigbee Waterway, the creation of Interstate 22 from Birmingham to Memphis (through his home of Walker County, of course) as well as the funding of community colleges and major universities in the state became some of his signature accomplishments. The multi-campus Bevill State Community College is named in his honor. Somehow, despite his work on the appropriation needs of the entire nation, Bevill and his in-state aide Charlie Watts managed to remain in close contact with his home district, the needs of his state, and his own community, including the First United Methodist Church of Jasper. Bevill's son, Don, notched his own place in local lore, playing college basketball, serving as a Walker County District Judge, and practicing law with his father in the firm of Bevill & Bevill.

After 30 years in Congress, Bevill retired, but the seemingly endless number of buildings and institutions bearing his name speak to the impact of a life of public service, one which began on the beaches of Normandy.

William Wyatt Bibb
Thomas Bibb
Alabama's first two Governors

The journey of the Bibb brothers began with the Broad River, traveled with the Alabama Fever, and ultimately led to their service as Alabama's first two governors.

In many ways, Alabama became a state because of the Broad River Group. After the Revolutionary War, General George Mathews led a group of Revolutionary War veterans from Virginia to homestead land in Georgia. This group included the Bibb family, along with future United

Did You Know??

Ten percent of all the freshwater in the continental United States originates or flows through Alabama. That's a whopping total of 52,000 square miles, or 33.3 million acres of water in our state.

States Senators William H. Crawford and Charles Tait. General Mathews served two terms as Governor of Georgia, and the network formed by these war veterans and pioneering families would shape Alabama's future. The group was nicknamed after the Broad River, which ran through the land they settled.

Then came the Alabama Fever. This was not a contagious disease, but rather a rush of pioneer settlers to the new land that would ultimately become the state of Alabama. By the late eighteenth century, the British Empire had developed global trading partners and had heightened the demand for cotton. Because cotton crops deplete soil nutrients over time, farmers in Georgia, South Carolina, and Virginia looked for new land and great soil.

And so they came, bringing not only new opportunities, but their old political networks from their former states. Georgia, as the next-door neighbor, provided the most new farmers and the deepest political connections.

Enter the Bibb brothers.

Although their father died during their youth, they inherited the means to afford college educations. William Wyatt Bibb studied at the College of William and Mary, then earned his medical degree from the University of Pennsylvania. At age 21, he was elected to the Georgia House of Representatives and by 25, he was a new member of the U.S. Congress. Later, he was elected to the United States Senate from Georgia. The young Bibb became an excellent networker, renewing political alliances with his fellow Broad River friends, including Senator Charles Tait, and the former Senator William H. Crawford. Bibb became a popular Senator, enough so that Georgia named a county after him. However, an ill-advised vote on a major congressional pay raise exhausted his popularity and he lost the Senate seat.

Now out of Congress, Wyatt looked to the west, and he liked what he saw. The Alabama Fever had transformed the area into a prosperous land, and Bibb's younger brother Thomas was one of its successful young pioneers. Thomas had settled in the areas now known as Madison and Limestone counties, becoming economically prosperous and politically influential. Thomas had used his own Broad River Group connections to forge his personal network. William followed his younger brother from Georgia, settling his family in the new land with new opportunities. He settled his family in St. Stephens, the territorial seat of government in the area that is now part of Washington County.

In 1817, the Alabama Territory was created out of the Mississippi Territory, and President James Monroe had to appoint a territorial governor. William Wyatt Bibb's old family friend from Georgia, William H. Crawford, had become the Secretary of the Treasury, and recommended his friend Bibb to the president as the territorial governor. President Monroe appointed the former Senator Bibb as Alabama's first and only territorial governor.

In Bibb, Alabama was blessed with a governor who was a former US Senator and extremely well connected. He immediately began exerting his influence to achieve statehood for this brand new territory. Just two years after becoming a territory, Alabama became the 22nd state in the union.

As governor, Bibb made one controversial decision that almost ended his leadership of Alabama before statehood. Although a commission had recommended Tuscaloosa as the state's first capital city, Bibb proclaimed that it would instead be Cahawba, in the Black Belt region of the state. Bibb angered many with this decision, which happened to have benefitted his Broad River friends who had made speculative land purchases in the Black Belt.

The Cahawba-Tuscaloosa issue gave rise to a political opponent from Tuscaloosa, but Bibb's north Alabama support and work to achieve statehood propelled him to victory as the first governor of the state of Alabama.

A fall from his horse caused injuries that ultimately resulted in his death at the age of 39. The state's constitution called for the president of the state Senate to succeed Bibb. That happened to be Thomas Bibb, the younger brother of the first governor.

Thomas Bibb had become highly influential in Limestone County and beyond, partially because of his Broad River network in Alabama and partially because of his own accomplishments. However, his perceived role as a caretaker of the governor's office, along with the fact that he was the little brother of the governor, lessened his influence as the state's chief executive.

During Thomas Bibb's term as governor, Bibb County was named after William Wyatt Bibb.

Trivia

Which Alabama city once boasted America's busiest airport?

During the Vietnam War, Selma had the busiest airport in America.

How was that possible?

Menzo Driskell, the former executive director of the Craig Field Airport and Industrial Park Board, described it to the *Selma Sun* newspaper in 2017. "Craig Field was an important base for training Army and Air Force pilots during World War II, the Korean War, and the Vietnam War," he explained. "In terms of takeoffs and landings, it was the busiest airport in the world during Vietnam."

Thanks to the foresight of local leaders, including Selma attorney John Pilcher, Craig Field has now become a thriving industrial park and municipal airport, featuring Hyundai contractors, local companies, and even a golf course on the property.

James G. Birney
Abolitionist, legislator
Madison County

Huntsville attorney James G. Birney forged his successful career and considerable talents into a lifelong steely mission to end slavery. Running for President of the United States in 1844, he received over 62,000 votes, swinging the state of New York and the presidency away from the legendary Henry Clay. James K. Polk, instead, became President of the United States.

Raised on a Kentucky plantation, Birney grew up with the conflicting tensions of parents and grandparents who were abolitionists, but also slaveholders. He was mostly educated by an abolitionist teacher, and then attended Princeton University, in New Jersey, where its president was also an abolitionist and a slaveholder.

Birney was elected to the Kentucky Legislature in 1816, but moved to Madison County, Alabama, two years later and was soon elected to the Alabama House of Representatives. He led the effort to enact laws granting new rights to slaves, including the right to trial-by-jury for serious crimes, and the requirement of food and clothes for slaves. Locally, he encouraged leaders in Huntsville to establish a public library and was a founding member of the Huntsville Library Co., the oldest public library in the state of Alabama.

A leading abolitionist on the national scene, Birney played an active role in abolitionist organizations, speaking boldly on the subject. He also gave a speech criticizing Andrew Jackson for his treatment of Native Americans, but his positions against Jackson were not well received locally. He left his Huntsville law practice in 1832 to pioneer freeing slaves and recolonizing them in Liberia, until later leaving that effort to focus solely on abolition.

In the late 1930s, Birney returned to Kentucky where he freed his family's slaves. He published an abolitionist weekly publication titled *The Philanthropist* from 1835-1837.

Birney was the presidential candidate of the Liberty Party in 1840 and 1844.

Hugo Black

U.S. Supreme Court Justice
U.S. Senator
Clay and Jefferson Counties

He authored some of the most important and controversial court decisions in American history.

In 1963, Supreme Court Justice Hugo Black wrote the opinion in *Gideon v. Wainwright*, giving poor people the right to an attorney in criminal cases. In almost four decades on the highest court in the land, Justice Black became one of its most consequential justices.

But this historic career was nearly snuffed out. In many ways, the journey began with a fire.

The fire had destroyed everything. Hugo Black's law office in his hometown of Ashland, Alabama, along with his books and papers, were gone. Uninsured, as many were in 1907, Black was left in dire financial straits by the fire. His career was clearly at a crossroads.

Hugo Black made what turned out to be an outstanding decision, as he would become famous for doing in his future, and moved his law practice to Birmingham. Leaving his beloved Ashland, however, was no small task. At the tender age of six, he had begun sitting in the Clay County courthouse, watching lawyers try cases and wondering how he would have asked the same questions. The only professional assets he carried to his new city were his outstanding intellect, his work ethic, and his willingness to fight for those neglected by society.

Black's intellect and work ethic came from his parents, Martha Toland and William Black, who worked hard and remained lifelong learners. His support for the underdogs of society might have come from his own status as the eighth and youngest child in his family. After rising to prominence in Birmingham through a local judgeship and his law practice, Black was elected to the United States Senate in 1927 to replace the legendary Oscar Underwood. By 1935, Senator Black had become Chairman of the Senate Committee on Education and Labor. He famously introduced a bill calling for a national minimum wage and limited workweek, that became the predecessor of the Fair Labor Standards Act.

In the 1920s, between his arrival in Birmingham and election to the United States Senate, Black was, in the words of his biographer (Virginia Van Der Veer Hamilton) a "joiner." In other words, he zealously joined groups and networked extensively to aid his future ambitions. One of those groups, unfortunately, was the Ku Klux Klan. The extensive reach of its social and political clout in the 1920s made it politically tempting even to people like Black, who had long fought for the rights of minorities and the oppressed. Although some have sought to discredit Black because of this membership, his credibility with the African American community is unimpeachable. The black NAACP Executive Secretary Walter Francis White, a personal friend, testified on behalf of his nomination to the U.S. Supreme Court in 1937.

That nomination was a natural choice for President Franklin Delano Roosevelt, as Black was a zealous supporter of the New Deal programs and an outstanding Senator. After the Senate quickly approved his nomination,

Trivia

Which former American vice president was arrested in Alabama?

If you drive from Tuscaloosa to Mobile on Highway 43, you will pass through the town of McIntosh, in Washington County. For many, the drive on Highway 43 is a pleasant journey southward on the way to the beach, or northward for a college football game.

For Aaron Burr, who had served as the third vice president of the United States, the journey through the area now known as McIntosh wasn't quite so pleasant. President Thomas Jefferson had ordered Burr's arrest, based on accusations that he was planning a treasonous assault on Spanish territories and raising an army to accomplish that feat.

On the 19th of February, 1807, Captain Edmund P. Gaines led the effort to apprehend Burr, who had been spotted traveling through the area with an assistant the night before.

A Virginia jury later found Burr not guilty of the charges.

Burr was most famous for killing Alexander Hamilton in a duel.

Captain Edmund P. Gaines, who arrested former Vice President Aaron Burr in the area now known as McIntosh, Alabama, in Washington County. Photo courtesy of the Encyclopedia of Alabama.

Black served on the court from 1937 until 1971, making a monumental impact on the nation's laws and judicial system.

After he joined in the court's unanimous decision in *Brown v. Board of Education of Topeka, Kansas*, outlawing segregation in public schools, he became, in the words of the *Encyclopedia of Alabama*, "arguably the most hated white man in the American South."

Wynton "Red" Blount
Business titan,
U.S. Postmaster General
Bullock & Montgomery Counties

Wynton "Red" Blount was one of those rare people who changed his country, his home state, and his community.

A native of Bullock County, Blount and his brother, Houston, borrowed $28,000 to buy tractors and start Blount Brothers Construction. Using his powerful personality and elite business skills, Blount built the business into Blount International. Blount built the Superdome in New Orleans, a NASA launch site at Cape Canaveral, Florida, and the $2-billion King Saud University in Saudi Arabia.

When President Nixon asked him to become the U.S. Postmaster General in 1969, Blount organized a complete restructuring of the U.S. Postal Service, turning it into an independent agency that ensured its success and survival. Jobs and promotions became based on merit instead of political appointment.

The system that provides your daily mail was a direct result of Wynton Blount's leadership ability.

Blount also saved the University of Alabama from a potential disaster during the Civil Rights Movement. When Governor George C. Wallace made clear his intentions to prevent African American students from enrolling in the university, Blount acted quickly. He attended the University of Alabama, though he did not graduate, and served on the school's board of trustees. Blount called U.S. Attorney General Robert F. Kennedy at Kennedy's home, and the result of the conversation, as described in the *New York Times* obituary of Blount, was the proposal that Wallace read a defiant statement in front of the television cameras and then step out of the way and let the students enroll. The result was an event without the violence that had become commonplace during that season of time.

Blount spent at least $40 million of his massive fortune constructing the Wynton Blount Cultural Park and the Alabama Shakespeare Festival (among the ten largest Shakespeare festivals in the world). He donated part of his art collection, valued at $15 million in the 1980s, to the Montgomery Museum of Fine Arts. Blount also donated millions of dollars to schools of higher learning during his lifetime, including over $8 million to the University of Alabama.

Jo Bonner
Congressman, Chief of Staff
Wilcox County

Jo Bonner has become one of the rare Alabamians who has led his state's people in the Congress, the state government, its educational system, and in the realm of economic development.

Born in Selma, Bonner was raised in Camden, the community that also produced Senator Jeff Sessions and Governor Kay Ivey. After graduating from the University of Alabama, Bonner joined the staff of Congressman Sonny

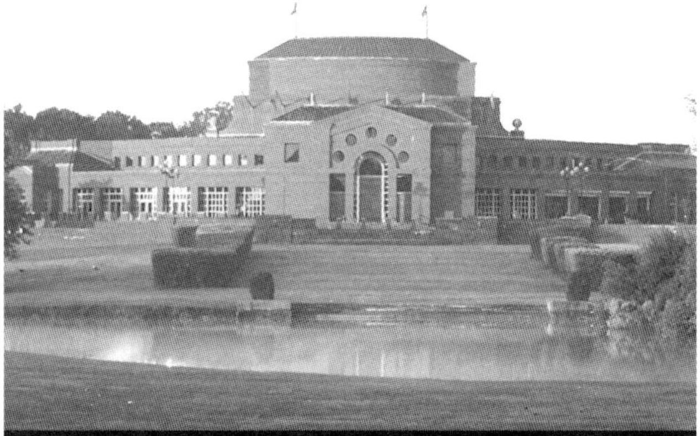

The Alabama Shakespeare Festival in Montgomery, built by the generosity of Wynton "Red" Blount.

Callahan, eventually rising to the position of chief of staff.

In 2002, Callahan announced his retirement from Congress, and Bonner successfully sought to succeed his boss. In Congress, Bonner established a reputation as a conservative who fought tax increases and sought economic development for his district. He served as chairman of the House Committee on Ethics, and later as a member of the Appropriations Committee.

In 2013, Bonner resigned from his seat in Congress to serve as vice chancellor of the University of Alabama System. His duties included roles in governmental relations and economic development.

In January of 2019, Bonner assumed the duties of chief of staff to Governor Kay Ivey, bringing extensive experience in leadership to Ivey's team.

Frank Boykin
Congressman
Washington & Mobile Counties

Frank Boykin was easily one of the most flamboyant, capable, wealthy, controversial and entertaining members of the U.S. Congress in modern times. In the 1950s, someone remarked that there were many millionaires in Congress, but Frank Boykin just might have been the only billionaire.

Boykin not only led a colorful personal life, he also made a substantial impact for the state of Alabama during his three decades in the U.S. House of Representatives, from 1935 to 1963. Boykin arranged funding to expand the Port of Mobile, laying the foundation for the city's future explosive growth. He also obtained funding to construct the Bankhead Tunnel under the Mobile River. He successfully appealed to International Paper Company and Vanity Fair Mills to open paper production plants in his district. In 1930, one of his corporations purchased most of Dauphin Island, and he later founded the Alabama Deep Sea Fishing Rodeo. Boykin and his partners later sold the rights to that event for just under a million dollars.

Boykin was a man of large appetites and many talents, none of which were more pronounced and public than his ability to make money. Known as the wealthiest man in Mobile, he didn't start out in the port city. Born in Choctaw County (Bladon Springs), his family moved to nearby Washington County (Fairford) during his childhood. In a sign of things to come, by age 15 Boykin had already be and operated by the Seaboard Manufacturing Company of Kansas City.

Along with his business partner in Washington County, John Everett, Boykin purchased a sawmill and pursued ventures involving land deals, timber, livestock, and the manufacturing of railroad ties. When Everett passed away, Boykin served as administrator of the estate and purchased all of Everett's interest in the business from the family for a mere $8,800. The acting probate judge who approved the amount was Boykin's brother, Matt.

Once in Congress, Boykin famously worked hard and played hard. He often brought legislative, military, and business leaders from Washington, D.C., to his vast hunting lands in the southernmost areas of Alabama. He also hosted lavish parties in Washington, which, along with the hunting trips, helped build relationships that made him a more effective congressman.

Boykin was known for saying that "Everything's made for love." His family decided on that for the title of his posthumously published biography. Boykin loved life and government service, excelling at both.

William "Bill" Brandon
Governor of Alabama
Tuscaloosa County

Governor William Brandon remains fondly remembered as a great builder of the state he served and loved.

Growing up as the son of a Methodist minister meant that Brandon and his family would move from time to time. Moving to new towns, and living in the local spotlight as the preacher's kid, prepared him well for a career in politics.

Brandon graduated high school in Tuscaloosa, and quickly became a rising star in local politics. He served as a local justice of the peace, and rose to the level of Captain in the Alabama National Guard during the Spanish -American War.

As always, Brandon was building any organization that he led. As a National Guard officer, he founded the military journal, *The Citizen Soldier*. When he was appointed Adjutant General of the Alabama National Guard, Brandon led its modernization and reorganization. Brandon's performance was undoubtedly clear to all, as he was reappointed to the position by the next two governors.

Elected State Auditor, Brandon continued his record of building better organizations, as he instituted modern accounting practices into the office. Later, he set his sights on the office of Tuscaloosa County Probate Judge, to which he was elected.

Brandon was elected Governor of Alabama in 1922, and, of course, began building. Before Brandon became governor, the state's industries had to use New Orleans rather than Mobile as their principal port. Brandon created the State Docks Commission and obtained a $10 million bond issue to deepen the port and make additional improvements that forever changed the Mobile area and saved massive amounts of expenditures for Alabama businesses.

At the 1924 Democratic National Convention in New York, Brandon became nationally famous when over 100 ballots were required to choose the party's presidential nomin nominee. It was also the first national political convention covered via radio. Alabama's legendary senator, Oscar Underwood, was a candidate and each round of balloting began with the words of Governor Brandon picked up by radio speakers: "Alabama casts its twenty-foahhh votes foahhh Senator Oscuuhhh Underwood."

Fittingly, a governor who built so much lived to see buildings and schools carrying the Brandon name, including the National Guard armory in Tuscaloosa, Brandon Memorial Methodist Church in Tuscaloosa (now Trinity United Methodist), and Brandon Elementary School in Florence, that educated children for decades.

Albert Brewer
Governor of Alabama
Morgan County

Governor Albert Brewer was the shooting star of Alabama government, entering at a record-breaking pace and leaving almost as quickly.

Raised in Decatur (Morgan County), Brewer studied at the University of Alabama, where he received both undergraduate and law degrees. By age 34, he had become the youngest Alabama House Speaker in Alabama history.

In less than 18 months, Brewer served as speaker, lieutenant governor, and governor, leaving the speakership when elected lieutenant governor in 1966 and then becoming governor 16 months later upon the passing of Governor Lurleen Wallace.

Brewer had spent his entire career acting boldly and quickly, and he brought that same energy to the governor's office. Brewer zealously sought, and achieved, passage of important legislation that vastly improved an education system that had been archaic and underachieving. He created the Alabama Ethics Commission, and may have changed the state the most by creating the organization that became the Economic Development Partnership of Alabama.

Brewer not only arrived at the governor's office quickly, he departed just as rapidly, thanks to a historically ugly campaign in 1970 for a full term as governor. The campaign has been included on lists of the nastiest political campaigns in American history. Former Governor George C. Wallace, who had run a historically strong third-party presidential campaign in 1968, wanted to regain the office of governor to aid his national ambitions for 1972. The stage was set for a clash between Governor Brewer and Governor Wallace.

Wallace deployed some of the darkest forces in the underbelly of Alabama society, resulting in an openly racist campaign designed to scare voters into opposing the "black bloc" of voters that had become part of the Brewer base. Wallace prevailed, and the rising political star of Albert Brewer flamed out before its time.

Despite the regrettable 1970 campaign, Brewer was best known for the powerful impact on the state he made during his brief time as governor. After leaving office, he remained deeply engaged and influential in the life of his state, serving as a professor at the Cumberland School of Law and an active civic leader.

William Jelks Cabaniss, Jr.
Ambassador, senator, businessman
Jefferson County

William Jelks Cabaniss, Jr., was born into a family legacy of public service. He has spent a lifetime making Alabama and the United States safer and more prosperous. His father, William, Sr., was awarded the Bronze Star for his service on the *USS Birmingham* during World War II. His great uncle, William Jelks, served as governor of Alabama and founded Protective Life Corporation, a major insurance company in the state.

After playing football at Vanderbilt University, Cabaniss enlisted in the U.S. Army and became part of the Army Special Forces, stationed in Germany, until an old football injury made that service impossible.

Cabaniss ultimately became the co-owner of Precision Grinding and Machining, Inc., and embarked on a business career until public service once again called. While on sales trips for his company, Cabaniss became disappointed that so many northern businesses were relocating in the Deep South in many states, but not in Alabama. The stigma of racial strife and the business climate combined to make the state unappealing. Ever the problem solver, Cabaniss sought to make changes. He was first elected to the Alabama House of Representatives, and then to the Alabama Senate, working diligently to improve the state's laws and image.

In 2003, President George W. Bush appointed Cabaniss as the U.S. Ambassador to the Czech Republic, where Cabaniss worked on issues arising from the Iraq War to the partnership between European automotive companies and the United States.

After his ambassadorship, Cabaniss has continued his life of public service, helping with a number of boards and organizations.

Clement Comer Clay
Governor, U.S. Senator,
Alabama's first Chief Justice
Madison County

If any Alabamian's life reflected the social, political, and financial turbulence of the early 1800s, it was Clement Comer Clay. The formation of the state of Alabama, the Panic of 1819, the advent of Jacksonian democracy, the Panic of 1837, and the American Civil War each left a lasting impact on the state, and on the career of Clement Comer Clay.

Perhaps no one in the state's 200-year history has served in more (and more powerful) positions of leadership. Clay served as chairman of the group of 15 that drafted the Alabama Constitution. He became the first Chief Justice of the Alabama Supreme Court. He served as Speaker of the Alabama House of Representatives. He served as Governor of Alabama, a United States Senator, and in the United States House of Representatives, where he became a powerful committee chairman.

Also an accomplished trial lawyer, Clay often represented large banking interests, with whom he sided politically as well. In one of the most unusual campaigns in American history, Clay ran for the U.S. Senate, while also serving as co-counsel with his campaign opponent in the second of the famous "big interest cases."

Clay was also a slaveholder, and the national financial panics of 1819 and 1837 affected his financial fortunes. When Andrew Jackson was elected president in 1824, Clay became determined to tie his fortunes to the new president's popularity and completely changed his pro-bank philosophy. The new paradigm for political prosperity had become populism, and Clay became a Jacksonian loyalist.

Despite the ups and downs of his political and financial careers, Clay was always able to rebound and recover his power and wealth until the Civil War, when he was imprisoned during the Yankee siege of Huntsville. While in captivity, his health rapidly declined, and Clay passed away in 1866.

Paul Compton
General Counsel, United States
Deptartment of Housing & Urban Development
Jefferson and Butler Counties

"Go where you can make a difference."

As a young law student, Paul Compton had the opportunity to meet the recently retired U.S. Supreme Court Justice Lewis F. Powell, Jr., at a reception. A native of Georgiana, Compton had excelled at the University of Alabama and was then a law student at the University of Virginia. Justice Powell asked the young Compton about what he might do after law school, and Compton described some opportunities, including one in New York.

Justice Powell's reply changed a young man's life.

"Go where you can make a difference," he advised. "You can go to New York, do well, and get a nice obituary from The *New York Times*, or you can go to Alabama and make a difference."

Over three decades later, in 2017, the United States Senate voted to confirm Paul Compton as General Counsel for the United States Department of Housing and Urban Development (HUD). Compton became the head attorney for an organization with a $50 billion budget, playing a key role in providing long-term disaster relief to states and local governments, businesses, and in turn for families.

Compton grew up in Georgiana, which to many Alabamians is the place where you turn off the interstate to go to the beach. For Compton, however, it was a place where values of hard work and integrity were instilled.

At the University of Alabama, those values bore fruit, as Compton was selected as a national Truman Scholar, and as the Outstanding Student at the College of Commerce and Business Administration.

Afterward came the University of Virginia School of Law with his bride Dana. He practiced law in Birmingham for almost 30 years at the firm now known as Bradley Arant Boult Cummings LLP, providing legal advice to developers, non-profits, public housing authorities, banks, and other financial institutions, until President Trump appointed him General Counsel for HUD.

By September of 2017, the U.S. Senate was moving slowly on confirmation votes on presidential appointments. Over 30 housing groups signed a joint letter asking the Senate to act quickly on the confirmation of Compton. Senator Richard Shelby joined the groups in supporting the Compton confirmation, as did Senator Luther Strange and a host of others.

The groups supported Compton because he was imminently qualified, and also because America needed him. The HUD General Counsel plays a crucial role in obtaining and distributing funds and credit support for housing, and resources for recovery, and rebuilding for hurricane victims, such as in Texas, Florida, and Puerto Rico. In doing so, Compton routinely deals with governors, mayors, White House officials, and HUD personnel across America on a daily basis.

When asked about the gravity of his work affecting so many lives, Compton explained that he relies on the Biblical admonition to "Do justly, love mercy, and walk humbly with your God." That, he added, takes care of any measure of self-importance.

Going where he could make a difference has accomplished exactly that, and has in turn made the people of his home state and hometown proud.

Braxton Bragg Comer
Governor of Alabama, U.S. Senator
Barbour County

Braxton Bragg Comer, elected Alabama's Governor in 1906, was a man of vast talents, zealous beliefs, and fearless governance in the face of opposition.

Born to prominent parents, Comer ultimately ran his family's Barbour County plantation and expanded it to a 30,000 acre operation.

Later, Comer moved to Birmingham and founded the historic Avondale Mills.

As a business leader and producer of goods, Comer was angered to learn that the railroad rates in Alabama allowed competitors in Georgia to undercut prices and steal business. Comer became a leading proponent of state control of railroad related matters, fighting fiercely for his cause at the Constitutional Convention of 1901.

Comer ran for governor in 1906, largely campaigning against the railroads. His progressive policies on some issues, but anti-reform positions on other issues created a curious mix of leftist and rightist politics. Comer supported educational, railroad, and environmental reforms, angering many in the business community. However, on the issues of child-labor and the rights of unions, he stood against employees. Presumably, his business interest in Avondale Mills influenced these positions.

After his term as governor, Comer was appointed to fill the unexpired term of U.S. Senator John Hollis Bankhead of Jasper, who had passed away.

B.B. Comer High School in Sylacauga is named after the former governor and business magnate. He is also the namesake of the Comer Library in Sylacauga and the Comer United Methodist Church in Alexander City.

Jeremiah Denton
U.S. Senator, Admiral, war hero
Mobile County

Senator Jeremiah Denton became the face of American courage during the Vietnam war, a United States Senator, a presidential confidante, an accomplished author, the subject of a movie, and the namesake of a U.S. Navy Destroyer.

Such an extraordinary life presents an impressive result when viewed...by the numbers:

By the Numbers

1...Denton became the first Republican elected as a U.S. Senator from Alabama since Reconstruction, gaining a narrow victory over future Governor Jim Folsom, Jr., as part of the Reagan landslide of 1980.

300...Denton's family traced its origins in the Mobile area to the original French settlers of Mobile, well over 300 years earlier (through his mother's side of the family).

91...After his plane was shot down during a bombing mission, Denton spent an unimaginable 91 months held as a prisoner of war by the Viet Cong, with a brutal 48 of those months in solitary confinement.

7...While being interviewed for a North Vietnamese propaganda film, Denton cleverly blinked seven letters in Morse Code: T...O...R...T...U...R...E, letting the world know that he and his colleagues were being tortured while in captivity. Denton became the face of American courage, and endured unspeakable torture after his efforts became known to his captors.

3...After landing with the first plane load of prisoners released after the Paris Peace Accords of 1973, Denton was the first to exit because of his status as the highest ranking officer. He thanked his Commander-in-Chief and the American people, and then tearfully exclaimed three words that once again inspired millions: "God bless America."

Jack Edwards
Congressman, attorney
Baldwin County

The U.S. Congress depended on his leadership. So did America's armed forces. So did the state of Alabama.

American Presidents Ford, Nixon, Carter and Reagan each met with him weekly during their years in the White House.

So who was so important?

Congressman Jack Edwards (William Jackson Edwards, III) was a longtime member of the U.S. House of Representatives from Mobile County (Point Clear) from 1965 to 1985. He still practices law at the firm of Hand Arendall in Mobile.

Leadershp, it seems, was always the path best suited for young Jack Edwards. Originally from Birmingham, Edwards graduated from Shades Cahaba High School in Homewood and entered the U.S. Navy, studying at the United States Naval School (1947-48). After his service, he enrolled at the University of Alabama, where he was ultimately elected president of the Student Government Association.

Edwards moved to Point Clear and practiced law, while also becoming involved in local community leadership. He ran for a seat in the U.S. Congress in 1964 as a Republican, no small task since the last Republican Congressman from the state of Alabama had served in 1901. Fittingly, it was Edwards' own great-great grandfather, Congressman William F. Aldrich.

Edwards won the election, serving ten terms in the U.S. Congress. His leadership included ten years as the ranking Republican member of the Defense Subcommittee of the House Appropriations Committee. In this capacity, Edwards established himself as an expert on America's national defense and its funding. Edwards was highly regarded as a fair-minded leader who pursued a conservative agenda while working well with those with whom he disagreed. Although Edwards strongly supported the defense buildup during the Reagan presidency, he opposed weapons systems which he thought were ineffective, such as the B-1 Bomber.

After retiring from Congress in 1985, Edwards remained a leader for both the state and nation. He served on multiple boards at the request of Reagan and subsequent presidents. He became a leader of the University of Alabama Board of Trustees, and resumed his role as a local leader through his practice at Hand Arendall.

Carl Elliott
Congressman
First Profiles in Courage Award winner
Walker and Winston Counties

When the family of President John F. Kennedy created the first *Profile In Courage* award, they chose Carl Elliott of Jasper (Walker County) as the first recipient.

Born and raised in Vina (Winston County), Elliott was

the eldest of nine children. Serving as the natural leader of nine kids prepared him to lead on the state and national levels. After graduating first in his class at Vina High School, Elliott paid his way through the University of Alabama by working a variety of jobs. For a time, he even spent nights in the abandoned campus observatory to save money.

A shortage of funds and the need to work multiple jobs did not prevent Elliott from becoming a leader on campus just like he was in his childhood home. Elliott ran for president of the Student Government Association, becoming an unlikely winner and defying the odds to become the first independent student (not in a social fraternity) elected to the position.

His victory in Tuscaloosa was only the first time Elliott won a victory as an underdog candidate. After serving in World War II, rising to the rank of first lieutenant, he ran and lost his first election (for judge in Walker County). In 1948, at only 34 years of age, Elliott ran for the U.S. Congress against the heavily favored Congressman Carter Manasco. After winning by an impressive margin, Elliott moved to Washington with his wife Jane and young family.

Because education had served as Elliott's personal vehicle out of poverty, he successfully sought to improve American schools. He was instrumental in the Library Services and Construction Act of 1956, and the National Defense Education Act of 1958. Elliott was ultimately appointed to the prestigious Rules Committee, where he helped advance the agenda of his friends and ideological allies, President John F. Kennedy and Attorney General Robert F. Kennedy.

In 1966, Elliott spent his retirement pension running against Lurleen Wallace in the Democratic primary election for governor, and the resulting loss left him in financial ruin. In 1990, he received the *Profile In Courage* award, and in 1992, he authored his autobiography, *The Cost of Courage*.

The Elliott name remains revered in Jasper, as his nephew, Hoyt Elliott, Jr., serves as a highly regarded circuit judge. The Carl Elliott Regional Library is named to honor his positive impact on the nation's libraries, and the Elliott Society at the University of Alabama preserves the name of one of its great student leaders.

Rankin Fite
Speaker of the House
Marion County

Rankin Fite called 9-1-1, in Haleyville, Alabama, even though there was no emergency.

The call by Fite made nationwide news, but Fite didn't find himself in trouble. In fact, two-time Speaker of the Alabama House of Representatives from Hamilton (Marion County) didn't just place a 9-1-1 call; he placed the very first such call, February 16, 1968. The ceremonial call showed the world that Alabama had just developed an important new way for people to contact local emergency services, just by dialing those three numbers. Legendary Congressman Tom Bevill of Jasper answered the symbolic call, and the system became a permanent part of American life.

Fite became the face of Hamilton, Marion County, and the entire region of the state between Tusaloosa and the Quad Cities for decades. Governor George Wallace called him a "legislative legend." Fite first served in the Alabama Senate, becoming a floor leader for Governor Jim Folsom, and later began his historic tenure in the Alabama House of Representatives.

Fite's legacy has touched virtually all Alabamians in various ways. He played a pivotal role in the establishment of the vast community college system that has provided countless Alabamians with access to post-secondary education.

James "Big Jim" Folsom
Governor of Alabama
Coffee and Cullman Counties

For much of the 20th century, James "Big Jim" Folsom stood larger than life in the state of Alabama. That was partially due to his height; at six-foot-eight, he was an enormous man for his time when he launched his successful campaign for governor in 1946.

Big Jim also stood tall in other ways, as the governor who forever changed transportation in the state of Alabama, as a brilliant campaigner, as a man far ahead of his time on issues of race and voting rights, and as the father of a future governor.

Big Jim was raised in Elba, Alabama (Coffee County), and at 11 years of age suffered the passing of his father. He attended the University of Alabama and Howard College (now Samford University) before returning to Elba to help with disaster relief after the devastating floods of 1929. Afterward, Folsom bounced from job to job, as a hotel doorman in New York, a sparring partner for professional boxers, and a sailor, among other adventures. He returned to Alabama, running against entrenched Congressman Henry Steagall twice, losing both times.

After his brother-in-law landed him an insurance job in Cullman, Folsom ultimately launched a bid for the governor's office in 1942, surprisingly coming in second place to Chauncey Sparks. At least it was surprising to the experts, but probably not to people in small towns who connected with the unforgettable big guy with legendary storytelling ability, personal rapport with a crowd, and a populist message that resonated with the economically downtrodden. Also, Folsom had two political hometowns, meaning that he enjoyed the support from surrounding counties because he was a Cullman County candidate, as well as support from areas surrounding his original home of Coffee County.

Because the Alabama Constitution forbade a governor from serving successive terms, Sparks was ineligible to run again in 1946, making Folsom frontrunner. He ran again and won, although an unfriendly legislature kept many of his proposals and ideas from becoming a reality.

But Big Jim had already become a political legend, and after waiting until he was again eligible to run, he sought the governor's office again in 1954, winning handily. This time, Folsom brought a number of like-minded legislators whom he had supported, and who now stood ready to support him. One result was a massive road expansion bond issue that turned many of the farm-to-market dirt roads in rural counties to paved roads now accessible with cars and trucks. The result was a revolution in transportation within the state, and a world in which access to goods, services, and schools were not lost after a good rain.

Folsom was a longtime supporter of full voting rights for minorities, and famously hosted New York Congressman Adam Clayton Powell in the governor's mansion. Unfortunately, the 1954 U.S. Supreme Court's decision in the *Brown v. Board of Education of Topeka, Kansas* case, outlawing "separate but equal" segregation, caused a political backlash that damaged his personal popularity through the state, rendering most of his civil rights goals unattainable.

Folsom passed away in 1987, only six years before his son and namesake, James "Jim" Folsom Jr., took the oath of office as Alabama's 50th governor.

James "Jim" Folsom, Jr.
Governor of Alabama
Cullman County

He will go down in history as the governor who helped launch the modern automobile manufacturing industry in the Southeast. James E. "Jim" Folsom, Jr., from Cullman (Cullman County) invested his governorship, his credibility, his time, and the state's resources to recruit Mercedes-Benz, a premier automaker, to Alabama. The success of Folsom and his team became the gold standard for getting things done in Alabama, forever changing the image of the state as a destination for corporations from across the globe.

While many aspiring leaders see the governor's mansion as a destination, Jim Folsom, Jr., recalled it as his childhood home. As the son of the legendary James E. "Big Jim" Folsom, Jim (often called "Little Jim") found that he inherited many of the same gifts and aspirations as his famous father. He also shared his father's ability to marry a smart and talented wife, Marsha Guthrie Folsom, who became a highly regarded professional and public servant in her own right.

During his political career, Folsom enjoyed great success, with two exceptions that arose not from Folsom himself, but from bad timing. In 1980 and 1994, America saw massive electoral landslides in favor of the Republican Party, with the 1980 election of Ronald Reagan as president, and the "tsunami" of 1994 that captured both houses of Congress for the Republicans.

In 1980, the 31-year-old Folsom stood on the brink of political greatness, having just unseated an incumbent U.S. Senator and having captured the democratic nomination for that office. Unfortunately for Folsom, the Reagan revolution swept candidates to office across America, and Admiral Jeremiah Denton rode that wave to a narrow victory over Folsom.

Folsom continued his service on the Alabama Public Service Commission, and was elected Lieutenant Governor twice. On April 22, 1993, Governor Guy Hunt was found guilty of a felony by a Montgomery County jury, and Jim Folsom, Jr., took the oath of office as Alabama's 50th governor.

That day set in motion the events that would lead to the decision to locate the Mercedes-Benz plant in Vance, Alabama. Alabama's new cache as a great location for automotive manufacturers would begat many more victories for the state, including the Hyundai plant near Montgomery, the Honda plant near Lincoln (Talladega County), and the massive Toyota-Mazda joint facility in Huntsville.

Unfortunately for Governor Folsom, his campaign for a full term as governor ran up against another great Republican landslide, the tsunami of 1994. As in 1980, he ran against a party on the rise while he carried the burden of an unpopular president leading his own party. He narrowly came up short to former Governor Fob James, the one-time Democrat running as the Republican candidate. Twelve years later, Folsom was once again elected to statewide office, returning to the job of lieutenant governor in 2006.

Just as his father had modernized the state's rural roads and changed life in Alabama's small counties, Jim Folsom, Jr., made his mark in history through transportation. Despite the abbreviated term as governor, Folsom managed to pull off a transcendent accomplishment when he and his team recruited Mercedes-Benz, changing the image and potential of a state and a region.

Trivia

Which Alabamian founded Veterans Day?

Thanks to Alabama's own Raymond Weeks, America celebrates Veterans Day each year.

Until 1947, Weeks was best known as a local veteran of World War II and an active Civitan Club member. Weeks decided to honor our nation's veterans with a special day.

He chose November 11, which before then was celebrated as Armistice Day, marking the end of World War I.

Weeks, from Jefferson County, earned America's gratitude for a second time with his enthusiastic efforts to launch the new national day of remembrance and honor for our greatest heroes.

Robert Gibbs
White House Press Secretary
Lee County

"Robert is the guy I want in the foxhole with me during incoming fire...If I'm wrong, he challenges me. He's not intimidated by me."

– Barack Obama,
on Gibbs' "tell it like it is" relationship with the president-elect (Wall Street Journal, Aug. 28, 2008)

In 2008, Auburn native Robert Gibbs became famous as the face of the Obama presidential campaign's brilliant communications team. He was so close to the future president that he earned the nickname "the Obama whisperer." It seemed only fitting for their great relationship that, when Obama gave the famous keynote address at the 2004 Democratic National Convention, he borrowed Gibbs' pale-blue necktie and put it on right before stepping out onto the stage. While serving in the White House, Gibbs joked about Obama never returning that necktie.

It's only fitting that Robert Gibbs would make a career crafting the right messages for voters or consumers, because that's precisely what he learned as a child in Auburn. As the child of two Auburn University librarians, Gibbs learned about the power of the written word early in life. But he learned much more when his mom, rather than hiring a babysitter, would take him with her to League of Women Voters meetings. They also involved Robert with local campaigns, and he grew up observing how to relate to people of all ages and backgrounds.

After graduating from North Carolina State University,

Gibbs worked for several different members of Congress, as well as the Democratic National Committee, before landing an important post with Senator John Kerry's presidential campaign in 2004.

Then came Barack Obama.

After serving as one of Obama's closest advisors during the 2008 presidential campaign, Gibbs was offered the position of White House Press Secretary, becoming the daily voice of the president and his administration to the world. Gibbs served successfully and admirably, before entering the world of private consulting in 2011 and resuming his role as a political advocate for Obama on talk shows and with media outlets.

Shar Hendrick, fellow Alabama native and former political operative, worked with Gibbs during the early years and appreciated the future White House aide's networking skills. "Robert and I first met when we were working for Congressman Glen Browder. Early on, I was impressed with Robert's ability to forge relationships with key staff members in the House and Senate," he explained. "However, the relationship that really sticks out, is the one he developed with Chuck Todd. Chuck was the editor of *National Journal's* 'Hotline.' I recall Robert routinely talking to Chuck. He would give him insights into the Blue Dog Democrats, and Chuck would give Robert insight into other things taking place on the Hill. As time moved on, Robert became President Obama's Press Secretary and Chuck became NBC's White House correspondent."

One of the world's most successful companies, the McDonald's restaurant chain, hired Gibbs to serve as executive vice president and global chief communications officer. Once again, he uses the relational and communication skills he learned in his Auburn childhood to connect messages with people.

By the way, years after borrowing that necktie backstage before the 2004 speech, President Obama returned it in style. During Gibbs' last appearance before the media as press secretary, Obama came into the room, presenting the necktie to Gibbs in a frame with two photos from the speech and a hand-written note card.

Bibb Graves
Governor of Alabama

He was the cousin of Alabama's first two governors. He became governor himself for two non-consecutive terms, helping guide Alabama through the Great Depression. After Senator Hugo Black was appointed to the U.S. Supreme Court, Governor Bibb Graves appointed his wife, Dixie Bibb Graves, to serve the remainder of the term. She became the first woman United States Senator from Alabama. She was also his first cousin.

After his unsuccessful gubernatorial bid in 1922, Graves assembled a coalition of prohibitionists, women's rights supporters, and Ku Klux Klan members to win the election of 1926 and become the state's governor.

While in office, Graves worked hard and spent aggressively, as the state and nation treaded unknowingly toward the Great Depression.

A signature achievement of his time in office was a massive road improvement project. The rights of laborers and better education for black students were also the object of his work.

In 1942, Graves prepared to seek the office of governor for a third time and stood as the prohibitive favorite until passing away as a result of kidney problems.

His curious mix of a progressive record, considered alongside his Klan membership, makes his legacy complicated. He was, however, a strong and popular leader, even during difficult economic times.

In honor of his vast contributions to education in Alabama, many Alabama college and high school facilities bear his name. The stately Graves Hall stands on the front corner of the campus quadrangle at the University of Alabama. Serving as the main academic building for the School of Education and its library, Graves Hall serves as a lasting monument to its namesake's leadership during difficult times.

Howell Heflin
U. S. Senator
Colbert County

He became famous as a U.S. Senator and judge, but he was also a warrior and a leader, even at a young age.

As a U.S. Marine officer during World War II, the young Heflin fought in the vicious war in the Pacific where his bravery earned two Purple Heart medals and the prestigious Silver Star Award. The U.S. Marines issued the following citation with the Silver Star to Heflin:

"Directing his troops in a vigorous, prolonged battle, he frequently exposed himself to devastating fire at close range in order to control the attack more effectively and, by his unflinching determination and aggressive fighting spirit, contributed materially to the defeat of the enemy and the attainment of his company's objective."

What does one do after becoming a war hero? Heflin launched the next season of his remarkable life with a highly successful law practice in his hometown of Tuscumbia. Politics, however, was never far from his mind, as he grew up the nephew of a U.S. Senator and the great-nephew of a Congressman. Heflin was elected Chief Justice of the Alabama Supreme Court, where he led the reorganization and modernization of the state court system from 1971 to 1977.

In 1978, Senator John Sparkman retired, and Heflin ran successfully for that seat in the U.S. Senate. Serving 18 years, Heflin served as an influential member of the Agriculture and Judiciary Committees, and as Chairman of the Ethics Committee.

The *New York Times* famously called him the "conscience of the Senate."

The son of a Methodist minister, Senator Heflin always remained loyal to the church, and in his last week as a candidate in 1990, delivered the sermon at Talladega's historic First United Methodist Church for Pastor Gary T. Ward.

Heflin graduated from Birmingham Southern College and the University of Alabama School of Law .

Guy Hunt
Governor of Alabama
Cullman County

In November of 1986, Guy Hunt was elected governor, heralding a seismic change in Alabama politics and achieving one of the most improbable victories in the state's 200-year history.

Raised in Holly Pond (Cullman County) Hunt served in the Korean War, earning a distinguished service medal for his outstanding performance of duties with the the 101st Airborne and the First Infantry divisions of the U.S. Army. He served for decades as a Primitive Baptist minister, and was twice elected Probate Judge of Cullman County.

Hunt's bravery in war and unlikely wins in Cullman County showed a growing record of a bold leader uninhibited by unfavorable odds against him. He continued taking on incumbent leadership in 1976, when he led the Alabama delegation to the Republican National Convention. He opposed the sitting President, Gerald Ford, opting instead to throw his support behind former California Governor Ronald Reagan.

Two years later, Hunt won the Republican nomination for governor, but was defeated by Democrat Fob James.

Then came the political tsunami of 1986. Hunt was again the Republican nominee, and again faced seemingly overwhelming odds. However, a dispute within the Democratic Party, resulting in a lengthy court battle, soured the public on that party and resulted in a victory for Hunt.

Hunt was elected to a second term, and served until an ethics conviction removed him from office in 1993. In 1998, he was officially pardoned by the Alabama Board of Pardons and Paroles.

Forrest "Fob" James

Governor of Alabama
Chambers, Lee, & Baldwin Counties

Forrest "Fob" James, Jr., has lived the American Dream, succeeding grandly in every realm of his life as an athlete, businessman, governor, and family man.

James became the only person ever elected Governor of Alabama as a Democrat (1978) and as a Republican (1994).

After growing up in Chambers County (and finishing high school at Baylor in Chattanooga), Fob James studied engineering at Auburn University and starred on the Tigers football team. Before his senior season, he eloped with the Auburn Homecoming Queen, Bobbie May Mooney of Morgan County (Decatur). Marriage suited Fob James well, as he was named an All-American running back that year. After Auburn, James played professional football with the Montreal Alouettes of the Canadian Football League.

After working at other jobs, James acquired the backing of both his father and a wealthy family friend (attorney Jacob Walker Jr. of Lee County) and founded Diversified Products in 1962. This company manufactured the product conceived by James, plastic-coated barbells. Fifteen years later, when the men sold the company, Diversified Products owned three manufacturing plants, yielding roughly a billion dollars in annual revenue.

In 1978, James decided to enter the world of public service, and as always, he did it his way. He sought election to the office of governor of Alabama, but there was a problem. The field of candidates was historically well-stacked with accomplished and talented people such as Lieutenant Governor Jere Beasley, Attorney General Bill Baxley, Senator Sid McDonald and former Governor Albert Brewer.

Armed with the strategic experience of a business executive, James was never captive to conventional wisdom if he believed in a cause. If he was the only candidate without extensive government experience, then he would use that to his advantage. Just as he built D.P. into a mammoth company, he employed a state-of-the-art media strategy with a folksy campaign style to deliver his message to the voters of Alabama, winning the election.

In his first term as governor, James sought to improve the battered image of the state. He applied business principles to run the state government. He appointed Oscar Adams as the first African-American Supreme Court Justice, and appointed minorities to multiple cabinet posts in his administration. The economic woes of the 1970s made governing and budgeting difficult for the James administration, especially in the area of education. "Proration" became associated with James, as did other economic problems, and he eventually decided against seeking reelection in 1982.

As always, James did things the unconventional way, and in 1994, almost twelve years after leaving office, he was elected Governor of Alabama as a Republican. During his second term, James, who was elected along with the national Republican wave of 1994, focused his energies more on social issues.

Frank M. Johnson

U. S. District Judge
Winston County

He was just a U.S. District Judge, but he was featured on the cover of *Time* magazine. Multiple biographies and documentaries have been created about him. He received the Presidential Medal of Freedom, as well as honorary degrees from institutions across America. His name became one of the most recognizable in an entire era of American history. He has been inducted into halls of fame.

Who is this judge, and what did he do to merit so much attention?

Judge Frank M. Johnson just did his job, but in the heat of the civil rights era, especially in Montgomery, Alabama, that meant interpreting the laws and constitution courageously in the midst of systemic oppression and institutionalized hate.

For most judges, their best job preparation includes law school and work at some type of firm or prosecutorial office. Johnson's best prep might have been his combat in World War II, in which he was wounded by gunfire on two different occasions. He was awarded a bronze star for his heroism in battle. Ironically, he carried a bullet in his body for the rest of his life.

A native of Winston County, Johnson practiced law in nearby Jasper and engaged in Republican politics, serving as chairman of "Veterans for Eisenhower," Eisenhower's presidential campaign effort in Alabama in 1952. President Dwight Eisenhower, a fellow Republican, appointed Johnson to the federal bench in 1955.

Johnson's appointment came merely a year after the U.S. Supreme Court's *Brown v. Board of Education* decision, outlawing segregation in public schools. In 1956, the *Browder v. Gayle* case came before Judge Johnson, who ruled that the *Brown* decision regarding public schools also applied to the Montgomery bus system, and that segregation on the bus system was unconstitutional.

The *Browder* decision was only the beginning for Johnson, who found himself in the midst of the most strife-laden, violent, and vile behavior in his home state's history.

As a judge, Johnson sometimes found himself handling cases in which both parties knew what was right, but elected officials wanted him to end discriminatory practices so the politicians could use him as cover and complain about him publicly.

Johnson handed down landmark rulings on the insufferable conditions of Alabama prisons, the rights of mental health patients to treatment, racial discrimination, and equal protection under the law.

Johnson paid dearly for his courage. He and his family became social outcasts in Montgomery. His elderly mother's house was bombed. His son developed issues with mental anguish and ultimately committed suicide. The governor of his home state and law school classmate, George Wallace, publicly called him "integrating, scalla wagging, carpetbagging liar." Others called him the most hated man in America.

President Carter wanted to appoint Johnson as Director of the FBI, but the judge respectfully declined because of heart surgery and the necessary recovery time. Carter later appointed him to the U.S. Court of Appeals for the Fifth Circuit (now the Eleventh).

President Bill Clinton awarded Johnson the Presidential Medal of Freedom in 1995.

In July of 1999, on the Sunday after Judge Johnson passed away, President Carter taught his Sunday school class at the Maranatha Baptist Church in Plains, Georgia. Carter began the lesson with a moving tribute to Johnson, whom he called an American hero and a great jurist who helped transform America as few others have.

Catesby ap R. Jones
Businessman, Confederate leader
Dallas County

In the American Civil War, the battle of Hampton Roads produced one of the most famous clashes in naval history. For the first time, two iron-clad ships fought against each other. The fight is now often known as the battle between the *Monitor* and the *Merrimack*, and the result of that battle still lives on today in Selma, Alabama.

While the battle between the two ships was inconclusive, the *Merrimack* was captained, on that day, by Catesby ap R. Jones, a former U.S. Navy Lieutenant who resigned his commission to assume the same rank in the Confederate Navy.

After artfully guiding the *Merrimack* (known as the *CSS Virginia* in the confederacy), through the battle, Jones was ultimately promoted to the rank of commander and assigned to lead the crucial Ordinance Works facility in Selma, Alabama. After the war, Jones became a leading businessman in the state.

Originally from Virginia, Jones was descended from leading colonial settlers, including the founder of Richmond. His mother was a cousin of Robert E. Lee. The "ap" in his name is a Welsh patronymic term, like "Mc" or "Mac" at the beginning of Irish or Scottish names.

Once in Selma, Jones became the founder of a lineage of elite leaders consistent with his own ancestry. The stately mansion in downtown Selma's Old Town area, where many antebellum homes still stand, remains inhabited by his family.

As Alabama enters its third century, the descendants of Catesby ap R. Jones have continued their service as pillars of the community. The current generation of leaders from the family includes Catesby Jones, who serves as chairman of First Cahawba Bank, Tommy Jones, a leading attorney in Selma and Dallas County, and Van Carter, the former general of the Alabama National Guard.

Dr. Martin Luther King, Jr.
Pastor, leader, legend
Montgomery County

His name appears on lists of the most important people in world history. He has been called the voice of not just a people or a movement, but of human rights in America.

Martin Luther King, Jr.'s ministry as the pastor of the Dexter Avenue Baptist Church in Montgomery vaulted him onto the front lines of the Civil Rights Movement, and into the spotlight of world events.

Delivering one of the most famous speeches in American history, Dr. King declared "I have a dream," describing a day in which people looked beyond race in relating to each other. Invoking both the Holy Bible and America's founders, King's 1963 speech at the Lincoln Memorial made an immediate impact that continues today. King added, "I have a dream that my four little children will one day live in a nation where they will not be judged by the color of their skin but by the content of their character."

Over a quarter of a million people had gathered for the event, which, at the time, was the largest of its type in American history.

Drawing on the power of nonviolence taught by Jesus Christ and India's Mahatma Ghandi, King did not seek an upheaval of society, but rather the opportunity for all to pursue the American dream.

King's leadership in the Civil Rights arena began in 1955, when he served as the public face of the Montgomery Bus Boycott. Later, in addition to the famous 1963 "I Have A Dream" speech in Washington, King led rallies, marches, boycotts, and initiatives to follow the dream of equal rights under the law.

King also served as the leader of the events in Selma, Alabama, in March of 1965. Lyndon B. Johnson, the 36th President of the United States, called Dr. King his "essential partner" in working for the passage of voting rights laws.

The night before he was assassinated in Memphis on April 4, 1968, King delivered an almost prophetic speech in which he declared to the audience that he had "been to the mountain top," and had "seen the promised land," but "might not get there with you."

Although born in Georgia, King became a citizen of the world as a Montgomery pastor, and the state claims him as the most famous Alabamian.

William Rufus King
Vice President of the United States
Dallas County

The only Alabamian elected to the office of Vice President of the United States, King spent decades serving in the United States Congress and as a highly successful diplomat.

He also named the City of Selma, proposing the name from *The Songs of Selma*, by Scottish poet James MacPherson.

A native of North Carolina, King was elected to the U.S. Congress and later served as an aide to the U.S. Minister to Russia.

King followed the land rush to the Alabama and Mississippi territories, on the advice of his brother, who had already settled in Tuscaloosa. King chose an imposing piece of property in the future area of Selma, a town standing majestically above the Alabama River.

King later spent two different stints in the United States Senate from Alabama, as well as time in Paris as the U.S. Minister to France. President John Tyler had appointed King to the ambassadorship, hoping he could convince the French to stay out of the turmoil over the Republic of Texas. King successfully entertained and lobbied King Louis Philippe and his court of advisors, and may have changed the course of American history.

King was elected Vice President of the United States to serve under President Franklin Pierce. During the campaign, however, he developed tuberculosis. By the time of the scheduled inauguration, King was recuperating in Cuba. Congress passed a special law allowing King to take the oath of office in Cuba.

Knowing that his death was imminent, King traveled

home to his beloved Selma to see it one more time. During the next night after his return, he passed away.

Although unable to serve in his highest office, William Rufus King led a life of service and enlightened leadership to a grateful nation, adopted state of Alabama, and his adopted home of Selma.

John Tyler Morgan
U. S. Senator
Dallas County

John Tyler Morgan was a national leader, thoughtful intellectual and the ideological father of the Panama Canal, yet a product of his antebellum upbringing on issues of race and social justice.

Named after President John Tyler, to whom he was related, Morgan passed the bar exam and became a lawyer despite not attending college. He had attended a private law school taught by his brother-in-law, Alabama Supreme Court Chief Justice William Parish Chilton. Morgan was born into political connections, but made his way in the world primarily through his impressive intellect and zealous advocacy for issues he held dear.

An ardent secessionist, Morgan enlisted in the Confederate Army at the beginning of the Civil War. He ultimately rose to the rank of general, and because of another colleague named John Morgan, he chose to use all three of his names, becoming known as John Tyler Morgan.

After the war, Morgan settled in Selma where he raised his family in a stately antebellum home in Selma's Old Town District.

According to many accounts, Morgan remained bitter about the result of the Civil War and resulting loss of what he perceived as the Southern way of life. He helped the Democrat Party regain control of the Alabama Legislature from Reconstruction Republicans, and was rewarded with the legislatively appointed U.S. Senate seat in 1876.

Once in the Senate, Morgan developed a reputation as a man of stark contrasts, an elite intellectual with an open mind for learning but with cemented beliefs on issues arising from the Civil War and race. Morgan became the Senate's leading voice for American expansion and imperialism, as evidenced by his leadership on a canal in Central America. Although he originally supported the Nicaraguan route rather than the Panamanian route, he still became known as its ideological father.

On issues of federal vs. state powers, Morgan sided with states' rights, especially on the subject of race. He often cited, with approval, the writings of U.S. Supreme Court Chief Justice Roger Taney, which advocated treating African-Americans as less than full humans.

Overall, John Tyler Morgan was a product of his times who served 30 years in the U.S. Senate and exerted vast influence over national affairs. He is buried in his adopted hometown of Selma, and the John Tyler Morgan home is now used as an office for a state agency. Morgan Academy in Selma was named in his memory.

William "Bill" Nichols
Congressman, hero
Talladega County

The remarkable life of William "Bill" Nichols was, amazingly, punctuated by two explosions that changed his life and propelled him to great acts of service.

The first explosion occurred in the beautiful forests of Germany. Things weren't so beautiful in the summer of 1944, as allied forces were pursuing the retreating German Army after the Normandy invasion. Nichols, a native of Sylacauga (Talladega County), had become a star athlete at Sylacauga High School and then captain of the 1940 Auburn Tigers football team. The young man was physically fit, with a powerful intellect and engaging personality. In the U.S. Army, during World War II, he served as gunnery officer in the Eighth Infantry Division. At least he did until the Battle of Hürtgen Forest, in Germany, one of the deadliest battles in the European theater. An exploding mine changed Nichols' life forever, causing serious injuries and the amputation of his left leg above his knee. His valor during the war, and especially in the Battle of Hürtgen, resulted in his receiving the Bronze Star, the Purple Heart, and three major battle stars.

Maybe it was his life-changing injuries, or perhaps it was his small-town Methodist upbringing, but after the war, Nichols embarked on a life of public service. Settling down in his hometown with his bride, Carolyn Nichols, he worked in the local business community and became a local leader before running for the Alabama House of Representatives. Serving in both the House and the state Senate, Nichols became one of the most consequential young leaders of the mid-twentieth century. He proposed and steered the passage of a law providing free textbooks for all Alabama school students, among other accomplishments.

By 1966, Nichols had sacrificed more for his country, and accomplished more for his state, than most would in a lifetime. His greatest impact on America, however, had not even begun. That year, he was elected to the United State Congress. After his first successful re-election in 1968, Nichols requested and received an appointment to the House Armed Services Committee. His intellect, concern for soldiers, and military experience made him a natural leader. He became a national expert on the subject, protecting soldiers, helping the military leadership, and expanding the national government's military presence in Alabama.

Then came the second explosion.

Nichols and several colleagues from the Armed Services Committee traveled to Lebanon to inspect the Army base in Beirut. Nichols and the others left with serious concerns about the safety of the soldiers, given the layout of the base, and what they perceived as the lack of proper security.

Not long afterward, in October of 1983 a truck filled with explosives crashed into the base, killing 241 American servicemen.

Unlike the explosion of 1944, Nichols wasn't physically wounded by the Beirut attack, but he was once again propelled into action to help others. He became a zealot for reform of the military that he loved. The result was the vote of 406 to 4 in the House of Representatives to pass the "Bill Nichols Department of Defense Reorganization Act of 1986." The Senate passed a similar bill, and it became known as the Goldwater-Nichols Defense Reorganization Act. As described by the *Washington Post*, the law "overhauled command structures in the upper levels of the armed forces, gave new authority to the chairman of the Joint Chiefs of Staff, created the post of vice chairman, and called upon the services to better integrate commands."

Nichols passed away at his congressional office desk in 1988, leaving a legacy of a hero, a consequential public servant, a devoted family man, and a caretaker of his nation's defenders.

Condoleezza Rice
U. S. Secretary of State
Jefferson County

She has been called the most powerful woman in the history of the United States government. She established herself as a talented stateswoman, a brilliant scholar, an accomplished pianist, and an elite achiever in American history.

Dr. Condoleezza Rice was born and partially raised in segregated Birmingham, developing a love for her native state while seeing, personally, how systemic government oppression can affect its victims.

Throughout the passage of time and her international success as a diplomat and author, Dr. Rice has maintained strong bonds with Alabama. Serving as President George W. Bush's National Security Advisor in the wake of the September 11 attacks, Rice convened meetings of the war cabinet in preparation for the responsive action in Afghanistan. She nicknamed the war cabinet the "Vulcans," after the former professional football team in Birmingham and the iconic statue in the city.

By the Numbers

2...Rice held two of the most important national security leadership roles during her career, including National Security Advisor and later as Secretary of State. She served in both capacities during the presidency of George W. Bush. She became the first African-American woman to hold each of those positions.

2...Although she began her college years as a music major, she became inspired by a political science class and changed her major to political science. She earned both her bachelor's and doctoral degrees at the University of Denver.

24...Rice has authored or contributed significantly to 24 books, including a political memoir, autobiographical works, public policy books, and academic works on global strategic planning.

1...During her years as a faculty member and provost at Stanford University, Rice has left a significant impact on the school, including an improvement in the institution's finances and the creation of the Center for a New Generation, a program for underprivileged students.

88...Notwithstanding her enormous accomplishments, her greatest talents might lie in her artistry with the 88 keys on a piano. She has retained the skill of a concert pianist, and has contributed time and resources to supporting the performing arts.

Bob Riley
Governor of Alabama
Clay County

Leaders often gain or lose approval by the way they handle a disaster or a crisis. Alabama Governor Bob Riley forever earned the gratitude of Alabamians because he wisely responded to a crisis before, rather than merely after, it struck.

In August of 2005, Tropical Wave 10 had almost run out of energy. As fate would have it, the tropical wave collided with another small storm, out in the Caribbean, and re-formed into a larger one. The National Weather Service actually gave it a new name, Tropical Wave 11, because the previous storm had died. By the time the new storm grew, it had been given the name "Katrina." The new storm began building ferocity while heading into the Gulf of Mexico.

When Governor Bob Riley was informed of the storm's possible paths, he and his administration sprang into action. Many wondered whether he was overreacting, because he had ordered the state to prepare for previous hurricanes that didn't turn out as badly as predicted. Maybe it was just business as usual for governments, some wondered.

For Riley, hurricanes would never become business as usual. Too many lives were at stake. He had become an enormously successful businessman, by acting early and planning for different outcomes. Bringing that expertise to the governor's office meant that Alabamians would benefit from that type of preparation.

Alabamians had seen Riley in action as a candidate, and as a political leader, but the summer of 2005 gave them the chance to see his character and work ethic in action. By the time the world understood that Katrina was a cataclysmic storm, Alabama had long since begun preparing. The contrast between Alabama's timely responses, compared to other states and major cities, was stark indeed.

The Katrina planning also gave Alabamians a glimpse into the patterns of Riley's success. He had spent his career navigating the challenges of the business world. He and his brother entered the poultry business decades earlier, becoming major poultry producers and then selling that business. In 1996, his home Congressman Glen Browder left his seat, running to replace the retiring Senator Howell Heflin. Riley defeated a strong candidate in the Republican primary, then won a cliffhanger election against Senator Ted Little (D-Auburn).

His campaigns for Congress and governor were notoriously well-run, in part because they were family events. His adult children played pivotal roles in his campaign successes.

In 2006, a different type of storm appeared on the political horizon. Facing re-election, it looked like Riley would face the political equivalent of a hurricane, with primary opponent Roy Moore and the general election foe Lucy Baxley. Once again, Riley was ready for the storms and easily defeated both.

Riley's second term brought mostly smooth sailing. The unemployment rate in the state hit a historic low, confirming what Alabamians had already seen from his handling of the storms and other issues facing the state. Even after the storms of the 2008 economic crash struck, the governor's steadying hand kept the ship of state running smoothly,

Riley left office at the end of his second term as one of the most popular two-term governors in the state's history.

Lee and Will Sellers
Government leaders
Montgomery County

One of Alabama's leading power couples has made their impact by focusing their considerable energy on the state's future. Alabama Supreme Court Justice Will Sellers began his career of service in high school, serving as governor of the Alabama District of Key Club International, the world's largest high school service organization. During his years practicing law, Sellers often fought on behalf of people and businesses against the IRS, something that most Americans would applaud.

Even while growing a family and legal career, Sellers never lost his focus on the state's future, serving as an influential trustee for Huntingdon College. He has also been active in the Alabama World Affairs Council and the Alabama State Committee for the Arts.

Sellers became Justice Will Sellers in 2017, when Governor Kay Ivey appointed him to the Alabama Supreme Court.

Sellers' wife, Lee Grant Sellers, has also led by focusing on Alabama's future. As the director of Alabama Girls State, she has helped mold and challenge rising leaders. The fruits of that labor will undoubtedly produce a harvest of leaders in the coming decades.

Along with the extensive work in Girls State, Lee Sellers serves as the Director of Special Projects in the office of Governor Kay Ivey.

Jeff Sessions
Attorney General of the United States
Wilcox and Mobile Counties

Anyone driving through Camden, Alabama, might think it's a long trip from this Black Belt town (it's in Wilcox County) to the nation's capital of Washington, D.C.

In many ways, they have marked each end of the career path of Jeff Sessions.

While serving as a United States Senator and later as the Attorney General of the United States, Sessions lived in Washington but held strong to the experiences, people, and values of his home. Born just up Highway 41 in Selma, Sessions spent his formative years in Wilcox County and remains a child of the state's Black Belt region. He became an Eagle Scout, graduated from the University of Alabama School of Law, and became and remains a loyal, engaged, and supportive member of the United Methodist Church. Sessions was elected to its General (worldwide) Conference in 1996, and attended that conference even during his first campaign for the U.S. Senate.

His career took him to the heights of America's government, legal system, and political arena. After President Ronald Reagan appointed him as United States Attorney, he served in that capacity during the 1980s and was elected Alabama Attorney General in 1994. Just two years later, Sessions ran for the U.S. Senate seat of the retiring Howell Heflin and was elected to the first of four terms.

During his Senate years, Sessions became an influential member of the Senate Armed Services Committee, especially important during wartime, and the Senate Judiciary Committee which oversees legal appointments and the legal system in America.

Sessions resigned from the U.S. Senate when President Donald J. Trump named him Attorney General of the United States, serving until November of 2018.

Don Siegelman
Governor of Alabama
Jefferson & Mobile Counties

Don Siegelman became, and remains, the only person ever elected to the four major statewide offices of Alabama Governor, Lieutenant Governor, Attorney General, and Secretary of State. He was surprisingly the first native of Mobile elected Governor of Alabama, as well as the first and only Roman Catholic, and the first and only student body president from the University of Alabama to do so.

After graduating from Murphy High School in Mobile, Siegelman entered the University of Alabama and was elected Student Government Association President, inducted into the prestigious Jasons Men's Senior Honorary, and pledged Delta Kappa Epsilon social fraternity. He served as a United States Capitol policeman to fund his law school education at Georgetown University. Afterward, he studied at Oxford University (in International Law) from 1972 to 1973.

As the Governor of Alabama, Siegelman played a major role in recruiting the Honda and Hyundai plants that have employed thousands of Alabamians, creating countless jobs for contracting companies and spin-off businesses, and giving Alabama a reputation for corporate recruiting resulting in even more businesses and jobs.

Siegelman also helped create the Alabama Reading Initiative, a program for young students that has been adopted in various forms by other states.

As legend has it, in late 2000, Governor Siegelman and his wife, Lori, were dining with Vice President and Mrs. Gore when the Gores received word of the U.S. Supreme Court decision in *Bush v. Gore*, resulting in Governor George W. Bush of Texas (rather than Gore) becoming the 43rd President of the United States.

The documentary *Atticus and the Architect*, released in 2017, chronicled, from a supportive perspective, the trial and incarceration of Siegelman arising from ethics charges while serving as governor.

In 2018, the second generation of public service in the Siegelman family emerged. Governor Siegelman's son, Joe, won the Democratic Party's nomination for attorney general, coming up short against incumbent Republican Steve Marshall.

Trivia

Was Alabama ever a separate country?

On January 11, 1861, the State of Alabama seceded from the United States of America. The resulting sovereign nation was named The Republic of Alabama.

At the time of the Republic of Alabama's formation, Alabama had one of the top economies in America, even though it lacked the major industries of many other states. Although it was one of the more populous states, approximately 44 percent of that population was enslaved.

The new nation even adopted a flag, featuring a lady holding an "Alabama" flag in her left hand and a sword in her right, all against a solid blue background. Above her lay the words: "INDEPENDENT NOW AND FOREVER."

Unlike the birth of the United States, Alabama's journey as an independent nation lasted only a month, as the state joined the Confederate States of America. Montgomery was chosen as its national capital city, and newly selected president Jefferson Davis took the oath of office on the steps of the Alabama Capitol building.

Mike Spann
American hero, first Afghanistan fatality
Marion County

In late November of 2001, only ten weeks after the unspeakable horror of the September 11 attacks, America mourned the loss of its first fallen hero in the war in Afghanistan. Across the nation, the outpouring was real, and it was patriotic.

In Winfield, Alabama, however, it was personal.

Before becoming a national hero, Johnny Micheal "Mike" Spann was a running back for the Winfield High School Pirates, and then a student at Auburn University. He joined the United States Marine Corps and served for eight years, rising to the rank of Captain, before joining the Central Intelligence Agency in 1999.

Just two years later, the September 11 attacks were conceived and orchestrated by the Al Qaeda terrorist network based in Afghanistan, and America responded swiftly and covertly in the wake of the attack. One of those covert operatives was Spann, a favorite son of Winfield and the product of a highly respected family.

The description of the events giving rise to the attack that ultimately took Spann's earthly life were described in a CIA account posted online on the eighth anniversary of Spann's passing, in 2009:

Mike was conducting initial interviews of extremists held in Qali-i-Jangi fortress at Mazar-e Sharif when hundreds of prisoners revolted and he was attacked.

His last act, just before he was killed by those who had supposedly surrendered, was to warn an Agency colleague of the imminent danger. Mike was killed on November 25, 2001: The first American killed in combat in Afghanistan.

Mike Spann became the first American fatality of the war in Afghanistan, and the Spann name became symbolic of the outstanding young warriors who take the ultimate risk to keep America safe and preserve the freedoms enjoyed by its people.

At Spann's funeral, C.I.A. Director George Tenet correctly remarked that "Mike understood that it is not enough simply to dream of a better, safer world. He understood that it has to be built – with passion and dedication, in the face of obstacles, in the face of evil."

John Sparkman
United States Senator
Morgan and Madison Counties

President Truman recommended him, and the Democratic Party followed their leader's advice by choosing Senator John Sparkman as their candidate for the vice presidency in 1952.

Sparkman, the running mate with presidential candidate Adlai Stevenson, proved a wise choice for their party. Even though they lost to General Dwight Eisenhower, Sparkman acquitted himself as a national leader and statesman.

As the seventh of eleven children in his family's Hartselle home, Sparkman learned diplomacy at a young age. During his years studying at the University of Alabama, he accomplished the rare feat of serving as editor of *The Crimson White* student newspaper, and later as president of the Student Government Association.

He followed his collegiate success by quickly immersing himself in the politics of Huntsville, where he had established a law practice. In just a few short years, he was elected to the U.S. House of Representatives in 1936. By 1946, he was elected Assistant Majority Leader (or Majority Whip). That same year, Jasper's Senator John H. Bankhead, Jr., passed away, and Sparkman successfully sought that seat.

Although most successful as the vice presidential candidate, Sparkman became a giant in the Senate, chairing several of its most prestigious committees and becoming an expert on complicated issues. He worked zealously and effectively to expand the scope of the federal government's role in providing affordable housing. He chaired the Senate Banking Committee, dealing with the competing interests of financial institutions and consumer advocacy groups. He left the Banking Committee to assume the chairmanship of the Foreign Relations Committee at a time in which the Vietnam War monopolized America's attention.

Notwithstanding his national stature and responsibilities, Sparkman paid careful attention to the needs of his home state in the realm of the federal government. He and his colleague, Senator Lister Hill, worked closely together for decades to direct countless millions of federal appropriations to Alabama.

Schools, buildings, and even a town have been named after one of the state's greatest statesmen and national leaders.

Luther J. Strange
United States Senator
Jefferson County

While other kids his age enjoyed their summer time at the beach or with friends, he was somewhere out in the North Atlantic Ocean, working long hours on a supply ship. The work was as hard as the hours were long, but Luther Strange was as grateful as anyone there to have that job, as it would help pay for his law school education.

Hard work was nothing new to Strange, who as a teenager developed a successful newspaper route in Homewood, became an Eagle Scout by age 13, worked at the power plant in Wilsonville (packing coal residue), and became a good enough basketball player to earn a scholarship. Clearly, he was not a typical teenager.

Working all those jobs became an important influence in his life. Even before he became a United States Senator, Homewood's Luther Strange worked tirelessly on bringing new jobs to Alabama. He helped negotiate to close the 1999 deal between Hyundai and the state of Alabama for the massive automotive plant near Montgomery. He was brought in to help the Russell Corporation from Alexander City save as many Alabama jobs as possible from ending up overseas.

Strange was especially proud of his work to close the Hyundai deal, because the timing of the automaker's arrival became so important.

"Hyundai came at a critical time when Russell Corp and the old textile industry were dying out and moving overseas," he explained. "The good news was that the people who were displaced in the textile industry were retrained and recruited for jobs in the automotive manufacturing sector."

Playing a role in the Hyundai project remains one of his favorite moments in serving the state. "It was nice to be in the economic development world during that time and to be a part of that fundamental transition in our state economy."

Strange has played an important role in many other events in the state's modern history. As Alabama Attorney General, Strange saved the taxpayers over $180 million by handling the BP oil spill lawsuit within his own staff rather than bringing in a private law firm. "That money shored up our general fund and Medicaid obligations," he added.

After being twice elected as attorney general, Strange was appointed to fill the Senate seat vacated by Jeff Sessions, who resigned to become the Attorney General of the United States. Serving on the Senate Armed Services Committee and the Senate Committee on Agriculture, Nutrition, and Forestry, he was able to guard existing industries in his home state and protect our heroes serving in harm's way around the world.

As a member of the U.S. Senate, Strange routinely worked with important figures in American history. Working with legends was nothing new to him, however. As a basketball player at Tulane University, he worked a summer job with the camp run by hoops legend Jerry West, getting the privilege of playing ball with him after sessions. So who was the best player he ever faced? "Good question, and there were some good ones, but the best player I ever played with was in practices, rather in games, because he was in New Orleans, and that was Pete Maravich. He was the best player I've ever seen."

Even while dealing with legislative battles and world affairs, Strange always remained focused on jobs for Alabamians. "I'm very used to hard work, and that's what makes me sympathetic to people who are working hard every day to do the right thing and take care of their families."

Strange's childhood friend, Bubba Smith grew up watching the future Senator doing the right thing every day. They played sports together for decades, winning championships together and dealing with the tough losses. They each had paper routes to earn spending money as kids. According to Smith, nothing has changed. "After being friends for going on 55 years, I now realize that the character all of his close friends observed back in middle school is the same character he displays today. To me that is amazing, and I am very proud to be his friend."

Oscar Underwood
Majority Leader, U.S. Senate
Jefferson Couny

Oscar Underwood was a giant of American politics and a true visionary leader. Future President Woodrow Wilson wanted Underwood as his vice presidential running mate in 1912, but the Alabamian turned him down, as the second highest office was not a common stepping stone to the top.

According to the U.S. Senate website, Underwood "holds the distinction of being the only person to serve as Democratic leader in both the House and Senate, and the first Senate Democrat to be officially designated as his party's floor leader."

Originally from Louisville, Kentucky, Underwood's father also served in both the U.S. House and Senate. Oscar graduated from the University of Virginia School of Law and followed his older brother to Birmingham.

He authored the "Underwood Tariff," and served as Chairman of the House Ways and Means Committee while also majority leader. He ran for president in 1924, but his opposition to the Ku Klux Klan and to prohibition cost him the votes of other southern states.

Underwood passed away in 1929 at his Virginia plantation, which had once been owned by George Washington.

Time magazine once described his politics as having "lofty purpose, great zeal, and not a little oratory."

The USS Alabama
By the numbers
Mobile County

The *USS Alabama*, one of America's great warships during World War II, now sits majestically in Mobile Bay as a monument to the Alabamians who have bravely defended our nation.

By the numbers

15 million...That's right; the *USS Alabama* has attracted over 15 million visitors and added over $1 billion to the Alabama economy.

2,500...The *USS Alabama* carried a cumulative total of 2,500 during its service in World War II.

1...The great honor of leading the American Fleet into Tokyo Bay on September 5, 1945, was bestowed on the *USS Alabama*.

9...No less than nine Battle Stars for meritorious service were awarded the "Mighty A" during her brief three-year tenure as the "Heroine of the Pacific," according to the *USS Alabama* website.

85,000,000...The *USS Alabama* weighed a whopping 85 million pounds (42,500 tons) when fully loaded

The Wallace family
Leaders of Alabama
Barbour & Montgomery Counties

The son of Clio, Alabama, became the most powerful, controversial, and influential governor in the state's history. George Corley Wallace was born in 1919, the year Alabama celebrated its 100th birthday. The next 100 years saw the state's reputation, politics, and image affected more by him than any other.

Volumes have been written about the Wallace family, including Governor George Wallace, Governor Lurleen Wallace, State Treasurer George Wallace, Jr., and Alabama Supreme Court Justice Mark Kennedy. Books about American history, from memoirs of the players to important works about the 1960s, credit the political genius of George Wallace with many of the campaign themes, tactics, and code-words used in the decades since his presidential campaigns.

The legendary stories about the Wallace political dynasty are almost endless. In his early years, as the legend goes, George Wallace would campaign at an event in one part of the state, but had his aides place calls to other events going on at the same time. They would ask the events' organizers and operators to please make an announcement asking George Wallace to call his office. The audience would hear Wallace's name on the public address system and believe he had taken the time to visit their event.

Another legend was told by a former state senator, who during his first term made comments critical of Governor Wallace to a newspaper reporter. The comments were published the next morning, and by the time that state senator went to lunch in the capitol building's cafeteria, he found himself dining alone. Not one of his colleagues wanted to sit at the table with anyone criticizing the governor.

Continuing the themes that vaulted him to the governor's office, Wallace campaigned for president on the issues of race, an interventionist federal judiciary, the evil media, and the pointy-headed intellectuals from up north who thought they had all the answers.

Through it all, to supporters and opponents alike, Wallace remained a compelling, powerful, entertaining, and even funny public speaker.

By the Numbers

5...The Wallaces were elected to the office of governor five different times, with Lurleen Wallace becoming the state's first female governor in 1967, and George Wallace becoming the only person elected governor four different times.

2...Wallace actually held two other offices from his native Barbour County: state representative, and circuit judge. Wallace dubbed himself the "fighting judge" because of his opposition to what he called excessive intervention by the federal government into the daily lives of Alabamians. The term had a double meaning; he was also a "fighting judge" because he had once been an amateur boxer. Perhaps that was his best training for the world of Alabama politics.

2...Wallace's 1962 election as governor was his second campaign for the job, after his failed try four years earlier. In that 1958 election, Wallace criticized the racially tinged campaign of his opponent. The NAACP endorsed Wallace in that race. After coming up short against the segregationist candidate, Wallace dropped his moderation on racial issues and became the candidate who had defeated him. Many biographers, students of history, and Wallace supporters claim that he only cared about the issues of race and segregation as a path to the governorship and presidency. As the *Encyclopedia of Alabama* described it, "During each election cycle, he modified his racial views to suit the times." Even the legendary national reporter Jack Germond, in his memoir described the Wallace presidential campaign he had covered and opined that Wallace didn't even care about the issue of race. The *Encyclopedia Britannica* concurred, explaining that: "The civil-rights issue was a means for him to enter the national spotlight." Regardless of his motivations, his infamous stand in the schoolhouse door to prevent integration of the University of Alabama campus cemented his reputation, and that of Alabama, for a generation to come.

1...Lurleen became the first female governor in the state's history with her election in 1966. She became a type of surrogate candidate for her husband, who was ineligible to run that year because state law forbade governors from serving consecutive terms. Unfortunately, she passed away while in office.

13...In 1968, one of the most tumultuous years since the Civil War, George Wallace ran for the American presidency and received 13 percent of the vote. That made him one of the most successful third-party candidates in American history.

1972...That was the year that Wallace once again sought the presidency, but was wounded in a near-fatal assassination attempt in Maryland. The gunman, Arthur Bremer, stalked Wallace around the country before shooting him in Maryland. The mystery as to how the unemployed Bremer had the resources to fund and organize the extensive travel remains a mystery.

20...When Wallace first became governor, Alabama had only 12 community colleges or trade schools. He worked with the legislature, including Speaker Rankin Fite of Hamilton, to create 20 new community colleges or trade schools.

Thanks to that effort, countless Alabamians have been afforded geographic and financial access to a college education.

2...The 1982 election became a second act for George Wallace. After apologizing to Alabamians, and particularly African-Americans, for his segregationist past, Wallace was elected to a fourth term as governor. In one of the state's great ironies, his margin of victory was provided mostly by African-American voters.

2...The second generation of Wallaces in public service arrived in 1986, when George Wallace, Jr., was elected Alabama State Treasurer. He was his party's nominee for the U.S. Congress in 1992, missing by less than one percent of the vote in a redrawn second congressional district. He was also elected to the Alabama Public Service Commission. His brother-in-law, Justice Mark Kennedy, served on the Alabama Supreme Court and later led the Alabama Democratic Party.

Joe Wheeler

American and Confederate General

Lawrence Counties

Joe Wheeler was the only person to become a general in the Confederate Army during the Civil War, and later become a commander in the Union Army.

During the Civil War, Wheeler quickly rose up the ranks due to his successes on the battlefields. His specialty came in using his troops of the Nineteenth Alabama Infantry Regiment to cover the movements of larger forces, such as the Confederate retreat during the Battle of Shiloh, in 1862.

Wheeler rose to the rank of major general during the war, and was accompanying Confederate President Jefferson Davis when they both were captured and imprisoned.

After the war, Wheeler married a widow he had met during the war and settled down in Lawrence County, Alabama. He was elected to the United States Congress, becoming a part of the government he had waged war against just a few years earlier.

If that seemed ironic to many, it may have paled in comparison to the sight of Wheeler in a U.S. Army uniform soon thereafter. With the Spanish-American War approaching, Wheeler enlisted in the Army and became a general of volunteer forces.

As in his entire career, Wheeler was quickly promoted to the rank of general in the United States Army, commanding troops in the war. One notable group under his command was the Rough Riders, led by future President Theodore Roosevelt.

In perhaps the greatest irony of them all, upon Wheeler's passing, the former general of the Confederate forces was laid to rest in the Arlington National Cemetery, among those he had fought.

The other president in the White House (Stewart Douglas McLaurin)

One of America's great civic leaders serves as president of the White House Historical Association, and his own history stands deeply rooted in Alabama.

Stewart Douglas McLaurin graduated from the University of Alabama, an institution that has placed many alumni in White House roles. He has also served as Executive Vice President, American Village Citizenship Trust in Montevallo.

According to WhiteHouseHistory.org, McLaurin has also "held senior positions with George Washingtons Mount Vernon Estate, The Ronald Reagan Presidential Foundation,the Motion Picture Association, Georgetown University, American Red Cross, and the Federal Government."

His social media posts provide a great public service by giving readers a well-crafted insight into White House history, along with interesting facts and unique photos. McLaurin's work as Executive Director for the Ronald Reagan Presidential Foundation earned the honor of PRWeeks 2011 Non-Profit National Campaign of the Year.

The White House Historical Association was established in 1961, in support of First Lady Jacqueline Kennedy's vision to preserve and share the White House's legacy.

Did You Know???

Alabama and the vice presidency

William Rufus King of Selma was elected the 13th Vice President of the United States in 1852.

Birmingham's Senator Oscar Underwood was asked by Woodrow Wilson to serve as the Democratic candidate for the vice presidency in 1912. Because the position was much less powerful then, Underwood turned down the job, and possibly forfeited his chance for the presidency.

In 1952, Senator John Sparkman was the Democratic candidate for the vice presidency. He and his running mate, presidential nominee Adlai Stevenson of Illinois, lost to General Dwight Eisenhower.

General.

Trailblazer.

Leader.

Alabamian.

Meet General Sheryl Gordon

On July 17, 2017, Governor Kay Ivey appointed Maj. Gen. Sheryl Gordon as the first female Adjutant General of the Alabama National Guard.

For Gordon, the appointment marked the latest in a career filled with achievement, honors, and massive responsibilities in the realm of the state's military forces.

Her previous duties with the Alabama National Guard included Deputy Adjutant General of the Alabama National Guard (2011-2013), Commander of the 62nd Troop Command (2009-2011), and Garrison Commander of the Ft. McClellan Training Center (2007-2009). She served as Brigadier General before her promotion to Major General.

"As adjutant general, she advises the governor on military affairs and commands the Alabama Army and Air National Guard and its more than 12,000 citizen Soldiers and Airmen," according to Governor.Alabama.gov.

Our Ultimate Heroes
Congressional Medal of Honor Recipients

The state of Alabama has made enormous contributions to the national security and wartime efforts of the United States of America. In no arena has that contribution stood more profoundly than with those Alabamians who have been awarded the Congressional Medal of Honor. Celebrating Alabama's first 200 years would fall incomplete without the names of those who have received America's highest citation of honor.

Paul Bolden
Staff Sergeant, U.S. Army
Madison, Alabama

Cecil Bolton
First Lieutenant, U.S. Army
Huntsville, Alabama

Charles Davis
Major, U.S. Army
Gordo, Alabama

Henry Erwin
Staff Sergeant, U.S. Army
Adamsville and Leeds

Rodney J. Evans
Sergeant, U.S. Army
Montgomery, Alabama

Howard Walter Gilmore
Commander, U.S. Navy
Selma, Alabama

Ross Franklin Gray
Sergeant, U.S. Marines
Marvel Valley, Alabama

Robert L. Howard
First Lieutenant, U.S. Army
Opelika / Montgomery, Alabama

Osmond Kelly Ingram
Gunner's Mate First Class,
U.S. Navy
Oneonta, Alabama

Gordon Johnston
First Lieutenant, U.S. Army
Birmingham, Alabama

William R. Lawley
First Lieutenant, U.S. Army
Leeds, Alabama

Matthew Leonard
Sergeant, U.S. Army
Eutaw, Alabama

Jake Lindsey
Technical Sergeant, U.S. Army
Isney, Alabama

Sidney Manning
Corporal, U.S. Army
Flomaton, Alabama

President Donald J. Trump awards the Congressional Medal of Honor to Gary Rose, who now resides in Huntsville, for valor during the Vietnam War.

David McCampbell
Commander, U.S. Navy
Bessemer, Alabama

Alford McLaughlin
Private First Class, U.S. Marines
Leeds, Alabama

Don Leslie Michael
Specialist Fourth Class, U.S. Army
Florence and Montgomery, Alabama

Ola L. Mize
Corporal, U.S. Army
Albertville and Gadsden, Alabama

John Dury New
Private First Class, U.S. Marines
Mobile, Alabama

Gary Rose
U.S. Army Special Forces
Huntsville, Alabama

William Seay
Sergeant, U.S. Army
Brewton and Montgomery, Alabama

James Sprayberry
First Lieutenant, U.S. Army
Montgomery, Alabama

Jack Treadwell
Captain, U.S. Army
Ashland, Alabama

George Watson
Private, U.S. Army
Bessemer, Alabama

Wilson Douglas Watson
Private, U.S. Marines
Tuscumbia, Alabama

Harold E. Wilson
Technical Support, U.S. Marines
Birmingham, Alabama

THE LEGEND OF LISTER HILL
by the numbers

Many historians believe that Lister Hill was the most important and consequential leader ever produced by Alabama. In the rich history of national leaders produced by the state, only Richard C. Shelby could lay claim to the type of power that Hill enjoyed during his decades in the U.S. Senate.

Both the state and nation still benefit from his service that defies measure. Nonetheless, his legacy is described...by the numbers.

2...Lister Hill wasn't the first in his family to achieve national prominence. His father, Montgomery physician Dr. Leonidas Hill, was the first American to surgically repair a human heart. Dr. Hill named his son Lister after Dr. Joseph Lister, another famous physician.

2...As a student at the University of Alabama, the young Lister Hill sharpened his political skills by founding two of the premier organizations on campus. He founded the Student Government Association and served as its first president. He also co-founded the Jasons Men's Senior Honorary, which has retained its prestige and elite status for over 100 years.

1931..Seven years before becoming a Senator, then-Congressman Lister Hill successfully lobbied to move the Tactical School to Maxwell Field in Montgomery, which would later become known as Maxwell Air Force Base.

500,000...Over half a million hospital beds were established across America because of the Hill-Burton Act, the landmark legislation that built rural hospitals across the country.

1...The Hill-Burton act was the number one source of funding for most buildings for the institution now known as The University of Alabama School of Medicine at UAB and the UAB Hospital. There could never be enough buildings named after Hill to sufficiently honor his impact on the state's medical community, and on UAB.

Pictured (above) President Harry Truman accompanied Alabama Senators Lister Hill and John Sparkman to the first Chilton County Peach Festival in 1947. Pictured, (L-R) are Congressman Pete Jarman, Senator Lister Hill, President Harry S. Truman, and Senator John Sparkman.

74...In 1945, only 24 percent of Southern black babies were born in hospitals. By 1960, thanks to the Hill-Burton Act, that number had climbed to 74 percent.

2...Not content to merely revolutionize our rural health care, Senator Hill set his sights on a second frontier, the nation's education system. After the Soviet Union (Russia) launched the first satellite to orbit the Earth, the American public feared that our schools were inadequately preparing our students for their individual futures and the nation's future.

Enter Lister Hill.

Hill and fellow Alabamian Congressman Carl Elliott authored the National Defense Education Act to help our schools in science and math, and to help make student loans available to students across America.

1948...Senator Hill and Florida Senator Claude Pepper, a fellow alumnus of the University of Alabama, passed the National Institutes of Health Act of 1948 that greatly aided and promoted medical research across America.

Pictured: Top left, Birmingham native Condoleezza Rice served as Secretary of State during he second term of President George W. Bush. Top right, President Donald Trump (left) confers with aide Cliff Sims. Middle, Governor Kay Ivey takes the oath of office, administered by Justice Will Sellers. The Bible is held by Dr. Cathy Randall of Tuscaloosa. Bottom, left, President John F. Kennedy (seated) signs legislation with Senator Lister Hill (left) and Mobile's own Congressman Frank Boykin. Bottom, middle, Dr. Regina Benjamin served as the Surgeon General of the United States. Bottom, right, First Lady of the United States Eleanor Roosevelt (center) enjoys a moment with Rosa Parks (left) and Autherine Lucy Foster (right).

ATHLETES

Players, Coaches, Broadcasters, Benefactors

Mobile native Henry "Hank" Aaron smacks his 715th career home run on April 8, 1974, breaking the most hallowed record in all of American sports.
Photo courtesy of the Encyclopedia of Alabama.

Henry Aaron
Baseball's home run king
Mobile County

At the biggest moment in baseball history, the state of Alabama stood center stage. The batter, who had grown up swinging cross-handed during sandlot games in Mobile, faced the outstanding Los Angeles Dodgers pitcher Al Downing. Millions across America and beyond watched as Downing hurled a fastball across the middle of home plate on April 8, 1974. The batter, Henry Aaron of the Atlanta Braves, timed the pitch perfectly, snapped his legendary wrists, and smacked the ball over the left field fence.

Aaron's home run was his 715th, surpassing the mighty Babe Ruth and breaking the most hallowed record in all of American sports.

For Aaron, who grew up in the Mobile area, that historical homer marked the successful journey from second-class citizen to America's most honored living athlete. In his early years, Aaron actually played briefly in the old Negro League before entering Major League Baseball. Back then, segregation was a systemic part of life. By the time of his retirement, he stood alone as the last remaining Negro League alumnus.

Those born after 1974 might be surprised by the reaction that the record's pursuit caused toward Aaron. As times were much different in the early 1970's, and because Babe Ruth was such an iconic figure, the hate mail and death threats poured in. The Braves actually hired a secretary just to help Aaron manage his mail, and the U.S. Postal Service awarded him a plaque for receiving over 930,000 pieces of mail during the 1974 season.

Aaron stood, singularly unaffected, as a model of class and humility. He maintained his dignity throughout his career, but especially during the chase to break Babe Ruth's record.

Even beyond his home runs, Aaron continues to stand alone in many ways, such as the holder of seemingly countless records. In addition to retiring as the all-time home run king (and many still consider him that today), Aaron also set records for the most RBI (runs batted in), selections to the MLB all-star game, total bases, and extra base hits. He also remains in the top five of baseball history in runs scored and hits.

Aaron's class and career transcended sports, and made him a role model for generations to come and one of Alabama's greatest contributions of the 20th century.

Rudy Abbott
National championship coach
Calhoun County

The state of Alabama has been blessed with many outstanding educators and coaches, and few have ever become the face of an athletic program more clearly than Coach Rudy Abbott at Jacksonville State University.

Born in Anniston, Abbott went just up the road for college at Jacksonville State and became a star pitcher for the Gamecocks, hurling two different no-hitters in 1962. After a brief professional career (he was drafted by the Pittsburgh Pirates), Abbott returned to his alma mater and served as the sports information director.

Hired as the head baseball coach, Abbott led the Gamecocks for an amazing 32 years, winning two national championships, 1,003 games, and 11 conference championships.

Scotty Ward, who played for Abbott and served as an assistant on a national championship team, explained that "Coach Abbott was one of the most influential men in my life; he expected the best out of you at all times on and off the field. He truly is one of the all time greats, not just at JSU or in the state of Alabama but on the national level."

Ameer Abdullah
NFL star running back
Jefferson County

As the 2010 Homecoming halftime show began at Homewood High School, few would have guessed that the band would make national news in the next few minutes. The Homewood Marching Band formed the words spelling "FEAR AMEER" on the field, honoring their star alumnus and then-Nebraska star running back Ameer Abdullah.

Abdullah had become one of the leading candidates for the Heisman Trophy and All-American honors after a record-breaking career for the University of Nebraska football team, and the Homewood band celebrated their friend and fellow Homewood Patriot. Abdullah, by then a nationally known athlete, finished the year with a seemingly endless string of honors and awards, including: 2014 Second-Team All-American; 2014 Doak Walker Award Finalist; 2014 Senior CLASS Award Winner; 2014 Pop Warner College Football Award; 2014 Paul Hornung Award Finalist; 2014 Wuerffel Trophy Finalist; 2014 Maxwell Award Semifinalist; and 2014 Second-Team All-Big Ten

Professional football teams agreed with the Homewood Marching Band, and the Detroit Lions chose Abdullah in the second round of the 2015 National Football League Draft. In November of 2018, his services were acquired by the Minnesota Vikings.

Tommie Agee
Auburn and NFL star running back
Chilton County

Tommie Agee's career has been defined by using elite talents to help others. After starring in four sports at his hometown's Maplesville High School (Chilton County), Agee could have chosen a college where he would become the primary star.

Thankfully, for Auburn University and Dallas Cowboy fans, Agee is a bigger man than that. He signed with Coach Pat Dye's Auburn Tigers to become a fullback, which meant that he occasionally carried the ball but more often blocked for other running backs. Agee's vast success speaks for itself, as he blocked for Auburn to win the 1983 Southeastern Conference Championship, and for his buddy Bo Jackson to win the 1985 Heisman Trophy.

After a few years with the Seattle Seahawks and one year with the Kansas City Chiefs, Agee was signed by the Dallas Cowboys and began blocking a path for another young star, Emmitt Smith. Agee was assigned to teach the Cowboys' offense to Smith, and the result was two Super Bowl victories together, and Smith ultimately becoming the league's all-time leading rusher.

After his football career, Agee has continued selflessly and tirelessly paving the way for others to succeed, just as he did at Auburn and in the NFL. Agee has worked with the parks & recreation in the Auburn-Opelika area, and now does the same in Andalusia, where he uses his vast talents, strong national connections, and natural team spirit to improve the life of his community. Agee and his wife, Anchylus, have three children (Tyler, Torey, and Angelique).

Shaun Alexander
NFL Most Valuable Player
The University of Alabama

If one word describes the career, personal, and spiritual life of Shaun Alexander, it would be "purpose." In his early years, his purpose in playing pee-wee football in his hometown of Florence, Kentucky, was to keep up with his older brother, Durran. Shaun grew up in the shadow of Durran, who was known as one of those kids who was seemingly good at everything and liked by almost everyone.

Shaun's purpose for playing football began to change in one of those pee-wee league games in which he returned two kickoffs for touchdowns. The coaches made him a running back, and he played the same position at Boone County High School. Alexander began his career as a backup player, just as he would in college and in the pros. In his senior year, Shaun Alexander set the Kentucky state record by scoring 54 touchdowns in one season. He was no longer just the little brother, but was instead now the official "Mr. Football" of Kentucky and was named a *Parade* All-American. Choosing among many scholarship offers, he decided on the University of Alabama.

Even twenty years later, Crimson Tide fans still complain that Alexander should have received more carries as a running back. During his freshman year of 1996, a teammate's injury forced him into the game against LSU in Baton Rouge, and he responded with a school-record 291 yards rushing. By his senior year at the Capstone, Alexander became the first player ever actively promoted by the university for the Heisman Trophy, although a mid-season injury derailed his prospects for the award. He became the SEC Player of the Year, and set the SEC single-season record for rushing touchdowns in a season. He was chosen in the first round of the National Football League Draft by the Seattle Seahawks.

Alexander's running style, purposefully following blockers before breaking into a full sprint, was under-appreciated in Seattle when Alexander first arrived. Just as in high school and college, Alexander began as a backup, but ultimately became the team's star player and broke every franchise touchdown record, and set NFL marks for total touchdowns in a season, rushing touchdowns in a season, and the most consecutive seasons with at least 15 touchdowns.

The purposeful running style, that had become his trademark through the years, was only one part of the purpose in his life. Since roughly the age of ten, Alexander became a committed Christian and has lived the totality of his life with a spiritual purpose that exceeds even his football intensity.

Mel Allen
Hall of Fame broadcaster
Bibb County

"How about that!"

It was more of a statement than a question, but for fans across America, it was the sound of the most recognizable voice in all of sports. For decades, Mel Allen served as the voice of national college football broadcasts, and most famously for the New York Yankees, who dominated Major League Baseball.

In addition to his signature "How about that!" Allen is widely credited with expressions like "Going...going...gone" to describe home runs.

And it all started in Alabama.

West Blocton claims Mel Israel (his birth name) as a native son. Birmingham and Sylacauga do as well, because his dad's work took their family to different parts of Alabama during childhood.

When he auditioned at CBS Radio in New York in 1937, he was hired and asked to change his last name from Israel to something less "Jewish." He took his father's middle name, Allen, and the rest is history. History, also, is part of the reason he landed the job in New York with CBS, because a veteran sportscaster had already heard Mel's broadcasts of his dearly beloved Alabama Crimson Tide football games.

Allen entered the University of Alabama in the 1930's, when the Crimson Tide was winning national championships and was led by a dominant coach (if that sounds familiar, some things haven't changed). Alabama head football coach Frank Thomas, who was impressed with Mel's work while a student, recommended him to WBRC-Radio in Birmingham as a play-by-play announcer for Crimson Tide broadcasts.

The *Encyclopedia of Alabama* artfully and accurately summed up the broadcasting style of one of sports' greatest voices.

Allen developed a broadcast style that became a model for subsequent generations of radio sports broadcasters. Audiences enjoyed Allen's ability to create word pictures that allowed them to visualize the action on the field. He developed catch phrases that often incorporated the names of cigar and beer sponsors, such as a "White Owl wallop" or a "Ballantine blast" which Mel Allen in uniform described home runs. Other Allen phrases, delivered in a smooth southern drawl, have become part of the general sports lexicon, including the famous "How about that!" and "Going, going, gone."

Allen was inducted into pretty much every hall of fame for which he was eligible, and was named the second greatest sportscaster of all time by the American Sportscasters Association.

Dr. Leah M. Rawls Atkins
Hall of Fame water skier
Jefferson County

In 1976, Dr. Leah Marie Rawls Atkins became the first woman inducted into the Alabama Sports Hall of Fame.

She became the first female water skiing champion produced by the state of Alabama. For a seven-year span, from 1951 to 1958, she became the dominant figure in her sport, winning international and national championships.

A native of Birmingham, Atkins earned master's and doctorate degrees from Auburn University after her professional skiing career ended.

Jay Barker
Championship quarterback
Jefferson County

The game had just ended, and Jay Barker walked off the football field after leading his team to victory on national television. It was September of 1994, and the early autumn air in Tuscaloosa was still filled with the noise of cheering fans. A reporter from the ESPN sports network caught up with Barker and asked for comments about the 29-28 comeback win over the University of Georgia. Rather than discussing his outstanding performance, Barker used the national platform to talk about his Christian faith.

Putting faith and teammates before himself has defined the career of Barker, who quarterbacked the Crimson Tide to the national championship in 1992, had a career record of 35 wins, with only two losses and one tie, became a finalist for the Heisman Trophy in 1994, and won the Johnny Unitas Golden Arm Award in 1994.

After a brief stint in professional football, Barker has once again become a humble star in a second career, as a sports radio talk show host. For over a decade, Barker starred in the Birmingham radio market, and now headlines a show originating in Homewood and airing on stations in multiple cities, including Tuscaloosa.

Charles Barkley
Hall of Fame basketball star
Jefferson County

Charles Barkley was voted one of the 50 greatest basketball players in history, and has remained one of America's most recognized and entertaining sports figures for almost 40 years. Along the way, he may have acquired more nicknames than any American athlete since Babe Ruth, becoming known by such monikers as "Sir Charles," the "Dough Boy," and "The Round Mound of Rebound."

Barkley crashed onto the national scene as a power forward at Auburn University, where he played for Coach Sonny Smith. The youngster from Leeds wasn't highly recruited out of high school, but soon became known for relentless rebounding, thunderous slam dunks, and a winsome personality. Chosen in the first round of the National Basketball Association draft in 1984 (by the Philadelphia 76ers), Barkley immediately seized the national stage with his aggressive play and portly frame. He quickly became one of the game's elite players and product endorsers, along with his good friend Michael Jordan and iconic stars of that era such as "Magic" Johnson and Larry Bird. In 1992, Barkley joined Jordan, Johnson, Bird and others on the United States Olympic Basketball Team, nicknamed the "Dream Team" and still considered the greatest collection of basketball players to ever play together.

After one of the game's greatest careers, Barkley took his talents to television, serving as a basketball studio analyst for Turner Network Television and other affiliated networks. Barkley has become almost as great in the studio as he was on the court, as his expertise and entertainment skills keep viewers tuned in long after the games have ended for the night. His trademark authenticity and willingness to criticize poorly performing players and coaches has brought controversy at times but has also cemented his reputation as an honest expert on the game.

A native of Leeds, Barkley has remained loyal to his hometown, visiting often (especially before his mom's passing) and keeping in touch with the family and friends who served as the foundation for his life and his success.

Gene Bartow
Hall of Fame basketball coach
Jefferson County

In every realm of his life, on and off the basketball court, Gene Bartow was a winner.

Already a nationally prominent coach, Bartow was hired by the University of Alabama at Birmingham to launch a basketball program. For many, the move to Birmingham might have seemed risky, as Bartow was leaving the premier job in college basketball at the time, the University of California Los Angeles (UCLA). In recent years, Bartow had already led two different universities (UCLA and Memphis State) to the Final Four of the NCAA tournament, the pinnacle of college basketball. He had also coached at Central Missouri State and Valparaiso.

For Bartow, the job might not have been a risk as much as it was an opportunity to pioneer a new program and shape young lives, which was part of his coaching genius. As many had hoped, the success came quickly for Bartow, who led UAB to the NCAA Sweet Sixteen round of the tournament in 1981 and the Elite Eight round in 1982 (just one game short of another Final Four). Bartow's building job at UAB was so successful that it helped vault the success of other UAB sports, and cemented his reputation as not only an elite coach, but as the father of UAB athletics.

Bartow retired in 1996, and UAB named their coliseum "Bartow Arena" the next year. Bartow's son, Murry, succeeded him as UAB's coach and won over 100 games, maintaining a winning conference record.

Bob Baumhower
Hall of Fame football star
The University of Alabama

Before lunch that day, it seemed clear that football would define the career of Bob Baumhower. After all, he had become a star of the NFL's Miami Dolphins, honored as Rookie of the Year and later named to five Pro-Bowls. In college, he was a two-time All-American and twice All-SEC, named to the all-decade team of the 1970s and a leader of a national championship and three conference titles at the University of Alabama.

But that was merely his first all-star career.

Then came the unforgettable lunch.

Steve Towle, a fellow former Dolphin player, wanted Baumhower to try a local restaurant in Ft. Lauderdale, Florida, that served Buffalo wings. Not having any idea what Buffalo wings were, he thought his friend was crazy. By the end of the meal, Baumhower was already planning his first restaurant. In 1981, the restaurant idea from that lunch became a reality, as Baumhower opened Wings & Whiskers in the home of his college alma mater, Tuscaloosa, Alabama. It was the first restaurant in the state to serve Buffalo chicken wings.

The menus have expanded, and so have the restaurants, with eleven restaurants in Alabama serving seafood, steaks, salad, delicious desserts, and of course the trademark Buffalo chicken wings.

Baumhower's name has become synonymous with outstanding food and entertainment, and of course football.

Jeff Beard
Auburn Athletic Director
Lee County

Simply put, Garland Washington "Jeff" Beard transformed Auburn University Athletics. Assuming leadership as athletic director in 1951, Beard quickly moved to name Ralph "Shug" Jordan as the head football coach. The result of Beard's judgment was a national championship and some of the greatest years and players in the program's rich history.

Beard also made drastic changes in the athletic facilities. The football stadium seated only 22,000 when he became athletic director, but under Beard's leadership, the seating capacity tripled. A tiny arena gave way to a major modern coliseum for the basketball teams. He led the charge to develop a ten-acre football practice facility, along with athletic dorms to house Auburn's student-athletes.

Beard was inducted into the Alabama Sports Hall of Fame in 1971.

Terry Beasley
All-American Auburn football player
Montgomery County

Legend has it that Terry Beasley could stand, flat-footed, and jump over a Volkswagen. They say he could have made the Olympic team as a sprinter if he had so chosen. They also say he ran the 40-yard-dash in a blazing 4.2 seconds.

Almost 50 years after he played at Auburn, they're still remembering, talking, and writing about the wide receiver from Montgomery's Lee High School who wowed fans across America and helped his teammate win the Heisman Trophy.

"Sullivan-to-Beasley" remains one of the premier broadcaster calls in the history of Southern football. Pat Sullivan would throw it, and Beasley would catch it. Even if the ball was thrown high, low, or over his head from behind, Beasley was ahead of his time in his ability to make the seemingly impossible catch.

Beasley accomplished much in college football, but was robbed of the opportunity to repeat that success in the professional ranks. After the San Francisco 49ers chose him in the 1972 NFL Draft, a series of concussions forced an early retirement. During his football career, Beasley was reported to have suffered as many as 19 concussions. After suffering health problems arising from his concussions, Beasley has bravely fought through those difficult times with the same tenacity that he showed on those Saturday gridiron battles in Jordan-Hare Stadium.

Cornelius Bennett
Hall of Fame football star
Jefferson County

In the rich history of football teams and players from the state of Alabama, Ensley's Cornelius Bennett stands among the elite. Named to both the College Football Hall of Fame and the Alabama Sports Hall of Fame, the kid nicknamed "Biscuit" by his friends excelled at a level enjoyed by few in the history of the game.

At Ensley High School, Bennett became a nationally recruited player on defense (as a linebacker) and at running back, where he rushed for over a thousand yards on just 101 carries. He became the crown jewel of the first post-Bear Bryant recruiting class at the University of Alabama, where he became only the second three-time All-American in school history, and received the coveted Lombardi Award. His 1986 ferocious hit, planting Notre Dame quarterback Steve Beuerlein, inspired a painting by renowned artist Daniel Moore titled "The Sack."

Bennett became the highest drafted Alabama defensive player, chosen second overall by the Colts. Rather than becoming a Colt, Bennett traveled in a different direction when a preseason three-team trade brought him to the Buffalo Bills.

Bennett became an elite NFL player in Buffalo, where he was twice named AFC Defensive Player of the Year, named All-Pro five times, and helped lead his team to four Super Bowls. He later played on a fifth Super Bowl team with the Atlanta Falcons.

At Ensley High School, the University of Alabama, and in the NFL, Bennett proved himself as one of the sport's greatest players.

Larry Blakeney
Hall of Fame football coach
Pike County

Simply put, Larry Blakeney has always been a winner.

That's why the Troy University football team plays its games on Larry Blakeney Field. That's why Blakeney was inducted into both the Alabama Sports Hall of Fame and the Troy University Sports Hall of Fame. That's why he won no less than eight conference championships while coaching the Troy Trojans.

Blakeney played his college football at Auburn University, where he started as quarterback and defensive back at different times in his career. After successful high school coaching stints at Southern Academy, Walker (now Jasper), and Vestavia Hills, he returned to his college alma mater in 1979 as an assistant coach. As a highly respected and pivotal member of the Auburn Tigers' coaching staff, Blakeney was a part of four consecutive Southeastern Conference championship teams.

As Troy's coach, his 23-year tenure included not only the eight conference championships, but also a move from Division II, to Division I-AA, to the height of college football in Division I-A. Troy defeated teams such as #17 Missouri (on national television), Mississippi State, and Oklahoma State.

Blakeney received the prestigious Johnny Vaught Lifetime Achievement Award by the All-American Football Foundation in 2000.

Ruthie Bolton
Hall of Fame basketball star
Auburn University

One of the most accomplished women basketball players ever, Ruthie Bolton has spent her post-career years helping others soar to new heights.

Born in Mississippi, Bolton joined her sister, Mae Ola Bolton, at Auburn University where they led the Lady Tigers to the Women's Final Four in both 1988 and 1989.

Bolton played an important role for the United States Women's Basketball team in the 1996 Olympics and the 2000 Olympics, winning gold medals in both Olympic Games.

Drafted by the Sacramento Monarchs of the WNBA (Women's National Basketball Association) Bolton enjoyed a long and highly successful career before her retirement in 2005. She has served as a collegiate head basketball coach, at William Jessup University (in California) and as a First Lieutenant in the United States Army Reserves. She currently resides in Sacramento, the home of her WNBA career, where she coaches high school basketball.

In 2011, Bolton was inducted into the Women's Basketball Hall of Fame. She has also authored two books detailing her life's journey, her basketball career and the darkness of an abusive marriage that she endured before going public with her struggles.

Charlie Boswell
Hall of Fame golfer, war hero
Jefferson County

For Charlie Boswell, blindness was not a handicap, but merely an inconvenience.

Originally a three-sport athlete at Ensley High School, Boswell went on to

THE HEISMAN TROPHY

Alabamians have enjoyed a rich history with the most prestigious award in American sports, the Heisman Trophy. In addition to the winners, several other athletes from the state have been honored as finalists at the Heisman presentation ceremony in New York. Also, the National Football Foundation named retroactive winners for years before the award was created, and the 1934 winner was Don Hutson from the University of Alabama.

Heisman Trophy winners from the State of Alabama

1985 Heisman Trophy winner Bo Jackson

1971
Pat Sullivan
Auburn University
John Carroll High School
Birmingham

1985
Vincent "Bo" Jackson
Auburn University
McAdory High School
Bessemer

2009
Mark Ingram
The University of Alabama
Tuscaloosa

2010
Cam Newton
Auburn University
Auburn

2013
Jameis Winston
Florida State University
Hueytown High School
Hueytown

2015
Derrick Henry
The University of Alabama
Tuscaloosa

play college sports at the University of Alabama and aspired to become a professional baseball player. World War II changed his plans, and while on a European battlefield, Boswell was rescuing a fellow soldier from a burning tank and sustained the injury that permanently blinded him.

After multiple surgeries, the Army sent Boswell to the Valley Forge General Hospital, which specialized in working with sight-impaired patients. It was there that one of the rehabilitation specialists introduced Boswell to golf, hoping that it might serve as an outlet for his athletic ability and competitiveness.

Boswell became one of the greatest golfers in the U.S. Blind Golfers Association, winning 17 American championships and 12 international championships. He served as president of the USBGA for 20 years.

Despite his inspirational achievements, perhaps the biggest accomplishment of Boswell's remarkable life was his leadership and fundraising for sight-related medical care and research. He founded the Charlie Boswell Celebrity Classic, joined each year by longtime friend Bob Hope and many others, raising over a million dollars for the Birmingham Eye Foundation Hospital.

Boswell was successful in every realm of life, operating a successful insurance practice, raising an outstanding family of three children with his wife, Kitty, and even serving as Alabama Commissioner of Revenue from 1971 to 1979.

Long after his passing in 1995, Charley Boswell's life remains a powerful and inspirational example to us all.

Bobby Bowden
Hall of Fame football coach
Jefferson County

Despite the national fame, the championships, the wealth, and the extensive travel, Bobby Bowden has always remained, in his heart, a child of Birmingham.

After graduating as a star student and athlete at Woodlawn High School, Bowden fulfilled a lifelong dream by entering the University of Alabama to play quarterback on the Crimson Tide's football team. After a year, he transferred to Samford University (then Howard College) and became an All-American quarterback.

Bowden's athletic success didn't foreshadow his future as much as his leadership success, as he was elected team captain, a two-time president of Pi Kappa Alpha fraternity, and nominated by his school for *Who's Who Among Students In American Colleges and Universities*.

After several coaching stops, including his alma mater of Howard College and the University of West Virginia, Bowden was hired as the head football coach at Florida State University in 1976.

Two national championships, twelve conference championships, and 304 wins later, Bowden retired as Florida State head football coach in 2009.

Bowden became the face of a major university, a leading figure for honesty and character in athletic competition, and a highly coveted public speaker. Bowden produced more professional players, All-Americans, assistant coaches promoted to head coaches, hall of fame inductions, and coaching awards than anyone could be reasonably expected to remember.

Maybe his most impressive statistic is the six children and 21 grandchildren about which Bowden and his wife Ann can rightfully brag.

Through it all, Bowden has faithfully spent time each summer with friends and classmates from Woodlawn High School. He has routinely spoken at events and charitable functions in his homeland of Alabama.

Robert Brazile
Hall of Fame football star
Mobile County

Robert Brazile's path has been a tale of two careers. In the first, he was known as

"Doctor Doom," and in the second, he found meaning, fulfilled his purpose, and changed lives.

In both careers, he became an all-star performer.

After graduating from Vigor High School in his hometown of Mobile, Brazile played football for Jackson State University. Already an elite player, Brazile was chosen as the sixth overall pick in the NFL Draft by the Houston Oilers (now the Tennessee Titans). His college teammate, Walter Payton, was chosen two picks earlier by the Chicago Bears.

Thus began the first of Brazile's two hall-of-fame-worthy careers. Brazile played ten years for the Oilers, never missing a game. He made an immediate impact for his team, earning Defensive Rookie of the Year. Ultimately, he won the greatest honors in the game when he was named to the All-Decade NFL team of the 1970s, was selected All-Pro five times (1976, 1977, 1978, 1979 and 1980) and was elected to seven consecutive Pro Bowls (1977-1983).

As wonderful as that might seem, Brazile told *USA Today* that he preferred his second career to his professional football days.

In his second career, rather than Dr. Doom, he was simply Mr. Brazile.

Brazile returned to his hometown of Mobile and taught middle school special education classes. The *USA Today* interview with Brazile came in 2018, upon his election to the Pro Football Hall of Fame. While embracing the joy of his sport's highest honor, Brazile nonetheless made a comment that grabbed a national headline: "If I had to choose it all over again, I would love being a teacher more than a football player."

That comment says more about Brazile than all the honors, wins, statistics, and accolades.

Dieter Brock
Hall of Fame football star
Jacksonville State University

They called him the "Birmingham Rifle" because when Dieter Brock threw a football, it seemed like the ball had been shot from a powerful gun rather than hurled by a mere human. A Canadian sportswriter once wrote that Brock's arm was so powerful that he "could throw a hole in the wind."

Ralph Dieter Brock began the unusual path of his football career as a backup quarterback at Auburn University. Even with his enormous physical talents, Ralph Brock fully understood that no one would replace the future Heisman Trophy winning Pat Sullivan as the Tigers' quarterback, so he transferred to Jacksonville State University. After an outstanding college career for the Gamecocks, Brock signed with the Hamilton Tiger Cats of the Canadian Football League and began using his middle name, Dieter.

Why did Brock not begin his career in the more American league, the NFL? Unfortunately, NFL talent scouts often focus more on "measurables" (height, weight, et al.) than they should. Tom Brady was the 199th player taken in the 2000 draft. A scout famously told Joe Montana that he would never play in the league. And, Warren Moon languished for years in the Canadian Football League before finally getting an opportunity. Brock was similarly misevaluated, and the NFL's loss was Canada's gain, as he led Hamilton to the Grey Cup finals. Brock was traded to the Winnipeg Blue Bombers, which he also led to the Grey Cup finals. Finally, at age 33, he became an NFL rookie with the Los Angeles Rams and set passing records in his one year before injuries forced his retirement.

Brock was inducted into the Alabama Sports Hall of Fame, the Canadian Football League Hall of Fame, the Winnipeg Football Club Hall of Fame and its Circle of Honor.

Johnny Mack Brown
Movie star and football star
Houston County

From a shopkeeper's home in Dothan to the unmatched glamor of Hollywood, the journey of Johnny Mack Brown launched Southern football into the national spotlight.

As one of eight children raised in Houston County, Brown might not have fit the profile for national stardom. A local high school football star, Brown was recruited to play football for the University of Alabama. Brown became an All-American running back and led Alabama to an invitation to the Rose Bowl in Pasadena, California, at the end of the 1925 season.

By all accounts, the game was expected to be a blowout win for the Washington Huskies, who were the nation's top team and the prohibitive favorite to win the game and the national championship. Also, the national media did not take Southern college football teams seriously.

At least, they didn't until January 1, 1926.

On that day, Southern football changed forever, as it was carried on the back of Johnny Mack Brown into the national spotlight. Perhaps the legendary columnist Clyde Bolton explained it best when he wrote that "The 1926 Rose Bowl was without a doubt the most important game before or since in Southern football history."

Alabama defeated the heavily favored Huskies, capturing the first of seemingly endless national championships. The players and coaches were treated as conquering heroes on the return trip. Crowds gathered to cheer players as the train passed through small Southern towns. Over 1,000 Tulane University students showed up to cheer the Southern heroes when the train arrived in New Orleans.

In the middle of nowhere, in a hamlet near Fordyce, Arkansas, a 12-year-old boy listened to the game on the radio. The kid listened as his fellow Southerners won the national championship, and as Johnny Mack Brown became a legend. That kid, Paul "Bear" Bryant, decided that day that he wanted to play football at Alabama.

Johnny Mack Brown not only scored two touchdowns in the Rose Bowl, he also impressed the pro scouts. Actually the pro scouts were Hollywood talent scouts, and he soon embarked on a second All-American career, as a matinee idol on the big screen.

Brown starred in movies about the Wild West, and played the good-guy role of cowboys. He became even more famous nationally through movies than via football, but the kid from Dothan will always stand tall as the All-American. He made his university, and all of Southern football, a respected part of the All-American sport.

Paul "Bear" Bryant
Hall of Fame football coach
Tuscaloosa County

He was born in the middle of nowhere, but when he passed away, his funeral drew national media, multitudes lining the streets of Tuscaloosa, and even banners on interstate highway overpasses.

In between those two events, Paul "Bear" Bryant lived a fully successful life, re-writing the college football record books with six national championships and fourteen Southeastern Conference titles.

Bryant seemingly spent his entire life as a legend. At

age thirteen, he wrestled a bear at a carnival and picked up the nickname. His momma wanted him to become a minister, but he explained to her that "Coaching is a lot like preaching." That would be the first of many Bryant remarks that are still quoted in Alabama and beyond.

As a college student at the University of Alabama, Bryant played in the rivalry game against Tennessee with a broken leg, and the legend kept growing. He won his first SEC championship as the head coach of the Kentucky Wildcats, but left after the university boosters gave him a watch, while presenting a new car to the head basketball coach Adolph Rupp. That was the next part of the Bryant legend, like baseball's "curse of the bambino," because Kentucky hasn't won another conference championship in football since Bryant left.

Bryant briefly coached for four seasons at Texas A & M, where his team's field trip to a place called Junction, Texas, became another part of his legend. Then, in another famous quip, he announced that he was returning to his alma mater in Tuscaloosa because "Mama called."

The Crimson Tide was at low ebb when he arrived, after posting dismal records in the previous few years. Bryant, however, spent the next 25 years at Alabama, winning his six national championships and capturing 13 SEC crowns, totaling more All-American and All-SEC players than anyone could remember.

Bryant's reign over the college football world came at a time when the people of Alabama welcomed their status as a winner. The 1960s and 1970s weren't the best time for media coverage of the state, so the enormous success was especially appreciated for the state's image...and its self-image.

Baseball's greatest contact hitter

The legend of Joe Sewell

He grew up in Titus (Elmore County) hitting rocks with a broom handle. He became the greatest contact hitter in baseball history. During seven remarkable seasons, Sewell had over 500 at-bats while striking out less that 10 times the entire year.

Sewell never forgot his fans, even in his elderly years. On a cold winter day in 1984, when the New York Yankees played an exhibition game in Tuscaloosa to benefit the Bryant Museum, Sewell signed autographs and chatted with youngsters asking him questions about hitting baseballs and playing with Ruth and Gehrig.

After Bryant passed away in January of 1983, legendary national columnist George F. Will wrote about the 205 area code overloading, as people called family and friends to share the news of his passing.

Decades after his passing, one can drive around the University of Alabama campus, travel on Paul Bryant Drive, pass the Paul Bryant Museum and Bryant Conference Center on the way to Bryant-Denny Stadium.

Even Bryant's wardrobe remains legendary, as his houndstooth hats have become a subtle way to honor the coach. *The Houndstooth* stands as one of the most popular establishments on campus. Houndstooth has become a subtle style pattern for Alabama fans in hats, jackets, dresses, skirts, and furniture. In the 2009 national championship victory, Heisman Trophy winner Mark Ingram scored a touchdown against the Texas Longhorns, and held up his houndstooth athletic gloves for the television cameras.

Seasons pass and records fall, but the impact of Paul Bryant on his state and his university remain unique, historic, and lasting.

Jennifer Chandler

Olympic gold medalist
Jefferson & St. Clair Counties

Sometimes, the smallest events can change lives and history.

One bit of motherly advice, combined with a coincidental visitor, converged like streams creating a river and sent the 8-year-old Jennifer Chandler on a path toward Olympic gold.

The motherly advice? Jennifer's mom was a swim coach at the Mountain Brook Swim and Tennis Club, and a former diver herself. She was trying to start a diving team, and suggested that Jennifer give it a try. She thought her daughter had the optimum body style to become a good diver. Also, athletic genes ran in both sides of the family, as her father played college basketball at Auburn.

And the other event?

As it turned out, one of the previous coaches for the Cuban Olympic swimming and diving team was in Birmingham, working with her mom at the club. His name was Carlos DeCubas, and he was willing to coach the young Jennifer. Apparently, he saw the same potential that compelled Jennifer's mom to suggest diving.

"He told me when I was 10, I could be a national champion, and we started training for the Olympic trials when I was 12," Chandler explained to the *Alabama Newscenter* in 2016. The coach's words proved prophetic, as Jennifer not only won the competition at the Junior Olympics as a 12-year-old, but was named the outstanding athlete of the entire event.

Even after DeCubas became the swimming coach at Georgia Tech, Jennifer's parents often drove her to Atlanta to take lessons. Ultimately she switched to another coach (Ron O'Brien), and her biggest competition to date would be the Pan American Games in 1975.

She won the gold at the Pan Am games, and then won her Olympic Trials. It was time, finally for the 1976 Olympic Games in Montreal.

Jennifer Chandler won the 3-meter springboard event by a margin of almost 50 points, capturing the gold medal and changing her life. No American woman has won a gold medal at springboard diving since.

After graduating high school in Anniston, Chandler enrolled at the Ohio State University on a diving scholarship. Notwithstanding two significant back injuries after the Olympics, Chandler qualified for the 1980 Olympic Games. The American boycott, a response to the Russian invasion of Afghanistan, prevented her from competing.

After her 1976 victory, the invitations poured in, whether it was for public appearances or to serve as Grand Marshall for parades. Forty years later, the Olympic glory remains a part of her life.

Bill Clark

National Coach of the Year
Jefferson County

After building a football dynasty at Prattville High School with a record 106 wins and only 11 losses, Clark was hired as defensive coordinator at the University of South Alabama, and then head coach at Jacksonville State University. Before the 2014 season, he was offered the job as head football coach of the UAB Blazers. One of his chief rivals, Hoover Bucs Coach Josh Niblett, commented that there was no doubt Clark would win quickly at UAB.

Clark coached the 2014 season for UAB, and went 6-6 with optimism spreading like kudzu for the future of the program. Then, suddenly, the program was terminated by the University of Alabama System Board of Trustees, and Clark's tenure with the Blazers ended.

Or so it seemed.

Students protested, and the national media joined their local counterparts in support of the team and its school. Clark worked behind the scenes while UAB alumni and supporters quietly gathered financial commitments and the support of influential people. By June of 2015, before the dust had seemingly settled on the decision to end the program, the public outcry and gathered support convinced the board of trustees to reconsider its decision.

The Blazers became a darling of the national media, and that was before they resumed play in 2017. In that season, UAB went to a bowl game, defying the odds weighing heavily against a program that was buried just two years earlier.

Then came the magical 2018 year. The Blazers won 11 games and captured UAB football's first Conference USA championship. Bill Clark was the recipient of three different national Coach of the Year awards, and the Blazers completed one of the wildest and most dramatic comebacks in the history of American sports.

Joe Cribbs
Auburn and NFL star running back
Lamar County

Growing up in Sulligent, Alabama (Lamar County), Joe Cribbs learned about teamwork because his entire childhood was a team effort. Because of an absentee father, Cribbs was basically raised by his mom, grandmother, aunts, and two brothers who were nine and 11 years older than he. The brothers coached Joe at home and prepared him for organized sports, but he understood teamwork because he had lived it.

Cribbs thrived at his hometown high school, becoming a two-time *Parade* All-American and signing a college scholarship with Auburn University. During his college years, Cribbs broke several Auburn Tigers rushing records and today his name still stands in the top ten of many offensive categories, including rushing touchdowns, rushing yards, and rushing attempts.

Cribbs began his professional career with the Buffalo Bills, and was named Rookie of the Year and the only rookie named a starter in the Pro Bowl that year. Around that time, the USFL had emerged as an alternative league, and Cribbs signed with Alabama's own team, the Birmingham Stallions. In 1985, as the league folded, Cribbs once again played for the Buffalo Bills, and then the San Francisco 49ers, the Indianapolis Colts, and the Miami Dolphins. He totaled over 5,000 career yards and three Pro Bowl appearances, which are especially impressive given the years he played in another league.

After football, Cribbs has remained active in teamwork to help others, establishing the Cribbs Foundation to help local youth, working to help former NFL players after retirement, and helping with disaster relief after the devastating 2011 tornadoes.

Otey Crisman, Jr.
Inventor, the Otey Crisman putter
Dallas County

No one had ever seen anything like it.

Selma's own Otey Crisman, Jr., showed up at a U.S. Open qualifying event in Birmingham, Alabama, with a putter he had designed and created himself. The Otey Crisman website described that first putter as:

"...a mallet style putter with a hickory shaft, ahead of its time, as a soft metal brass insert was embedded in the aluminum head. Two lead weights on either side of the insert created a "center balance", reducing torque and improving solid contact."

The putter became an instant hit, and by the next year (1947), Jimmy Demaret won the 1947 Masters at Augusta National, using an Otey Crisman putter.

Countless champions, including hall of famers such as Ben Crenshaw, Arnold Palmer, Nancy Lopez, and Miller Barber won tournaments using an Otey. Palmer won the 1958 Masters with an Otey.

Many putters in today's world of golf employ the concepts created by Selma's Otey Crisman, and his name remains legendary in the sport.

The Croom family
Coaches, players, pioneers
Tuscaloosa County

Sylvester Croom, Sr., was an All-American player, a pioneer of civil rights, a shepherd to his ministerial flock, an accomplished educator, and a stabilizing influence during turbulent times.

After becoming an All-American at Alabama A & M, Croom became a spiritual and athletic leader in the Tuscaloosa community. For decades, he served as the team chaplain for Paul "Bear" Bryant's Alabama football team. Many credit Croom with helping Bryant successfully navigate the stormy waters of integration and unrest during the 1960s and 1970s. He stood tall and broad, with an imposing bass voice that made him a powerful preacher. Even as he neared retirement as an educator, at Holt High School, he remained engaged in the progress of his students, even making sure that new students were hanging around the right kids and thriving academically. Alabama A & M University named him one of their alumni pioneers in the realm of race relations and civil rights.

In his footsteps, Sylvester Croom, Jr., was named an All-American player for the University of Alabama Crimson Tide. After a year playing in the NFL, the younger Sylvester became an assistant coach for the Tide, earning two national championships and multiple conference titles.

He headed to the Tampa Bay Buccaneers of the NFL for the 1987 season, spending most of his career in the league and coaching for several different teams. He did head back to college, as the head coach at Mississippi State University, becoming the first African-American head coach in SEC history.

Also walking in their dad's footsteps was Dr. Kelvin Croom, who succeeded as an Alabama football player, educator, and pastor. Just as older brother Sylvester, Jr., was rebuilding football teams and mentoring players, Kelvin spent his career mentoring students and shepherding his flock as a minister.

On April 27, 2011, College Hills Baptist Church in the Alberta area of Tuscaloosa was leveled by the historically destructive F-4 tornado that ripped through the city. Almost five years to the day, the church's pastor, Dr. Kelvin Croom, led the dedication of the new sanctuary, marking yet another way in which this remarkable family has so greatly improved their community.

Rece Davis
National sports broadcaster
Colbert County

Many young souls dream of becoming sportscasters hosting the biggest programs in America, but for Rece Davis of Muscle Shoals, Alabama, the dream has become a weekly reality.

After graduating from Muscle Shoals High School (Colbert County), William Laurece "Rece" Davis enrolled at the University of Alabama, where he graduated cum laude from the School of Communication. While in school, he found local reporting roles and after graduation worked for television stations in Columbus, Georgia, and Flint, Michigan.

Then came ESPN.

Working for America's flagship sports network, Davis began his upward climb at the network by hosting smaller-profile shows, finally breaking in to occasionally anchoring SportsCenter, the nightly show.

Davis now serves as host for *College GameDay,* the top college football preview show, winning multiple EMMY Awards for his excellence and talent. He also serves as one of ESPN's top basketball studio hosts and sportscasters for college basketball broadcasts.

In addition to the EMMY Awards, Davis has been recognized as an outstanding alumnus of the University of Alabama's School of Communication and Information Sciences.

Al Del Greco
Hall of Fame football star
Auburn University

Whoever said records were made to be broken might have had Al Del Greco in mind. When he retired from football, the former Auburn University kicker had re-written the record books at the college and professional levels.

As a placekicker, he was one of the top ten scorers in the history of the National Football League. At Auburn, and with four different professional teams, Del Greco established dozens of team and league records. On the 1983 Southeastern Conference Championship team, he scored all the points in the thrilling 9-7 victory over the University of Michigan in the Sugar Bowl. He helped lead the Tennessee Titans to the 2000 Super Bowl.

After spending no less than 17 years playing in the NFL, as one of its greatest kickers, Del Greco was inducted into the Alabama Sports Hall of Fame.

Since his playing days, Del Greco has expanded his sphere of achievement to teach, challenge, and inspire others. He has coached young kickers at Spain Park High School, and achieved a second type of celebrity status as longtime co-host of the Morning Drive radio show with former Alabama quarterback Jay Barker and local radio legend Tony Kurre. He has also served as the men's head golf coach at Samford University, the Birmingham Steeldogs' kickers coach, and the kickers coach for Spain Park High School.

T. R. Dunn
Hall of Fame basketball star
Jefferson County

Michael Jordan famously described T. R. Dunn as the best defender he ever faced on a basketball court. That perfectly describes the selfless but elite game of Theodore Roosevelt Dunn, the guy who always seemed to go through life doing things the right way.

In high school, Dunn sported a 3.91 grade point average at Birmingham's West End High School. Dunn signed with the University of Alabama and became an All-American, as well as one of the most popular athletes ever at the school. Drafted by the Portland Trailblazers in the second round of the 1977 NBA Draft, Dunn played 14 years in the league. Along with three seasons in Portland, Dunn played ten years with the Denver Nuggets and a season with the Phoenix Suns.

Experts still list Dunn as one of the greatest defensive players of all-time, and easily one of the best rebounding guards the game has seen. His post-playing days have been spent as a successful assistant coach for different NBA teams and also for a season at his alma mater in Tuscaloosa.

Pat Dye
Hall of Fame football coach
Lee County

"Sixty minutes."

With those words, the history of Auburn University athletics changed.

That two-word answer was given by Pat Dye when a search committee from Auburn asked him how long it would take to defeat their arch-rival, the University of Alabama Crimson Tide. Led by Dye's coaching mentor, Paul "Bear" Bryant, Alabama had defeated Auburn nine years in a row, and patience was running thin in the loveliest village on the plains.

Fortunately for Auburn fans, the university hired Dye, and he led them to five Southeastern Conference Championships, a four-year winning streak against Alabama in the 1980s, and the title of the *New York Times* National Champions in 1983. Also, and to some most importantly, Dye brought to Auburn a newfound status as the equal in their rivalry by moving Auburn's Iron Bowl home games (every other year) to Jordan-Hare Stadium rather than Birmingham's Legion Field.

During his college years at the University of Georgia, Dye earned football All-American, Academic All-American, and Academic All-SEC honors. After serving in the United States Army, he played briefly in the Canadian Football League. As a young coach, he served as an assistant football coach at the University of Alabama for almost a decade, winning two national championships and several conference titles with Bryant.

Dye coached countless all-conference players, many All-American players, and sent more players to the professional ranks than most other college coaches. Dye's teams, no matter the season, were known for hard-nosed play, a ferocious defense, and a strong running game that typically left opponents fatigued in the second half of their games.

Dye was inducted into the Alabama Sports Hall of Fame, the National Football Hall of Fame, and the prestigious University of Georgia Circle of Honor.

Vonetta Flowers
Olympic gold medalist
Jefferson County

Birmingham native Vonetta Flowers traveled one of the most improbable journeys to a gold medal in modern Olympic history.

Vonetta's trek to the Olympic Games began on a more traditional path. A track star at Birmingham's Jackson-Olin High School, she signed a track scholarship with the University of Alabama at Birmingham. She became one of the most highly accomplished athletes in the school's history, winning 35 conference titles and becoming the school's first seven-time All-American.

Vonetta qualified for the U.S. Olympic Trials in 1996 and again in 2000, but a variety of injuries had extinguished her dreams of an Olympic medal.

Or so she thought.

Depending on one's perspective, what happened next might be considered providential or merely serendipitous. A couple of days after the 2000 Olympic Trials had ended, her husband, Johnny, found a flyer seeking athletes to try out for the U.S. Olympic Bobsled Team. Vonetta dismissed the idea, but Johnny, also a track athlete, asked her to accompany him as he tried out for the team.

As the tests began, Johnny pulled a hamstring, and asked his bride to take his place and give it a shot for both of their Olympic dreams. Amazingly, Vonetta made the team, began competing on the international stage, and ultimately qualified for the 2002 Salt Lake City Olympic Games.

There, along with her bobsledding partner Jill Bakken, Vonetta Flowers won the gold medal at the Olympic Games on February 19, 2002.

Vonetta became the first person of African descent, as well as the first Alabamian, to ever win a medal in the Winter Olympic Games. She was inducted into the Alabama Sports Hall of Fame in 2011.

For all Alabamians, especially those with UAB and Jackson-Olin roots, Vonetta Flowers remains a role model for hard work, determination, and the willingness to seize even the most unlikely of opportunities.

Jim Fyffe
Hall of Fame broadcaster
Lee County

The numbers explain it all.

The hall-of-fame career of broadcaster Jim Fyffe, one of the great talents and gentlemen of his profession, produced some amazing numbers.

9...He was named Alabama Sportscaster of the Year nine different times.

22...He served as the voice of Auburn University football for 22 years.

20...He served as the voice of the Talladega Superspeedway for over twenty years.

20...He was the voice of the national Blue-Grey All-Star Classic in Montgomery for over 20 years.

70...Way back in the 1970s, he pioneered sports talk radio in the state of Alabama, with his talk show in Montgomery that was one of the first of its type.

Fyffe did it all during his illustrious career, but was of course most famous for painting vivid word pictures for football fans as his beloved Auburn Tigers battled rivals on autumn Saturdays. His tenure saw many great successes for his Tigers, including the four consecutive Southeastern Conference championships in the 1980s, the Heisman Trophy season of the great Bo Jackson, and the first Iron Bowl rivalry game played in Auburn's Jordan-Hare stadium in 1989.

And then there was the unforgettable ring of his signature call: "Tooouuuchdoowwn Auuuubuuurn!!"

When he passed unexpectedly in 2003, the state's media, and fittingly its sports talk shows, became a day of tribute to the legend. Tributes and memories were shared by friends, fans, and rivals alike. Fyffe remains on any list of the greatest Southern football announcers.

The Legend of "the Hawk"

Clay Carroll from Chilton County became the premier relief pitcher in baseball

His teammates called Clay Carroll "the Hawk" because of his intensity.

He was one of nine children, growing up working in a cotton mill and taking any other jobs he could find. At the age of 15, he took a trip to Tallahassee with a friend's family; it was the first time he had ever left home.

As a youngster, Clay Carroll might not have known much about the world, but everyone who saw him pitch knew he was really good. The Atlanta Braves knew it too, and signed him to a contract for $1,000. In 1966, he set the team record for pitching appearances in one season, with 73. After he was traded to the Cincinnati Reds, he and his team saw grand success. In 1972, Carroll set the major league record for the most saves in a season, with 37. He was named "Fireman of the Year," as the game's best relief pitcher.

Carroll was also the winning pitcher in the seventh game of the 1975 World Series, one of the greatest series ever played.

Rowdy Gaines
Olympic gold medalist
Auburn University

Rowdy Gaines traveled a unique path, from the brink of the Olympic Games, to working at a gas station, to the first of his amazing comebacks, to Olympic gold medals, to a paralyzing disease, to the second and even more improbable comeback, and finally to his role as one of the sport's great ambassadors, speakers, and commentators.

Ambrose Gaines IV got his nickname from Clint Eastwood's character in the television series Rawhide. His nickname described his journey over so many difficulties that became mere hurdles on his sprint to success. His accomplishments can be understood, and appreciated, by the numbers:

11...As a young swimmer, Gaines had already broken 11 world records and seemed poised to become one of America's greatest Olympians.

5...At Auburn University, Gaines became a five-time national champion swimmer.

1980...That was the year that the United States boycotted the Summer Olympic Games, denying Gaines the ability to compete for the championships and fame that arise from Olympic victories.

1...One piece of advice from his dad changed Rowdy's life. He was working at his dad's gas station, remaining saddened about the career he could have enjoyed after Olympic stardom. His dad's advice? "Stop feeling sorry for yourself." Even though he had not competed in over a year, Rowdy returned to the sport in an improbable comeback and qualified for the Los Angeles Summer Olympic Games in 1984.

3...Rowdy Gaines won three gold medals in the 1984 Olympics, earning his place in history.

0...In 1991, Rowdy was tragically diagnosed with Guillain-Barre Syndrome. Guillain-Barre is a neurological disorder paralyzing the nervous system. He could have become paralyzed for life, or he could have died from the disease. After a two-month hospital stay, he finally went home, and his wife took him directly to... you guessed it...a swimming pool.

2...In his second miraculous comeback, Rowdy had to learn to walk and perform basic functions all over again. By the 1996 Olympic trials, he stood in the top ten in multiple freestyle events and was ready to compete for a place in the Olympic games.

1...Because the number-one priority in life was his family, Gaines decided to accept an offer to serve as a television commentator for the Olympics, setting aside the draconian training schedule yet remaining an important part of the sport he loved.

Chan Gailey
Hall of Fame football coach
Pike County

Chan Gailey became the only person to ever coach two different college football teams and a professional football team in Alabama. As the coach of Troy State, Gailey led the Trojans to the 1984 Division II national championship. He also coached at Samford University and the Birmingham Fire of the World League of American Football.

Gailey has served as a head coach in the NFL, leading the Dallas Cowboys, and the Buffalo Bills. He also served as head coach of the Georgia Tech Yellowjackets.

Known as an innovative thinker in the realm of offensive football, Gailey built a reputation for imaginative play calling and brilliant strategies.

Gailey was inaugurated into the 50th anniversary class of the Alabama Sports Hall of Fame in 2018.

Harry Gilmer
Hall of Fame football star
Jefferson County

He was the pride of East Lake and Woodlawn High School. Harry Gilmer became famous as a teenager, but it never would have happened without his first failure.

As a three-sport star at Woodlawn High School in Birmingham, Gilmer fully understood that his college years would be delayed, as it was 1943 and the world was at war. He had been drafted shortly before graduating from Woodlawn, and that was when he encountered the event that launched a career. The United States government doctors flunked Gilmer on his medical exam to enter the military, because a stomach condition made a specific diet necessary.

Deprived of the opportunity to serve his country, Gilmer enrolled at the University of Alabama, where he immediately launched one of the great careers in football history. He was twice a finalist for the Heisman trophy, and became the first (and still only) Crimson Tide player chosen first overall in the NFL Draft (December 19, 1947). In 1946, he amazingly led college football in major categories on offense (497 rushing yards) on defense (eight interceptions) and on special teams (436 punt return yards).

In his first team practice as a professional, Gilmer sustained a leg injury and never became the player in the NFL that he was in college, although he was chosen twice for the Pro Bowl. He also became the first U of A alumnus to become a head coach in the NFL, leading the Detroit Lions in 1965.

Artis Gilmore
Hall of Fame basketball star
Houston County

They called him the "gentle giant," but Dothan High School's legendary Artis Gilmore became one of the most ferocious rebounders and greatest players in basketball history.

Gilmore came to Dothan from Chipley, Florida, where he badly wanted to play football as a 6-foot-5 freshman tight end. Ironically, his big break came when the health insurance required for the football players was too expensive, and young Artis had to concentrate on basketball. The Gilmore family lived in poverty, often struggling to find food and clothing for their ten children. After the feet of young Artis grew past a shoe size of 13, he often had to go barefoot.

He then sprouted to a towering 7-foot-2 inches tall, yet maintained the hand-eye coordination that allowed him to dominate at every level. By the time his college career at Jacksonville University had ended in 1971, he averaged a whopping 22 rebounds per game for his entire career. Almost 50 years later, the record still stands.

Poverty disappeared from Gilmore's life when the professional leagues came calling in 1971. At the time, there were two major professional basketball leagues, the NBA and the ABA. Having the luxury of choosing his league, Gilmore opted to sign with the Kentucky Colonels of the ABA and in his first year was named Most Valuable Player and Rookie of the Year. After that league ultimately folded, Gilmore signed with the NBA's Chicago Bulls and later played for the San Antonio Spurs and the Boston Celtics.

Gilmore still holds the NBA record for the highest career shooting percentage, sinking 59.9 percent of all shots over his many years.

Eli Gold
Legendary sports broadcaster
Jefferson County

Eli Gold is, quite simply, "The Voice."

For the past 30 years, he has served as the voice of Alabama Crimson Tide football, calling games for legions of fans across the state and beyond since 1988 through six head coaches, six national championships, and eight SEC titles.

For decades, he served as the voice of NASCAR, calling the sport's biggest events, and hosted a variety of shows on multiple networks, including ESPN.

NBC tapped him as the voice of the Arena Football League, relying on his vast talents and large fan base to help bootstrap the league to higher ratings.

Gold has served as the voice of seven different professional hockey leagues, including stints as the voice of two different National Hockey League teams.

He serves as a lead weekly radio voice of the NFL, calling a premier game each week for America's most successful sports league.

He was the voice of the UAB Blazers basketball team for the first six years of their existence, and the voice of the Birmingham Barons baseball team.

Gold also gave voice to his fans, as he helped pioneer sports talk radio, beginning with the *Calling All Sports* show he hosted in the 1980s.

Gold has been honored with seven different Alabama Sportscaster of the Year awards, and also with a seemingly countless number of additional honors, awards, and commendations.

The offers keep coming, and Gold has served as the voice of so many sports teams and leagues that he has become one of THE voices in all of American sports.

He may have grown up in New York, but he has become a fixture of both the sports world and the culture of Alabama. His legions of fans consider him as much an Alabamian as anyone, and his continued excellence and achievements make him one of the state's great broadcasters, joining Mel Allen, Douglas Edwards, Jim Fyffe, and many others.

Kerry Goode
Football star, inspiration to many
Lawrence County

In its 200 years, the state of Alabama has rarely seen someone who has more courageously and effectively inspired and motivated others than the pride of Town Creek, Alabama, Kerry Goode.

During the 1983 football season, the freshman at the University of Alabama burst onto the national scene, becoming the Southeastern Conference Freshman of the Year. With his blazing speed and winsome personality, the tailback made jersey number 35 one of the cool numbers to wear in Alabama. His sophomore year promised to be even better, beginning on national television against Boston College and its future Heisman Trophy winner Doug Flutie at Birmingham's Legion Field.

In the first half of the game, Kerry dominated once again, scoring a touchdown on a Mike Shula pass and then returning a kickoff for a touchdown. In the game's second half, a devastating knee injury ended Goode's season and deprived him of that blazing speed that had set him apart from other running backs.

Goode made a comeback and even played four years in the National Football League, with the Tampa Bay Buccaneers and the Miami Dolphins before coaching in the league for several years.

Despite his fame and notoriety, the signature event of Kerry Good's amazing life began in 2015, when he was diagnosed with Amyotrophic Lateral Sclerosis (Lou Gehrig disease).

For Kerry Goode, the diagnosis became an opportunity to reach out, inspire, motivate, and witness to countless multitudes of people through social media messages. He has posted about his aspirations to inspire, but has also given a window into the pain and frustration that arises from the gradual worsening of his condition. Rather than covering up his issues, or complaining, he has given a voice of dignity and acceptance while refusing to submit to the disease.

In his first career, Kerry Goode excited and entertained fans across Alabama and beyond. But in his second career, he has become one of the most inspirational Alabamians in the state's history. Kerry Goode teaches and reminds, each day, of the power of living beyond circumstances. He also teaches and reminds of the power of living for a higher purpose, and of the opportunities we have, in daily life, to love and serve others.

Trivia

Which native of Etowah County won a football national championship as a 33-year-old coach?

The Clemson Tigers have become an annual championship contender, but they had never won a national championship until they hired Danny Ford.

Ford, a native of Gadsden, was an All-SEC player at the University of Alabama. He was hired at the age of 30 to lead the Tigers, and won the program's first title in 1981.

After 11 seasons, Ford posted an impressive 96-29-4 record, becoming Clemson's second winningest coach, behind only fellow Alabama alumnus Frank Howard. In 2017, Ford was displaced as the number-two coach in victories by yet another alum of Alabama, Dabo Swinney.

Ford later coached at the University of Arkansas, where he won the SEC Western Division championship for the first time since Arkansas had joined the Southeastern Conference.

Ford remains a popular figure in Alabama, where many fans wanted him to return as a coach.

Hubert Green
Golfing legend
Jefferson County

Sporting an unusual swing and a unique personality, Mountain Brook's Hubert Green stood tall as one of the great modern golfers.

Green won 19 PGA tournaments over a sparkling two-decade career, capturing two majors (the 1977 U.S. Open and the 1985 PGA Championship). As with his trademark quick, business-like swing, Green did things his own way, like hitting irons off the tee on all par-five holes in the '85 PGA Championship win. On a personal level, many found him difficult, and he didn't relate to throngs of golf fans in the same lovable way as favorites like Arnold Palmer or Chi Chi Rodriguez. In his defense, however, his interpersonal difficulties may have arisen from a childhood with a father who rarely expressed affection or approval.

No one, however, could dispute that Hubie Green was blessed with the toughness and mental tenacity of a true champion. His 1977 U.S. Open victory came despite a death threat that provoked heavy security during the tournament's final round.

Despite the reputation, Green also had a sharp sense of humor, as seen in his recollection to *Golf Digest* of bad advice he once gave to President Gerald Ford:

"We're playing a par 5 at Eldorado, and President Ford is

looking over his third shot. I slid over and see he's got 128 to the hole, the pin back. 'What are you gonna hit, Mr. President?' I ask. 'A 9-iron,' he says. 'The pin's in the back, Sir–better hit the 8,' I said. President Ford hits the 8-iron–and airmails the green. I can feel him sort of glaring at me. I just shrugged. 'I'm a private in the National Guard, you've been the Commander-in-Chief of the Armed Forces, and you're listening to me?' I got out of there."

Green lived his final years on Smolian Avenue in Birmingham's historic Redmont area before passing away in 2018 after a lengthy battle with cancer. Not surprisingly, his small yard, in front of the historic home, was perfectly manicured like a U.S. Open fairway.

Kevin Greene
Hall of Fame football star
Auburn University

He started out as an Auburn walk-on (non-scholarship) player, meaning that he would likely never see the football field during an actual game. Clearly, his future lay with the military, where he was commissioned during college as a Second Lieutenant in the Alabama National Guard.

Or so it seemed.

Kevin Greene continued his military career during college and beyond, ultimately attaining the rank of captain and the expertise of a paratrooper. But a funny thing happened to his career at Auburn.

The walk-on became a star, and Greene became the 1984 Southeastern Conference Player of the Year at Auburn. He was ultimately drafted by both the NFL and the USFL.

In the NFL, Greene became one of the all-time greats, retiring as the third leading sack artist in league history. He retired holding the record for most career sacks by a linebacker. Greene was named Player of the Year, All-Pro multiple times, Linebacker of the Year in multiple seasons, and was a multi-time player in the Pro Bowl. He also led the NFL in sacks in multiple seasons.

Greene played for the Los Angeles Rams, the Pittsburgh Steelers, the Carolina Panthers, and the San Francisco 49ers.

Mia Hamm
Hall of Fame soccer star
Dallas County

Perhaps biography.com put it best: "Mia Hamm is largely considered the best female soccer player in history...building one of the biggest fan bases of any American athlete."

Born in Selma in 1972, Mia Hamm grew up in the lifestyle of an Air Force family, moving frequently from one base to another. Her father had been stationed at Craig Air Force Base in Selma.

By her teenage years, Mia had proven beyond doubt that she held great potential as a soccer player. Then came the college years. Hamm chose the University of North Carolina at Chapel Hill, and led the Tarheels to the women's soccer NCAA national championship in each of her four years.

Mia competed for the United States, winning the Olympic gold medal with her team in 1996 and 2004. She played for 17 years, and added to her Olympic success with two Women's World Cup championships, five consecutive Soccer USSA Female Athlete of the Year awards, and two ESPY Awards. She also set the record for the most career goals scored in international competition.

Hamm established the Mia Hamm Foundation to fund further bone marrow research, in response to the passing of her brother Garrett from a rare blood disease.

With her playing days behind her, Hamm generously lends her time to many charitable groups and events, appearing many times in her birthplace of Selma to help great causes in that community.

Chris Hammond
Major League Baseball star
Randolph & Jefferson Counties

Amazingly, Chris Hammond was not supposed to pitch that day. He wasn't even a regular pitcher for the UAB Blazers baseball team. For some reason, perhaps providentially, Hammond pitched in the game on the very day the professional baseball scout showed up.

The rest, as they say, is history.

A native of Vestavia Hills and star player for the Vestavia High School Rebels, Hammond made it to the big leagues in 1990, on the Cincinnati Reds team that won the World Series that year. In his fourth season, he was traded to the Florida Marlins in their first year of existence. After pitching with the Marlins and the Boston Red Sox (and briefly for the Marlins again), Hammond underwent shoulder surgery and retired from baseball, living on his land in Randolph County, Alabama.

Or so it seemed.

Just as providentially as that day he pitched in front of the big league scout, Hammond tried a comeback, signing with the Cleveland Indians, but not making the team. He did, however, impress the Atlanta Braves, who signed him for the 2002 season.

Hammond didn't merely make a comeback; he enjoyed a transcendent year in which he posted a historic 0.95 earned run average that included almost 30 consecutive scoreless innings. After that epic year, Hammond signed with the New York Yankees and found himself on another team headed for the World Series, this time facing his former teammates with the Florida Marlins. Hammond also pitched for the Oakland Athletics and San Diego Padres before closing out his career where it began, with the Cincinnati Reds.

After baseball, Hammond has worked tirelessly to help young people and share his Christian faith with people of all ages and backgrounds. Hammond speaks regularly to groups, including churches, and actively engages in prison ministry to reach those whom society has seemingly left behind. He founded the Chris Hammond Youth Foundation as a vehicle to help others, and actively posts on social media to reach the world for his faith.

The Hannah family
Championsip coaches and players
Marshall County

Herb Hannah played for the University of Alabama football team from 1948 to 1950, but that was only the beginning of his contributions to the school.

Herb was a lineman who excelled at Alabama and played professional football with the New York Giants. His three sons weren't too bad at the game either.

John Hannah was called the greatest offensive lineman in NFL history by *Sports Illustrated*, and named the second greatest all-time lineman by the *Sporting News* in 1999. After an All-American career at Alabama, he spent his entire professional career with the New England Patriots.

He was inducted into the college and pro football halls of fame, and every other hall of fame for which he was eligible. Hannah had also played at the Baylor school in Chattanooga, and then played his senior high school year back in the family's home town of Albertville, where he was named all-state.

Charlie played at Alabama as a defensive lineman and then in the NFL with the Tampa Bay Buccaneers and the Oakland Raiders as an offensive lineman. Charlie played a particularly good game for the Raiders in Super Bowl XVIII, clearing space for legendary tailback Marcus Allen to have one of the great rushing games in championship history.

David not only played at Alabama, but was an All-SEC performer for the Crimson Tide. In high school, at Baylor in Chattanooga, he became a top player on their 1973 high school national championship team. David also won a national championship in college, in the 1978 season. In the famous goal line stand against Penn State in the national championship game, David helped make the third-down tackle, and then got his hand on the running back in the famous fourth-down play.

Derrick Henry
Heisman Trophy winner
The University of Alabama

At every stage of his career, Derrick Henry has done what no one else ever has.

It began in high school, at Yulee High School in Yulee, Florida, where he ran the football for more yards than anyone in the history of American high school football. Henry amassed an incredible 12,124 yards, breaking the 59-year-old national record. In his senior year he averaged an unbelievable 327.8 yards per game.

Those numbers made him a top national recruit, rated a five-star athlete, and he signed an athletic scholarship with the University of Alabama.

Henry played for three years at Alabama, winning the 2015 Heisman Trophy, setting the Alabama and Southeastern Conference records for most rushing yards in a season (2,219). That same year, he won the Maxwell Award for national player of the year, the Walter Camp Award for the nation's best football player, and the Doak Walker Award for college football's best running back, as well as SEC Player of the Year and All-American honors. He led Alabama to the 2015 national championship, carrying the ball 36 times in the national championship win over Clemson. He carried the ball a whopping 46 times against Auburn in the Iron Bowl rivalry game that year.

In the National Football League, Henry has already set or broken records for the Tennessee Titans, including the longest run in NFL history (99-yards), the most yards rushing in a game, and the most yards accumulated from scrimmage in a playoff game.

At his birth, his grandmother nicknamed him "Shocka" because he shocked them all at birth. The rest of us, however, have no reason to be shocked by any of Derrick Henry's accomplishments, records, and championships, as he has already established himself as one of the great legends of football history.

Howard Hill
Hall of Fame archer
Shelby County

Wilsonville native Howard Hill was indisputably the world's greatest archer.

Although the Shelby County native played baseball for Auburn University, he found that his greatest talents lay with the bow and arrow. His victories included a winning streak of 196 field archery tournaments, occurring between 1926 and 1942.

Hill became the first man to kill a bull elephant with a bow and arrow. He was the go-to guy to perform archery stunts in Hollywood movies, most famously for Errol Flynn in his portrayal of *Robin Hood*.

Hill was inducted into the Alabama Sports Hall of Fame in 1971.

Evander Holyfield
World champion boxer
Escambia County

The remarkable journey of Evander Holyfield has taken him from Atmore, Alabama, to Atlanta to Las Vegas, and television sets around the world.

Born in Atmore (Escambia County), Holyfield found his future path as a teenager in Atlanta in Golden Gloves competition. He ultimately made the U.S. Olympic Boxing Team, winning a bronze medal in the 1984 Olympic Games in Los Angeles.

He won his first 29 professional fights and captured the world heavyweight title by knocking out champion Buster Douglas in only seven minutes.

Holyfield would ultimately become a four-time heavyweight champion, but that was only the beginning of his legacy. He carved out a reputation as a fierce competitor, a ferocious hitter, and an equally zealous advocate for children outside of his boxing career.

His faith would also emerge as a guiding principle of his life, albeit in a bizarre circumstance. The 1996 bout between Holyfield and Mike Tyson was one of boxing's most anticipated fights in years, if not decades. Holyfield won the match and the WBA world heavyweight title, and a rematch was quickly scheduled. Their second fight, which once again captured the attention of the sports world, became legendary not for the fighting, but for the two times in which Tyson bit Holyfield's ear. Holyfield publicly forgave Tyson, and the public got a true glimpse into the life and world of an athlete whose life rose above mere competition.

During his career, and especially afterward, Holyfield has generously donated time and money, and raised funds, for charitable causes. He also founded the Holyfield Foundation to support a variety of causes, especially those helping the lives of children in urban areas.

Robert Horry
Basketball star
Covington County

They called him "Big shot Bob."

They were right.

Covington County's Robert Keith Horry played on seven NBA championship teams, and earned the distinction as the only player to win at least two championships with three different teams (the Houston Rockets, Los Angeles Lakers, and San Antonio Spurs). No matter where he played, Horry's teams won, and he was a major reason why. He led his Andalusia High School team to the state's Final Four, and at the University of Alabama, he led the Crimson Tide to a three-peat of SEC tournament championships (1989, 1990, and 1991).

By the end of his third year of pro basketball, Horry already sported two NBA championship rings, and had quickly developed a reputation as a player who could hit the big shots at the crucial times. Horry established himself as a pivotal player who could play multiple positions, defend multiple positions, and pass the ball with the precision of a seasoned veteran.

Horry went on to the Los Angeles Lakers, with Shaquille O'Neal and Kobe Bryant, where he sank shots that remain legendary, such as his three-pointer with 47 seconds left in game three of the 2001 NBA Finals. He scored 12 in that game's crucial fourth quarter, before hitting the shot that created a dynasty. Then there was the buzzer shot to win game four of the 2002 Western Conference Finals against Sacramento, prompting Magic Johnson to proclaim Horry as one of the 10 best clutch shooters in NBA history.

David Housel
Auburn Athletic Director
Pickens and Lee Counties

David Housel has been, and remains, the face of the Auburn fan nation. Alabama has begun its 200th year as a state, and for over one-fourth of those years, Housel did not miss an Auburn football home game.

As a high school student in Gordo (Pickens County), he took the ACT test (to attend Auburn) and missed the Auburn vs. Georgia game on November 14, 1964. He did not miss another one until 2018. Between those two games, David Housel has become the leading supporter of Auburn sports, the one whose words rallied the fans during tough times, and the one who seemingly loved the university more than anyone. The inspirational talks broadcasted before games on the Auburn radio network have inspired, challenged, motivated, and sometimes even consoled fans.

After studying journalism at Auburn, Housel quickly rose in the world of newspapers, becoming news editor of the *Huntsville News*. When his alma mater called, however, Housel answered and accepted an administrative job in the athletic ticket office. In 1980, he became the assistant sports information director. As with everything Housel has done, his talents and work ethic propelled him upward at Auburn and he became sports information director only a year later.

For the next 13 years, he spent his time joyfully trumpeting the achievements and stories of Auburn sports to the world. In 1985, Auburn running back Bo Jackson won the Heisman trophy by the narrowest voting margin in the award's history. Jackson later became an international superstar, but at the time, the outstanding promotional campaign by Housel is credited with helping Jackson receive more votes than Iowa quarterback Chuck Long.

From 1994 to 2006, Housel served as athletic director at Auburn, leading the athletic department in an era of expanding facilities, building programs, and unprecedented excellence in most of their athletic teams.

Wendell Hudson
All-American basketball player
Jefferson County

When Wendell Hudson and his little sister were small children, they were already learning about family love, hard work, and defying odds to succeed. Their mom, Mildred Hudson, worked in a Birmingham department store, raised her two kids (with her mom's help), and studied as a full-time high school student.

With that powerful example as his foundation, Wendell Hudson was undeterred by potential strife when a life-changing offer was given to him in his family's living room. The offer came in 1969 from the University of Alabama head basketball coach C. M. Newton, and it was a basketball scholarship. If he accepted, Hudson would become the first African-American athlete ever signed by the university, and that would likely mean plenty of strife when the Crimson Tide played in the arenas of schools that had not yet integrated their athletic programs. Ironically, he also faced pressure from supporters of traditionally black colleges who wanted him to play ball at one of their schools.

This was no ordinary scholarship offer, but then the son of Mildred Hudson was no ordinary young man. Hudson accepted the offer, and repaid the courageous Newton by elevating the Alabama basketball program to national prominence, including a breakthrough 1973 season in which he was named an All-American player and the Southeastern Conference Player of the Year.

After a brief professional career, Hudson became a career coach in the college game that he loved. After serving as an assistant coach for several schools, Hudson became the women's basketball head coach at his alma mater. He remains one of the university's most popular alumni.

The Humphrey family
Athletes, leaders
Jefferson County

After gaining fame at a young age, Birmingham's Bobby Humphrey has made the successful transition from sports star to community leader and patriarch of a high-achieving family.

After starring at Glenn High School in the Birmingham area, Bobby Humphrey took his considerable talents to Tuscaloosa, where he played running back for the University of Alabama football team. Although his senior season was cut short by a knee injury, Humphrey left college as the Crimson Tide's all-time leading rusher, a two-time All-American, and an honored athlete with a top-ten finish in the 1987 Heisman Trophy voting.

His professional career began with a bang, as he was named the AFC Offensive Rookie of the Year and played in the Super Bowl with his Denver Broncos. Over the next few years, however, intervening off-the-field issues cut his career short.

Using the same determination that defined his football success, Humphrey made a personal comeback and now serves as Vice President of Bryant Bank. He has also served as head coach of the Birmingham Steeldogs professional team, and as a member of the Parks and Recreation Board in Hoover.

Barbara Humphrey, herself a former star athlete at UAB, serves on the University of Alabama System Board of Trustees and has forged a career as a highly regarded educator. Carrying on the family tradition, their son Maudrecas played football for the UAB Blazers after beginning his career for the Arkansas Razorbacks. Daughter Breona, like her mom, starred in track and field at UAB. Son Marlon followed his dad's legacy to the University of Alabama, where he led the Crimson Tide to the 2015 national championship and two SEC championships, and now plays cornerback for the NFL's Baltimore Ravens. Daughter Brittley became a track star at Louisiana State University. In 2018, son Marion Humphrey became the state's top track athlete, capturing state championships in the 400-meter dash, 110-meter hurdles and 300 meter hurdles, and was named the Super All-State Track Athlete of the Year.

Scott Hunter
Football star, sportscaster
Mobile County

In the twenty first century, prime time college football games are a weekly event, in homes, at gatherings, in restaurants, and in dorm rooms.

All of that began, however, in the late 1960s when a television network's risky move pitted the University of Alabama against Ole Miss in the autumn air at Birmingham's legendary Legion Field.

The hero of that historic game was Scott Hunter, and he led the Alabama team to a dramatic, last-moment comeback that was watched and admired from sea to shining sea.

Hunter rewrote the Alabama record books, putting up numbers that lasted for decades with his passing wizardry, long before the days of spread offenses and the liberal rules for offensive linemen.

The year was 1969, and the national news was dominated by a president who was new (Nixon), a war that was anything but new (Vietnam), a concert that was beyond the understanding of many Americans (Woodstock), and the amazing sight of Americans actually walking on the Moon.

Earlier that year, ABC television had decided to roll the dice and televise a college football game in the prime time hours. The setting was Birmingham, the mecca of Southern football...and the venue for the clash between Alabama and Ole Miss. The home team was (and remains) the gold standard of college football, and the visiting team personifies the heart of Southern culture, sporting names like William Faulkner Johnny Vaught, John Grisham, and as of that night, Archie Manning. As the outstanding sportswriter Lars Anderson described it, Manning ran around like his shoestrings were on fire for three years at Ole Miss. Even today, the speed limit on campus is 18, in honor of Manning's jersey number.

But it all started that night in Birmingham, on prime time television.

The duel between Hunter and Manning was one for the ages, with each quarterback blazing through the opposing team's defense like a knife through some of that banana pudding served under a white tent on The Grove. Both Hunter and Manning passed for over 300 yards each, and the 20th ranked Rebels seized the lead late in the 4th quarter.

And that was when the legend of Scott Hunter was truly born.

And that was also where the best story at the Selma Quarterback Club began.

It was fourth down, and the game was in its waning moments. As Hunter tells it, Coach Bryant called a time-out, and Hunter ran to the sidelines to learn which play the coaches would call. After hearing Coach Bryant talking to a coach on the sideline who relayed each message to former Alabama quarterback Steve Sloan, who called plays from the booth in the press box, no play had been called.

"The referee came up and explained that the car commercial had just ended on ABC, so it was time to go back on the field," Hunter explained to the riveted group of football fans of the Selma Quarterback Club. "I had to run back on the field, and no play had been called, and then I heard Coach Bryant's voice call out my name. I turned around, and he yelled for me to run the best play I've got."

Ole Miss blitzed their linebacker, who ran a direct path right at Hunter. However, the play Hunter had called included keeping star running back Johnny Musso near him to block for him, and Musso blocked the linebacker perfectly. That block afforded Hunter the time to throw a perfect strike to the open receiver and win college football's first prime-time game.

The seemingly unstoppable Manning was trumped by the kid from Mobile who called his own play and executed it flawlessly with the game on the line.

The suspenseful game and the play of the two quarterbacks generated such great ratings, that the ABC gamble proved a brilliant decision and the game was forever changed.

Hunter spent many years as a professional football quarterback with the Green Bay Packers and the Atlanta Falcons. Since his playing days, he has become a different type of star, and for years entertained sports fans as a television sportscaster in his native Mobile.

Did You Know???

The legend of George Foster and the "black beauty"

In the 1970s and 1980s, baseball fans knew exactly what the "black beauty" was. One of baseball's most feared hitters was Tuscaloosa native George Foster, and his black bat carried the nickname "black beauty." Foster was the cleanup hitter for the mighty Big Red Machine, one of the greatest teams in baseball history. He was named the 1977 National League Most Valuable Player, and led the National League in home runs (twice), runs batted in (three consecutive years), capturing two World Series championships.

Jalen Hurts and Tua Tagovailoa
All-American quarterbacks
The University of Alabama

They began their careers as mere teammates and competitors, but their stories have become intertwined as one of the greatest quarterback redemption stories in the history of college football.

As a freshman, Jalen led the University of Alabama football team, seizing the quarterback job and leading the Crimson Tide to the SEC championship. He orchestrated a dramatic, fourth quarter comeback in the national championship game, leading with just one second remaining until a controversial no-call on a pick play cost his team the game.

As a sophomore, Hurts again led Alabama to the national championship game, but struggled against the Georgia Bulldogs and the Crimson Tide trailed at halftime.

Enter Tua Tagovailoa.

Before that fateful night, most Americans, not to mention many Alabama fans, still couldn't pronounce his last name. That would change quickly, after the freshman led a comeback for the ages, capped by the second-and-26 pass play that won the championship and became the most famous pass in college football history.

The next year, Tua seized the starting job, and Jalen handled his backup role with the same poise and class that had defined his career. As the season progressed, Tua established himself as a leading candidate for the Heisman Trophy, leading Alabama to an undefeated regular season.

In the SEC Championship Game, however, Tua found himself back in the same Atlanta stadium against the same Georgia Bulldogs. This time, he struggled with two in-game injuries, and the Crimson Tide faced another seemingly insurmountable deficit.

Enter Jalen Hurts.

In a scene that only happens in a Disney movie or the mind of a novelist, Jalen entered the game in the second half against Georgia, just as Tua did the year before against the Bulldogs, seized the reins of the team and led the march to victory with a fourth quarter comeback.

The nation watched as each young man showed the class and character that defined their athletic careers. Hurts grew up in Texas and Tua in Hawaii, but the two were clearly raised with the same types of values. As young men of faith, they weren't trying to steal the job from each other; they had each other's back during the most difficult on-field circumstances.

Even as they travel on different personal and professional paths, their names will always stand for the camaraderie and class to which young athletes will always aspire.

Don Hutson
All-Pro, All-American, All-everything
The University of Alabama

In 2017, the writers at *AL.com* named him the number-one football player ever produced by the state of Alabama.

For roughly 50 to 60 years, he was considered the greatest receiver in the history of football. His name still stands as one of the truly elite players of all-time. The NFL Network named him as the greatest player in the history of the Green Bay Packers, and most experts consider him the greatest player in the history of his college team, the University of Alabama. The *Sporting News* named him the sixth greatest player in NFL history, and that might have been a lowball estimate.

He was so famous as an end on the 1934 national championship team at Alabama that the team's other offensive end, none other than Paul "Bear" Bryant developed a second nickname: "the other end."

Like Bryant, Hutson hailed from Arkansas (Pine Bluff). In fact, Hutson had achieved such fame during high school that Bryant hitchhiked with friends to Pine Bluff just to see his future teammate play.

By the time Hutson and Bryant headed to Alabama, the Crimson Tide had already won national championships in 1925, 1926, and 1930. Led by their two ends from Arkansas, the Crimson Tide won the 1934 title as well, and Hutson was named to the All-American team. Hutson and Bryant also started a laundry business together in Tuscaloosa, called "Captain Kidd Cleaners."

When the National Football Foundation awarded retroactive Heisman Trophy recognition for seasons before the trophy was created in 1936, the award for the 1934 season went to Hutson.

In his 11 years in the NFL, Hutson became what ESPN has described as the first modern wide receiver. He broke every major career record in the sport, including catches, yards, and touchdowns receiving. His was the first jersey number ever retired by the Green Bay Packers. In one season, he even led the NFL in interceptions when he played defense as well as offense.

Hutson put up 21st century receiving statistics in the 1930s and 1940s, when the offenses, defenses, and rules made the NFL a running league. In the context of his time, Hutson's stats almost defy belief; it was six decades before anyone could break his career touchdown receptions record. Hutson was named to the Pro Football Hall of Fame, the College Football Hall of Fame, the Wisconsin

Trivia

Which native of Ensley changed the game of Major League Baseball?

For most baseball fans, the ideas of brightly-colored uniforms, night games in the World Series, and the designated hitter are just routine parts of the game.

But when Alabama's own Charlie Finley first suggested or supported those ideas, he was ridiculed and called crazy or revolutionary.

Born and raised in Birmingham's Ensley community, Charles O. Finley began his involvement with professional baseball as a 12-year-old bat boy for a local minor league team. Finley found himself working in coal mines in Indiana, and ultimately selling insurance.

More than anything, Finley was a man of ideas, and when he was struck with tuberculosis in 1946, he underwent a long but successful recovery. All of the down time, however, gave Finley time to think, and he was poised to make his fortune with a novel idea when his health returned.

Sure enough, Finley pursued his idea, which was selling group insurance to medical doctors. His success brought a multi-million dollar fortune, and he decided to pursue his longtime goal of acquiring a Major League Baseball team.

In 1960, Finley bought the Kansas City Athletics, and began proposing and trying new ideas. Some, like using orange baseballs, didn't work out. Others, like the brightly-colored uniforms, became the standard for the game. He later moved the team to Oakland.

Finley and his talent scouts had extraordinary discernment in signing young ball players. He and his staff brought in historically good talent, like future stars Reggie Jackson, Jim "Catfish" Hunter, Rollie Fingers, and Vida Blue. Finley bestowed entertaining nicknames on many of the players, and gave them monetary bonuses for growing mustaches.

Finley's team won three consecutive World Series titles, in 1972, 1973, and 1974. However, the advent of free agency made it almost impossible to afford so many great players, and the team mostly disbanded over the course of a few years.

Finley's bombastic personality and uninhibited creativity caused personal difficulties at times, but resulted in the child of Ensley bringing entertainment and joy to his fans, and changing the game he loved.

Hall of Fame, the Alabama Sports Hall of Fame, and every list of the all-time greatest NFL players, including #6 on the *Sporting News* list of the 100 greatest NFL players.

Mark Ingram
Heisman Trophy Winner
The University of Alabama

In 2018, Mark Ingram became the leading touchdown scorer in the history of the New Orleans Saints football team. That was only the latest milestone in a career that has taken Ingram from Flint, Michigan, to Tuscaloosa, Alabama, to New Orleans and now Baltimore, for his current team the Ravens.

That journey also included an evening in lower Manhattan, at the PlayStation Theatre in New York, on the night that he was awarded the 2009 Heisman Trophy, becoming its first recipient from the University of Alabama. In his three-year career, Ingram not only won the Heisman, he achieved unanimous first-team All-American honors, SEC Player of the Year honors, and the MVP of the national championship game, among many other accolades.

Known as a player who competed with both ferocity and class, Ingram gave the nation a glimpse into his character with his Heisman acceptance speech. Standing on the New York stage, surrounded by a semi-circle of former Heisman winners, Ingram delivered a heartfelt tribute to his family, coaches, teammates, and fans that still stands as one of the best in the illustrious history of the award.

Ingram has gone on to the fame and fortune of professional athletics, but remains a supporter of his alma mater and can still occasionally be spotted at times on the sidelines at Crimson Tide games.

Bo Jackson
Heisman Trophy Winner
Jefferson County

Simply put, Vincent "Bo" Jackson may be one of the greatest pure athletes the world has ever seen.

Perhaps the best fact to explain the greatness of Bo Jackson is that he was a baseball phenom and the Most Valuable Player of the Major League Baseball All-Star game...yet baseball was probably his third best sport.

Jackson is best known as the guy who won football's Heisman Trophy as an Auburn University running back, and was the overall first pick in the 1986 NFL Draft. He played both sports at a historically elite level, prompting apparel giant Nike to air a famous "Bo Knows" television ad featuring Bo "knowing" baseball, football, and every other major sport.

On the football field, he famously outran speedy defensive backs and plowed through linebackers as if they were high school players. Opponents never conquered the great one, but unfortunately an injury cut short his brilliant football career and robbed him of the elite speed that had helped define his baseball play as well.

In baseball, he was one of his era's great talents, and in football, he was one of the all-time greats.

And then there was track and field, possibly Jackson's best sport. Legend has it that, in his senior year at McCalla's McAdory High School, Jackson earned enough points in different events to win the team state championship all by himself. He also qualified for the United States Olympic team during his years at Auburn.

Bo Jackson stands alone in athletic history because of his world-class speed and strength, but he has continued soaring long after his playing days ended. In recent years, Jackson started "Bo Bikes Bama," a long-distance charity cycling event, to raise funds for tornado shelters in rural Alabama communities. Jackson remains one of America's greatest celebrities, and one of Alabama's great ambassadors to the world.

Michael Johnson
Football star, benefactor
Dallas County

Anyone looking for a role model in the world of sports should search no further than Dallas County's own Michael Johnson.

But the reasons why he's such a great model for us all lie beyond the football field.

Sure, he's a highly successful defensive end for the Cincinnati Bengals of the National Football League. Sure, he gets to play football on national television each week. Sure, he has been blessed with the fame and fortune that accompany professional football.

Michael Johnson, however, has worked hard to become anything but a typical pro athlete since graduating from Dallas County High School and Georgia Tech. He works tirelessly, even during the off-season, to train himself physically and eat like a champion.

Even more importantly for Alabamians, Michael Johnson gives generously, throughout the year, for families and youth to improve lives, sharpen minds, and strengthen family relationships.

In short, Johnson works as hard to improve the lives of others as he does to better himself. He sponsors football and cheerleading camps for young people in his hometown of Selma. He also sponsors family outing days to give local families a day to spend time together and create memories. Johnson has formed a partnership with Wallace Community College Selma to create and fund educational programs for youth and families, including career guidance and training.

If that weren't enough, he raises significant funds for the Selma Area Food Bank, helping to feed the hungry in Selma and surrounding areas of Dallas County. His parents are active supporters and board members of the Selma Area Food Bank.

But why does he do so much?

"I care because my parents taught me to care," he told the *Selma Sun* newspaper in 2017. "My parents raised me, and the community of my school also raises our students to become the best we can be. I learned to work hard and to invest what I have to help pull others up."

In 2018, the NFL announced that Johnson had been honored as a finalist for the NFL Man of the Year award. The national recognition taught America what the people of Dallas County already knew.

Bill Jones
National championship coach
Calhoun County

The Bill Jones Court at Jacksonville State University bears witness to his remarkable career and impact on so many young lives. Seen by the numbers, his career ranks with the absolute best.

By the Numbers

1985...That was the year that Jones captured the national championship for his alma mater, the Jacksonville State Gamecocks.

31...The Gamecocks pulled off a remarkable 31-game

winning streak during their national championship season in 1985.

30...In the 1965-66 season, Jones became an All-American player for the Gamecocks, twenty years before the national championship.

6...Bill Jones won a whopping six different Gulf South Conference championships during his coaching tenure at JSU.

The Jones family
Coaches, athletes
Lauderdale County

The Jones family has compiled a remarkable record of great accomplishments over three generations of success and championships.

A visit to the University of North Alabama could include the Bill Jones Athletic Complex, named after the grandfather and family patriarch. Jones, originally from Lexington (Lauderdale County), remained in his home county to study and play basketball at UNA. He later became the head basketball coach, winning the Division II national championship, and leading his team to four different Final Four appearances, six different conference championships (tournament and regular season), and five regional championships. He was twice honored as Coach of the Year.

His son, Rex, grew up around basketball and learned the discipline and attitude of a champion from his dad. Rex played basketball at the University of Alabama from 1981 to 1984, playing a role in an SEC Championship, a NCAA Sweet Sixteen appearance, and three NCAA tournament appearances. Although not a starter during his years at Alabama, it was not without good reason, as seven of his teammates were chosen in the N.B.A. draft. Rex serves as CEO of the Christian Community Foundation in Memphis. Tennessee, where he and wife Leslie chose to emphasize faith over sports for their three sons.

And then came Barrett.

Barrett Jones wasn't exactly built like his father or grandfather, with a 6-4, 300-plus pound frame making him much better suited for football than basketball. Like his father, he signed an athletic scholarship with the University of Alabama, in the historic recruiting class that included many future All-Americans and professional stars such as Julio Jones, Mark Ingram, Terrence "Mount" Cody, Mark Barron, and Courtney Upshaw.

By the time he played his last game for the Crimson Tide, Barrett had become one of the most highly decorated offensive linemen in the history of the sport. He became the only player in college football to ever win the coveted Outland Trophy and the Rimington Award in two different years, playing two different positions. He was named All-SEC at guard, tackle, and center in different years. He started and excelled on three national championship teams (2009, 2011, and 2012) and won the Jacobs Blocking Trophy (best offensive lineman in the SEC) the Jim Parker Trophy (college football's best lineman), and several other awards for combining athletic excellence with academic achievement and community service. He was also named an Academic All-American.

But Barrett wasn't the only Jones in the third generation of athletes. Harrison Jones was a highly recruited tight end who also played for the Crimson Tide. He made a strong contribution to two national championship teams until injuries forced him out of the world of college football. Walker Jones, the youngest brother, was the only defensive player of the three but signed with Alabama as a linebacker and played on the 2015 national championship team.

The Jones family has stood out, through three generations, as models for those who aspire to succeed through hard work and doing things the right way. Their championships serve as a testament to their beliefs and values.

Julio Jones
Football star
Baldwin County

In February of 2008, a father checked his third-grade daughter out of elementary school for a doctor's visit. She had a sore throat and maybe a slight fever. While sitting in the waiting room, the father checked the news headlines on his smart phone. The daughter looked up and asked a surprising question.

"Did we get Julio?"

It happened to be National Signing Day for high school football players, and the "we" was the University of Alabama football team that their family enjoyed following. Julio, the person she asked about, was a high school senior in Foley (Baldwin County) and the number-one high school player in America that year. The father laughed and asked how she knew who Julio was.

"That's all the boys at school are talking about. They think he's the greatest."

"They're right," the father replied with a smile.

Julio did indeed choose Tuscaloosa as his college home, and left after winning the national championship, the Southeastern Conference championship, two SEC Western Division titles, All-SEC honors, and a permanent place in the hearts of Crimson Tide fans.

Before the accolades, and before third-grade boys in the state knew the high school senior's name, Julio was raised by a courageous single mom who made all the success possible. Queen Marvin found the time and resources to raise, teach, and support her children while working in a fast-food restaurant. After her older son suffered a gunshot wound to his arm, she became more determined than ever to protect her kids from the violence that was part of life in their neighborhood. Julio was not only the best high school player in America, he also earned the state track and field athlete of the year award for his superior performance in multiple events.

At 6-foot-4, 220 pounds, and with a 40-inch vertical leap, Julio may have been the most talented receiver coming out of college football since Randy Moss. Even beyond his enormous physical gifts, Julio became famous for his relentless work ethic. Nobody, it seemed, cared more about improving and winning than the guy who was already the best athlete on the field.

The Atlanta Falcons recognized what some other teams did not, and traded five draft choices to the Cleveland Browns for the fifth overall pick in the 2011 draft. In the days following that draft trade, some cynical fans complained that the Falcons gave up too much to acquire Jones, but the critics were quickly silenced. Julio has become the best receiver in football, averaging more yards receiving per-game than any player in history. He became one of six players to accumulate 300 yards receiving in one game. In late 2018, he became one of only five players in history with three different seasons of 100 catches and over 1,500 yards. He has been named All-Pro and has led the Atlanta Falcons to the Super Bowl.

Lee Roy Jordan
Hall of Fame football star
Monroe County

The scene might look familiar to football fans of 2018. The Orange Bowl game featured the University of Alabama facing the University of Oklahoma, and the sporting world was watching. It was New Year's Day of 1963, and President John F. Kennedy joined the capacity crowd to take in the game.

In front of a national television audience, the president, and the crowded stadium, a kid from Excel, Alabama, became a legend.

Lee Roy Jordan dominated the game; the senior linebacker recorded a historic 31 tackles as the boys from Tuscaloosa shut out the Oklahoma Sooners, 17-0.

In his three years, Jordan was named All-SEC all three years, an All-American, and the MVP of that Orange Bowl game. With Jordan at linebacker, Alabama lost a total of two games in three years and won a national championship in 1961.

Thankfully, Lee Roy's friends, family, and fans back home in Excel (Monroe County) enjoyed the opportunity to watch their hometown hero for many years after he left college. The Dallas Cowboys drafted Jordan with the sixth overall draft pick, and offered him $17,500 and a car to sign with them rather than the Boston Patriots of the rival American Football League. For the next 13 years, Jordan became a Super Bowl champion, as well as a Pro Bowl and All-Pro player. He was chosen for the Dallas Cowboys Ring of Honor, and remains beloved in both his football city of Dallas and his home state of Alabama.

Ralph "Shug" Jordan
Hall of Fame football coach
Dallas and Lee Counties

His journey took him from Selma, to Auburn, to the history books, winning the hearts of Auburn people and earning the reputation as a class act.

Ralph Jordan grew up in Selma, living in one of the stately Victorian homes just a block from Dallas Avenue in the Olde Town area. They called him "Shug," in Selma and they loved him. They still do. He earned the nickname through his love of sugar cane. People fondly recall stories of how he was a national success as a football coach but an equally more successful person.

Jordan was hired as the Auburn University football coach in the 1950s, and brought immediate success on the gridiron. He won the 1957 national championship, and followed it with another undefeated season the next year. He coached plenty of big-time stars such as Heisman Trophy winner Pat Sullivan, and he coached winners such as Morris Savage who were good players on the field but great success stories afterward, as Savage was with the law firm of Bankhead & Savage in Jasper.

During his college years, Shug was named Most Outstanding Athlete at Auburn, excelling in three different sports. He coached basketball at the University of Georgia and later at Auburn, and served as an assistant coach at each school.

By the time he was named Auburn's head football coach, he was well prepared for the battles of SEC football. That readiness came not just from coaching experience, but from fighting real battles. Jordan was wounded in the 1944 invasion of Normandy (during World War II). Amazingly, after recovering from those serious injuries, he returned to battle in the Pacific part of the war.

With that experience, he would never become intimidated by any team, coach, players, or big game.

Jordan retired as Auburn University's all-time winningest coach, and the most revered leader in the storied program's history. People still nickname children and pets after him. Auburn's Jordan-Hare football stadium, seating over 87,000 people, was named in his honor.

Trivia

Which two Jefferson County natives became the first brothers to win batting titles in Major League Baseball?

Their dad was a big league pitcher for the old Washington Senators, "Dixie" Walker, who roomed with the great Walter Johnson on their team's road trips.

Dixie Walker's boys, Fred and Harry, grew up to become major league ball players in their own right.

Fred had the highest batting average in the National League in 1944, posting a scorching .357 for the Brooklyn Dodgers. Three years later, Harry joined his brother in MLB history with an even better .363 for the St. Louis Cardinals and the Philadelphia Phillies (he was traded during the season).

Known as "the hat," Harry didn't just excel during the regular season. He batted a whopping .412 in the 1946 World Series, and knocked in the winning run in game seven to clinch the title. Harry later became one of the game's great hitting teachers.

Bryan Kirkland
Paralympic gold medalist
Blount County

He became America's top Paralympic athlete, and then became a source of inspiration throughout America.

Bryan Kirkland, a native of Oneonta (Blount County), has won multiple gold medals on both the Paralympic Games and the World Wheelchair Games, in rugby and track and field events.

He was named the 2003 National Athlete of the Year by the USQRA.

In 2007, he was named to the Ambassador Program of the U.S. Olympic Committee, and in 2009, he was named as a Hartford Athlete, commissioned to inspire, comfort, and challenge.

Kirkland has carved out a place in Alabama history as one of its most inspirational athletes.

Freddie Kitchens
Football player and coach
Etowah County

An Attalla native leads the NFL's Cleveland Browns.

On January 12, 2019, the Cleveland Browns named Freddie Kitchens as the team's head football coach. For the native of Attalla (Etowah County), it was just the latest achievement in a football career filled with honors, accolades, and victories.

As a highly-touted quarterback at Etowah County High School, Kitchens signed a scholarship to play at the University of Alabama. He started as quarterback in 1996 and 1997, accumulating over 4,800 career passing yards and leading the dramatic, fourth-quarter comeback over

Auburn in the 1996 Iron Bowl.

In his playing and coaching days, Kitchens learned from some of the biggest names in football, such as Gene Stallings, Nick Saban, Bill Parcells, Bruce Arians, Ken Whisenhunt, and Mike DuBose.

In one of his biggest victories, he fully recovered from a 2013 aortic dissection that required emergency, life-saving surgery.

Tackhole Lee
Hall of Fame marksman
Jefferson County

Birmingham's Thomas K. "Tackhole" Lee became one of the great shooters in recorded history. He set at least 38 world records, and had a standing offer to bet $15,000 against anyone willing to compete in rifle, shotgun, and pistol combined competition. He invented the Lee Tomic shell and the Lee Dot gunsight.

Tackhole Lee was inducted into the Alabama Sports Hall of Fame in 1971.

Carl Lewis
Olympic gold medalist
Jefferson County

He was born in Birmingham, and by the time he was 15 years old, he had to spend significant time on crutches, even though he had not been injured.

So why the crutches?

After his family relocated to New Jersey, Carl Lewis had grown 2 1/2 inches in a single month. The crutches were necessary until the rest of his body caught up with the growth. After that, however, Carl Lewis became an athlete for the ages.

He was named "Sportsman of the Century" by the International Olympic Committee, and the "Olympian of the Century" by *Sports Illustrated*. Lewis won a staggering nine gold medals in four different Olympic games-1984, 1988, 1992, and 1996. Even before his Olympic fame, as a college star at the University of Houston he won both the 100-meter and the long jump events. Only Jesse Owens, his hero and fellow Alabama native, had accomplished that feat.

Long after his Olympic heroics, Lewis remains one of the most revered athletes in track and field history.

Walter Lewis
Football star
Escambia County

Walter Lewis was the most highly celebrated athlete in the history of Brewton (Escambia County). He became the first African-American quarterback at the University of Alabama. Lewis starred as the most exciting player of coach "Bear" Bryant's last team, and later of the USFL's Memphis Showboats.

But Lewis was much more than an athlete. He epitomized the idea of a scholar-athlete, majoring in engineering. In a 2008 interview with *Birmingham News* columnist Kevin Scarbinsky, Lewis recalled preparing for the 1983 Iron Bowl while also preparing for three major exams (in engineering classes) in the two days before the game. He earned the reputation of the rare person with an elite intellect, athletic skill, and a winning personality.

Lewis entered coaching after his football years, serving at both the University of Alabama and the University of Kentucky before taking his talents to the business world.

Above all, Lewis made his hometown of Brewton proud as a man of class who has succeeded in every realm in which he has competed.

Joe Louis
World boxing champion
Chambers County

This native of Chambers County became one of America's greatest athletes and heavyweight boxers of all times. He was the first boxer ever honored with a postage stamp, and has been inducted into more halls of fame than anyone can probably remember.

Joseph Louis Barrow endured a difficult childhood, living in poverty after losing his dad to confinement in a mental institution. Years later, his mother remarried, and the family moved to Detroit, Michigan. There, he embarked on a journey that brought fame, championships, and even national honor over that of Nazi Germany.

The career of Joe Louis matches up with any in boxing history when viewed...by the numbers.

By the Numbers

2...Joe Louis only used his first two names, avoiding the use of his last name. Some believe he did this to keep his mom from finding out that he used money allocated for violin lessons for boxing. The other legendary tale had him signing up to box and, limited in literacy, writing too large for the form and only fitting his first two names.

12...Louis held the world heavyweight championship for almost 12 years, the longest in the sport's history at that time.

1...His first round knockout of the German boxer Max Schmeling in 1938 rallied the American people of all races behind him. Before this rematch of their bout two years earlier, German Nazi Chancellor Adoph Hitler remarked that Schmeling was the superior fighter because of his racial superiority. The early knockout proved ominous for Hitler's delusional rants, and made Louis a transcendent figure in American sports.

5...Joe Louis volunteered to join the U.S. Army at the height of his career and served five years during World War II, attaining the rank of sergeant.

68...Joe Louis won 68 of his 71 professional bouts, with 54 of the victories coming by knockout.

Gus Malzahn
Championship football coach
Auburn University

At every stop in his career, Auburn University head football coach Gus Malzahn has earned the reputation as a genius in the realm of offensive football.

As a high school coach, he led different teams to state championships, setting records for scoring and yardage along the way. As a college offensive coordinator, his teams won even more championships and set records for points and yardage.

His indisputable acumen as an offensive play caller quickly brought him from the high school ranks to positions as a college offensive coordinator and then as a head coach at Auburn's elite football program. Few in the history of the game have risen to such heights as quickly as Malzahn.

For Malzahn, his creativity extends far beyond play calling. He uses his unmatched creativity to confuse opponents and slow the pursuit of opposing defenders. He uses such unconventional formations as having linemen line up near the sideline, in front of receivers. He will hide a small player behind the center and snap the ball before defenders realize what has happened.

Malzahn took over as Auburn's head coach in the wake of the disastrous 2012 season that included no SEC victories. Immediately, Malzahn propelled the Auburn program back to national success, winning the SEC title and leading the Tigers to the national championship game. Auburn held the lead, and seemingly the championship, until a late fourth quarter comeback by Hueytown native Jameis Winston captured the championship for Florida State University.

Other highlights of his early years include Malzahn's strategically placing Chris Davis in the end zone as Alabama attempted a last-second field goal in the 2013 Iron Bowl at Jordan-Hare stadium. The resulting "kick-six" return for a touchdown remains one of the most re-played moments in the sport's history.

Through it all, fame, fortune, and public adoration have not changed the guy from Arkansas. After Auburn wins, he and his wife still enjoy their victory meals at the local Waffle House.

Willie Mays
Hall of Fame baseball player
Jefferson County

Many believe Willie Mays was the single greatest baseball player ever.

Raised in Fairfield (Jefferson County), Willie Howard Mays, Jr., began by playing alongside his father for the Fairfield Stars of the Birmingham Industrial League. After playing in the old Negro Leagues and becoming one of its last young stars, he was signed by the New York Giants. He played in the minor leagues for the Minnesota Millers, but after hitting a whopping .477 in 35 games, it was time for the big leagues. He was called up to the Giants in May of 1951, and by the end of the season he was the Rookie of the Year.

Mays was called into military service early in the 1952 season, and then returned for the 1954 season.

From his return in 1954 through 1973, Mays became a transcendent athlete. He was chosen for the all-star team a record-tying 24 times. His 600 home runs were third in history, trailing only Babe Ruth and Henry Aaron, but he had lost two seasons due to military service. His two Most Valuable Player Awards and four consecutive stolen base titles were great accomplishments, as was his legendary over-the-shoulder catch in game one of the 1954 World Series. Sprinting through the vast center field area of the Polo Grounds stadium, Mays caught the ball over his shoulder, and in one motion, turned and threw a perfect strike back to the infield. It was actually two plays in one.

Despite being one of the biggest athletic celebrities in America, Mays still found time to play stick-ball with local kids in Harlem while the Giants were located in Harlem. His nickname, "the say hey kid," described his gregarious personality and his accessibility to kids.

Mays has remained a favorite celebrity in his home state, and a legend in his hometown of Fairfield.

Willie McCovey
Hall of Fame baseball player
Mobile County

"If you pitch to him, he'll ruin baseball. He'd hit 80 home runs. There's no comparison between McCovey and anybody else in the league."

–Sparky Anderson, Manager
The Cincinnati Reds

From Siluria to San Francisco

Today, Siluria is a neighborhood area within the Shelby County city of Alabaster. Back in the day, it was an old mill town famous for placing two of its kids on the 1958 roster of the San Francisco Giants baseball team.

Jim Davenport was an outstanding infielder for the Giants who played a dozen years for the team. Today, he remains locally famous as the namesake for Davenport's Pizza in Mountain Brook.

Willie Kirkland was born in Siluria, just six months after his future teammate Davenport. Although Kirkland spent much of his childhood in Detroit, the sons of Siluria made their debut in the big leagues together and remained teammates for three years.

They called him "Stretch" because of his 6-foot-6 frame and his long arms that helped make him an excellent first baseman in the major leagues.

It was no stretch, however, to call him one of the best to ever play the game.

Born and raised in Mobile, Willie McCovey joined fellow Alabama native Willie Mays with the San Francisco Giants in 1959, playing together until the 1970s and becoming the most feared back-to-back hitters in the game. In 1959, McCovey played only 52 games, but was still named the National League Rookie of the Year. Mays used to say that McCovey could hit a ball farther than anyone he had ever seen.

McCovey finished his career with 521 home runs, two Most Valuable Player Awards, and an almost endless string of honors and awards.

Just as importantly, McCovey was known as a gentle giant off the field, someone accessible to fans and easily approachable by the media. His popularity with fans lives on, as the area outside the waterfront stadium where the San Francisco Giants play is named "McCovey Cove."

Ronald McKinnon
Hall of Fame football star
Coffee County

He was called "one of the most honored athletes in college football history" by the Alabama Sports Hall of Fame.

He remains the only defensive player to ever win the Harlon Hill Award, the Division II equivalent of the Heisman Trophy.

Overlooked by the state's larger universities because of his size, Elba's Ronald McKinnon signed with the University of North Alabama, playing for legendary head coach Bobby Wallace. McKinnon became one of the few three-time All-Americans in Division II history, and finished as the all-time leading career tackler at UNA, and in the history of the Gulf South Conference.

In his three All-American seasons, UNA also won the national championship all three years, as well as the Gulf South championship in each season.

After his college career, the NFL didn't make the same mistake as the big schools in Alabama. He signed with the Arizona Cardinals, playing nine seasons with them and one season with the New Orleans Saints. In his ten NFL years, he made a whopping 1,000 tackles, along with 12 sacks and 10 pass interceptions.

McKinnon was inducted into the College Football Hall of Fame and the Alabama Sports Hall of Fame.

Mal Moore
Football player, coach, athletic director
Crenshaw & Tuscaloosa Counties

It's a long journey from Dozier, Alabama (Crenshaw County) to Tuscaloosa, but the journey of Mal Moore changed the University of Alabama and the lives of countless young college students.

If success is measured in championships, then Mal Moore is one of the most successful people in the history of college sports. As a player, coach, and athletic director, he played a role in an unprecedented 10 national championships in football for the University of Alabama. His vast success includes calling plays for Coach Paul "Bear" Bryant's national championship teams in the 1970s, and for the 1992 national champs under head coach Gene Stallings. After his coaching days, Moore became the athletic director and began a massive building program resulting in new or enlarged buildings and additions to Bryant-Denny Stadium that increased the seating capacity to over 100,000. Moore also helped build the charitable infrastructure in Tuscaloosa, chairing the committee to raise funds to build the Caring Days Facility in Tuscaloosa that assists patients afflicted with Alzheimer's and other illnesses associated with traumatic memory losses. His seemingly endless charitable work also included the Boys and Girls Clubs of Tuscaloosa.

Despite accomplishments that may be unparalleled, younger Alabamians might remember Moore most for a visit he made to the Miami area after the 2006 football season, a mission marked by his determination not to return to Tuscaloosa until he had convinced Nick Saban to return with him as the new coach at Alabama. Saban, then coach of the NFL's Miami Dolphins, had previously declared that he would not take the job. That, however, was before Mal Moore met with him personally.

Moore was inducted into the Alabama Sports Hall of Fame, and named the nation's top athletic director by the National Football Foundation and Hall of Fame.

Joe Namath
Hall of Fame football star
The University of Alabama

They called him "Broadway Joe," even though he was a kid from small-town Pennsylvania who arrived via Tuscaloosa, Alabama.

Despite his origins, however, there was never anything small about the persona, presence, or celebrity of Joe Willie Namath.

Raised in Beaver Falls, Pennsylvania, Namath was the grandson of Hungarian immigrants and the son of a steel worker. The youngest of five, Namath became a multi-sport athlete who made his way to the University of Alabama, where he played quarterback for the legendary Coach Paul "Bear" Bryant.

Namath possessed eilte quarterback skills, awing fans, teammates, and professional scouts as he led the Crimson Tide to the 1964 national championship. He set records, and became known as a dominant athlete who had a bright future.

That future became a reality when the New York Jets signed Namath to a record 3-year, $427,000 contract. Jets owner Sonny Werblin, a movie producer, fully understood the value of Namath as both a quarterback and a celebrity. The Jets played in the American Football League (AFL), which was widely considered inferior to its rival league, the NFL.

Namath, as Werblin had hoped, quickly became much more than a football player. He was the face of New York sports, the hard-partying bachelor who dated movie stars, endorsed products, and heightened the importance of events with his presence.

Within five years, Namath was setting passing records in the AFL and led his 1969 team to the Super Bowl. Their opponent, the Baltimore Colts, were prohibitive favorites to win the game. Namath, ever the brash athlete on and off the field, guaranteed a win for the Jets. That guarantee seized national headlines. Following Namath, athletes and coaches will publicly guarantee wins, but it all started with the quarterback from Alabama.

When Namath led the Jets to the Super Bowl victory, Broadway Joe had become one of the sport's great legends, and the AFL had become a legitimate football league.

After Namath's career with the Jets and Los Angeles Rams ended, he remained one of America's greatest sports celebrities. Namath has also remained loyal to Tuscaloosa, where he continues to be extremely popular. He has become involved in various business interests in Tuscaloosa, and annually attends multiple Crimson Tide football games at Bryant-Denny Stadium. Through the years he has generously contributed his time and name to charitable causes in Alabama.

Tony Nathan
Hall of Fame football star
Jefferson County

Of all the stars produced by Birmingham's legendary Woodlawn High School, none have shone more brightly than Tony Nathan. He has been portrayed in a major motion picture. He has been the subject of countless articles and features. He has played in the Super Bowl, college football's national championship game, and the biggest game in the history of Alabama high school football.

Through it all, he has remained the same, humble kid who never lost sight of his true self, his family, and his home community of Woodlawn.

As a high school student, Nathan became a *Parade* All-American, featured in *Sports Illustrated* after his seven touchdowns against Ramsay High School. Things just couldn't get any better, it seemed.

Then came November 8, 1974.

Woodlawn faced off against nationally ranked Banks High School at Birmingham's Legion Field. Over 42,000 fans came out to see the matchup between two great teams and two *Parade* All-Americans, Nathan and Banks quarterback Jeff Rutledge. Banks won the game, but high school football in the state of Alabama was the biggest winner.

Nathan took his talents to the University of Alabama, where he excelled as a running back on the 1978 national championship team. The quarterback was none other than his high school rival, Jeff Rutledge.

After college, Nathan played for the Miami Dolphins, joining several former Alabama teammates and leading the Dolphins to two Super Bowls.

After his playing career, Nathan remained part of the game as a coach, and remains a great legend in Birmingham and Woodlawn. He was portrayed in the movie *Woodlawn* and authored a book about his life's journey.

Ozzie Newsome
Hall of Fame football star
Colbert County

Ozzie Newsome, Jr., became one of the great modern sports executives after a hall of fame career as a player. Not bad for a kid from Colbert County who didn't consider football to be his best sport.

A native of Leighton, Newsome had excelled in baseball and basketball at Colbert County High School, but when the scholarship offers began arriving, he reconsidered and decided that he was a football player after all.

The next stop of Newsome's journey was the University of Alabama, where he was a star receiver on three Southeastern Conference championship teams. He was selected as the Alabama Player of the Decade for the 1970s.

Drafted in 1978 by the Cleveland Browns, Newsome spent his entire 13-year career with the team. He retired as the NFL's all-time leading tight end in receiving yards, catches, and touchdowns.

He was elected to the Alabama Sports Hall of Fame in 1992, the College Football Hall of Fame in 1994, and the Pro Football Hall of Fame in 1999.

Even during his playing years, Newsome's community involvement beyond the football field made an impact, as he received the Whizzer White Award for public service by the NFL.

After his retirement from football, Newsome became the first African-American to run an NFL team, becoming the Vice President and General Manger of the Baltimore Ravens. Newsome's great legacy came as the architect of the Ravens 2000 team that won the Super Bowl.

Cam Newton
Heisman Trophy winner
Auburn University

In 2018, ESPN released its World Fame 100, listing the most famous athletes from around the globe. Auburn University legend Cam Newton was the highest ranking athlete with Alabama connections. The list revealed the fame that the extraordinary athlete has achieved after his historic success at Auburn.

Newton came to Auburn as a highly celebrated recruit, having just quarterbacked Blinn College to the National Junior College Athletic Association national championship. He enrolled at Auburn and immediately became a transcendent player. Newton led the Tigers to the 2010 national championship, including a historic comeback win over arch-rival Alabama in Tuscaloosa and a dramatic, last-second drive to set up the game-winning field goal over Oregon in the championship game.

Newton has always been blessed with a strong arm, but complimented his passing with outstanding running when needed. In a 24-17 win over LSU in 2010, Newton dominated the game with 217 yards rushing, which included two touchdowns and several critical third-down conversions.

The monument to Olympian Jesse Owens (see page 112) captures the poise and power of the world-famous native of Oakville, in Lawrence County. (Photo courtesy of the Encyclopedia of Alabama).

In roughly a year, Newton achieved what no one else has ever done before or since. He won the national championship, received the 2010 Heisman Trophy, was chosen first overall in the NFL draft, and won the NFL Rookie of the Year award. He became the only player in league history to throw for over 400 yards in his first game.

Newton became the modern face of Auburn football in 2010, and has remained its most celebrated player since Bo Jackson and one of the biggest stars in American sports.

Newton won the NFL's Most Valuable Player award in 2015 and led the Carolina Panthers to the Super Bowl.

At any level, with any team, Cam Newton is a winner.

C.M. Newton
Championship basketball coach
The University of Alabama

He began his career as a backup player under a legendary coach. Years later, C. M. Newton would defeat his mentor, personally resurrect three basketball programs, achieve the status of a hall of fame coach, and become known as the most powerful person in his sport.

Newton was born in Tennessee and raised in Florida, but his move to Kentucky placed him on the path to greatness. He played college basketball at the University of Kentucky under Adolph Rupp, considered by many as the sport's greatest coach. During his playing years, Kentucky's football coach was Paul "Bear" Bryant, also considered by many as the greatest coach in his own sport. Newton and Bryant would cross paths a few years later.

After college, Newton became the head basketball coach at Transylvania College in Kentucky, where he made history by signing the first black player in the school's history. By 1968, the University of Alabama was searching for a new basketball coach. Bryant had become the football coach and athletic director, and called his old colleague Rupp to recommend a new coach in Tuscaloosa. Rupp recommended his former player, and Bryant offered the job that would launch a historic career.

Newton forever changed basketball at Alabama, winning at an unprecedented level and integrating the team as he did at Transylvania by signing the first black basketball player, Wendell Hudson. Under Newton, Alabama became the first team other than Kentucky to win three consecutive Southeastern Conference championships (1974, 1975, and 1976). He was twice named SEC Coach of the Year, and produced professional players at a rate normally reserved for the football team.

Newton left the rigors of coaching to become assistant commissioner of the Southeastern Conference in 1980, but just one year later, Vanderbilt University convinced him to return to the court. Once again, Newton resurrected a program, winning at a historic level at Vanderbilt, producing a high graduation rate expected at the school, and putting players in the professional ranks.

Then, his alma mater called.

Kentucky had encountered stormy weather as a basketball program, with NCAA probation, scholarship losses, and a struggling won-loss record, Once again, Newton brought a program back from the graveyard of the sport, recruiting the sport's top young coach, Rick Pitino, as the new leader of the program. Pitino won just as Newton himself had in younger days, capturing a national championship. After Pitino left for the professional Boston Celtics, Newton hired Kentucky's first black head basketball coach, Tubby Smith, who won another national championship in his first year.

Amazingly, these weren't his biggest contributions to the game.

Newton headed the NCAA committee governing college basketball, and led the charge to implement the shot-clock, the three-point shot, and a host of other improvements to the game. He retired in 2000 and later moved back to Tuscaloosa, a great compliment to the city and state. When he passed in 2018, the tributes poured in from coaches, players, media figures, and appreciative fans.

C.M. Newton is still considered by virtually all to be the one of the most influential people in basketball history.

Dr. Lloyd Nix
Hall of Fame quarterback
Walker & Morgan Counties

The journey of Dr. Lloyd Nix has revolved around service to others, but he will always be best known for his leadership as a mere college student.

Nix wasn't just any college student, though. He quarterbacked the 1957 Auburn University football team to the national championship under legendary head football coach Ralph "Shug" Jordan, cementing his name in the great history of Auburn University. He led the Tigers to another undefeated (9-0-1) and top-five finish the next year as well. Nix was named All-SEC twice in football, and was also named All-SEC in baseball as the first baseman for the SEC champion Tigers his senior year.

Before his college years, Nix had become a legendary athlete in Walker County, at Carbon Hill High School. According to the Walker County Sports Hall of Fame website, "During his four years of varsity sports, he lettered 11 times, was selected All County 9 times, and helped lead the Bulldogs to 7 county championships. He was selected twice as an All-State quarterback and was the MVP of the 1955 5th District basketball tournament."

After college, Nix studied at the University of Alabama School of Dentistry before joining the U.S. Air Force. After serving his country, Nix served as both a dentist for 35 years in Decatur (Morgan County) and as a community leader. He became the model of a servant leader, in Central United Methodist Church, the board of the Alabama Institute for the Deaf and Blind, chairman of the Auburn Research Advisory Board and member of the Auburn University Foundation, among many others.

Bill "Brother" Oliver
Hall of Fame football coach
Sumter County

Perhaps no one has lived the nation's top college football rivalry in the way that Bill "Brother" Oliver has.

Known as a genius of the defensive strategies and tactics, Oliver became, at various times, a hero or villain for both teams in the Iron Bowl rivalry between the University of Alabama and Auburn University.

A native of Epes (Sumter County), Oliver was one of only eight (of 107) players in Coach Paul "Bear" Bryant's first recruiting class at Alabama to stay for four years. Oliver's legendary perseverance paid off, as he played defensive back on the 1961 national championship team that only surrendered 25 points the entire year.

By 1966, Oliver had become the defensive backs coach at Auburn, hired by another legend, Ralph "Shug" Jordan. He quickly became known as a guru of defensive backfield coaching.

In 1971, Bryant brought Oliver back to Tuscaloosa in the same capacity, defensive backs coach. The result was a backfield that stifled opposing passers and helped bring home three more national championships in 1973, 1978, and 1979. In 1980, Oliver left to become the head coach at the University of Tennessee at Chattanooga, and later as defensive coordinator for the USFL's Memphis Showboats.

After years of successful defensive coaching at Clemson University, Oliver returned to Alabama as the defensive coordinator for head football coach Gene Stallings. The result, of course, was another national championship (1992), a 28-game winning streak, and another undefeated regular season in 1994. His innovations became famous, such as playing eight defensive backs at a time or placing all 11 defenders on the line of scrimmage before the ball was snapped.

At one point, Oliver was reportedly told he would succeed Stallings as the head coach, but conflicts within the program convinced Oliver to leave his alma mater.

His next stop? Auburn University, of course. Tigers head football coach Terry Bowden hired Oliver as his defensive coordinator, and when Bowden was fired during the 1998 season, Oliver was named interim coach for the rest of the campaign. In his only Iron Bowl as head coach, Auburn jumped out to a commanding 17-0 lead, until a historic Andrew Zow-led comeback propelled Alabama to a 31-17 win on November 21, 1998.

Oliver's impact went well beyond the football field, as he mentored and propelled the careers of future head coaches Dabo Swinney and Will Muschamp.

Vickie Orr
Hall of Fame basketball star
Morgan County

In many ways, Hartselle's legendary Vickie Orr launched women's basketball in Alabama.

In the early 80s, all things were still new in the sport. The state had just begun holding a state championship for women's hoops in 1978, and college coaches weren't exactly flocking to the state for talent.

All of that would change with Vickie Orr.

Her Hartselle High School team won 62 consecutive games and two state championships. She led her AAU team to the national championship as well. Not surprisingly, the college coaches flooded the state to recruit Orr.

She chose Auburn, and led the Tigers to an incredible record of 119 wins and just 14 losses. She led Auburn to three final four appearances and the national championship game two consecutive years, coming just two points shy of a national title in 1988 and six points short in 1989.

Orr played for the U.S. Olympic Team, winning the bronze medal in 1992. She won gold medals for the U.S. team in the Goodwill Games and the 1990 world championships.

Orr was inducted into the Alabama Sports Hall of Fame and the Morgan County Sports Hall of Fame.

Jesse Owens
Olympic gold medalist
Lawrence County

Almost halfway between Cullman and Florence, just off of state highway 157, sits the Jessie Owens Memorial Park in Oakville, Alabama (Lawrence County).

The park is named after Oakville's favorite son, the track and field star who would be honored as America's greatest Olympic athlete.

But before all the fame and the awards, he was just a kid from Oakville, and his name wasn't even Jesse. James Cleveland Owens and his family moved to Ohio later in his childhood, as part of the mass exodus of African Americans to northern states. His family called him J.C., but a teacher misunderstood his name and called him "Jesse." The nickname stuck, and J.C. became Jesse Owens.

As a high schooler, Jesse became a highly regarded track star and chose the Ohio State University for his education and track competition. In 1935, at Ann Arbor, Michigan, Owen delivered what is considered the greatest track performance in history, breaking three world records and tying a (third) world record, all in less than 60 minutes.

His greatest fame arose in 1936, in the Olympic games held in Berlin, Germany, which was ruled by Adolph Hitler. The event captured the attention of the American public, as Hitler's racism and elitism would co-exist with Owens on the world stage.

Owens won gold medals in the 100-meter dash, the 200-meter dash, the long jump, and the 4 x 100-meter relay. The child of Oakville became the hero of an adoring public and the symbol of achievement from anyone not born to the top tier of society.

Ironically, his college, the Ohio State University, claimed to be integrated but did not allow Owens to live in its dorms or participate fully in student life. Owens, however, approached such societal inequities with the same quiet dignity with which he dealt with any other difficult circumstance. Owens was sometimes criticized for not taking a more combative approach to racially charged situations, but never wavered from his philosophy of peaceful coexistence.

In the succeeding decades after his accomplishments and peaceful example, Owens remained a role model for athletes and for those hoping to rise above hate.

Trivia

Which two future NBA stars came from Marengo County in 1991?

When Marengo County attractions come to mind, many might think of Christmas on the River or the deliciously great Crawfish Festival in Faunsdale. In the 1990-91 basketball season, however, anyone who saw the Demopolis High or Linden High teams got a glimpse at the future of the sport, with each team sporting a future NBA first-round draft choice.

They were born 121 days apart, and then both became two of the great shot blockers in college basketball in the 1990s.

Demopolis High School had a 6-foot-10 forward named Theo Ratliff, who signed with the University of Wyoming and was then chosen by the Detroit Pistons with the 18th pick of the 1995 NBA Draft. Ratliff left Wyoming as the school's leading career shot blocker, with a record 425 rejections that still stands. He retired as one of the NBA's top 20 all-time shot blockers.

Roy Rogers also finished high school in 1991 in his own hometown of Linden. He signed with the University of Alabama, joining the roster for the 1991-1992 season that included no less than five future first-round draft choices. He sat out that season as a redshirt because of knee issues, but ultimately joined his fellow Marengo County native Ratliff as one of college basketball's premier shot blockers. Against the University of Georgia, Rogers blocked a whopping 14 shots in one game. He was drafted by the Vancouver Grizzlies with the 22nd pick of the 1996 NBA Draft.

Terrell Owens
Football and television star
Tallapoosa County

He became the star of his own television show, a national celebrity, and one of the greatest receivers in football history. Terrell Owens, nicknamed "T.O.", rose above difficult childhood times to achieve his dreams with a combination of great talent and a relentless drive to succeed.

Owens grew up in the home of his grandmother, where he, his mom, and his siblings moved during difficult times. Owens was eleven years old when he first met his father, who lived on the same street but remained disengaged from his life. Tough times aside, Owens excelled in four sports at Benjamin Russell High School in his hometown of Alexander City (Tallapoosa County). He signed a football scholarship to the University of Tennessee at Chattanooga, and became the greatest player in Mocs history. The San Francisco 49ers chose him in the third round of the 1996 NFL Draft.

After a splendid career with the 49ers, the Philadelphia Eagles, the Dallas Cowboys, the Buffalo Bills and the Cincinnati Bengals, T.O. retired as the second leading receiver in NFL history in both touchdowns and receiving yards.

T.O.'s propensity to speak out boldly and promote himself caused issues at times, but also made him an appealing subject for his own television show.

Through it all, with each team, each controversy, and each phase of his life, T.O. has always remained a star and the sports pride of Alexander City.

Satchel Paige
Hall of Fame baseball player
Mobile County

On September 25, 1965, Mobile's Leroy "Satchel" Paige pitched three scoreless innings for the Kansas City A's against the Boston Red Sox.

He was 59 years old.

Becoming the oldest pitcher in Major League Baseball history was just one of the many records and firsts in the career of Paige. As a teenager in Mobile, he worked a job carrying luggage at a train depot, and picked up the nickname "Satchel."

He enjoyed a long illustrious career in the old Negro League, sometimes pitching both games of a double header and setting a number of pitching records. He became such a draw for fans that his employer, the Birmingham Black Barons, would sometimes rent him out to other teams to increase the crowds and help those teams with attendance.

Before the color barrier was broken in the big leagues, Paige did have opportunities to face major league teams in exhibition teams. In 1930, he faced major league hitters for the first time against the Babe Ruth all-stars and struck out 22 batters.

His teammate with the Kansas City Monarchs, Jackie Robinson, broke the major league color barrier. Paige followed his friend into the league a year later at age 42, setting the record for the oldest rookie to debut in Major League Baseball.

Paige was inducted into the Baseball Hall of Fame in 1971.

Sarah Patterson
Hall of Fame gymnastics coach
Tuscaloosa County

She just might have been the greatest coach in the history of her sport.

If most Alabamians were asked to name all their head coaches who have won six national championships, most answers would name only football coaches.

Sarah Patterson, however, was arguably the equal of Paul "Bear" Bryant or Nick Saban in her sport. Just a few months after graduating from Pennsylvania's Slippery Rock State College in 1978, Patterson was hired by Paul "Bear" Bryant to coach the University of Alabama gymnastics team.

Nice choice.

Patterson quickly turned the Crimson Tide into a national power and a consistently big draw to Coleman Coliseum, as large crowds watched her lead the gymnasts to six national championships and eight Southeastern Conference titles. She was named National Coach of the Year four different times (1986, 1988, 1991, and 2001), and SEC Women's Gymnastics Coach of the Year in four seasons (1985, 1995, 2000, and 2010).

Especially in the 1990s and early 2000s, when the University of Alabama athletic department became a carousel of coaching changes, Patterson remained a stable coach achieving predictable excellent results.

And there's more. Patterson didn't just win; she turned Alabama gymnastics meets into exciting events, often drawing more than 10,000 to see the girls compete on their journey to their next national championship.

Champions Plaza, sitting between Coleman Coliseum and Sewell-Thomas Stadium on the University of Alabama campus, is named after Patterson in honor of her six national titles and her impact on countless young lives.

The Person family
Basketball stars
Crenshaw County

If you drive through Crenshaw County, anywhere near Brantley, you'll probably see a sign for the outstanding recreation center named after Chuck and Wesley Person. The brothers became two of the talented shooters in the NBA and two of Auburn's greatest players in the program's history.

As for Chuck, it's only fitting that one of the elite shooters of his era would be nicknamed "The Rifleman."

Chuck Person grew up in Brantley (Crenshaw County) and played the game with a style far ahead of this time. In the 21st century, players like Steph Curry light up the scoreboard hitting shots from long distances. Even in the 80s and 90s, Chuck Person shot the ball from ridiculous distances and fully earned his nickname.

He played college basketball for the Auburn University Tigers and finished as their all-time leading scorer. The three-point shot didn't enter the college game until the season after he had left Auburn. One can only imagine the points he would have scored if the three-point line had been introduced earlier.

Chosen with the fourth overall pick in the 1986 NBA Draft by the Indiana Pacers, Person attacked the league with the same ferocity that he used to lead Auburn. After averaging over 18 points per game, he was named the NBA Rookie of the Year. In only six seasons with Indiana, he scored so many points that he left as one of the franchise's top ten all-time leading scorers.

Person continued his professional career with Minnesota, San Antonio, Charlotte and Seattle before becoming a coach in the NBA and college ranks.

Little brother Wesley Person also dominated at Brantley High School, then followed his brother to Auburn. In college, Wesley became the Tigers' best player and joined his brother as one of the greatest shooters in the team's history.

Wesley, like Chuck, was a first-round pick in the NBA Draft, chosen by the Phoenix Suns. Like Chuck, Wesley also enjoyed an outstanding debut season, resulting in his place on the NBA All-Rookie team.

Wesley possessed a lethal long-range shot, terrorizing opponents in the Person family tradition. He enjoyed a long and successful career in the NBA, playing 11 seasons and averaging double-figure per-game scoring for his career and in the NBA Playoffs.

Then came the next generation.

Brantley High School enjoyed another Person family member ripping up the nets from far away, as Wesley Person, Jr., followed in the family footsteps.

Playing at Troy University, Wesley, Jr., became the school's all-time leading scorer, the all-time three-point shooter in Sun Belt Conference history, and only the sixth player in conference history to be named to the All-Sun Belt team four consecutive years.

Wesley Person, Jr., signed with a professional team in Italy in 2018, starting the next generation of Person family members who made it to the pros.

Chris Porter
All-American basketball player
Henry County

Those who saw him play recall Chris Porter as one of the most exciting-to-watch players in SEC history, joining legends like "Pistol" Pete Maravich, Dominique Wilkins, Gerald Wallace, and Jason Williams.

It began in his hometown of Abbeville, when Porter became the biggest thing to come out of Henry County since Great Southern Wood. Leading Abbeville to the state championship, he was also named Class 4A Player of the Year.

Porter's journey took him first to Chipola College, where he was named a Junior College All-American.

Then came the Auburn Tigers, where Porter became the marquee player on a team loaded with talent and coached by Cliff Ellis. Porter was named the SEC Player of the Year and an All-American as he routinely provided highlights for ESPN's SportsCenter program with his thunderous dunks and acrobatic rebounds.

Despite his elite athletic ability, at 6-foot-7, Porter was undersized to play his natural position of power forward. He played briefly in the NBA and then played for several foreign teams, the NBA Developmental League, and the USBL.

Rick Rhoades
Championship football coach
Pike and Jefferson Counties

Few Alabama coaches have ever succeeded as grandly as Rick Rhoades at the high school, small college, and major university levels.

In 1976, he was hired as the head coach of the Mountain Brook High School Spartans, but the team stood in turmoil after the dismissal of its previous coach. To make matters worse, they were the defending state champions, so the expectations would be almost impossible to meet.

Rather than seeking to lower expectations, Rhoades embraced them, even while changing the team's style from a defense-first, regimented team to a more laid-back unit that emphasized offensive scoring.

The result? Mountain Brook's 1976 state championship team remains one of the most celebrated in the history of the Birmingham area. Running back Major Ogilvie became a high school All-American, and later a college All-SEC performer at the University of Alabama and the first player to ever score a touchdown in four different bowl games.

Rhoades coached at other high schools after Mountain Brook, and made his way to the college game. As the head coach of Troy University (then Troy State), he led the Trojans to the 1987 national championship.

By 1989, Rhoades had moved to the Southeastern Conference, coaching the offensive line at the University of Alabama. His O-line paved the way for running back Siran Stacy and protected the conference player of the year, quarterback Gary Hollingsworth, en route to an SEC title.

Rhoades coached in other small colleges and professional leagues, always maintaining the reputation as an excellent teacher of the game, mentor to young players, and as a winner of championships.

Sanders Russell
Hall of Fame harness racer
Jackson County

In 1971, Sanders Russell was inducted into the Alabama Sports Hall of Fame, and with good reason.

Russell, a native of Stevenson (Jackson County), was one of the world's premier harness racers for almost 50 years, from age 15 (in 1915) to age 62 (1962).

Before entering the world of horse racing, Sanders played both baseball and tennis at Auburn. Once he began harness racing, however, his success made that decision worthwhile.

According to the U.S. Trotting Association, Russell was credited with 1,166 wins.

One-and-done in Greenville

Za'Darius Smith was a high school basketball player for Greenville High School. For his senior year, he decided to play football, too.

Nice choice.

After playing junior college ball and later starring at the University of Kentucky, Smith entered the NFL, where he played his first four seasons with the Baltimore Ravens.

After the 2018 season, Smith had become one of the league's most highly coveted free agents. In March of 2019, he signed a mammoth contract with the Green Bay Packers.

The Rutledge family
Football stars
Jefferson County

These two brothers have done what no one else has.

It started with Gary, who graduated from Banks High School in Birmingham and quarterbacked the University of Alabama football team. In his three seasons on the team, Alabama won a national championship (1973) and three Southeastern Conference titles.

Gary was the starting quarterback in 1973, when the Crimson Tide kicked off the season by defeating the University of California, 66-0, and steamrolled to an undefeated regular season and the most powerful offense in the school's illustrious history (at least until 2018).

No one at Alabama had ever led his team to so many scores. Gary had etched his name into the history books, and two seasons later, little brother Jeff had signed with Alabama and now hoped to play quarterback as well.

Would the little brother sink from the challenge or rise to it?

Jeff Rutledge, as it turned out, was no ordinary little brother.

Jeff was a *Parade* All-American in high school, winning championships and leading Banks in the biggest high school game in the state's history, the clash against Woodlawn at historic Legion Field. Woodlawn sported its own All-American, Tony Nathan, and the game had become a classic even before kickoff.

At Alabama, Jeff matched his brother's feat by quarterbacking the Crimson Tide to the 1978 national championship, and also becoming a part of three Southeastern Conference championship teams. His teammate and fellow leader on the team was none other than Tony Nathan, the former Woodlawn star. Nathan was portrayed in the hit movie Woodlawn.

Then, Jeff went a step further. He was drafted by the Los Angeles Rams of the National Football League, and went on to play in three Super Bowls with three different teams (the Los Angeles Rams, the New York Giants, and the Washington Redskins).

Plenty of brothers have played college football in the state of Alabama, but no other brothers have quarterbacked teams to national championships.

Banks High School closed years ago, but its legacy of producing champions on and off the field continues.

Nick Saban
Championship football coach
The University of Alabama

Nick Saban's championship team went undefeated, following him as its leader, by famously working long hours and playing relentlessly physical football.

However, the team was not the Alabama Crimson Tide, and Saban was not the coach.

The 1968 Monongah High School football team won the West Virginia state championship, and was led by its senior quarterback, Nick Saban. That was the year that Saban's indefatigable work ethic and physical style of football begat results so satisfying that he has spent his entire adult life winning championships, and developing young athletes into personal champions.

In his early years, Saban learned under some of the game's great coaches, such as Don James and Bill Belichick. Success at his first head coaching job, Toledo, earned him a shot at the big time, in the Big Ten conference at Michigan State University. When Louisiana State University (LSU) of the Southeastern Conference called, Saban won his first national championship in 2003 before leaving a year later for the NFL's Miami Dolphins.

Then came Mal Moore's trip to Miami.

A pillar of Alabama's success since the early 1960s and by then the athletic director, Moore was determined not to return home to Tuscaloosa without Nick and Terry Saban. Even before talks began with Saban's agent, Jimmy Sexton, Moore and Saban had valuable common ground because Moore's nephew, Chuck Moore, built the Saban's lake home in Georgia several years before and had become a friend of the coach. When the Sabans landed at the Tuscaloosa airport as the new first family of Alabama football, thousands of excited fans cheered their arrival and celebrated future victories and championships.

Their hopes were not misplaced; in fact, they were exceeded, as Saban entered the state's bicentennial year having won five of the last nine national championships and five conference championships, including a three-peat in 2014, 2015, and 2016. On the week of the game vs. Mississippi State in 2008, Alabama became the number-one-ranked team in the first regular season poll since losing to the same MSU team in 1980. Since then, Saban has broken records relating to coaching the number one ranked team as well.

Saban actually changed college football before his first game, when the annual "A-Day" spring scrimmage brought a packed Bryant-Denny Stadium and sparked nationwide competitiveness over spring game crowds. Both the 92,000 fans who packed the stadium and the tens of thousands who surprisingly couldn't get in can tell that the actual crowd was much, much larger than the official attendance.

Even the most hopeful Alabama fans might be pleasantly surprised with so many championships in such little time, but Terry Saban and those teammates from Monongah High School recognize the same fierce determination, attention to detail, and love of winning that makes their Nick the same person he has always been.

The funniest coach

If you defeat your opponents and they still like you, you're probably a pretty good person.

Coach Sonny Smith took the Auburn University basketball team to the Elite Eight of the NCAA tournament. He won the championship of the SEC tournament. He recruited All-American players like Charles Barkley, Chuck Person, and Chris Morris.

He was also likable and funny. Really funny. In fact, Smith and his arch-rival, former Alabama coach Wimp Sanderson, hosted a sportstalk radio show together for years after their retirement. Smith's comedic skills and Sanderson's dry wit created a perfect combo to inform fans and also keep them laughing.

With his coaching and broadcasting experience, Smith was the natural choice for his current work, providing commentary for the Auburn basketball radio broadcasts.

Wimp Sanderson
Hall of Fame basketball coach
Lauderdale & Tuscaloosa Counties

According to legend, when Winfrey "Wimp" Sanderson walked home from playing with friends, his mom could tell whether he had won or lost when he was still a block away.

After growing up in Florence (Lauderdale County), Wimp Sanderson coached a year at Carbon Hill High School in Walker County and then moved to Tuscaloosa for an assistant coaching job with the University of Alabama. After spending 20 years as an assistant coach, Sanderson had been through the athletic wars, recruited successfully, and understood both the players and the university. Seeing that, Athletic Director Paul "Bear" Bryant hired Sanderson as the head basketball coach in 1980.

Sanderson quickly became a legend, winning both championships and the hearts of Crimson Tide fans. His plaid jackets and side court rants whipped the crowd into a frenzy at just the right times to maximize the home court advantage in Tuscaloosa. In his second year, he guided Alabama to a stunning SEC Tournament championship, defeating Kentucky in Rupp Arena with a buzzer-beating tip-in by Eddie Phillips. A poster-sized photo of that moment remained in his office during his tenure in Tuscaloosa. That team fell short to North Carolina (with Michael Jordan and James Worthy) in the Sweet 16 round of the NCAA Tournament.

Sanderson's teams went on to win a total of five SEC Tournament championships, including a three-peat from 1989-91. Around the time of his departure from Tuscaloosa, Alabama was tied with North Carolina for having the most former players on NBA rosters. His 1992 team sported no less than five future first-round draft choices

(Robert Horry, Latrell Sprewell, James "Hollywood" Robinson, Jason Caffey, and Roy Rogers).

After a few years coaching at the University of Arkansas at Little Rock, Sanderson returned to the state of Alabama and has enjoyed a second career as a sportscaster, radio host, and guest on sports shows.

Ozzie Smith
Hall of Fame shortstop
Mobile County

When he was born in Mobile, Alabama, his parents named him Osborne Earl Smith, but the world would forever know him as "Ozzie," and the "Wizard of Oz."

During his childhood, the Smith family moved to the Los Angeles area, where little Ozzie became a talented defensive shortstop for his high school baseball team, which amazingly produced two members of the Major League Baseball Hall of Fame: Smith, and first baseman Eddie Murray. Murray was the star, and Smith's only offer beyond high school was to play shortstop for California Polytechnic State University-San Luis Obispo.

Playing at a small school didn't keep Smith from catching the attention of professional teams, and he was chosen in the fourth round of the 1977 draft by the San Diego Padres. After playing only one year in the minor leagues, Smith quickly became the starting shortstop for the Padres and established himself as a star for his defensive wizardry (hence the nickname) with seemingly unlimited ability to get to sharply hit balls beyond the reach of other mere mortals. He was traded to the St. Louis Cardinals before the 1982 season, and promptly led the team to the World Series championship that year and two more World Series appearances (1985 and 1987).

Smith won a whopping 13 consecutive Gold Glove Awards, was selected to the Major League Baseball All-Star Game 15 different years, and set the record for career assists by a shortstop (8,375). Although known mostly for his defensive greatness, he developed as a hitter during his career and knocked the famous home run in 1985 to defeat the Los Angeles Dodgers in the National League Playoff Series, sending the Cardinals to the 1985 World Series.

Ken Stabler
Hall of Fame quarterback
Baldwin County

He was the swashbuckling pirate with the beard and long hair and the attitude.

They called him the "Snake."

That might seem like some type of sinister nickname, unless you saw him running around a football field. Defenders chased in vain as he scrambled around until either finding an open receiver or running with the ball himself.

He was a kid from the beach, from Foley (Baldwin County), with an eccentric personality and playing style. He was the authentic guy who played football the way he lived: uninhibited. He didn't really throw a football as much as he launched it. Not just at Alabama during his college years, but during those Super Bowl seasons leading the bad-boy Oakland Raiders, or with the New Orleans Saints or the Houston Oilers.

He won high school state championships, college national championships, Southeastern Conference championships, NFL division titles, AFC Conference championships, and a Super Bowl championship. Kenny Stabler represented Oakland and its people in ways that so many NFL teams did in the1970s. New York had Broadway Joe Namath, the Pittsburgh Steelers had the gritty defenders with whom the steel workers could identify. Stabler represented Oakland, the rougher side of the San Francisco Bay, and he did it with panache.

He put up hall of fame-type numbers, and won all the awards. He was named AFC Player of the Year in 1974 and 1976, the NFL's Most Valuable Player (by the Associated Press) in 1974. Stabler won the Hickok Belt in 1976 as professional athlete of the year and was named to the Pro Bowl in 1974, 1976, and 1977.

But Stabler was always bigger than numbers. He was a one-man personality cult, the good-old-boy whom Southerners appreciated, the beach guy that with whom coastal Californians identified, and the bad boy that so many everywhere appreciated, even if quietly.

Stabler was inducted into the NFL Hall of Fame. He passed away in 2015.

Trivia

Which Alabamian became the state's high school "Mr. Basketball," played in the SEC, and then coached a team to the national championship game?

Mike Davis was a strong offensive player but an absolutely ferocious defender. After the Fayette County High School star was named Mr. Basketball, he played his college ball at the University of Alabama, where he was named to the All-Defensive team.

Davis was drafted by the Milwaukee Bucks, but never played in the big show. Instead, he played and later coached international ball. After returning to his alma mater in Tuscaloosa as an assistant coach, he was hired as an assistant at Indiana University.

After coach Bobby Knight was dismissed for behavioral reasons, Davis was named head coach during the 2000 season. The next season brought enormous success, as Davis led the Hoosiers to the Final Four and the national championship game.

Gene Stallings
Hall of Fame football coach
The University of Alabama

On the field, Gene Stallings won just about everything that can be won. He won the national championship as the Alabama football coach. He won multiple coach of the year honors, and a Southeastern Conference championship. He was inducted into several halls of fame, and remains a highly coveted public speaker and guest on radio and television programs. In short, he is a living legend.

But those have not been his biggest victories.

During his career and afterward, Stallings has worked tirelessly to help the underprivileged and challenged in society. After his late son, John Mark Stallings, was born with Down syndrome, Stallings became one of America's leading spokesmen and fundraisers to help those with that condition, and their families.

It was also common knowledge that Stallings would often visit Tuscaloosa's Druid City Hospital to visit with families of patients in the Intensive Care Unit. Unlike many coaches, Stallings fully understood how important the Alabama football coach was to the Tuscaloosa community, and he understood that just stopping by and checking on people made a meaningful impact.

More than a coach, Gene Stallings became a lifelong champion.

John Stallworth
Hall of Fame football player
Tuscaloosa and Madison Counties

He began as an undersized, overlooked high school player and became one of the greats in the history of football. Later, he started an undersized, overlooked start-up business and and turned it into a major company with 375 employees in 15 states. Afterward, he has directed his focus on the John Stallworth Foundation, a family-oriented organization raising scholarship funds for students attending his alma mater, Alabama A & M University.

But it almost didn't happen.

As a senior in Tuscaloosa, Stallworth wasn't attracting interest from college coaches. That changed when the Rev. Sylvester Croom, Sr., a local pastor and father of Stallworth's best friend, called the coaches at Alabama A & M, his alma mater.

That call altered the path of Stallworth, the Pittsburgh Steelers franchise, and countless families in Huntsville who would later benefit from his foundation.

After a record-setting career at Alabama A & M, Stallworth went to the NFL and then set virtually every receiving record in the history of the Steelers. He was named All-Pro three times and won four Super Bowl championships, including his iconic catch against the Los Angeles Rams that landed him on the cover of *Sports Illustrated*.

Stallworth and his wife, Flo, have continued benefitting the City of Huntsville.

JoJo Starbuck
Olympic athlete, television star, author
Jefferson County

Born in Birmingham, Alicia "JoJo" Starbuck became one of America's darlings as part of the youngest pair skaters America had ever sent to the Olympic Games.

After gaining fame as a two-time Olympian and multi-time national champion, Starbuck expanded her realm of achievement. She enjoyed a multi-faceted career as an athlete and artist, and now as a producer, spokesperson and coach.

From the Ice Capades to Broadway shows to the Rink at Rockefeller Center to an autobiography, she has entertained, instructed, and inspired millions from across America and beyond.

Bart Starr
Hall of Fame football star
Montgomery County

Bart Starr won games, Super Bowls, MVP Awards, the respect of opponents, and the hearts of Alabama and Green Bay Packers fans.

After quarterbacking the Sidney Lanier High School team in his hometown of Montgomery, he was named a high school All-American. Starr then made his way to the University of Alabama, but had the misfortune of playing at Alabama during some of the football program's leanest years. Based in part on wins and losses, he and his teammates didn't rack up too many individual awards.

His professional career, however, was another story, but it hardly began with the glamor of a future gridiron hero.

People still talk about Tom Brady lasting until the 199th pick of the 2000 draft, but the future two-time Super Bowl MVP lasted until the draft's 17th round, when the Packers chose the Alabama quarterback.

That became one of the best draft choices in American sports history, as Starr propelled the team to five NFL championshps and victories in the first two Super Bowls. Starr was named the Most Valuable Player in both Super Bowl I and Super Bowl II. He led the NFL in passing three different times, and was ultimately (and easily) voted into the Pro Football Hall of Fame and the Alabama Sports Hall of Fame.

When Starr passed away in May of 2019, media outlets from across the globe, from ESPN to the British Broadcasting Company, featured it as a front-page story. Tributes from across the world of sports hailed him as an outstanding athlete, leader, and person.

Pat Sullivan
Heisman Trophy winner
Jefferson County

Pat Sullivan won the Heisman Trophy. He led Auburn to great victories. He defeated Alabama. He defeated Georgia, Florida, and Ole Miss. He battled cancer in a public battle that made all sports fans his supporters.

The state of Alabama has produced more than its share of elite athletes, but few have become as successful, likable, and strongly supported as Auburn's first Heisman Trophy winner, Pat Sullivan.

Sullivan first became a star at Birmingham's John Carroll High School, where he excelled at three sports. Legendary Auburn football coach Ralph "Shug" Jordan offered him a scholarship, laying the foundation for one of the great eras of success in the storied program's history.

Sullivan did almost everything an athlete can do in college ball. In addition to winning the Heisman Trophy, the most glamorous and coveted award in American sports, he was the two-time Southeastern Conference Player of the Year. He broke all of Auburn's passing records and defeated all of its rivals.

He was drafted by the NFL's Atlanta Falcons, but in the days before spread offenses, his 6-foot frame just wasn't tall enough for the professional game in that era.

He worked in private business and served as a sportscaster for Auburn radio broadcasts, until Tigers coach Pat Dye hired him as Auburn's quarterbacks coach. Sullivan coached at his alma mater for six years, winning three Southeastern Conference championships and cementing his reputation as a mentor to young quarterbacks.

Sullivan was hired as head coach at Texas Christian University, laying the foundation for that program's future success. After coming back to Birmingham he became the offensive coordinator at UAB for six seasons. It was during that tenure that he was first diagnosed with cancer and fought an uphill battle, recovering by 2004. But the chemotherapy and radiation he endured did have long-lasting effects on his body. In 2006 Sullivan was named head football coach at Samford University, where his father once played with future coaching legend Bobby Bowden. He retired from coaching in 2014, assuming a new role within the university.

Through his playing, coaching, and health successes, Sullivan has remained one of the state's most popular and admired sports figures.

Don Sutton
Hall of Fame pitcher
Barbour County

He was born in a shack made of tar paper. His parents were teenage sharecroppers in Clio, Alabama. By age 21, he was a starting pitcher for the Los Angeles Dodgers, and by the end of his 23-year career, his success landed him in the Baseball Hall of Fame. By any statistical measure, Sutton was one of the ten greatest pitchers in baseball history, as he finished in the top ten all-time in shutouts, strikeouts, innings pitched, winning percentage, and games started. Sutton holds the record with seven games of nine innings of shutout ball without a decision, and for the most at-bats without a home run in Major League Baseball history (1,354). His 324 career wins are in the top 15 in the sport's history.

Sutton pitched the Dodgers to several World Series appearances, and also helped lead the Houston Astros to the playoffs, the Milwaukee Brewers to the World Series, the Anaheim Angels to the playoffs, and then his beloved Dodgers again, including their World Series championship season of 1988. The Dodgers, for whom he pitched in 17 of his 23 seasons, retired his jersey number 20 in 1998.

After his playing days, Sutton began a second hall-of-fame career as a broadcaster. Sutton was inducted into the Atlanta Braves Hall of Fame, in 2015, for his many years as an outstanding broadcaster for the team.

Dabo Swinney
Championship football coach
Shelby County

Pelham's Dabo Swinney has become one of the great winners in American sports, but his path to football fame and fortune took him on the ROY bus, the world of real estate, and a job that he didn't even want.

After his playing days at Pelham High School, Swinney became a non-scholarship player (nicknamed a "walk-on") at the University of Alabama for Coach Gene Stallings. Years later he joked that the walk-ons had to ride a different bus to games, called the ROY bus (for Rest-of-Y'all), meaning the players who didn't matter. Seeing the world of college athletics through the eyes of a walk-on gave him a perspective that still guides his relationships with players. Swinney played on the Crimson Tide's 1992 national championship team.

One day, as Swinney has hilariously told the story, he visited a team practice after graduation and said hello to Coach Stallings. During that chat, Stallings told Swinney that a job as a graduate assistant coach awaited him, and he would start work in July. Swinney explained to his former coach that he was engaged to be married, and already had a job lined up. Stallings replied that Dabo must not have heard him, because his graduate assistant job would begin in July. Swinney, like most people, was afraid to tell Stallings no, so he suddenly found himself heading for a coaching career.

He coached for several years, including the 1999 SEC championship team at Alabama, but soon found that a head coaching change left him jobless. He entered the world of commercial real estate, building the foundation for a strong career until Clemson coach Tommy Bowden, one of Dabo's position coaches at Alabama, offered him a job.

Swinney joined the staff, and in late 2008 found himself as the head coach. By the beginning of Alabama's bicentennial celebration, Swinney's Clemson Tigers had faced his alma mater, Alabama, for the past four years in the College Football Playoff. Each team won two of the games, each won two of the previous four national championships, and two teams' senior classes stand tied together for the record of the most wins ever by a senior class, with 55.

Frank Thomas
Hall of Fame baseball star
Auburn University

In 1986, the Auburn University football team welcomed a high school tight end recruit whom they believed was a future member of the Pro Football Hall of Fame.

In 1986, the Auburn University baseball team also welcomed a high school first baseman recruit whom they believed was a future member of the Baseball Hall of Fame.

Amazingly, the football and baseball players were the same person, Frank Thomas. He ultimately chose baseball, and was inducted into the Baseball Hall of Fame in 2014. Football coaches and fans still believe he had a hall-of-fame career in that sport as well if he had chosen it.

Clearly, his choice of baseball turned out well. Thomas retired after an 18-year career with 521 career homers, 1,704 RBIs and .555 slugging average, all of which ranked among the Top 25 of all time when he retired.

After Thomas suffered a leg injury playing football and decided to pursue only baseball, Tigers coach Pat Dye kept Thomas on a football scholarship, considering him part of the Auburn family and wanting to help him make his dreams come true.

In many of his major league seasons, his batting stats more closely resembled video game numbers rather than the results against big-league pitching. In his rookie year of 1991, he torched the American League for .318 with 32 homers and 109 RBIs. Perhaps the most impressive stat from his rookie season was his league-leading 138 walks, unheard of for a rookie and indicative of a disciplined, patient hitter.

Justin Tuck
NFL star and businessman
Coosa County

No one knows for sure, but it's possible that the highest Super Bowl ratings in history might have been achieved in Kellyton, Alabama, two different times. The Coosa County town has a population of 217, and just about one hundred percent of the town was tuned in to watch the New York Giants win America's biggest game in 2008 and 2012.

That's because Justin Tuck, the football hero of Coosa County, was one of the Giants' best players and a vital part of both championship victories.

Justin was one of eight children, raised in the Kellyton home their father built mostly by himself. Like most professional football players, Justin was blessed with size, speed, and toughness. As a truly elite football player, he developed the drive to succeed by disciplining himself on and off the field. Before entering the NFL with the Giants, he starred in college for the illustrious Notre Dame Fighting Irish.

But that's not all.

Justin Tuck's intellect just might exceed his athletic ability. After graduating from Notre Dame's business school, he waited patiently for the end of his playing days, then entered the nation's top business school, the Wharton

Steadman Shealy

Then: championship quarterback
Now: championship lawyer

He was undefeated. He was an all-star. And that was just in the classroom. After graduating as valedictorian of his class at Dothan High School (Houston County), Steadman Shealy, also a football star, played quarterback in college for the University of Alabama.

Once again, he was undefeated, and he was an all-star. In his four years with the Crimson Tide, Shealy won two national championships and three Southeastern Conference championships. In his junior year, he was the backup quarterback to future NFL player Jeff Rutledge, playing often, and helping the team to the national championship. The next year, as the starting quarterback, Shealy was an outstanding leader and triple-option quarterback, leading the Crimson Tide to an undefeated season and another national title. Shealy played a major role in the 28-game winning streak from 1978 to 1980.

After college, Shealy graduated from the University of Alabama School of Law, and ultimately became the senior partner in the law firm of Shealy, Crum & Pike in his hometown of Dothan. An accomplished courtroom lawyer, Shealy has once again become the all-star, just as he had at Dothan High School and on his college campus.

Eric Davis

Then: championship defensive back
Now: championship broadcaster

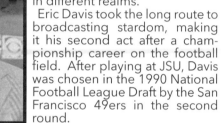

There's something about Jacksonville State University and the many excellent communicators the school has produced. Pulitzer Prize-winning Rick Bragg, nationally known radio host Rick Burgess, and the legendary singer Randy Owen are just a few of the JSU products who have mastered communication in different realms.

Eric Davis took the long route to broadcasting stardom, making it his second act after a championship career on the football field. After playing at JSU, Davis was chosen in the 1990 National Football League Draft by the San Francisco 49ers in the second round.

For the next 13 years, Davis performed at an elite level, becoming one of the best defensive backs in the game. He still holds the all-time NFL record for the most consecutive playoff games with an intercepted pass. He helped lead the 49ers to the Super Bowl championship in 1995, and was selected to the Pro Bowl in the following year.

After football, Davis has made his alma mater just as proud as a broadcaster. His expert analysis has made the airwaves for the NFL Network and ESPN, in years past. He now lends his expertise to various media outlets and social media followers.

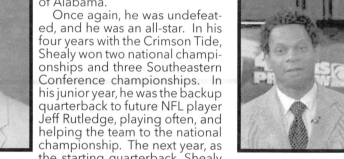

UWA's stars shine in the NFL

Butler, Hill prepared for pro ball in Livingtson, Alabama

Thanks to the NFL, the world of sports has learned plenty about the University of West Alabama.

It was one of the biggest plays in the rich history of the Super Bowl. Social media exploded and trended the his name, Malcolm Butler, and his college, the University of West Alabama.

With seconds left in Super Bowl XLIX, Butler, the New England Patriots defensive back, made an acrobatic and historic interception of a pass, from the one-yard-line, by Seattle quarterback Russell Wilson. According to ESPN, 109 passes were thrown from the one-yard-line in the 2014-2015 season, and Butler's pick was the only interception of them all.

After the Super Bowl ended, and quarterback Tom Brady was named the game's Most Valuable Player, he received a new truck from Chevrolet as part of the award. Brady immediately announced that he would give the truck to Butler, who deserved it more than he.

Butler, however, isn't the only University of West Alabama alumnus to seize the NFL stage. Tyreek Hill has become one of football's elite receivers and kick returners, and is generally regarded as the fastest player in the sport. He has made the All-Pro team, the Pro-Bowl, and the All-Rookie team, but he is best known for his world-class speed.

In 2017, Hill became the fastest player ever tested by ESPN and its Sports Science program, hitting a speed of 22.3 miles per hour in a 20-yard sprint.

The NFL Draft

The NFL draft stands tall as one of the premier off-the-field events in all of American sports. The success of Alabama's football teams and players, at the high school and college levels, has long extended to the NFL draft.

No less than eight number-one overall picks were either natives of Alabama or players from a state university.

The first choice

Overall number-one draft picks from Alabama

2007 top overall draft choice JaMarcus Russell

1948
Harry Gilmer
The University of Alabama

1961
Ken Rice
Auburn University

1965
Tucker Frederickson
Auburn University

1986
Vincent "Bo" Jackson
Auburn University

1988
Aundray Bruce
Auburn University

2007
JaMarcus Russell
Louisiana State University (from Mobile)

2010
Cam Newton
Auburn University

2015
Jameis Winston
Florida State University (from Hueytown)

School at the University of Pennsylvania.

Armed with his Ivy League degree, Tuck then became a vice president of Goldman Sachs in Manhattan, once again making Kellyton and Coosa County proud.

Ben Wallace
NBA basketball star
Lowndes County

He was featured on the cover of an ESPN video game. A basketball shoe was named after him. He was named NBA Defensive Player of the Year four times.

Not bad for a kid from Lowndes County, whom no colleges wanted.

Ben Wallace graduated from Central High School in Hayneville, and then played junior college basketball before landing at Virginia Union.

Then came the NBA.

Wallace was not chosen in the NBA Draft, but later became the only undrafted player in league history named a starter in the NBA All-Star Game.

Wallace was named to the All-NBA team five times. He was named to the All-NBA Defensive Team six times. He won the NBA championship, led the league in rebounding twice, and led the league in blocked shots.

Ben Wallace's jersey number 3 was retired by the Detroit Pistons.

Jameis Winston
Heisman Trophy winner
Jefferson County

He won the Heisman Trophy as a teenager. Becoming the youngest winner of the most prestigious trophy in sports was only one of the remarkable feats in the meteoric rise of Hueytown's Jameis Winston.

After leading the Hueytown High School Golden Gophers to the state championship, Winston became the most celebrated recruit in America. He signed with Florida State University, choosing college football over an offer from Major League Baseball's Texas Rangers, who had chosen him in the 15th round of their league's draft.

The experts pegged him as a future star, and they were right. In his first year of playing for the Florida State Seminoles, he won every major player of the year award, captured the national championship on his 20th birthday, and won the Heisman Trophy, finishing ahead of fellow Alabamian A.J. McCarron, who finished second.

Winston became the top overall pick in the NFL Draft, and embarked on a career with the Tampa Buccaneers.

Swede Umbach
Hall of Fame wrestling coach
Lee County

One of the great coaches in wrestling history, Arnold "Swede" Umbach was born in 1903 in the Oklahoma Territory (it would become a state four years later). In 1944, Umbach, then a high school coach, accompanied his mentor, Carl Voyles, to Auburn University. Two years later, Umbach began a historic run as wrestling head coach at Auburn, resulting in four national champions and 127 SEC champions.

In his years at Auburn, his record in dual meets was almost beyond belief, at 249-28-5.

The 1971 national championships were held at Auburn, which was probative of the prestige and acclaim that Umbach had brought to the school's wrestling program.

In 1981, Umbach was inducted into the National Wrestling Hall of Fame, and in 1991, he was enshrined into the Alabama Sports Hall of Fame.

Golf Greats
From Alabama

Jerry Pate

After becoming an All-American at the University of Alabama, Jerry Pate became a smash, and then a famous splash. The smash was his smashing debut, as a rookie professional (1976), in which he won the U.S. Open, the Canadian Open, the Japan Masters, and was Co-Player of the Year with Jack Nicklaus.

After winning multiple tournaments the next couple of years, Pate had a string of second place finishes without a win, By 1982, when he won the PGA event in Memphis, he made his most famous splash by jumping into a lake adjacent to the 18th hole to celebrate his win. According to the *New York Times*, "No incident in recent years has done more to enhance the popularity of the PGA Tour than that plunge, which Pate took last June 18, after he won the Memphis Classic. Photographs of his shallow racing dive were published everywhere, from Saudi Arabia to Alaska." Pate made another splash after a win at the Tournament Players Championship the next year, and later starred in a famous television ad for a camera company reenacting the famous dive.

Pate has become one of the sport's top consultants and golf course designers.

Sam Byrd

Samuel Dewey Byrd grew up in Birmingham, and enjoyed an elite golfing career after playing baseball for the New York Yankees. As a Yankee, he was part of the all-Birmingham outfield of the 1944 team featuring him, Dixie Walker, and Ben Chapman.

As a golfer, Byrd had multiple top-tier finishes at The Masters, and won the Philadelphia Open in 1944, which according to the Alabama Sports Hall of Fame was the wartime equivalent of the U.S. Open.

Byron Nelson, one of the game's legends, once remarked that Byrd was the greatest long-iron player in the history of the game.

Gardner Dickinson

Dickinson became one of the early stars in the rich legacy of athletes from Dothan (Houston County). Dickinson won a whopping 37 tournaments as an amateur. Turning professional in 1952, he went on to win nine PGA tournaments.

A prote`ge` of golfing legend Ben Hogan, Dickinson was also chosen as a member of two Ryder Cup teams (1967 and 1971).

Jason Dufner

He entered the final round just one stroke down, but that quickly changed when he birdied the fourth hole. The 2013 PGA Championship brought a thrilling final round between the Auburn alumnus Dufner and Jim Furyk. Dufner had come up short two years before, in the 2011 PGA Championship, losing in a playoff. That had been especially frustrating because of a tee shot into the water on the 15th hole that began a three-hold slide and a lost lead.

But 2013 appeared to be his year. Two days earlier, Dufner shot a blazing 63 to break the Oak Hill Country Club course record, previously held by legends Ben Hogan and Curtis Strange.

After his fourth hole birdie, Dufner and Furyk traded the lead, but Dufner eventually won his first major championship

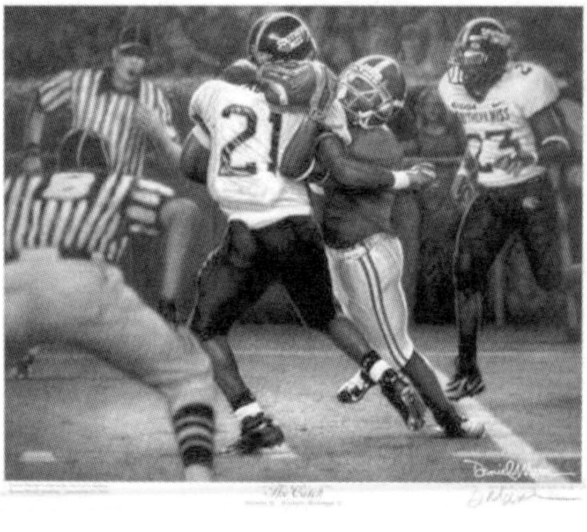

The Catch
Cleburne County's Tyrone Prothro honored in art, and in history

When the game began, no one would have imagined that it would be recreated in art and in the history of college football.

In the first half of the 2005 football game between the University of Alabama and the University of Southern Mississippi, Alabama quarterback Brodie Croyle launched one of his trademark tightly-spiraled long passes to a receiver, about 40 or 50 yards downfield.

This however, was no ordinary play, and Tyrone Prothro was no ordinary receiver. Somehow, Prothro reached with both arms around the defensive back, making the no-look catch while hugging the defender. All of this happened at full speed, and the two tumbled onto the ground with Prothro pinning the ball against the defender's back to complete the catch. The catch was soon immortalized in a painting by the renowned sports artist, Daniel Moore.

Cleburne County High School fans were probably not surprised by the feat. Prothro had made outstanding catches and had proven himself an even better person than football player. After an injury derailed a promising career, Prothro now coaches young players in the game he loves.

and his place in history, with a two-stroke win.

Known for his laid back personality, Dufner quickly became a popular player on the PGA Tour, especially with Auburn fans.

Virginia Derby Grimes

A native of York (Sumter County), Grimes has become the face of Auburn Women's Golf and a leading coach of the game as well.

After playing her college golf at Auburn, Grimes accumulated a staggering number of wins, including the Alabama Women's State Amateur five times ('89, '93, '94, '95, & '98), the USGA Women's Mid-Amateur ('98), the South Atlantic Amateur ('98), the Women's Southern Amateur ('87 & '96), the USGA State Team Championship ('97), and the 1980 Women's Alabama State Junior Championship.

Grimes later returned to Auburn as the head women's golf coach. Two different tournaments have been named in her honor.

John Huston

He has been described as the fastest player on the Champions Tour, with no one a close second. John Huston has made fast work of his opponents many times during a successful golfing career at Auburn University, the PGA Tour, and the Champions Tour.

A native of Illinois, Huston won an impressive seven PGA Tour victories and an equally imposing 80 top-ten finishes in PGA tournaments. At the United Airlines Hawaiian Open in 1998, he broke the 53-year-old course record with a 28-under-par victory.

Hank Johnson

He has been featured on the cover of *Golf Digest* magazine seven different times.

He has literally written the book on how to win at golf.

Born in Birmingham, the Auburn University alumnus became an outstanding golfer, finishing second in the 1962 SEC golf championship and playing on the PGA Tour for two years. He became famous, however, as an elite teacher of the game.

He routinely wins state, regional, and national accolades for his teaching, such as the Dixie Section PGA Horton Smith Award (1978, '80, '82, and '83, for outstanding contributions to golf education), Top Teacher of the Year-*Travel South Magazine* (1989), Professional of the Year by the Alabama Golf Association (1984), Professional of the Year by the Dixie PGA (1985), and finalist for the PGA National Teacher of the Year (1998). Most weekend golfers would be well served to read his book, *How to Win the Three Games of Golf.*

Steve Lowery

For over 15 years, the Hoover native remained one of golf's most consistently outstanding players. Lowery was a two-time SEC Player of the Year at the University of Alabama. He became the first player in the history of Alabama golf to have won both the Alabama State Open and the Alabama State Amateur Championship in the same year (1981).

Always a mentally strong, clutch player, all three of his PGA Tour wins came in playoffs. He ranks among the top 50 on the all-time PGA money list, and his accomplishments included nine second-place finishes, ten third-place finishes, 64 top-tens and 138 top-25 finishes.

Larry Nelson

The Fort Payne (DeKalb County) native is the only Alabamian to have three PGA major tournament wins. In 1981 and 1987, he won the PGA Championship, and in 1983 he captured the U.S. Open title with a record-setting 10-under par in the final two rounds.

Nelson won 10 tournaments on the PGA Tour, and was a three-time selection for the Ryder Cup team.

After his PGA Tour days, he joined the Senior Tour in 1997 and ultimately became the Player of the Year and leading money winner in 2000.

Conrad Rehling

In 1971, Peru native Conrad Rehling made his way to Tuscaloosa as the new University of Alabama golf coach. Actually, he was from Peru, Indiana, but it was still a long way from Indiana, to the University of West Florida, to Tuscaloosa.

Once he arrived, Rehling made himself at home, winning the SEC championship in 1979, finishing second in the national tournament in 1975.

Rehling mentored several future PGA professional golfers, but his signature pupil was Jerry Pate, who won three tournaments as a professional rookie, including the U.S. Open. Rehling's generosity toward teaching the game, especially to the disabled, has been honored in many ways, including the Special Olympics golf trophy bearing his name.

TRACK AND FIELD GREATS
From Alabama

Harvey Glance

He became a legend in the world of sports, and the face of Auburn University's rich track and field tradition.

Harvey Glance, a native of Phenix City (Russell County), won pretty much every award and competition that a sprinter can win. He won a gold medal in the 1976 Olympic Games. He earned a place on three different Olympic teams. He won several national championships in college, a host of SEC championships, broke multiple world records, and won multiple gold medals in both the Pan Am Games and the Goodwill Games.

After his illustrious career, Glance has served as the head track coach at Auburn University, and later at the University of Alabama.

Danette Young Stone

The Alabama A & M athlete became one of the great female track stars of the 1980s. She won Olympic gold in 1988 with the 4 x 100-meter relay team. She won a silver medal in the 1992 Olympics in the same event.

At Alabama A & M, she simply dominated, earning 13 different All-American honors and losing only one race in four years of competition. She won nine different national titles in various events over her collegiate career.

Although originally from Florida, Danette Young Stone captured the hearts of her school, of Huntsville, Alabama, and of future runners who can admire and appreciate her vast accomplishments.

Percy Morris Beard

From his arrival at Auburn University in 1925, Percy Beard seemed destined for greatness. He became the star of the track team, setting a variety of records. He won a silver medal at the 1932 Olympic Games in Los Angeles.

But Percy Beard was no ordinary athlete. He was also an intellectual, a broad thinker who addressed challenges with the mind of the engineer he had studied to become. After graduation, he remained at Auburn to teach engineering and prepare for post-college track and field events.

Along with his Olympic medal, he won seven different national championships in AAU competition. After his Auburn years, he became the long time track coach at the University of Florida, holding the job from 1937 to 1964.

According to the Alabama Sports Hall of Fame website, "Beard also invented the brushed cement shot and discus ring used throughout the world. These inventions have contributed to great improvements in track records."

Alice Coachman Davis

Her gold medal in London's 1948 Olympic Games made her the first black woman to earn such a prize.

She was a four-time All-American at the Tuskegee Institute, where she competed under the tutelage of famed track coach Cleve Abbott.

She won an amazing 25 national championships, and ultimately returned to her alma mater in Tuskegee to teach, inspire, and challenge her students.

Richmond Flowers

Only elite athletes can compete in more than one college sport, but Richmond Flowers earned six different All-American designations in two sports. He was named one of the 20th century's 25 great college football wide receivers. Several of his track and field records still stand, 50 years later.

A native of Dothan (Houston County), Flowers opted to compete athletically for the University of Tennessee. He became the university's first individual national champion in track, in the indoor championship in the 60-yard high hurdles event. He became a four-time All-American in track, and a two-time All-American for the Volunteers football team.

In 1968, poised to compete as one of the favorites in the 1968 Olympic Games in Mexico City, a torn hamstring prevented Flowers from pursuing his Olympic dreams.

Chosen in the second round of the NFL Draft by the Dallas Cowboys, Flowers played an important role with the 1970 Super Bowl team.

Willie Smith

By the time he enrolled as a college freshman at Auburn University, Willie Smith was already a national track star. A native of Long Island, New York, Smith was named National High School Athlete of the Year in 1974.

At Auburn, Smith made the 1976 Olympic team, joining forces with his Auburn teammate, Harvey Glance. He was a two-time national champion at Auburn, and made the Olympic team again in 1984, winning a gold medal.

At age 40, he competed in an intercollegiate track meet and finished in the top six, winning his individual meet.

Mel Rosen

Sometimes, the numbers say it all.

A native of Bronx, New York, Mel Rosen made Auburn his home and he made the SEC championships his personal home turf.

He led the Auburn University track team for 27 years, producing 162 All-Americans, 134 SEC champions, and 11 Olympic athletes.

Rosen was chosen as the head coach of the U.S. Olympic team in 1992, and as head coach of the U.S. team in the world championships of 1987.

His Auburn teams won four consecutive SEC indoor titles and the school's first SEC outdoor team title.

Rosen was named NCAA Coach of the Year three times, and SEC Coach of the Year four different times.

Alabama and the ***Final Four***

Until 2019, no college basketball team from Alabama had ever reached the Final Four of the NCAA Division I Mens College Basketball Tournament.

Auburn University Head Basketball Coach ***Bruce Pearl*** took his high-octane, three point-shooting team all the way to the Final Four, pinnacle of the college game. The Tigers defeated traditional powers Kansas, North Carolina, and Kentucky to take their place among that year's elite programs. Auburn was led by stars ***Bryce Brown, Jared Harper, Chuma Okeke***, and ***Austin Wiley***. For Wiley's family, the NCAA Final Four was familiar territory, as his mom, ***Vickie Orr (Wiley)***, led Auburn to the Women's Final Four in the 1980s.

Orr's coach at Auburn, ***Joe Ciampi***, led the Tigers to three Women's Final Four appearances, and eight SEC championships (tournament and regular season).

Duane Reboul led Birmingham-Southern to two national championships and a whopping 402 victories in his 17 seasons with the Panthers.

The improbable Final Four run by the Mississippi State Bulldogs was fueled by two outstanding guards from Alabama. ***Darryl Wilson***, from Lamar County, was a sharp-shooting guard who could seemingly score from anywhere. ***Bart Hyche*** wowed crowds with dazzling passes and team leadership. Both players drew crowds wherever they played in high school and remained popular athletes during their college years.

Antonio Lang starred at Mobile's LeFlore High School before taking his talents to Duke University. Adding Lang and fellow freshman Grant Hill to an already talented team gave the Blue Devils the team that won national championships in 1991 and 1992.

Parker High School (Birmingham) legend ***Gerald Crosby*** was a third team Parade All-American in 1981, but was overshadowed by legends ***Ennis Whatley*** and ***Bobby Lee Hurt***. Crosby sank a sizzling 22 of 29 shots in the 1983 SEC tournament, leading the University of Georgia to the NCAA tournament and ultimately to the Final Four.

That 1983 Final Four featured another player from Alabama, ***Walt Densmore***, a freshman on the national champion North Carolina State Wolfpack. Densmore's team won the championship in a thrilling finish that remains one of the great moments in American sports.

The 1994 season began in tragic circumstances for the University of Alabama Women's Crimson Tide, who mourned the sudden passing of an assistant coach before the season. The Crimson Tide banded together under head coach ***Rick Moody*** to achieve a Final Four run and an overall record of 26-7.

Pictured (above) Bruce Pearl, men's head basketball coach of Auburn University.

ACHIEVERS

Alabamians reaching the pinnacle

This historic photo shows the Robertsdale High School yearbook staff in 1978. The photo is significant because the young man kneeling, front left, is a trombone player and honor student. His name is Tim Cook, and he became the CEO of Apple, the world's first trillion-dollar company. Photo courtesy of the *Encyclopedia of Alabama*.

Ralph David Abernathy
Civil Rights legend
Marengo County

Ralph David Abernathy was a titan of the American Civil Rights Movement, the chief partner of Dr. Martin Luther King, Jr., and a model for young people, especially from his native Marengo County, Alabama.

Born and raised in Linden, Abernathy spent his life fighting for causes greater than himself. That began when he left his beloved Marengo County to serve in the United States Army in World War II. After serving his country, Abernathy enrolled in Alabama State University, where he successfully pursued a degree in mathematics in 1950. During his college years, Abernathy led a protest over housing conditions at the university, which included a lack of heat and hot water.

After earning a second degree (sociology) at Clark Atlanta University, Abernathy was named the pastor of the First Baptist Church in Montgomery. In Alabama's capital city, he became the closest of friends with another local pastor, Dr. King, who served the Dexter Avenue Baptist Church. They famously became two of the primary organizers of the Montgomery Bus Boycott (1955) and their lives were inextricably joined thereafter. King became president of the newly formed Southern Christian Leadership Conference (SCLC) and Abernathy became secretary-treasurer and later vice president of this organization that they co-founded.

After Dr. King was assassinated on April 4, 1968, Abernathy succeeded his dear friend as leader and continued the struggle for just causes that had defined his life and his success. Abernathy authored an autobiography, *And the Walls Came Tumbling Down*, a year before his passing in 1990. Abernathy received numerous honorary degrees from colleges and universities, and a major stretch of Interstate 20 in Atlanta is named in his memory.

Scott Alexander
Radio broadcasting legend
Dallas County

When a sixteen-year-old Selma kid named Scott Alexander decided on a career in radio, neither he nor anyone else was surprised. "This has always been a family business," Alexander said of the award-winning Selma company, Scott Communications, which now owns and operates radio stations across the Black Belt, from Montgomery to Meridian, Mississippi. "I spent time in WALX that my parents founded in 1973, and my dad was a great teacher, so my career choice didn't surprise anyone. The radio bug hit me pretty hard."

For the 2017 Alabama Broadcaster of the Year, the journey has taken him to great heights. The expanding business and the new radio stations have never tempted him to leave the hometown he loves. "Everything we do in other places is subbed out of Selma, and the great thing about today's technology is that we can run and monitor operations from Selma."

Scott Communications, which his parents named after him, operates radio stations with a variety of formats, offering classic rock music, country music, Christian music, and talk radio. The result has been a years-long streak of ABBY Awards as, the best in broadcasting. Scott Alexander runs the company with his son, Paul, succeeding while believing strongly in the future of radio, and in the bright future of their hometown of Selma.

Did You Know???

The Birmingham Shuttlesworth International Airport is named after a pioneer of civil rights

------

Birmingham's international airport serves millions of travelers each year. Fittingly, it is named after a giant of civil rights who helped lead millions to equal protection under the law.

Fred Shuttlesworth, a Birmingham native, co-founded the Southern Christian Leadership Conference with Dr. Martin Luther King, Jr., and Ralph David Abernathy. Known as Birmingham's nemesis to Bull Connor, Shuttlesworth led voting rights and desegregation efforts that achieved historic victories.

Evelyn Daniel Anderson
Renowned educator
Hale County

Life didn't start out so well for Evelyn Daniel Anderson, who was struck by a stray bullet at age four, in 1930. From the moment that bullet entered her tiny body, she was never again able to walk, stand, or even sit up.

While that tragic event ended her personal mobility, it served as the beginning of a life of courage and selfless giving that brought accomplishments and many honors to the native of Greensboro, Alabama.

Refusing to wallow in her misfortune, Anderson referred to the gunshot wound and resulting paraplegia only as a "physical inconvenience." Amazingly, Anderson earned a degree from Judson College (graduating with honors with a double major in Art and History) and began teaching, unofficially, in her beloved Greensboro.

At first, Anderson wasn't allowed to officially teach because state law prohibited the hiring of severely handicapped persons. Inspiring her local state senator to lead the charge, she lobbied successfully for a change in the law, and was able to teach in Greensboro.

Anderson later earned a master's degree from the University of Alabama, and received numerous awards for her accomplishments, determination, perseverance, and outstanding work as an educator.

Alabama Public Television aired a documentary about her story in her later years. In addition to a host of other honors, Anderson was inducted into the Alabama Women's Hall of Fame.

The Anderson family
Books-A-Million
Lauderdale County

He was only trying to help his family. Instead, he made business history.

Roughly a hundred years ago, the 14-year-old Clyde Anderson began selling newspapers in his hometown of Florence to help his family survive economically. He also began selling newspapers to workers on the massive Wilson Dam project, and learned that many of them were out-of-state workers who missed their hometown newspapers.

Learning of the workers' desire to read news from home, the seeds of a publishing dynasty would soon be planted in the brilliant mind of Clyde Anderson. Acting on the opportunity before him, the young Clyde cut a deal that changed his life and his family for foreseeable generations to come.

Swampland.com described what happened next: "Anderson made a deal with the northern publishers to have them delivered to Florence. He constructed a makeshift newspaper stand out of old piano crates, and within five years he and his brother were able to open a bona fide bookstore."

In the 1950s, Anderson's son, Charles, took over the business and continued the innovative thinking that had been his father's signature mode of operation. After the Alabama national championship win over the University of Miami on January 1, 1993, *Sports Illustrated* magazine did not feature the Crimson Tide on the front cover. Anderson convinced them to print 200,000 copies commemorating the game, then he bought them all and sold every single copy, making a $200,000 profit.

Every *Sports Illustrated* commemorative issue can be traced back to the brilliant business minds of the Anderson family.

The Anderson family also owns Anderson Media Corporation, American Promotional Events, Anderson Press, and their signature store, Books-A-Million.

Books-A-Million has become the second largest bookstore chain in America, and has played a major role in the revival in the book industry over the last decade.

Dr. James Andrews
Globally renowned surgeon
Jefferson County

For the last 30 years, the world's premier athletes, movie stars, heads of state, and royal families have made the trip to Birmingham for needed orthopedic surgeries.

The medical needs and surgeries are usually complex, but the reason for the common destination of Birmingham is simple. Dr. James Andrews, and his team have developed a globally prominent reputation for state-of-the-art, highly skilled surgical procedures.

The journey into the world of sports medicine was a natural one for Andrews, who starred as an athlete at Louisiana State University. In fact, Andrews won two individual Southeastern Conference championships, in the indoor pole vaulting and outdoor pole vaulting. After medical school at LSU and his residency at Tulane, Andrews completed fellowships at the University of Virginia, and then in Lyon, France, under the renowned Albert Trillat, M.D., who has been called the "Father of European Knee Surgery."

Andrews has been inducted into the Alabama Business Hall of Fame, the Alabama Sports Hall of Fame, the Louisiana Sports Hall of Fame, the LSU Alumni Hall of Fame, the American Orthopaedic Society for Sports Medicine (AOSSM) Hall of Fame and was presented the Gerald R. Ford Award, and the 2009 Distinguished American Award by the Auburn Chapter of the National Football Foundation and College Hall of Fame. Dr. Andrews serves as Medical Director and Orthopaedic Surgeon for Auburn University Intercollegiate Athletics.

His colleague and prote`ge`, Dr. Lyle Cain, serves as the team physician for the rival University of Alabama, among other college, professional, and high school teams.

The Piggy Bank

that launched an empire

America's great portrait company was launched from a Selma piggy bank.

They were broke. Their business had gone kaput. Mary and Olan Mills, Sr. had started a photography business in Selma, the home of Mary's family, but the business had failed.

Unfortunately, this wasn't the first failed business for Olan. He had gone to Florida in the late 1920s to pursue a career in real estate. The Great Depression sabotaged the dreams of Olan and virtually all other real estate salesmen, and he had to start a new career. Hitchhiking through Alabama, he had been given a ride by two men who operated a photography business. Olan tagged along with them, worked with them, and learned the business.

After studying art at the University of Alabama, Olan married Mary. They moved to Selma, borrowed the money to purchase a car, and started their photography business. They used an old shed, in downtown Selma on the banks of the Alabama River, as their studio.

When it failed, they found themselves in serious straits.

Fortunately, maybe miraculously, they heard about the Clements photography studio in Tuscaloosa that had also failed. They decided to move to Tuscaloosa and find a way to obtain ownership of that studio.

How did they pay for their move to Tuscaloosa? They borrowed ten dollars from the piggy bank of their son, Olan Mills II.

The business quickly grew, thanks in part to a contract to take portrait photos of University of Alabama students for the 1933 school yearbook, *The Corolla*. In just six years, the company's 650 employees produced over 12,000 portraits each year. The color treatment of the photos and the distinctive Olan Mills signature made their portraits works of art rather than merely photos. The innovative pre-paid three sessions in a year developed lasting customer loyalty.

Although the company scaled back its operations during World War II, the Olan Mills company quickly rebounded and became a premier studio once again. Olan Mills II, who unknowingly financed the original move to Tuscaloosa with his $10 piggy bank savings, sold the company in 2011.

The Arendall family
Legal and ministerial leaders
Mobile and Jefferson Counties

A young family's journey from Richmond to Mobile might not have seemed unusual in 1924, but it changed the history of a state.

Rev. Charles and Kate Arendall moved their families

Did You Know?

Samford University's Memory Leake Robinson Hall was named for the attorney who brought the Cumberland Law School to Birmingham

It was a team effort rather than a solo performance, but there was never any doubt that attorney Memory Leake Robinson made it happen.

Robinson, a name partner in the historic law firm of Lange, Simpson, Robinson & Somerville, was accustomed to succeeding. When the possibility of obtaining the law school arose, Robinson pursued it with the full force of the litigator he had become over the years of practicing law.

Robinson also came from a family that supported education. Barnwell Hall at the University of Alabama is named after his father-in-law.

As he typically did in life, Robinson succeeded in the pursuit of the Cumberland School of Law. In honor of his lasting work on behalf of the university, Memory Leake Robinson Hall houses the law library.

The Robinson legacy continues, as Robinson's grandson, Greg Robinson, practices law in Birmingham. After serving as an assistant attorney general, Greg Robinson now serves as a leading trust attorney with BBVA Compass Bank, handling matters across the state and region.

(Pictured, below, Memory Leake Robinson Hall)

including two sons, to Mobile because Charles had become the pastor at the Dauphin Way Baptist Church. While the parents made their own impact in Mobile, two sons would each become the fathers of institutions that have made the Arendall name indispensable to any history of the state of Alabama. Interestingly, they both followed the path of their father.

Edgar Arendall followed his father's footsteps into Christian ministry, serving first at Atmore Baptist Church (1945-48) and then Dawson Memorial Baptist Church in Homewood from 1948 through his retirement in 1984.

Dr. Arendall's dynamic leadership, shepherd's heart, and powerful preaching helped propel Dawson to its role as a pillar of the Southern Baptist Convention. When Dr. Arendall preached his first sermon at Dawson, the church had a membership of between 600 and 700. Under Arendall's leadership, the church membership had increased ten-fold to over 6,000 by the time of his retirement. The reach of Dawson's impact on the state of Alabama and beyond arose, in no small part, from the faithful ministry of Dr. Arendall.

Charles Arendall, Jr., also followed his father's path, by settling in the Port City of Mobile, and quickly became a prominent attorney. In 1941, as a mere 26-year-old lawyer, Arendall formed a partnership with Charles C. Hand, named Hand Arendall, that quickly emerged as a leading Mobile law firm.

In 2016, Hand Arendall celebrated its 75th anniversary of success in its many areas of legal expertise. The vision of Charles Arendall, Jr., that of serving as zealous advocates for their clients, has resulted in a law firm with over 70 attorneys, providing hundreds of jobs in their offices across the State of Alabama and the panhandle of Florida.

Dr. Neal Berte
Longtime president,
Birmingham-Southern College
Jefferson County

In January of 2018, when Dr. Neal Berte received the Jemison Visionary Award, one of Alabama's great modern leaders was once again recognized for the impact of his service.

For almost three decades, Dr. Berte served as president of Birmingham-Southern College, propelling the United Methodist school to a nationally recognized institution for both academic excellence and public service.

Despite his enormously successful tenure as Birmingham-Southern's president, Berte somehow found time to lead in other realms, even as he was a presence at BSC athletic events, student performances, and in classrooms. He became known for his ability to recognize and interact with hundreds of students on campus. Berte was a founder of Leadership Birmingham, and served as either president or chairman of the Birmingham Chamber of Commerce, the United Way, the Birmingham Kiwanis Club, and the Birmingham Civil Rights Institute.

Before assuming the presidency of Birmingham-Southern, Berte served as dean of the New College at the University of Alabama, earned a doctorate at the University of Cincinnati, and was named a Ford Foundation Scholar, Rockefeller Foundation Fellow, and Omicron Delta Kappa National Scholarship winner.

Berte also served the church tirelessly, serving in leadership roles in his local church (Canterbury United Methodist) and as a delegate to the General and Southeastern Jurisdiction Conferences (representing the North Alabama Conference).

No matter how wide and deep his civic leadership has been, the signature impact of Dr. Neal Berte's career has been his dynamic leadership that has made Birmingham-Southern College one of America's leading liberal arts institutions.

Buford Boone
Pulitzer Prize winning publisher
Tuscaloosa County

Buford Boone courageously endured threats to his business and safety as he built the *Tuscaloosa News*, and his family's Boone Publishing, into institutions still growing and thriving today.

Originally from Georgia, James Buford Boone, Sr., moved to Tuscaloosa to become the publisher of the *Tuscaloosa News* in 1947. Before his arrival in Alabama, Boone had served as a speechwriter for FBI Director J. Edgar Hoover, and as editor of the *Telegraph and News* in Macon, Georgia.

Ten years later, Boone himself became the news when he authored a Pulitzer-Prize-winning editorial that levied a scathing rebuke of the University of Alabama leadership for its handling of the Autherine Lucy admission into the university. The predictable threats poured in, directed at his newspaper, his personal safety, and his family. Boone consulted with local leaders, university officials, and even the new Alabama football coach, Paul "Bear" Bryant, about ways in which the extant racial issues could be handled peacefully.

If anyone believes that newspapers no longer thrive in the internet age, they can look no further than the BNI, the Boone family-owned company. Buford Boone's courageous handling of difficult issues was just one example of his outstanding contributions to the world of news and media. Another lies in the enormous success of his son and prote'ge', Jim Boone, who has led BNI to acquire and/or manage 82 newspapers along with websites, shopping guides and magazines in communities in Alabama, Georgia, Kentucky, Louisiana, Michigan, Minnesota, Mississippi, Virginia, North Carolina, Ohio, and Tennessee.

Amelia Boynton
Civil Rights pioneer
Dallas County

At the age of 103, Amelia Boynton was an honored guest, hosted by Congresswoman Terri Sewell, at the 2015 State of the Union address. Boynton and Sewell spent time with President Barack Obama after the conclusion of his speech. Later that year, Boynton passed away just eight days after her 104th birthday. Boynton spent most of the century that was her life fighting and winning battles for basic civil rights, equal protection under the law, and equality of opportunity.

After graduating from the Tuskegee Institute she ultimately landed in Dallas County, Alabama, for a job with the U.S. Department of Agriculture. There, in Selma, she met and married a local extension agent named Samuel Boynton. The two were a perfect match, with matching aspirations for voting rights, equal rights, and civil rights for all types of Americans. Amelia Boynton co-founded the Dallas County Voters League, and carried out a number of voter registration drives in Selma and Dallas County. She also became the first African American woman to run for Congress in Alabama, in 1964.

According to multiple sources, including biography.com, it was Amelia Boynton who asked the Rev. Dr. Martin Luther King, Jr., and the Southern Christian Leadership Conference to come to Selma. Dr. King did exactly that, and the Selma-to-Montgomery March, and the resulting Bloody Sunday, resulted in a number of marchers suffering unmerciful beatings at the hands of Alabama State Troopers.

An iconic photo of the bloody and beaten Amelia Boynton helped capture the nation's imagination, and most importantly its attention, leading to the passage of important voting rights legislation. So when Boynton and Sewell met with President Obama in 2015, it did not mark the first time Boynton had spent time with an American president. She was the guest of honor at President Lyndon B. Johnson's signing of the Voting Rights Act of 1965.

Did You Know???

Two Alabama college students changed the world just by enrolling

----

Many college students aspire to one day change the world, but Vivian Malone and James Hood did exactly that, just by enrolling as the first two African-American students at the University of Alabama. Their admission into the university was the result of lengthy litigation.

While a nation fearfully watching hoped that violent scenes in other states would not be repeated, the stand in the schoolhouse door by Governor George C. Wallace, while not helping the state's image, actually helped prevent violence.

In 1965, Jones became the university's first African-American graduate. Hood left school, but returned in the 1990s to earn his doctorate. He later attended George Wallace's funeral as a symbol of reconciliation.

That new law, in no small part, arose from the public sentiment inspired by the courageous Amelia Boynton and her fellow heroes who risked their lives at the Edmund Pettus Bridge in Selma.

Upon her passing in August of 2015, Congresswoman Sewell wrote: "Let us be inspired by the extraordinary life of Mrs. Amelia Boynton Robinson to keep striving and working towards a more perfect union. May we honor her by continuing her life's work."

Dr. Ed Bridges
Author, historian, archivist
Montgomery County

"He's more connected than Google."

Dr. Ed Bridges has become so deeply connected to Alabama's past, path, and people that he himself has become one of the state's treasures.

The remark about Bridges becoming more connected than Google was given by Leslie Sanders, president of the Montgomery Museum of Fine Arts Board of Trustees. The article was published by *The Montgomery Advertiser,* fittingly, on December 14, 2018, Alabama's 199th birthday and the official countdown to the bicentennial.

Bridges never would have foreseen his role as the state's great historian, mainly because he was born and raised elsewhere. A native of Bainbridge, Georgia, Bridges grew up learning about local history from the best local tour guide: his father. Although his dad hoped Ed would pursue a career in medicine, the tours left a profound impact on the younger Bridges, sparking a fascination with the path on which people, events, art, culture, and ideas converged to create history.

Bridges graduated from Furman University in Greenville, South Carolina, then earned his M.A. and Ph.D. in history from the University of Chicago. After teaching at the high school and college levels, he began his career as an archivist with the Georgia Department of Archives and History in 1976. After rising to the position of assistant director, he was appointed Director of the Alabama Department of Archives and History in 1982.

Dr. Bridges didn't just compile and preserve records; he shepherded the Alabama Department of Archives and

History into great growth in facilities, prestige, and user-friendliness for the public.

Even years after retiring, Bridges remains a highly valuable resource for the state, providing wise counsel for a variety of projects, from economic development to historical research. He accepted the call to serve as Interim Director of the Montgomery Museum of Fine Arts, and has served on a variety of boards.

All of his contributions and accomplishments, however, fall short of painting the picture of this still-significant career. Dr. Bridges has authored some of the most important historical books of the modern era, including most recently, *Alabama: The Making of an American State*. Among other works, Bridges co-authored *Of Goats & Governors: Six Decades of Colorful Alabama Political Stories* with the state's top political commentator, Steve Flowers.

In the same *Montgomery Advertiser* article of December 14, 2018, Bridges described writing a book as analogous to walking ten miles, because one just starts walking and does not stop until it's finished. Thankfully for Alabama, each step in the 200-year path has become better preserved, appreciated, and understood because of Dr. Ed Bridges.

Bobby Bright
Congressman, mayor of Montgomery
Montgomery County

The son of a sharecropper in Alabama's Wiregrass region (Dale County), Bobby Bright spent much of his childhood and youth working on a farm with his 13 siblings. After working to pay his way through Troy University, Bright was inspired toward a legal career by a job working as a corrections officer at a prison. He pursued a legal education at Montgomery's Thomas Goode Jones School of Law and practiced law for well over a decade.

Elected in 1999 over longtime incumbent Emory Folmar, Montgomery Mayor Bobby Bright led the charge to change the face of his adopted home city. The beautiful development along the river, Riverfront Park, includes the sports stadium, hotel, and convention center. Bright was instrumental in recruiting the Montgomery Biscuits (a Class AA minor league baseball team) back to Montgomery in 2004.

Although later elected to the United States Congress (2008), Bright will remain best known and appreciated for the decade he spent revitalizing the city of Montgomery.

Katie Boyd Britt
President, Business Council of Alabama
Coffee County

Katie Boyd Britt's meteoric rise, to the height of influence and power in Alabama, has become one of the signature stories of Alabama's bicentennial year.

It all began in Enterprise, Alabama, where achievement and responsibility became her trademark. Katie became governor of Alabama Girls State as a rising high school senior. She also made her debut on the national stage as the first runner-up in the America's Junior Miss Pageant (now called Distinguished Young Women).

College life at the University of Alabama presented a new arena, but the results were equally impressive, as Katie was elected president of the Student Government Association.

A natural leader, her talents, drive, and work ethic propelled her to a rapid journey up the ladder of leadership in the world of national and state politics. At age 23, she became the youngest press secretary in the U.S. Senate, when the legendary U.S. Senator Richard Shelby appointed her to that position on his staff.

After intervening years brought law school graduation, marriage to New England Patriots football player Wesley Britt (also a University of Alabama graduate), and practicing law, Katie returned to Washington as Shelby's Chief of Staff.

In 2018, Britt was named President of the Business Council of Alabama, the state's premier advocate for business interests on both the state and national levels. The BCA also stands atop the world of Alabama politics in endorsing and electing state, federal, and local candidates for public office.

Britt's rise to the pinnacle of government and politics has redirected the spotlight to a new generation of leaders, unencumbered by demographic categories, who are continuing Alabama's modern journey of success.

Despite the success and influence, Katie has remained well-grounded by the community and values that originally shaped her. In 2016, as she explained to her hometown newspaper, the *Southeast Sun*, "You know, I've had the opportunity to live in D.C., New England, Montgomery and Birmingham but when people ask me where I'm from I always say, Enterprise is home," Britt said. "Family and community, they're what make opportunity possible, and we have a really special one in our city."

David Bronner
CEO, Retirement Systems of Alabama
Montgomery County

Growing up in the small town of Austin, Minnesota, David Bronner was able to see what successful investments could do for a community. After all, Austin is known as SPAM-town, USA, as the home of Hormel foods and the place where most of the SPAM lunch meat is produced. Making lunch meats employs many people, but Hormel wasn't content with operating a major corporation. Austin also serves as home of the Hormel Institute, one of America's leading cancer research facilities, operated and funded by the University of Minnesota and the Mayo Clinic.

Maybe it was the Hormel example that inspired him, but regardless, the work of David Bronner for the state retirees of Alabama has yielded quality of life improvements for the state, along with financial benefits.

When Bronner left the University of Alabama to become head of the Retirement Systems of Alabama, the RSA had roughly half-a-billion dollars in assets and a 1.5 billion dollar I.O.U. from the state of Alabama.

Today, the RSA stands as one of the world's 50 largest retirement systems, holding over 40 billion dollars in assets, owning the largest commercial building in Manhattan, and maintaining enormous success through the energy crises of the 1970s, the crash of 1987, the tech-stock crash of 2000, and the Great Recession crash of 2008.

Bronner has used the RSA's investment in the Robert Trent Golf Trail to not only make massive financial returns, but to also play an important role in transforming the image of Alabama. The long-term national marketing campaign for the RTJ Golf Trail has yielded benefits that cannot be measured, as the improved image of the state has played a role in the recruitment of high-tech corporations, military contractors, and automotive manufacturers.

Jeff Brooks
National real estate developer
Shelby County

From an unassuming office in Shelby County, Jeff Brooks has become an emblem of Alabama's business success across America.

Brooks operates a national investment company managing hundreds of millions of dollars in assets for his clients. He has partnerned with major companies such as KKR of New York, one of the great global investment firms. Brooks is the founder and CEO of HighPoint Holdings which specializes in acquiring high-end properties in emerging markets.

His success has brought notoriety, even though he tries to limit his public profile. As AL.com described him: "Operating from its offices tucked away near Greystone off U.S. 280, chief executive and HighPoint founder Jeff Brooks said word-of-mouth and a track record have been all the publicity the firm has needed to add new business and investors."

The KKR deal involved an energy company in Texas in 2011, showing that the scope of HighPoint Holdings extends beyond real estate. The company has also led an investment group into a major media company with holdings across America. The media venture, like so many others orchestrated by Brooks, turned out grandly successful for his investors.

Brooks learned how to evaluate properties by growing up as part of Birmingham's Berry family, a longtime pillar of the community and deeply involved in the local real estate market. The experience and knowledge from his family served as a foundation for Brooks, empowering him to invest wisely, understand how and when to purchase properties, and most importantly, when to sell.

Working hard and playing by the rules, Brooks has propelled his investors and the image of Alabamians to greater heights while expanding his company's investment footprint across America.

Stephanie Bryan
CEO, Poarch Band of Creek Indians
Escambia County

Stephanie Bryan spends her life creating a bright future for her tribe and her family. As the Tribal Chair and CEO for the Poarch Band of Creek Indians, Bryan works to expand both educational opportunities and health insurance for tribal members. She played a significant role in the opening of both the new health clinic and its assisted living facility.

Bryan also leads on the national level, serving on legislative committees and Native American organizations such as the United South and Eastern Tribes, the National Indian Gaming Commission, and the National Indian Gaming Association.

Beyond tribal organizations, Bryan lends her considerable talent to local groups in Alabama, such as Support ACH (Atmore Community Hospital), the Escambia County Alabama Community Hospital Board, and the Mobile Area Chamber of Commerce Board of Advisors.

Bryan and her husband, Keith, also lead at home, having three children and ten grandchildren, thriving in the modern world while maintaining the values, traditions, and culture that have defined their tribal heritage for centuries.

Did You Know???

A star football player gave up a promising career to help children

John Croyle was an outstanding athlete who gave up the chance to play professional football.

Why? He felt called to start the Big Oak Boys' Ranch in 1974. He not only gave up his own financial gain, but as legend has it, he persuaded football legend and Alabama Crimson Tide teammate John Hanah to give up his signing bonus with the New England Patriots to help fund the ranch.

Through the years, the ranch has become a haven for boys, and now features a separate home for girls who have been abused, neglected, or left homeless.

Croyle's own children, Brodie Croyle and Reagan Croyle Phillips, now lead the team. Both of them, along with Reagan's husband John David Phillips, were star athletes at the University of Alabama.

Paul Bryant, Jr.
Founder, Bryant Bank
Tuscaloosa County

Paul Bryant Jr., has spent his life winning. In every realm of his career, Bryant has succeeded grandly in creating businesses, creating jobs, and creating opportunities for future generations. Blessed with a mind for business and timing, Bryant has succeeded at everything from running a professional baseball team, to founding a prominent bank, to leading the University of Alabama System Board of Trustees during a period of unprecedented growth.

Although he grew up as the son of a legend, Alabama Coach Paul "Bear" Bryant, Paul Jr. has been unaffected by the aura of his father as he forged his own path of success. Bryant has either founded or built companies in insurance, catfish farming, concrete (Ready Mix USA), gaming (Greenetrack, in Greene County, Alabama) and Bryant Bank (founded in 2005). Bryant has also co-authored two books about the University of Alabama football program.

Bryant's success, however, is only the beginning of the story. His generosity and zeal for helping others have combined to become the source of his greatest impact. Bryant has donated tens of millions of dollars to make his alma mater, the University of Alabama, a world-class institution. He used Bryant Bank as a tool to play a major role in financing the rebuilding of Tuscaloosa after the devastating 2011 tornadoes.

Dr. Peter Bryce
Mental health pioneer
Tuscaloosa County

Many people complain about their large or crazy families, but Peter Bryce spent his life loving his large family and making their lives better.

When Bryce and his newlywed wife, Ellen, arrived in Tuscaloosa from their native South Carolina, the patients at the Alabama Insane Hospital became their family.

At the tender age of 26, Bryce was hired as the director

Starting at the **TOP**

An Alabama Governor founded a nationally known insurance company

------

One of Alabama's greatest businesses was founded by the state's leading citizen.

William Jelks served as Alabama Governor from 1901 to 1907. In 1907, after his term as governor ended, Jelks founded the Protective Life Insurance Company. According to the *Encyclopedia of Alabama*, the company had expanded to six states while holding $7 million in assets by the time Jelks retired in 1929. Jelks was the great uncle of Ambassador William Jelks Cabiness of Birmingham.

Protective has been blessed with extraordinary leaders, including Col. William Rushton, who assumed leadership in 1937 and grew the company.

Then came Billy Rushton, a dynamic leader who became the company's head in 1969 and transformed it into a truly national company.

Future Chief Justice of Alabama Drayton Nabers successfully led the company for years, as did his successor, John D. Johns. Nabers, who clerked for Justice Hugo Black after law school, also authored a motivational and spiritual book that has been used for studies by individuals and groups.

Current CEO Richard Bielen served as CFO for ten years before taking the reins of leadership and a grand tradition of success.

Johns, who serves as executive chairman, has led a philanthropic drive to donate more than $23 million to charitable causes by 2020. Johns was named to Yellowhammer's 20 most powerful people in Alabama in 2018.

of the hospital in 1860. Despite his youth, Bryce had already developed an impressive background of experience and study of the mentally challenged in Europe, New Jersey, and back home in South Carolina. He had been educated at the institution now known as the New York University School of Medicine. Bryce had become particularly known for advocating the moral treatment of the mentally ill as opposed to the straight jackets, shackles, and other tortuous instruments used to imprison people whom society did not yet understand.

Bryce required absolute courtesy and manners from his staff to the patients. The patients, in turn, were trusted with meaningful and educational work such as farming, sewing, carpentry, and undergoing therapy. Bryce believed that providing a daily purpose and routine for the patients, as well as avoiding idle time, would give their minds rest and acceptance of normal behavior.

In the height of irony, the outside world may have become more insane than the hospital just one year into his tenure, when the Civil War began in 1861. The state and its people would soon be ravaged by war, and the funding for the hospital would sink far down the priority list.

Thankfully, the farming and other work at the hospital provided needed revenue that helped keep the hospital open. So as the outside world was overtaken with organized violence, Dr. and Mrs. Bryce, and their patients, continued their routine of working hard and treating each other peacefully and respectfully.

Bryce became nationally known for his pioneering of the moral treatment philosophy, and served as president of the American Psychiatric Association.

Now, the hospital is named after Dr. Bryce, and the countless success stories can be explained by the fact that Peter and Ellen loved their family.

Bush Hog

Nationally known equipment company
Dallas County

It happened on a local farm, near Selma, in the heart of Alabama's Black Belt. It was likely a winter's day, because each of the nine people were wearing long-sleeved shirts and three wore jackets. All of the trees were bare, except for the pines.

That's when he said it.

The words were simple, but they rang out from Selma across the globe, to farms, to industrial sites, and in road medians where cities and states keep their highways beautiful.

As people from the newly founded business in Selma were demonstrating their device that was designed to clear pasture and crop residue, one of the men exclaimed that, "That thing eats bushes like a hog!"

And that's the moment when the name of Bush Hog was born.

Today, Bush Hog products mow over 30 million acres per year. The mighty machines are still produced in Selma, where a highly skilled work force of 350 produce over 17 different product lines. The state-of-the-art facility now includes robotic welders.

Clearly, the combination of skilled workers and complex technology works well, as many of the Bush Hog products in use today are over 30 years old.

The name began with those words, but in many ways the first cleverly designed Bush Hog machine was created in the same way...meeting the needs of customers.

While operating a farm equipment dealership in Selma, brothers Orby and Forby Lawrence grew to understand that cutting equipment wasn't typically reliable. There was too much down time because of breakdowns. The Lawrence Brothers worked hard, and designed a machine that would be different from anything on the market.

As Bush Hog President Jerry Worthington described it, the equipment had three original features that ultimately launched an international company. "First was the way that the blade is attached to the gear box," he explained. "The blade actually retracts when it hits a big object. The second is that it was covered by metal, with an enclosed rear."

A third feature also helped the product sell quickly.

"Their product would fit with all tractors, so it was universally accepted in the market," Worthington added.

The timing could not have been better, as companies such as John Deere, Massey Ferguson, Ford, and others were basically coming of age with their tractors on the market, and Bush Hog's rotary cutter fit each of them.

And then came the salesman.

The Lawrence brothers hired a decorated Air Force veteran, Earl Goodwin, whose name many might recognize as the long-serving state senator from Selma. It was his Bush Hog service, however, that really put his name, and his company, on the map as a big local success. "Goodwin promoted Bush Hog and helped it grow," Worthington added. "He didn't just travel from Selma, but had sales reps in all areas of the country." Today, Bush Hog has 38 territories in the United States, with 40 to 50 dealerships in each territory.

As with many growing companies, Bush Hog began to expand their product line. But it was the way they did it, according to Ricky Pendley, that was brilliant. "They called it the 'voice of the customer,' through which customers and dealers would suggest new products," Pendley explained.

Pendley knows plenty about Bush Hog's history, having worked for the company during a majority of its existence...a whopping 39 years before retiring in June of 2018.

The King
of Huntsville

Olin King became one of the great business leaders in Alabama history, pioneering the involvement of private companies with the space program in Huntsville.

By the Numbers

1..SCI Systems (originally called Space Craft Inc.) became #1, as the largest contracting electronics company in the world.

17...SCI, by the time of King's retirement, had operations in 17 different countries.

31,500...Over 31,500 employees worked for SCI at the height of King's career. Many of those jobs were based in Huntsville and Arab, and that amazing number does not include the employees of contracting companies.

$6 billion...In 2001, the Sanmina Corporation from California purchased SCI Systems for a whopping $6 billion.

Paul Butrus
Health care and insurance pioneer
Jefferson County

Paul Butrus was one of those consequential leaders of business and government whom only insiders know about...and that is just how he liked it.

Butrus earned degrees from Notre Dame and Northwestern Business School (Kellogg) in the 1960s before beginning his career at Vulcan Materials working for CEO Bernard Monaghan. Over time, he moved in a mix of the business and political worlds. After working on the campaign of U.S. Senator John Sparkman in the 1960s, he became a key advisor in his 1972 re-election. Relying on his organizational skills, he also became an advisor to other political leaders including Senator Howell Heflin and Governor Jim Folsom in later years.

Alabama was still a "one-party" (i.e., Democratic) state in the 1970s and Paul Butrus was chosen to be vice-chair of the state party where he represented the business perspective at a time when the business community shared in the leadership of the party. Butrus was part of the generation of leaders who were working under the leadership of one-time party chair (and later federal judge) Robert Vance to positively shape the post-Wallace focus of government in Alabama.

While he was one who clearly liked politics, Paul Butrus turned down opportunities for public appointments over the years. He was happy to work behind the scenes and let others take credit and be recognized. He also turned down those opportunities because he was first and foremost a businessman. He had an MBA from the Kellogg School at Northwestern and he knew how to use it. Following his time at Vulcan Materials, he led several young businesses in the health and technology area in the early 1970s.

By the mid-1970s, a nationwide medical malpractice insurance problem was being felt in Alabama. Paul Butrus had helped turn around and lead businesses that various Alabama doctors (including Dr. Derrill Crowe who would become his long time business partner) had invested in. Thus, he was the logical person for Alabama doctors to recruit to help them follow the national trend and start an Alabama-focused "med mal" mutual insurance company to insure (and ultimately provide stability for) the medical profession in Alabama. Some state requirements were modified and the Mutual Assurance Society of Alabama was founded and licensed in 1976. Butrus worked for the company for over three decades, as it grew, before retiring as vice chairman. Today, that company is known as ProAssurance, and it is a national insurance leader that operates in all 50 states and has a market capitalization of several billion dollars.

Even as ProAssurance grew, Butrus and Crowe helped launch a number of other successful businesses in the health care area that produced positive results for investors and Alabama. At the same time, Butrus continued to participate in state politics and policy including working on various tort reform efforts over the years.

Profile provided courtesy of Greg Butrus, the son of Paul Butrus and an attorney with the law firm of Balch & Bingham.

Pat Byington
Environmental activist and leader
Colbert and Jefferson Counties

Pat Byington has established a legacy as one of the great environmentalists in Alabama's 200-year history.

A native of Sheffield, Byington graduated from the University of Alabama, where he studied in the university's

New College, became a leader in campus politics and an environmental activist. He served as executive director of both the Alabama Environmental Council and Wild South. For over 18 years, he served as publisher of the *Bama Environmental News*.

Byington played a pivotal role in creating the Alabama Forever Wild program. He also served in an active role with the Little River Canyon National Preserve, and with efforts relating to regulations on mercury standards in the environment.

Ehney Camp, Jr.
Businessman, benefactor
Shelby and Jefferson Counties

Ehney Camp, Jr., led a two-track life in which his professional accomplishments were matched by his tireless work to improve the health and education of Alabamians.

Born in Maylene, Alabama, Camp's family moved to Columbiana during his childhood, where he excelled in school. At the University of Alabama, Camp was named the Outstanding Male Scholar of the class of 1928, and inducted into the prestigious Jasons Senior Men's Honorary, Phi Beta Kappa, and Sigma Nu fraternity.

Camp then blazed a legendary path in the insurance industry, primarily with Birmingham's Liberty National Insurance Company. An expert in the fields of mortgage banking and life insurance, Camp served on a variety of national boards, and was asked by President Dwight Eisenhower to serve on the Special Advisory Committee on Government Housing Policies and Programs.

Beyond his professional expertise, the work of Ehney Camp, Jr., in the community left a lasting impact. He became a leader in the fight against tuberculosis, serving as the president of the Jefferson County Anti-Tuberculosis Society and as a member of the boards of directors of the County Tuberculosis Sanitarium and the Campaign Against Tuberculosis.

Camp led many other organizations that benefitted the community, because leadership was his life's calling. Camp also led the Birmingham Kiwanis Club, the Jefferson County Community Chest Campaign, and (in several different capacities) the lay leadership of Birmingham's First United Methodist Church, and the University of Alabama Board of Trustees.

Camp's legacy continues, through both endowed scholarships and the public service of his descendants, including his son, leading Birmingham businessman Ehney Camp, III, and grandson David Faulkner, who serves in the Alabama House of Representatives.

Dr. Charles Carter
Leading Southern Baptist minister
Jefferson County

Dr. Charles Carter has been called "the most respected Alabama Baptist leader of our generation."

At the age of six, Charles T. Carter was invited by a neighbor to Calvary Baptist Church in Birmingham. During his childhood, he realized that he had been called to preach the Word of God. By the age of 16, he became the pastor of the West End Baptist Church in Birmingham.

He graduated from Samford University in 1956, and within ten years he became the pastor of Whitesburg Baptist Church in Huntsville. Known as a dynamic preacher who also shepherded his flock of members and visitors, Carter became a pastor highly coveted by churches.

In 1972, he became the pastor of Shades Mountain Baptist Church in the Birmingham suburb of Vestavia Hills. By the time Dr. Carter retired, the church had grown to almost 7,000 members, and Dr. Carter was regarded as a giant of the Southern Baptist denomination. He also helped lead the denomination, serving two terms as president of the Alabama Baptist State Convention (1988, 1989) and nine years on its International Mission Board.

In 2012, Samford University's Beeson Divinity School announced an endowed chair to honor Carter, a longtime trustee. "We are honoring Charles Carter because he is the most respected Alabama Baptist leader of our generation, a great preacher and pastor for many years and a faithful professor at Beeson Divinity School," said Dean Timothy George.

Many years after his retirement, Carter continues bringing messages of salvation and healing, occasionally serving as interim pastor at various churches. As Alabama began its bicentennial celebration, Dr. Carter had returned to his roots, serving as interim pastor of Whitesburg Baptist Church in Huntsville.

Sonny Cauthen
Cattleman, lobbyist, political strategist
Montgomery County

As legend has it, Senator Al Gore was in flight on the way to meet with Governor Bill Clinton about becoming the vice presidential candidate in 1992. On the way to Arkansas, he called Sonny Cauthen for advice. Harvey E. "Sonny" Cauthen, Jr., has long been a fixture on Alabama's political scene. He has socialized with presidents and heads of state.

Cauthen began his political career as a volunteer in the 1970 Alabama gubernatorial campaign, advancing to the ranks of a paid campaign staffer in the 1974 race. He later worked as the executive assistant to a former Public Service Commissioner, allowing him to develop an expertise in the electricity industry and the legislative and executive branches of Alabama government. Shortly thereafter, he founded Cauthen & Associates.

A former member of the Alabama State Democratic Executive Committee and a veteran of several state and national campaigns, Cauthen served both the Clinton/Gore '96 reelection campaign and the 2000 Gore/Lieberman campaign as vice chairman for Business Outreach. He was a trustee of the Democratic National Committee and member of the National Finance Board and the Democratic Business Council.

Cauthen also provided important lobbying work on the massive Telecommunications Act of 1996 during the Clinton presidency.

Outside the firm, Cauthen is involved in several agricultural operations, including a diversified, family owned cattle ranch. He also holds an interest in the Teague Crossing Development Company, with properties adjacent to the Hyundai Motor Manufacturing Alabama plant near Montgomery. As an avid outdoorsman, Cauthen maintains the family ranch as a hunting preserve. He sits on the board of directors of the Alabama Wildlife Federation.

Born in Montgomery, Alabama, Cauthen graduated from the University of Alabama and is married to the former Florence Minor Mangum, also a native of Montgomery. She is an attorney and former U. S. Marshal for the Middle District of Alabama. They have two children, Belle Churchwell Cauthen and Eugene Preston Mangum Cauthen.

Richard Cohen
President
Southern Poverty Law Center
Montgomery County

As a highly skilled lawyer with degrees from Columbia and the University of Virginia School of Law, Richard Cohen could practice law anywhere.

He has chosen to spend his career fighting for the rights of the mistreated.

As president of the Southern Poverty Law Center in Montgomery, Cohen has led the fight against hate groups, served as a leading advocate for the rights of prisoners, and used the justice system to bring about more equitable educational opportunities for all American children.

One national magazine named him one of the 45 public sector lawyers who was changing lives through his work.

In 1998, Cohen won a 37.8 million dollar judgment against a South Carolina Ku Klux Klan organization involved in a church burning. As the SPLC website described it, "On the evening of June 21, 1995, members of the Christian Knights poured flammable liquids on the floor of a 100-year-old black Baptist church, ignited a fire and watched the building go up in flames."

Cohen was named a finalist for national Trial Lawyer of the Year based on his work in that case. In 2000, he sued an Aryan Nation leader and won a 6 million dollar verdict against the individual and the organization. In 2001, Cohen filed the lawsuit against Alabama Chief Justice Roy Moore that ultimately resulted in Moore's first expulsion from office.

Using the judicial system, Cohen has crippled the capacity of domestic terrorist groups. Using SPLC resources such as Hate Watch, he has helped shine the light of public scrutiny on groups that promote hate and domestic terror.

Tom Coker
Leader, lobbyist
Montgomery County

Over the last 50 years, Tom Coker has helped shape Alabama's political landscape through serving our national government and later representing institutions and businesses.

His ascent to the top of Alabama politics began when Senator James Allen appointed Coker as his Chief of Staff in Washington. Allen was no ordinary senator, as his mastery of parliamentary procedure and cordial relations across party lines distinguished him as a leader. As his top aide, Coker learned the art of government and politics, empowering his future rise to influence.

Coker also served as the first director of Senator Howell Heflin's in-state operation, expanding both his expertise in government and his growing personal network.

In the early 1980s, Coker played a pivotal role in helping Alabama Power President Elmer Harris form the Business Council of Alabama. Serving as vice president, Coker was placed in charge of developing the new organization's membership, a critical factor in the BCA's future grass-roots success.

As the head of Tom Coker and Associates, he has represented a variety of important institutions in the state. According to one account by *The Birmingham News*, his client list has included Alabama Power, Altria, the Alabama Medical Association, the Alabama Hospital Association, the Alabama School of Fine Arts, Troy University, the University of Alabama, as well as the state's district attorneys and district and circuit court judges associations.

In his five decades at the center of Alabama government, Coker has become an important resource of wise counsel for institutions, elected officials, and those who aspire to public service.

The Gold Rush
In Alabama

In 1985, Gold Ridge Baptist Church, near Ranburne, celebrated its 150th anniversary. The origin of the church's name might be lost on many in the 21st century, but back in the day, the area of northern Randolph County and southern Cleburne County was the site of a major gold rush.

Things have changed quite a bit since 1835, when the area was dominated by gold mines of the Arbacoochee gold district.

At its height, the Arbacoochee district was home to as many as 5,000 people while employing 600 gold miners. Other communities in Alabama, like Goldville, were equally prosperous.

Everything changed in 1849, with the California gold rush, as most miners left for the promise of riches in the Golden State.

Gold Ridge Baptist Church remains a leading church in the community, and one of the few testaments to a largely forgotten era of Alabama history.

The Collat family
Business leaders, benefactors
Jefferson County

The journey of Mayer (formerly Mayer Electric) began in 1930, and continues on the paths of great success and generosity to the City of Birmingham.

One doesn't have to look far to see the impact of the Collat family. The Collat School of Business at the University of Alabama at Birmingham, the vast contributions to Alzheimer's research, the Collat Congregational Center and Collat Jewish Services represent just a few of the ways in which this family has made their hometown a better place.

Originally founded by Ben S. Weil, the Great Depression harmed his business and forced a sale to Max Mayer, who placed his own name in the company's title. By 1934, Weil was able to repurchase the company.

Weil's daughter (Patsy) and son (Leonard) joined the company, and ultimately Patsy's husband, Charles Collat, joined the team as well. In 1979, Charles and Patsy Collat purchased full ownership of the company. Exponential growth followed.

As it thrives in the digital age, the former Mayer Electric has dropped the word "Electric" from the title and now uses only the name "Mayer," signifying its adjustment to modern technology and the dynamics of 21st century market forces.

Nancy Collat Goedecke (daughter of Charles and Patsy) now serves as Mayer Chairman and CEO, making Mayer

one of the largest female-owned companies in America.
Mayer now employs over 1,200 associates in 11 states, generating over $800 million in annual revenue.

Tim Cook
CEO of Apple
Baldwin County

In 1998, Tim Cook was offered a job at a company that had lost a billion dollars in the previous year. In many ways, taking the offer would amount to a career-risking move, but Cook, a graduate of Auburn University, thought he saw the potential for greatness.

Cook did indeed take that job as a vice president at Apple, and his contributions played an important part in transforming the company from a loser to history's biggest winner.

A native of Robertsdale, Alabama (Baldwin County), Cook majored in engineering at Auburn, and then earned a master's degree in business at Duke University. He rose quickly within the ranks of his first employer, IBM, and was ultimately promoted to North American fulfillment director. He spent the next three years as chief operating officer of the Reseller Division at Intelligent Electronics, and then was hired as vice president of Compaq Computer Corporation before Apple came calling.

Somehow, Cook felt compelled to join the Apple team. That might seem like an easy decision looking back, but at the time, many thought the company's future was doomed. Even the chairman of Dell Computers remarked that the best move for Apple would be just to close the company and give the investment money back to its shareholders.

But Cook took on the challenge, and was hired as a company vice president. He was placed in charge of the company's distribution and supply chains, which were poorly organized and serving as an unnecessary cost center for the company. The Auburn alumnus quickly orchestrated a turnaround of the company's system, as well as its bottom line. His changes allowed Apple to more efficiently and affordably connect its customers with its products. He rose to become Apple's chief operating officer under Apple's legendary leader, Chairman Steve Jobs.

In 2011 Jobs, faced serious health issues, and Cook was named as the acting head of the company during his leave. Ultimately, Jobs retired, just months before his passing. Alabama's own Tim Cook was chosen as the new chief executive officer of Apple, and the company has soared to even greater heights under his leadership. Cook's previous work as temporary leader had prepared him for the job, so the move wasn't unexpected. Still, Cook was a largely unknown commodity when tapped to lead the tech giant. CNN pondered the future of Apple's unknown Cook taking over the company, describing him as "a workaholic whose only interests outside of Apple appear to be cycling, the outdoors, and Auburn football."

Cook has led Apple to introduce products and services such as Apple Pay, the Apple Watch, burst-selfies, and countless new innovations. One innovation relates to the company's culture, rather than its products. Tim Cook has famously promoted a culture of harmony, even forcing out senior executives at Apple who were abrasive, unfriendly, and unable to get along with others in the Apple family. Through cultural changes, product unveilings and the force of his personality, Cook's leadership has resulted in Apple becoming the first trillion dollar-company in world history.

Did You Know?

One of Hollywood's newest stars grew up in the Presbyterian Home for Children?

Motell Foster has established himself as a rising movie star. After years in foster homes, Motell was blessed by the care of the Presbyterian Home for Children in Talladega. Founded in the wake of the Civil War to care for orphans of the war-ravaged Alabama, the home has remained a beacon of love and stability for children and families for over 150 years.

Foster earned his way to the prestigious New York University, and then made it to the big stage. At the celebration of the state's bicentennial, his most recent movie was *A Dog's Way Home*. Unlike some who succeed grandly, Motell has not forgotten his roots. He enjoys returning to the Presbyterian Home for Children, and became an inaugural member of the Children's Rights Young Professional Leadership Council.

The Cooper family
Shipping magnates
Mobile County

For over 100 years, the Cooper family has employed local workers, provided valuable services, and donated generously to the Mobile and Baldwin County communities.

Angus Cooper was the 13th of the 14 children born to Henry and Matilda Cooper. Angus, through hard work and ingenuity, began the family business of providing stevedoring services in port cities.

In 1905, he founded the Cooper/T. Smith company, and the company has never stopped growing. Today, Cooper/T. Smith has an important presence on all three American coasts, Central America, South America, and Canada, employing thousands of workers and consistently expanding the scope of its services and its holdings.

One of the largest maritime firms in the world, Cooper/T. Smith handles not only stevedoring, but also logistics, tugboats, barge services, terminal operations, forestry services, shipyard facilities and vessel repair.

The company now owns a variety of popular restaurants along the Gulf Coast region in Alabama and Mississippi.

No measure of success or international acclaim has prevented the Cooper family from generously giving of their time and resources to their local community, and to institutions such as the University of Alabama.

Cooper Riverside Park honors the memory of Ervin S. Cooper (1911-1982). The elegant statue depicts Ervin Cooper watching over the Mobile waterfront.

Angus Cooper II, grandson of the company's founder, has shepherded the company to international success while remaining in his hometown and state. Cooper has served on the boards of directors of Whitney National Bank of New Orleans, the National World War II Museum, the Coast Guard Foundation, Crescent Towing & Salvage Company, the Gulf Coast Conservation Association, the University of Alabama, and the Mobile Red Elephant Club. He has served as a director of the Federal Reserve, and as Chairman of the Port of New Orleans.

Continuing the parallel family traditions of commercial success and public service, Angus Cooper III has served as Chairman of the Board of Directors for the Alabama State Port Authority, Chairman of the Board of Trustees for UMS-Wright Preparatory School, Alabama Forever Wild Land Trust Board of Directors, 1st Vice Chairman of the Board of Alabama Wildlife Federation, Alabama Sports Hall of Fame Board of Directors, Bryant-Jordan Student Athlete Program Board of Directors, Bryant Bank Board of Directors, Treasurer for National Association of Waterfront Employers (NAWE), and University of Alabama Delta Kappa Epsilon House Corporation Board of Directors.

Miles Copeland, Jr.
CIA Spymaster
Jefferson County

Miles Copeland, Jr., was one of America's greatest spies, spy masters, and provocateurs rolled up into one magnificent, outsized personality. After his retirement from the CIA (Central Intelligence Agency), he authored multiple books and columns, including many pieces for William F. Buckley's iconic *National Review*. He was part-James Bond, part-*Mission Impossible*, part-Jack Ryan, part-Gabriel Allon and all-Alabama.

Born the son of a doctor in Birmingham, Copeland found himself in the National Guard during World War II. Presumably through the help of his father, Copeland was introduced to legendary spymaster William "Wild Bill" Donovan by Alabama Congressman John Sparkman. With the aid of his CIA sidekick Kim Roosevelt (grandson of President Theodore Roosevelt), Copeland orchestrated the overthrow of the Iranian government in 1953, the forced exit of Kwame Nkrumah of Ghana, and development of a personal rapport with the Egyptian leader, Gamal Abdel Nassar. Copeland was widely known as Nassar's closest confidante from the Western world. He opposed the disastrous "Bay of Pigs" operation in Cuba, believing that the operation was too large to remain undiscovered in advance.

His obituary in *National Review* described his "good-ole-boy Alabama drawl, that fluency in Arabic and a half-dozen other languages, and nearly fifty years of living in London, had done nothing to erase."

His last column for *National Review* in 1988 was titled "Spooks for Bush," endorsing George H.W. Bush for the presidency based on his worldview and understanding of the world's nations and leaders.

Even in his later years, Copeland remained an unabashed advocate of the CIA's aggressive posture in world affairs that had defined it during the Cold War years. In an interview with *Rolling Stone* magazine, he grabbed headlines with his opinion that the CIA should be conducting more, not less, of its cloak-and-dagger, government-overthrowing adventures.

Copeland's son, Stewart, was the drummer and a founding member of the rock band *The Police*. Son Copeland Miles, III, founded I.R.S. Records, one of the industry's most successful record labels. Daughter Lorraine is a highly successful writer and producer. Son Ian made his own impact on American music; as an acclaimed promoter, he helped launch the *New Wave* movement in the United States, promoting groups like *The Police*, the *B-52's* the *Go-Go's*, *The Cure*, and countless others.

Did You Know???

Some of America's most sacred monuments were constructed with Sylacauga Marble

———

Marble mined from Sylacauga, Alabama was used for the Lincoln Memorial, the U.S. Supreme Court building, and the bust of President Lincoln in the U.S. Capitol building

Marble was first discovered in the Sylacauga area by Edward Gantt, who was traveling through the area with General Andrew Jackson in 1814.

Tom Corts
President, Samford University
Jefferson County

Thomas Corts not only led a major university for two decades, he spent a lifetime serving as the ideal model of a servant-leader.

He came to Birmingham in 1983, to serve as president of Samford University, and spent the rest of his life serving in Alabama and on the international scene.

Born in Indiana and raised in Ohio, Corts graduated from Georgetown College (in Kentucky) before earning both his master's and doctorate from Indiana University. After working at his alma mater of Georgetown, Corts served as president of Wingate College (North Carolina) before being tapped to lead Samford in 1983. For the next 23 years, Corts led Samford to a period of unprecedented growth and expansion in academics, facilities, endowment, and reputation. He also stood tall as a reformist within the state of Alabama.

After his retirement in 2006, Corts was appointed, by President Bush, as coordinator of The President's Initiative to Expand Education and subsequently as Coordinator of Basic Education in the Office of the Director of Foreign Assistance, U.S. State Department. His work helped educate over four million in at least six different impoverished nations.

For Corts, serving came naturally because he loved people. That love propelled him into leadership, and that leadership impacted countless people at his beloved Samford University, and across the globe.

Mark Crosswhite
President, Alabama Power Company
Jefferson County

Mark Crosswhite has spent his career providing Alabama with a brighter future.

As chairman, president and chief executive officer of Alabama Power Company, he has literally made the state brighter to over 1.4 million customers across the state of Alabama. Before taking the helm at Alabama Power, he led Southern Company Operations, and was responsible for Southern Power, which provides energy to municipalities, electric cooperatives, and investor-owned utilities.

Even though he has risen to the pinnacle of the world of energy, Crosswhite has worked tirelessly to make the state brighter in other ways as well. He has vaulted Alabama Power Company back into a pivotal leadership position in the Business Council of Alabama, helping restore that organization's prestige and influence. He serves as chairman of the board of both the Economic Development Partnership of Alabama and the United Way of Central Alabama. He has generously lent his time to organizations across the state, such as the Birmingham Zoo, Birmingham Business Alliance, Business Council of Alabama, Mercedes-Benz U.S. International Inc., Southern Research, the University of Alabama Law School Foundation, and Leadership Birmingham. He also serves on the President's Advisory Council of the Freshwater Land Trust and is a member of the President's Cabinet of the University of Alabama.

Leading Alabama means that Crosswhite has come a long way since his teenage years, working at the wave pool at Decatur's Point Mallard Park. Crosswhite's life of service has already made a difference for the people of Alabama, in recruiting new industry to the state, developing the *Alabama News Center*, or through the seemingly endless charitable contributions made by Alabama Power.

The deGraffenried family
Leaders, legislators
Tuscaloosa County

For many generations, the deGraffenried family has led the state of Alabama, in both the United States Congress and in the halls of the state capitol in Montgomery.

Edward deGraffenried, who was affectionally known as "Mr. Ed," grew up in the tradition of public service, as his father (Edward) was an appellate judge in Alabama. After continuing the family tradition by graduating from the University of Alabama School of Law in 1921, Mr. Ed became a Solicitor (now known as a District Attorney) and was twice elected to the United States Congress.

Mr. Ed was an exceptionally effective mentor, as he not only guided his own sons to great success, but also taught the art of politics to a young prote`ge`, Richard C. Shelby, who became one of the greatest national statesman ever produced by Alabama.

Ryan deGraffenried, one of Mr. Ed's sons, was elected to the Alabama State Senate at a young age, and quickly developed a large and loyal following in Tuscaloosa and beyond. Taking a courageous stand in favor of racial integration, Ryan deGraffenried ran for governor against George Wallace in 1962. State law prevented Wallace from seeking reelection in 1966, so he ran his wife to succeed him, and deGraffenried once again became the opponent.

Senator Ryan deGraffenried had become a rising star in state politics and the face of the opposition to the politics of George Wallace. He had become a formidable opponent of the Wallace family until a fatal airplane crash, in Dekalb County, took his life during that 1966 campaign.

His son, Ryan deGraffenried, Jr., assumed the mantle of public service at an early age, serving as a Key Club lieutenant governor during high school. Ultimately, he ran for the Alabama Senate, filling the seat of his grandfather's prote`ge`, Richard Shelby, who had just been elected to the U.S. Congress. Ryan Jr. became an accomplished member of the Legislature, rising to the position of president pro tempore of the Alabama State Senate in the 1990s. After his years in the Senate, Ryan deGraffenried, Jr. continued another family tradition, the practice of law, and also served as a popular adjunct professor at the University of Alabama School of Law.

Augusta Dowd
Leading attorney
Jefferson County

Augusta Dowd has become the model 21st century woman of influence and power, reaching the height of professional excellence while successfully raising a family. That journey reached yet another peak in 2017, as she assumed the duties of office as the 142nd President of the Alabama State Bar.

Dowd, a native of Birmingham, graduated from the University of the South and the Vanderbilt University School of Law. She entered the professional world as a law clerk to longtime U.S. District Court Judge Seybourn H. Lynne. She practiced with the Lange-Simpson firm until leaving the practice of law, upon the birth of her third child, to raise her children while her husband practiced law with Burr & Forman.

Dowd returned to the practice of law in 2000, with the firm now named White Arnold & Dowd, using her vast experience in defending white collar crime cases, class action, complex litigation, personal injury, mass tort, pharmaceutical, environmental tort, and whistleblower actions.

Some of her many honors and accomplishments include the highly coveted AV-rating from Martindale-Hubbell, The Best Lawyers in America (2007-Present); *B-Metro Magazine*, Top Women Attorneys (2015); Mass Tort Lawyer of the Year; Top 10 Lawyers in Alabama (2011); Super Lawyers, Top 25 Women Lawyers in Alabama (2008-Present); and Top 50 Lawyers in Alabama (2008-Present).

Dowd somehow finds time to contribute to the Birmingham community, including service with the YWCA of Central Alabama, where she has been a member of the board of directors since 2010, and the Episcopal Diocese of Alabama, where she has served as assistant chancellor to the Bishop of the Episcopal Diocese of Alabama since 2009.

Dr. Nancy Dunlap
Medical community leader
Jefferson County

Dr. Nancy Dunlap has spent her career placing Alabama's medical community in a posture to provide the best in health care and to produce the best research. Her seemingly inexhaustible energy and willingness to serve the greater good has made her one of Alabama's great public servants.

After earning a biology degree at Wellesley College and a medical degree from Duke University, Dunlap studied at UAB, where she earned a Ph.D. in microbiology. After earning an MBA from the University of Michigan, Dunlap embarked on a journey that would lead her into the field of pulmonary critical care, and then as a leader in the medical profession.

After serving as Interim Dean of the University of Virginia School of Medicine, Dunlap now leads as a director of Southern Research Institute, Inc., and also as a Scholar at the UAB's Lister Hill Center for Health Policy. At the request of the National Governors Association, she has also served as physician-in-residence at the organization's Center for Best Practices Health Division. In that capacity, Dr. Dunlap helped develop recommendations for states to contain health care costs, manage diseases and improve technology.

Dr. Dunlap has used her considerable talents to help both individual patients and our entire society through her tireless efforts to improve health care for all.

Clifford & Virginia Durr
Leading activists
Montgomery County

Clifford and Virginia Foster Durr devoted their lives to the cause of individual liberties. Along the way, they sacrificed wealth, status, and even their own safety for their life's central cause.

But it didn't start out that way.

Clifford Durr was raised as the son of a prominent Montgomery family, and he charted a course of leadership, achievement, prominence, and wealth. He became class president at the University of Alabama, and then a Rhodes Scholar, studying two years in Oxford, England. He joined the law firm of Martin, Thompson, Foster, and Turner (now Balch & Bingham), and the sky was the limit for his career. The law firm, founded by Logan Martin, represented utilities, banks, and other financial interests, so Clifford Durr had entered the world of representing the big mules of society.

But then he met Virginia.

Virginia Foster was the daughter of a Presbyterian minister who had already sacrificed for his own cause, leaving the church over a doctrinal dispute. Virginia had turned down multiple suitors, and her family feared she would never marry until she met Clifford. The two married, and Virginia's brother-in-law, U.S. Senator Hugo Black, recommended Clifford for a post in the New Deal administration of President Franklin Delano Roosevelt.

Clifford left the lucrative practice of law for the cause of the New Deal.

The Durrs spent many years in Washington developing a network of friends and allies more leftist in outlook than they had befriended in the past. Clifford Durr's worldview and outlook changed dramatically, as he became more alike in thought and deed to his wife and his brother-in-law. He took increasingly liberal and combative positions for the causes and issues in which he strongly believed.

Virginia was no less zealous in her own path of service and leadership. She was a co-founder of the Southern Conference for Human Welfare, a coalition whose membership crossed racial lines and fought to achieve progress in human rights and civil rights. At the groups's first conference, the attending guests included First Lady of the United States, Eleanor Roosevelt, and Virginia's fellow member and brother-in-law, Supreme Court Justice Hugo Black.

The Durrs ultimately returned to Montgomery, and predictably immersed themselves in the Civil Rights Movement. When a lady who had done seamstress work for them, Rosa Parks, was arrested for refusing to give up her bus seat to a white person, Clifford Durr bailed her out of jail that night, along with Fred Gray. Durr also served as a key legal strategist to famed attorney Fred Gray in the appeal of the Parks conviction. The Durrs were also friends with Rev. E.D. Nixon, and Martin and Coretta King of the Dexter Avenue Baptist Church.

In that same era, in which the McCarthy hearings pressed the national fear of communism, Virginia Durr was called to testify in a hearing held in New Orleans. Many suspected the hearing's chairman, Senator James Eastland of Mississippi, of calling her as a witness as payback for her brother-in-law's vote on the U. S. Supreme Court case outlawing "separate but equal" segregation, in *Brown v. Board of Education of Topeka, Kansas*.

The Durrs were subjected to public ridicule and threats, to the point that they sent two of their five children to out-of-state boarding schools for their own peace and safety.

Clifford had become a legendary attorney, and upon his passing in 1975, multiple memorial services were held, including a large event in Washington, D.C. Virginia continued her advocacy for individual rights and a more peaceful world until her passing in 1999. After her death, much of her correspondence from the civil rights years was published by Patricia Sullivan as *Freedom Writer: Virginia Foster Durr, Letters from the Civil Rights Years*.

20 National Championships By one coach

She was simply the best at what she did.

Professor Annabel Hagood was much like some other Alabamians including Coach Nick Saban, athlete Bo Jackson, chef Frank Stitt, Apple CEO Tim Cook, Coach Sarah Patterson, or Olympian Jesse Owens.

Professor Hagood was the head debate coach at the University of Alabama, where she won championships. She won big, and she won often. In 1949, she gained recognition for winning the first of her 20 team national championships. That's right; 20 national team titles.

Professor Hagood wasn't just an elite debate coach; she was a leader on the national scene as well. She served as an original member of what would become known as the Commission on Presidential Debates, and kept a letter from Senator John F. Kennedy, expressing his willingness to participate in the debates of the 1960 campaign. Kennedy's history-making performance in the first debate made the letter especially important to her.

Even with the debate team and national work, she never lost sight of her primary mission as a university professor in the School of Communication. Her goals were always educating and challenging minds. In one of her classes, in the summer of 1986, she explained much of what would likely happen at the debate in Alabama's Democratic gubernatorial runoff election that featured his former prized student, Lieutenant Governor Bill Baxley. The debate would take place that night, and she explained the rationale behind certain color shirt-and-necktie combinations, how and where each candidate might stand, how they would address each other, when they would look directly into the television cameras, the issues they would address or avoid, and the types of action words each might use.

She was a walking gold mine of information, stories, insight, and love for her students.

John England
Supreme Court Justice, UA trustee
Tuscaloosa County

The historic path of Justice John England, Jr., began in the U.S. Army police force, wove its way to college chemistry classes, and eventually led all the way to the Alabama Supreme Court.

England was born in Uniontown (Perry County) and spent his formative years in Birmingham, where he graduated from local public schools. After service in the United States Army, he successfully pursued a Chemistry degree from Tuskegee Institute.

After graduating from Tuskegee, England enrolled at the University of Alabama School of Law, where he became one of its first African-American graduates. He remained in Tuscaloosa to establish his law practice and family life.

Simply put, England quickly became the type of lawyer that a community expects, meaning a true scholar of the law who also plays an active role in the community. England became (and remains) a leader on more boards and in more organizations than most people could handle as a full-time career. He was elected to the Tuscaloosa City Council, and immediately became one of the city's most prominent leaders.

He was elected Circuit Court Judge in 1994 (after being appointed to the post in the previous year by Governor Jim Folsom, Jr.) and served with distinction. In 1999, the honor of a lifetime came when Governor Don Siegelman appointed England to the Alabama Supreme Court.

Even during England's years as a supreme court justice, Tuscaloosa remained close to his heart. After his tenure on the court, England was once again elected to the Circuit Court bench in Tuscaloosa, and resumed his vast involvement and leadership in the community. He was also honored with an appointment to the University of Alabama System Board of Trustees.

Joe Farley
President, Alabama Power Company
Jefferson County

Alabama Power Company is well known as one of the state's premier corporate leaders, but once upon a time, the company endured great hardships and uncertainty. That was when Joe Farley emerged as the leader-hero who guided both Alabama Power, and his own family, through turbulent waters to the safe harbor of stability and success.

Even before he took the helm of leadership at Alabama Power, Farley had already established himself as a rising young leader. He earned degrees from the Harvard Law School, Princeton University (Mechanical Engineering), the University of Alabama (graduate degree in business) and Birmingham-Southern College.

After earning his law degree, Farley entered the practice of law with Martin, Turner, Blakey & Bouldin (now Balch & Bingham). That firm, founded by Logan Martin, represented utility companies and helped Farley develop expertise in that realm, which along with his engineering and business degrees left him highly qualified to join the Alabama Power Company.

Farley became president of Alabama Power in 1969, a difficult time on several different fronts. Inflation and economic woes of the 1960s and 1970s drove up the company's costs, but the political climate made rate increases increasingly difficult. Alabama Governor George Wallace, elected to another term the year after Farley assumed office, decided to find an issue beyond racial strife to use as a common enemy for himself and his supporters. He chose the utility companies, and campaigned hard against Alabama Power and each of the state's other utilities, promising the voters that he alone would stand up against them.

Through careful and wise shepherding of the company, its resources, and its public presence, Farley became a legend in the utility world through his successful leadership. He somehow managed to successfully lead a major corporation even while becoming a single parent at home. In 1978, his wife, Sheila, passed away (at age 48). That left Farley as the single father of three, but his intense love for his children and tireless energy empowered him to succeed just as grandly as a father as he did as Alabama Power's leader.

Joe Fine & Bob Geddie
Leaders, lobbyists
Franklin and Montgomery Counties

Through the decades, their names have become almost inseparable in the world of Alabama politics. The oldest government relations firm in Alabama, Fine Geddie has become a pillar of the political community as it nears the completion of its fourth decade of service.

Joe Fine began as a public servant from Russellville (Franklin County), serving two terms as a state senator (in the 1970s), including one term as its president pro tempore. The Alabama Press Association named him the most effective state senator. He also served as Franklin County District Attorney, and as a longtime member of the University of Alabama System Board of Trustees. He practiced law for 33 years.

Bob Geddie began his career with the legendary Senator John Sparkman, serving as legislative assistant and later as the coordinator of his state offices.

After serving as Legislative Liaison and Executive Assistant to Governor Fob James, Geddie became the Director of State Governmental Affairs for Alabama Power Company.

The two co-founded Fine Geddie in 1984. As described in *The Birmingham News*, "No other lobbying firm in Montgomery commands the cache and client list of Fine Geddie."

Autherine Lucy Foster
Civil Rights pioneer
Marengo County

In May of 1992, Grazia Foster earned her bachelor's degree in finance from the University of Alabama, and her family made national headlines. Actually it wasn't Grazia's degree that captured attention, but the graduate degree earned by her mother, Autherine Lucy Foster, who courageously became the first African-American enrollee at the university in 1956.

Today, students can apply for the Autherine Lucy Foster Endowed Scholarship, and they can walk to the Autherine Lucy Clock Tower in front of Foster Auditorium. Today, Grazia's mom and fellow 1992 graduate stands as a revered figure in the history of their state and their alma mater.

But it surely didn't start out that way.

Only through the courage of Autherine, the legal skill and persistence of lawyers, and the support of a budding national Civil Rights Movement was she able to enroll, and one day graduate from the state university.

Autherine had grown up as the youngest child (of 10) of Milton Cornelius Lucy and Minnie Maud Hosea Lucy in Shiloh, Alabama (Marengo County). She graduated from Linden Academy, earned a two-year teaching certificate from Selma University, and then earned a degree in English from Miles College in Birmingham. A friend persuaded her that the two of them should enroll in the University of Alabama together and pursue graduate degrees, and they applied. Not realizing their race, the university admitted them and even assigned dorm rooms and accepted a five-dollar deposit from each.

Expecting the inevitable, the girls contacted the NAACP, and legendary attorney Arthur Shores began preparing for the legal response when the university realized they were black and denied enrollment. Sure enough, it happened, and the resulting court action lasted until Autherine was finally admitted in 1956.

The 1956 admission of Autherine Lucy was met with demonstrations that bordered on riots. The question about the raucous crowd that day, as it is with protests in 21st century America, is whether the crowds were driven by passion or merely a well-organized and staged event. In either event, the university's board of trustees revoked her admission, ostensibly on the grounds of her personal safety, using the crowd as an excuse. Autherine's attorneys, Shores and future Supreme Court Justice Thurgood Marshall, filed a complaint alleging that the university conspired with the organized crowd to provide grounds to revoke her admission to the university. The university, in turn, expelled Autherine for taking part in the conspiracy complaint filed by her lawyers. The university didn't allow another African- American student until the 1960s.

In 1988, the university's board of trustees revoked their decision expelling Autherine, and she enrolled in graduate school the next year. Finally, in 1992, she earned her long-sought and well-deserved degree, walking across the stage on the same day that her daughter Grazia did in 1992.

Autherine Lucy Foster stands tall as a symbol of courage, persistence, and class.

Edward M. Friend, III

Attorney, civic leader
Jefferson County

"Happiness is a byproduct of helping others."

Edward M. Friend, III, of Birmingham, Alabama, learned those words from his father, General Edward Friend, Jr. They became the directional compass of his life, as he practiced law and engaged himself in his family and community.

After graduating from Shades Valley High School, Friend attended the University of Alabama, where he distinguished himself as president of the prestigious Jasons honor society, as well as Omicron Delta Kappa.

Upon graduating from the university's law school in 1971, Friend joined the prestigious law firm of Sirote & Permut, one of the state's leading firms.

Always a leader and provider of wise legal counsel, Friend typically seemed the natural choice to lead any organization he joined. Friend chaired the Birmingham Chamber of Commerce, the United Way of Central Alabama, Big Brothers Big Sisters, the American Red Cross, Farrah Law Society (University of Alabama School of Law), the National Conference of Christians and Jews, and Birmingham International Festival. He also serves on the board of numerous organizations including the Children's Hospital of Alabama, Metropolitan Development Board and the Boy Scouts.

Whether in the realm of law, public service, or family, Friend found his father's words rang true as he finds great joy in helping others.

Friend was inducted into the Alabama Academy of Honor in 1996.

Dr. Jane N. Geiger

Founder, Grace Ministries
Counselor, author
Jefferson County

So, why have you probably never heard of Rev. Dr. Jane N. Geiger? The reason is because it is her job to keep her mouth shut. She's still not talking.

Geiger is the founder and president of Grace Ministries, Inc., a nonprofit Christian counseling practice. In 1996, in Birmingham's Southside area, she established Grace Ministries with just $200, a Yellow Pages ad, a landline phone, some help from friends and a whole lot of faith. Today, she wears the hats of a minister, counselor, coach, and author each day.

But it almost never happened.

Today, she wears the hat of a peacemaker and counselor, but as a youth, she had to wear a battle hat in the most unlikely of places: her own home.

Raised by atheist parents, she had to fight for her faith, her belief and worship of God. When she opened her heart to the possibility of a God, it marked the beginning of the battle of a lifetime with her earthly father, who disowned her, and later, disinherited her. In doing so, he broke her mother's heart. Jane N. Geiger was named after her Mother, Noreen. Sadly, her father did nearly everything to crush her and her faith. However, paying an immediate price for her faith only strengthened it. Decades later, while counseling clients through family and spiritual strife, she wears the hat of experience.

Wearing many hats is nothing new to Geiger. Before opening the counseling practice, she wore the hat of a leader at the University of Alabama, where she founded the Coordinating Council of Honor Societies. She served in the Student Government Association, which named an award after her, while leading Bible studies and quietly sharing the Gospel of grace with others via lifestyle evangelism. She also wore the hat of a history maker as UA's first and only independent (non-sorority/fraternity) Homecoming Court attendant – elected twice, selected both her junior year and her senior year. She wore a hat of honor, selected for the Algernon Sydney Sullivan Award (for the top female and male students, given at select universities across the country) and the inaugural class of the XXXI Honor Society. Before the university, she wore the hats of a five-sport athlete, math team nerd, and Miss Vestavia Hills High School.

After earning her master's hat at UAB (4.0), where she was president of the counseling association, she earned the hat of a doctor, with a doctorate from Ashland Theological Seminary in Ohio.

Most of the credit, though, she easily awards to her parents, the balance of tender warmth and steely perseverance. The dynamic duo raised her right, and the Fifth Commandment, to honor your mother and father, has never been far from her heart, despite their religious differences. She honored them with a tribute, inspired by Dennis Rainey's work, *The Tribute*.

Throughout her life, Geiger has worn the hat of a builder and re-builder. Each day, she lives and teaches her motto: "GRACE HAPPENS." Each day, she sees clients reach for the hem of Jesus's garment for re-building lives through healing, marital miracles, deliverance from addiction, breaking the bondage to booze, escaping excessive spending on self and/or shopping, overcoming narcissism, or defeating any one of the strongholds of the seven deadly sins.

She also wears the hat of a published author, having written three books, a weekly newspaper column, a doctoral dissertation, a doctoral project, and her current work, set for release in 2019, *Social Media Sanity*. Geiger is also launching GRACE MODELS, Inc. in 2019, promoting the ideas that "fabric is your friend, class counts, and dress to bless" as a ministry to young girls and grown women who are challenged by Instagram and all of social media's temptation to show more skin.

Over 50,000 clients, throughout 27 years, have sought her counsel and the counsel of TeamGRACE at Grace Ministries, Inc.

Geiger still wears plenty of hats, but her preference is a good wide brim or baseball cap, lots of sunscreen. She's survived melanoma, skin cancer, twice. Thus, lots of hats.

Charles Graddick
Attorney General of Alabama
Mobile County

He won the election to become Alabama's new governor.

And then he didn't.

A career prosecutor and devoted public servant, Charles Graddick prosecuted criminals as Mobile County District Attorney before his election as Attorney General of Alabama. In both capacities, he developed a reputation as a tough prosecutor and advocate for stronger sentencing in criminal cases.

In 1986, Graddick ran for governor in a crowded field that included Lieutenant Governor Bill Baxley, former Governor Fob James, and former Lieutenant Governor George McMillan.

In that era, winning the Democratic Party nomination for governor was tantamount to winning the office. After making the runoff against heavy favorite, Baxley, Graddick then surprised the political world by winning the runoff as well. Graddick had assembled a talented group of young operatives, including several who had learned the art of politics on the University of Alabama campus. His campaign manager and close friend, publishing magnate H. Pettus Randall, joined Graddick to form a remarkable campaign team.

He had won, or so he thought.

Opponents claimed that illegal crossover voting from the Republican primary to the Democratic runoff improperly provided the margin of victory. A court battle ensued, provoking a public backlash.

After Baxley was ultimately declared the winner, a mini-revolt at the ballot box punished the Democratic Party leadership, choosing unknown Rev. Guy Hunt of Holly Pond as the new governor.

After his political career on the state level, Graddick returned to his roots and once again excelled in the practice of law.

Fred Gray
Attorney, activist
Montgomery County

His first big case launched a national movement. He argued before the U.S. Supreme Court, and his client list included Rosa Parks, Dr. Martin Luther King, Jr., and the victims of the horrific Tuskegee Study of Untreated Syphilis experiments.

If ever there was a hall-of-fame lawyer, it was Fred Gray.

Gray was raised in Montgomery, though he received his high school education at the Nashville Christian Institute, a boarding school operated by the Church of Christ denomination. His mother wanted him to become a preacher. Gray was recognized as a talented scholar with unusually strong public speaking skills. The school's president would take Gray along on fundraising tours as a student speaker and future pastor.

During his college years at Alabama State University, Gray was advised by a professor that he should pursue a career in the law. He did precisely that, studying at Cleveland Western Reserve School of Law before returning home to Montgomery.

On the day that Rosa Parks refused to give up her bus seat to a white person, Gray had eaten lunch with her just a few hours before. Gray and another legendary attorney, Clifford Durr, bailed her out of jail that evening. The arrest of Parks led to the Montgomery Bus Boycott and served as the foundation for the entire Civil Rights Movement of the 1960s.

Gray served as lead counsel for Parks in her criminal case arising from the bus incident, gaining national notoriety for the first of many occasions. He also served as an attorney on the tax evasion case against Dr. King, obtaining a "not guilty" verdict from the all-white jury.

In the case that resulted in George Wallace's famous stand in the schoolhouse door, Gray represented Vivian Malone and James Hood, obtaining a court order allowing them to enroll at the University of Alabama.

The case arising from the Tuskegee syphilis study shined the light of public scrutiny on the inhumane experiments, and resulted in a $10 million verdict obtained by Gray.

Gray also served as president of the American Bar Association, the first black president of the Alabama Bar Association, and as the pastor of the Newtown Church of Christ in Montgomery, fulfilling his mother's aspirations.

John Harbert
Titan of business
Jefferson County

The first investment might have begun with a little luck, but the empire was created by brilliant management and seasoned with generosity to the public.

John Harbert became one of the most successful businessmen in Alabama's 200-year history. He returned from service in World War II prepared to launch his business career. According to the *Encyclopedia of Alabama*,

"He used the winnings from playing dice on board a troop transport ship and the sale of some war bonds to start Harbert Corporation in 1949 with his brother Billy L. Harbert and two other engineers. His first project was the construction of a new bridge near Prattville in Autauga County financed with borrowed money and constructed from surplus war equipment."

After that first project, Harbert Construction began its meteoric rise to the upper tier of American business. Its projects included work across the Deep South, in Africa, and in the Middle East.

Understanding the mercuric nature of the construction industry, John Harbert led his company to acquire massive holdings in Kentucky and an oil company in Texas. He once joined legendary billionaire T. Boone Pickens in an unsuccessful attempt to acquire Gulf Oil.

In the 21st century, BL Harbert International is led by

Billy Harbert, as the company continues expanding its footprint and impact across the globe. His work with the company, before taking the reins, included positions as project manager and project engineer on pipeline and commercial projects. He graduated from Auburn University with a B.S. in Building Science, and from Emory University with an MBA.

Jack Hawkins
Chancellor, Troy University
Pike County

Jack Hawkins has spent the last 50 years as a hero, helping and elevating the lives of countless people in each season of his life.

In 1967, Hawkins graduated from the University of Montevallo, was commissioned a Lieutenant in the U.S. Marine Corps, and served as a platoon leader during the Vietnam War. For his heroic service to his country, he was awarded the Bronze Star, along with a Purple Heart and citation certificate from the U.S. Marines.

Then, he became a different type of hero. After earning his doctorate from the University of Alabama and serving as an Assistant Dean at UAB, Hawkins was named president of the Alabama Institute for the Deaf and Blind in 1979. There, he worked tirelessly to improve all aspects of the school, empowering the students to achieve the type of tasks and personal improvement that might have been impossible in the past. He led the school for ten remarkable years of success and growth.

And that was when Troy called.

Troy University (then known as Troy State), tapped Hawkins as the university's chancellor in 1989. Since then, under his leadership, the school has enjoyed skyrocketing growth, the creation of an international multi-campus system, strong endowments, a nationally known athletic program, a world-class art collection, and a student body greater in both number and academic credentials. The university has established a strong relationship with the American military, empowering soldiers and officers to achieve remote learning even while serving our country in a full-time capacity.

The dynamic presence and leadership of Dr. Jack Hawkins has placed Troy University firmly on the international stage as a destination for a quality education in an ideal learning environment.

Dr. Hawkins' wife, Janice Hawkins, has served as a full partner in leading the university. She has been instrumental in the University's dance, theatre and musical events. She opened the chancellor's home to students and student groups on a regular basis. She has also served as chair of the Alabama Historical Commission, the boards of directors for the Alabama Humanities Foundation, the Alabama Board of Interpreters for the Deaf, and the Alabama Institute for the Deaf and Blind.

Dr. Hawkins has long been the face of Troy University, and thankfully for that institution, they have a true hero at the helm.

Marillyn Hewson
CEO, Lockheed Martin
The University of Alabama

In 2018, Marillyn Hewson was number one on the list of 50 Most Powerful Women in Business, by *Forbes*. She has also been named as one of the most powerful businesswomen in the world. She has won numerous awards, honors, and listings throughout her career.

Did You Know???

Bobby Joe Seales,

Alabama's Bicentennial Ambassador, travels the state promoting the year of celebration

------

At events, institutions, and gatherings across the state, Bobby Joe Seales has become the most well-known and popular celebrant of Alabama's bicentennial year. His Victorian-Era top hat and morning coat have become an emblem at events and in social media.

It would be hard to imagine a more qualified ambassador than Seales, who was appointed by legislative act. He has become a leader in the Sons of the American Revolution, the Shelby County Historical Society, and the General Society of the War of 1812.

He and Mrs. Seales travel tirelessly and add to every event and gathering they attend.

Hewson stands tall in the world of business, not just as a woman, but as one of its most important leaders. As the CEO of Lockheed Martin Corporation, she leads one of the most important private companies in the worldwide effort to keep Americans, and freedom-loving people everywhere, safe from ever-changing threats.

Lockheed Martin's presence in Alabama includes its operation near Troy, which performs final assembly of the Javelin, the Terminal High Altitude Area Defense (THAAD) missile, the Joint Air-to-Surface Standoff Missile (JASSM) and air-to-ground missiles.

Hewson graduated from the University of Alabama, where she remains deeply engaged as a member of both the University of Alabama's President's Cabinet and the Board of Visitors of the Culverhouse College of Business. Her husband, James, also graduated from the university, with a bachelor's degree in communications.

In 2018, the university announced a $15 million gift from the Hewsons to the Culverhouse College of Business, the largest individual gift in the business school's history.

Mike Hubbard
Legislator, broadcaster
Lee County

Mike Hubbard made his mark in the world of sports, and then propelled the Republican Party to its first major victory in over 100 years. Despite the turbulence that would follow, he established himself as one of the greatest communications strategists and message crafters in Alabama political history.

Communication was always a vital part of Hubbard's skill set. In his youth (in his native Georgia), Hubbard won a statewide speech contest, besting future national politico Ralph Reed. He studied in the prestigious journalism program at the University of Georgia, where he played a significant role in the marketing campaign for Herschel Walker's 1982 Heisman Trophy.

Hubbard then took a job at Auburn University, where he helped once again with a Heisman campaign, this one for the great one, Bo Jackson, in 1985.

Hubbard ventured into electoral politics in 1996 for the campaign of Bob Riley for the U.S. Congress. Two years later, he was elected to the first of his four terms in the Alabama House of Representatives.

Then came his greatest campaign, to take over the Alabama Legislature for the Republican Party. By 2010, Hubbard and his team had achieved what was previously unthinkable, a Republican majority for the first time since post-Civil War Reconstruction.

Hubbard then helped write one of the great recent books about Alabama politics. Along with David Azbell, Hubbard co-authored *Storming The State House: The Campaign That Liberated Alabama from 136 Years of Democrat Rule*. The book chronicles the path, the players, and the politics of the historic victory.

Although legal issues and a high-profile trial in a Lee County criminal courtroom derailed his speakership and have led to affirmed convictions, Hubbard's place in the state's political lore and legislative history has been secured.

Dr. Paul Hubbert
Leader, lobbyist
Fayette & Montgomery Counties

He has been called the smartest person to ever serve as a lobbyist in Alabama. He cleverly took a struggling teachers union and transformed it into a political juggernaut. In his heyday, as legend has it, legislators would look up from the floor into the public gallery, where Dr. Paul Hubbert sat, and watch him hold his hand in the air. If he pointed his thumb upward, they were to vote for the pending legislation, and they would vote against it if his thumb pointed downward.

Hubbert, a native of Hubbertville, worked with his friend and ally, Joe Reed, to merge the white and black teachers unions that had previously remained segregated. This teamwork gave the newly revised Alabama Education Association a ready-made political infrastructure in every county and community in the state.

After spending years getting other candidates elected, Hubbert sought the Democratic nomination for governor in 1990. He turned out to be a dynamic speaker as well as an excellent organizer, and defeated a field of highly qualified and competent candidates. In the general election, he faced the incumbent, Republican Guy Hunt. In the final weeks leading up to election day, many thought he would win. Late in the campaign, a devastating television ad by the Hunt campaign associated Hubbert with a routine union-provided legal defense of a teacher accused of a sexual crime against a student. The ad was cleverly conceived and highly effective. Hunt ultimately won the race, and Hubbert returned to the world of lobbying.

One event helps to explain why he was so successful. A teacher had seen her retirement delayed by an entire year because of one faulty calculation within the state system. Her son, a young attorney, drove to Montgomery on another matter but stopped by the AEA office to inquire about his mother's situation. Without an appointment or any prior notice, Dr. Hubbert met with the attorney, listened carefully, and helped him develop a strategy to overturn the bureaucratic decision.

When the grateful attorney asked how he could return the favor, Hubbert asked if he knew a newly elected legislator in the attorney's home county. As it turned out, they were friends, so Hubbert asked for advice on how to connect and develop a friendship with the new senator.

It wasn't much to ask in return, but Hubbert was always building relationships and alliances. He was also always helping teachers, which remained the central calling of his illustrious career.

The Ireland family
Business leaders, benefactors
Jefferson County

One leading historian described the Irelands as one of the most generous and charitable families in Alabama's history. "It is hard to even imagine how much they do for the state, and for so many great causes," explained Dr. Wayne Flynt, the state's premier author on its history.

Originally from Gadsden, William Reynolds Ireland moved to Birmingham after serving in the U.S. Navy during World War II. After the war, he came to Birmingham and began his career with Vulcan Materials, which "is the nation's largest producer of construction aggregates–primarily crushed stone, sand and gravel–and a major producer of aggregates-based construction materials including asphalt and ready-mixed concrete," according to its website.

Through hard work, Ireland ultimately served as president of two different subsidiaries of the company. Vulcan Materials grew, expanding the scope of its operations and becoming one of the most successful of its type in America.

In turn, the Ireland family has prospered, and because of their vast generosity, many others have been helped.

How so? One need look no further than Alabama's "Forever Wild" organization founded in part by William Reynolds Ireland. Upon his induction into the Alabama Academy of Honor, Ireland was described as "one of the best friends the environment of Alabama has ever had."

He received both the 1994 Walter L. Mims Lifetime Achievement Award in Wildlife Conservation and the 1995 Ducks Unlimited Marsh Project Award. He was also inducted into the Alabama Sports Hall of Fame and the Alabama Men's Hall of Fame.

The family's generosity extends well beyond its patriarch. There's also the Nina Ireland Lung Disease Center at the University of California at San Francisco. Or one could visit the Glenwood Mental Health Services, founded by its namesake, Glenn Ireland, or the Glenwood Autism and Behavioral Health Center.

Students at Auburn University have benefitted from its Ireland Center Lab at the E.W. Shell Fisheries Center Station.

Both achieving students, and many who would have otherwise been left behind by society have been helped or cared for because of this extraordinary family.

The Irelands have continued expanding their benevolent impact on the state, and their generosity will no doubt continue helping the ill, less fortunate, and forgotten people of society for generations to come.

Tom Joyner
National radio legend
Macon County

He has become one of the biggest radio show personalities in American history.

And it happened because his family was wrong.

Tom Joyner grew up in Tuskegee, in a prominent and prosperous family. His grandfather was one of the few black physicians in America, having obtained his medical degree in 1909.

For college, Joyner enrolled at his hometown school, Tuskegee University. He loved music, and joined a band called The Commodores with his good friend, Lionel Ritchie. Because his band didn't really make any money at first, his parents insisted that he quit the band and find ways to earn more immediate income.

In retrospect, the comically bad advice would have deprived most people of their big chance, but Tom Joyner has never been like most people. Still wanting to associate with music, Joyner began working his way up the ladder in the world of radio.

Joyner had begun his career and proved popular with audiences. At one point, he received two job offers, with one being a morning show in Dallas and the other an afternoon show in Chicago. Amazingly, he took both offers and commuted between the two cities. He became legendary as the hardest working guy in the world of radio, and logged millions of frequent flyer miles over the eight years in which he handled both shows.

The success and legend of Tom Joyner continued to expand, and he became the host of nationally broadcasted radio and television shows.

For Joyner, his name says it all. His shows needed no other title other than *The Tom Joyner Show*, because his name has meant quality entertainment across America.

Helen Keller
Inspiration for millions
Colbert County

The legendary Mark Twain said it best: "The two most interesting characters of the 19th century are Napoleon and Helen Keller."

As an infant in Tuscumbia, she suffered an illness that made her blind and deaf. She had a restless mind and plenty of energy, but without the right approach to channeling those, she was just an insufferable child.

Enter Anne Sullivan.

Helen's parents had brought in Sullivan to work with Helen, and at first, it wasn't helping much. Sullivan tried teaching words through spelling their symbols to her by hand, but Helen wasn't able to understand that the words named the objects.

Then came the water pump, and the famous movie in which Sullivan pumps the water into one of Helen's hands and spells w-a-t-e-r into the other. Finally, it resonates with Helen, who wants to learn more words. She learned 30 more words before bedtime.

After that miracle, Helen spent the rest of her life working for others to have their own miracles. She inspired innumerable people, including Heather Whitestone, who also lost her hearing at a young age due to a fever and ultimately became Miss America.

Amazingly, Helen Keller met every American president from Grover Cleveland to John F. Kennedy. A statue of her stands in the United States Capitol. Her autobiography became a worldwide bestseller and the inspiration for a major motion picture. A theatrical production about her life remains a top tourist attraction in her hometown of Tuscumbia.

The list of her accomplishments, however, pales in comparison to the number of people whom she has inspired, comforted, and challenged.

John Lewis
Congressman, activist
Autauga County

John Lewis wrote a letter, and the reply changed his life and American history.

Lewis, who grew up in Prattville (Autauga County), wanted to attend Troy University (called Troy State at that time). As was typical with segregated schools, Troy had simply not responded to his application for admission.

Deprived of his first choice of schools, Lewis instead went to Nashville, studying at American Baptist College. During his college years, he decided to continue pursuing an education at Troy. He wrote a letter to the prominent young minister at Montgomery's Dexter Avenue Baptist Church, Dr. Martin Luther King, Jr., asking for help and advice.

The reply to that letter changed his life.

Dr. King sent a reply letter, with an enclosed two-way bus ticket to Montgomery for a meeting. After meeting with King and Ralph David Abernathy, Lewis dropped the Troy issue because of the potential harm to his parents and their economic livelihood. Instead, he decided to join King and Abernathy, pursuing a lifetime of devoted service to the issue of civil rights.

Lewis became a prote`ge` of King, even speaking before King at the 1963 March on Washington. After Lewis spoke, Dr. King delivered his iconic "I Have A Dream" speech.

In 1965, Lewis joined his mentor, King, in Selma. Just a few miles from his home in Autauga County, Selma was charged with strife on the weekend of the Selma-to-Montgomery March. They expected trouble, but it became even worse than they feared when law enforcement officers attacked marchers on the Edmund Pettus bridge. Lewis was brutally beaten by law enforcement personnel, sustaining a fractured skull.

The great irony arising from that day in Selma was that the same people who beat him down were unknowingly lifting his national stature and standing, empowering him to achieve much more for civil rights because of his personal sacrifice that day.

Undeterred, the son of Autauga County became a leader in the Civil Rights Movement and an iconic member of the U.S. Congress, where he has served for over three decades.

In events that revealed the ultimate success of that movement, Lewis was honored in two cities that had brought him great pain. Troy University held a "John Lewis Day,"

Did You Know???

Jim & Nick's started in the building of a failed pizza joint

When brilliant business minds combine with delicious food, the results can become unbeatable. The father and son combo of Jim and Nick Pihakis started their Bar-B-Q restaurant on Clairmont Avenue in Birmingham, in a closed pizza joint. In the beginning, there were many things they didn't have, like a famous name or exotic location.

Now, their names are known throughout the South, as Jim & Nick's sports almost 40 locations across the region. Their Bar-B-Q and catfish have become legendary, and their cheese biscuits are absolutely addictive.

There is, however, one thing that they still don't have: a microwave. None of their restaurants serve any re-heated items.

celebrating him after his election to the U.S. Congress. It was surely redemptive to the pain of their ignoring his application.

Then in Selma, where the pain was physical, Lewis once again marched to the foot of the Edmund Pettus Bridge. This time, however, he walked arm-in-arm with President and Mrs. Barack Obama. Speaking to a crowd exceeding 100,000 in number, he delivered a powerful introduction of the president on the 50th Anniversary of Bloody Sunday.

Don Logan
CEO of Time, Inc.
Owner, the Birmingham Barons
Jefferson and Morgan Counties

What do *Time* magazine, *Southern Living*, and the first major internet provider have in common? They have each been led by the same son of Alabama.

A native of Morgan County, Don Logan has risen to the top of the media world. He graduated with honors from Auburn University, and was hired by Southern Progress Corporation, the parent company of *Southern Living* magazine.

At Southern Progress, Logan became a prote`ge` of the company chairman and *Southern Living* founder, Emory O. Cunningham. When Time Warner purchased Southern Progress, Cunningham recommended Logan as his successor.

Logan became the CEO of Southern Progress, and by 1994 he had become the CEO of Time, Inc. Then, by 2002, he became the CEO of Time's newly acquired internet service provider, AOL.

After retiring from Time Warner, Logan returned home to Alabama and has invested his considerable talents back into his home state. He and his sons purchased the Birmingham Barons professional baseball team, and have transformed the team into a downtown summer destination for families and the singles scene.

But Logan and his family didn't stop there. The innovative leadership that propelled national media companies to greatness is now used to better the City of Birmingham. The elegant and family-friendly Regions Field has served as the hub for a revitalization of the entire area of Birmingham's Southside, serving as a year-round venue for meetings, conferences, receptions and parties.

Walt Maddox
Mayor of Tuscaloosa
Tuscaloosa County

To truly understand the public service career of Walt Maddox, look no further than April 27, 2011. That day became the defining moment for the City of Tuscaloosa in the early 21st century, and the signature of Maddox's outstanding tenure as mayor.

Two different tornados hit Tuscaloosa County, including a massive F-4 tornado that devastated much of the city and many families.

The numbers were staggering. The storms caused 1.5 billion yards of debris. Twelve percent of the entire city was damaged. Over 7,000 people were left unemployed. Sixty-five citizens were killed, but by unofficial accounts, many illegal workers lost their lives. Officially, over 1,500 people were injured. The wind speed of the larger tornado exceeded 190 miles per hour, and that tornado plowed its way across the state for an unbelievable seven hours and 24 minutes, traveling 380 miles on the ground and devastating almost everything in its path.

The damage estimate was at least $2.45 billion.

Maddox was in the basement of the Tuscaloosa City Hall when the tornado struck. Even before learning anything about the extent of the damage, he instituted the city's emergency protocol, putting rescue and recovery plans in action immediately, Those plans included urgently performing reconnaissance work, such as getting reports of the severity of damage, amount of damage, and potential cost of damage, sending out local emergency response teams, bringing in the National Guard, and staying in close contact with the governor's office.

Maddox immediately employed every imaginable avenue of help. Faith-based groups were brought on board quickly. Habitat for Humanity, along with churches of all denominations, played a vital role in meeting the individual needs of those within the city. While the municipal officials were working alongside governmental organizations such as FEMA to make sure the city's needs were met, the churches took it upon themselves to make sure the citizens' needs were met.

In the immediate aftermath of the storm, Maddox was proud to see the people of Tuscaloosa come together without regard for personal agendas, and he was proud to see the authentic care and help from President Obama.

In the years since the storms, the City of Tuscaloosa has waged a comeback for the ages, and Maddox proudly still leads the city he loves.

Doug Marshall
CEO, Presbyterian Home for Children
Shelby & Talladega Counties

Following his heart led Doug Marshall on the unlikely path from business executive to non-profit leader and father figure for hundreds of children.

As a Birmingham executive living in Shelby County, Doug Marshall seemingly had it all. He had risen to great heights in a major corporation, serving as director of tax for Energen, and vice president and controller of Alagasco.

Despite the success, Marshall had always felt a call to serve others.

It was time, he decided, to redirect his energy and the purpose of his career. That decision propelled Marshall on the path that has now defined his career, and landed him in Talladega on a cloudless afternoon in February of 2017.

On that day, the Presbyterian Home for Children, then celebrating its 150th year, held an investiture service for its new president and CEO, Doug Marshall. His new role has brought the best of both worlds, handling the duties of an executive leader while also receiving the joy of helping at-risk and underprivileged children each day.

For Marshall, the PHFC presents the perfect dovetail of his business abilities and his heart for service. That's a good thing, because the opportunities for service are endless. Marshall leads the staff at the home in Talladega, as well as the network of supporters, volunteers, and alumni of the home that extends across Alabama and beyond. The PHFC provides a wide variety of services, including the following programs and more:

******The Moderate Care Residential Therapeutic Program*** serves adolescents ages 13-17 who have been removed from their homes by the Alabama Department of Human Resources;

******The Transition to Adult Living Program*** helps young

women ages 19-24 who are facing challenges;

The Secure Dwellings Program is a program providing safe and affordable housing on the PHFC campus to homeless children and their female caregiver;

The Ascension Leadership Academy, the accredited private school, does everything in its power to help children succeed academically.

Marshall did not have to look far for great examples for educating children. His parents constantly educated their children, at school and at home. Caring for the children and showing them a male authority figure came naturally for him because of his great relationship with his own father, and because of his own role as a father to his three children.

Marshall's heart for service, in the private and nonprofit sectors, have not gone unnoticed. He was named to the "Top 50 Over 50" by *Modern Maturity*. Among many honors and board memberships, he was named to the "20 Making A Difference" in St. Clair & Talladega counties.

Marshall succeeds as a heart-driven leader looking out for at-risk children, homeless children and their moms, children and adults with disabilities and other individuals in need. In many ways, he has become a father to the fatherless.

Thankfully, Marshall followed his heart, and that has made all the difference.

Matt & Aunie
Political talk show hosts
Jefferson County

They have been featured by the national media. They have become the virtual morning water cooler for political talk in Alabama. After traveling vastly different paths, their careers intersected for a radio show, *The Matt & Aunie Show*, with whom their audience has lived through great moments, strife, and scandals in the state.

Matt Murphy was originally a native of Georgia, although he has become part of Alabama's political lore. After hosting different shows throughout his career, he had become the unusual radio personality who was perfectly comfortable and capable carrying the show by himself. As a serious student of public policy and politics, he combines a knowledge of issues with what one colleague kiddingly calls a curmudgeonly persona.

Then came Aunie.

Andrea Lindenberg has been a popular presence in the Birmingham media market for two decades. On television, the combination of reporting experience and Auburn communications education made for long-term media success. The female television personality and the brash radio personality provided a perfect balance.

Former Talk 99.5 General Manager David Walls conceived the idea of putting them together for a daily talk show, and the result has yielded a harvest of high ratings and an audience that is engaged on a daily basis.

Morning commuters and people at home are treated to a show that never shies away from reporting the difficult stories or interviewing the controversial guests.

During the national frenzy of media coverage for the 2017 United States Senate special election in Alabama, *The Matt & Aunie Show* was featured on national media outlets as the top political show in the state. Both CNN and ABC aired segments with Matt and Aunie to get the lay of the land of the Alabama political scene and the dynamics of that election campaign.

America's

Morning Joe

by way of Alabama

Anyone beginning their day by watching America's top political morning show will see an Alabama education in action.

Joe Scarborough, host of *Morning Joe*, has been named one of the *Time* 100 most influential people in America. Raised in Pensacola, Scarborough graduated from The University of Alabama, where he received his academic education and much more. He was also immersed in the legendary campus politics of the university. That experience propelled him to the U.S. Congress, to which he was elected in 1994 and served until 2001. His a strong intellect with gifted media skills made Scarborough a natural talk show host after his days in elected office.

Scarborough has authored two books that made the *New York Times* bestseller list. After many years, *Morning Joe* still enjoys superior success, in no small part because of Scarborough himself, his talented co-host (and wife) Mika Brzezinski, and the outstanding regular studio experts who include the audience in a virtual coffee-shop-chat each morning.

No matter how famous or successful Scarborough has become, he has remained loyal to his Alabama roots, hosting at least one show each year from the University of Alabama campus and supporting his alma mater on national television.

Dr. David Mathews
Educator, innovator
Clarke County

He was known in Grove Hill (Clarke County) as a bright kid with an equally bright future. Just a few years later, still in his thirties, David Mathews had already become America's youngest university president when the University of Alabama tapped him to lead the institution at the age of 33.

Mathews graduated from the university in 1958 and obtained his masters in 1959 before earning his doctorate at the Ivy League's Columbia University.

The seminal moment of his education occurred not in the classroom, but during a summer break. In 1963, Mathews worked with men's housing for the university during summer break from graduate school. The infamous stand in the schoolhouse door by Alabama Governor George Wallace captured the attention of a nation, and of the young David Mathews.

Two years later, Mathews had his doctorate and returned to his home state to work and teach at his alma mater.

The leadership skills and intellect were not lost on the university's leadership, and Mathews became the university's president in 1969. Mathews led the university from 1969 until 1980. He led the school through the height of integration and modernized both the campus and its image. His presidency was interrupted, as the university was not the only institution that recognized the value of Mathews' leadership. President Gerald Ford tapped Mathews to serve in his cabinet as Secretary of Health, Education, and Welfare. Even during his presidency, Mathews continued teaching a history class, keeping in touch with students and the happenings on campus.

In 1980, Mathews moved on to the next challenge of his career, becoming president of the Kettering Foundation.

Founded in 1927, the foundation's stated mission is "to sponsor and carry out scientific research for the benefit of humanity." In recent years, the mission of the Kettering Foundation has expanded to include the furtherance of democracy.

Mathews remains active in the life of Clarke County, serving the Clarke County Historical Society and maintaining the personal connections in his hometown.

Sid McDonald
Businessman, legislator, innovator
Marshall County

Many people spend their lives searching for the right calling or opportunity. As a child, Sid McDonald only had to glance to the other side of his family's living room in Arab, Alabama.

That's where his parents, one of four family generations operating the Brindlee Mountain Telephone Company, kept the switchboard that routed telephone calls in much of Marshall and Blount Counties.

McDonald was blessed with a sharp mind and the ability to take something good and transform it into something great. He took over his family's business in 1961, leading it to new growth and heightened profitability. He also founded DeltaCom Long Distance Services, which at its height became the state's second largest cell phone service provider after AT&T.

Never one to limit his ideas or vision, McDonald decided to direct his energy toward state leadership. He was elected twice to the Alabama House of Representatives and once to the Alabama Senate. A candidate for governor in 1978, McDonald later served as the State Finance Director, arguably the second most important position in the executive branch of government. .

After succeeding grandly in business and government, McDonald turned his considerable talents toward the future, meaning the world of education. Always a supporter of his alma mater, the University of Alabama, McDonald served on the University of Alabama System Board of Trustees, eventually becoming its president pro tempore. Many of the decisions leading to the university's explosive growth and national academic success can be traced back to the McDonald era of the board of trustees, including the creation of the UAB Health System.

McDonald's wife, Jane P. McDonald, has also played a leadership role in the realm of education, serving as the first female chairperson and longtime member of the Alabama Commission on Higher Education. She now serves on the Birmingham-Southern College Board of Trustees. Her son, Judge Liles C. Burke, serves as a United States District Judge for the Northern District of Alabama.

Robbie McGhee
Poarch Band of Creek Indians
Escambia County

What do the United States Senate, the Troutman Sanders law firm, and the Poarch Band of Creek Indians have in common?

The answer is: Robbie McGhee.

Robert R. McGhee has become a leading advocate for the rights of Native Americans in virtually all issues arising at either the federal or state levels. He brings expertise developed from his government experience, including work with the Department of Interior-Bureau of Indian Affairs, and the United States Senate Committee on Indian Affairs.

Following his heart, McGhee returned to Atmore. He currently serves as vice president of the Poarch Band of Creek Indians Tribal Council. He has been invited to serve on a variety of White House initiatives. His public service has included National Indian Child Welfare Association, Children First Alabama, Chairman of the Native American Rights Fund Board of Directors, Vice President of the United South and Eastern Tribes Board of Directors and the Board of Advisors for the Center for Native American Youth.

The Mitchell family
Business titans, benefactors
Mobile County

Many people talk of giving back to their home communities, but the Mitchell family has turned generosity into an art form.

Abe Mitchell has been named one of America's most generous donors by philanthropy.com. His and his brother Mayer's charitable gifts have changed the face of a university and created an important cancer center. Mayer and Abe graduated from the Wharton School of Finance at the University of Pennsylvania. The two brothers were best friends and partners in virtually every venture.

Along with a business partner, Mayer and Abe founded The Mitchell Company Inc. Together, they built a real estate empire that owned or managed over 25,000 houses, 20,000 apartments, and 175 shopping centers.

The Mitchell family has donated over $108 million to the University of South Alabama, including the $50 million donation by Abe in 2013. The family has endowed a cancer research institute at the university, along with enormously generous gifts to the university's academic and scholarship programs.

Johnny "Iron Man" Montgomery
Realtor, Inspirational leader
Jefferson County

The prison warden escorted him to the front gate. The man was about to leave and return to the free world. But before the man left, the warden stopped him for some final words.

"We've had many speakers here for the inmates, but they've never sat in silence for anyone until you delivered your message today. Thank you."

Johnny (Iron Man) Montgomery is no ordinary speaker, and he has led no ordinary life.

As he stood before the audience of prisoners, he began by telling them how he visited another prison, years before, to forgive the man on death row who had murdered his momma.

That got their attention.

"I tried to cope with the murder of my momma with alcohol. I drank enough alcohol to kill an entire third-world country, but it couldn't make the pain go away." Montgomery then shared that his relationship with God, rather than alcohol, had filled the emptiness in his life, one day at a time, caused by his momma's murder.

A former star track athlete at Livingtson University (now the University of West Alabama), Montgomery has become one of Alabama's premier speakers to recovering addicts, and to those who desperately need to become recoverers. He speaks to recovery centers, to small recovery groups, to prisons, to churches, and to just about any other group that invites him.

Montgomery, along with his wife, Liz, have become some of Birmingham's most successful real estate agents. He was featured on the popular HGTV's *House Hunters,* and the episode was so popular that they've asked him to star in another one. He was inducted into the Livingston University Hall of Fame, and nominated for the Alabama Sports Hall of Fame. He earned the nickname "Iron Man" through his triathlon competitions and his relentless physical training.

For Montgomery, the honors and real estate success matter little when compared to the impact on the lives of people who struggle with addictions, anger, or both.

When he encounters those who have just begun recovery, he promises an autographed copy of his book to them when they reach 30 days of sobriety. He typically inscribes the book: "If I can forgive the man on death row who murdered my mom, can you forgive the person who got your parking spot at Wal-Mart?" The message is amusing but profound.

On the day he was interviewed for this book, Montgomery mailed copies of his book to newly recovering addicts in Atlanta, San Francisco, and Opp.

For so many who struggle daily with addictions and anger, Johnny (Iron Man) Montgomery has become a hero of the type who doesn't seize media headlines, but who makes Alabama and its people better, one day at a time.

Roy Moore
Former chief justice
Etowah County

A native of the Gadsden area, Roy Moore was elected Etowah County Circuit Judge, and twice elected as Chief Justice of the Alabama Supreme Court. He was the Republican nominee for the U.S. Senate in the special election of 2017.

Moore graduated from West Point (the U.S. Military Academy), and from the University of Alabama School of Law.

He has made national headlines with his advocacy for the public acknowledgement of God in the judicial system. During his years on the Etowah County court, Moore became a nationally known politician through his refusal to remove a depiction of the Ten Commandments from his courtroom.

Moore's philosophy has become known as the "natural law" theory, arising from Thomas Jefferson's words in the Declaration of Independence describing the "laws of nature and of nature's God."

Although famous for his stances on the degree of church-state separation, Moore's duties as chief justice involved cases of all types and the administration of the state's entire judicial system. Moore's reputation as an unconventional maverick extended to the courtroom as well, as many of his rulings and opinions strayed from his party's orthodoxy when he believed that the law required a different result. Judicially, Moore often sided with individuals and victims over corporate interests in civil cases.

As the Chief Justice of Alabama, Moore disagreed with a federal court order mandating the removal of a monument depicting the Ten Commandments. Moore refused to obey the court order as an act of civil disobedience in the long American tradition of peacefully protesting what he perceived as a miscarriage of justice. However, a specially appointed panel of judges ruled against Moore and removed him from office.

After an unsuccessful run for governor, Moore again sought election as chief justice. Again, he won. Again, Moore found himself in opposition to federal court orders involving the issue of same-sex marriages. He resigned from the Alabama Supreme Court over the issue in 2017.

Did You Know???

Who's Who began in Tuscaloosa

Across America, students aspire to see their names *and bios included in the Who's Who Among Students in American Universities & Colleges*. What many don't know is that this publication was founded by a brilliant businessman from Tuscaloosa, H. Pettus Randall, Jr.

Randall Publishing had one asset that many businesses lack, which is an outstanding successor to its founder. Randall's son, H. Pettus Randall, III, had already shown his leadership potential during high school when he was elected Key Club International President and Boys Nation President. Amazingly, he found a wife who was his equal in Cathy Randall, who had served as president of Girls Nation and was a student leader at the University of Alabama. They became two of the outstanding leaders ever produced by Tuscaloosa. The University of Alabama's Catherine J. Randall Research Scholars Program was named after Cathy. She was named a 2018 Yellowhammer Woman of Impact.

Pettus, like his father, ultimately turned the company over to the right person. Mike Reilly had served as vice president of Randall Publishing before accepting a job in Houston. All it took was one phone call from his old boss to bring Reilly home.

Later that same year, Moore entered a crowded field of talented candidates for the Republican primary special election to succeed Jeff Sessions, who had resigned to become Attorney General of the United States. Moore defeated Senator Luther Strange in the runoff, becoming the party's candidate for the special general election. Moore's vast grass-roots network propelled him to a hard-fought primary victory. The general election campaign quickly became a national event, with the media focusing daily attention on the race. Intra-party Republican conflict, combined with well-timed scurrilous accusations turned the race into a spectacle in its final weeks.

Although Senator Doug Jones won the general election, Moore remained a hero among many for his support of the "natural law" philosophy of jurisprudence, and for the acknowledgement of God in the public domain.

Dr. Lloyd Noland
Medical innovator
Jefferson County

In 1912, an executive with a Tennessee Coal, Iron, and Railroad Company subsidiary traveled from Birmingham, Alabama, to the nation of Panama. The mission was to offer an important job to Dr. Lloyd Noland, a physician who had spent years in helping to control the spread of mosquitos and disease. Noland had assisted Dr. William Crawford Gorgas, the Alabamian who had become famous by leading the efforts to make the Panama Canal construction areas safe for workers.

Dr. Noland was exactly whom the Tennessee Coal, Iron, and Railroad Company needed for the mine fields of the Birmingham area. After a trip to inspect the areas he would serve, Dr. Noland accepted the position of superintendent of the company's health department. According to a description in the *Encyclopedia of Alabama*, the mosquito infestation was as bad in those mine fields as it was in Panama. Other health problems necessitated Dr.

Noland's immediate attention, such as hookworm, smallpox, typhoid, dysentery, and enteritis.

Within the first year, malaria cases decreased by 90 percent. In the first full year (1914), Dr. Noland and his staff handled over 129,000 visits to their clinics and conducted over 84,000 home visits.

Fortunately for the people of Birmingham, Dr. Noland convinced his employer to build a 350-bed facility in the Fairfield area of town. It was later named Lloyd Noland Hospital and became a landmark facility for medical care. It remained open for 85 years, until the economics of West Birmingham outweighed the desire of the medical community to keep it open. Before a medical school was established in the state, the hospital became an important training ground for future physicians and nurses.

Dr. Noland's impact on the health of workers, the growth of the mining industry in Alabama, and the patients of the hospital he founded cannot be overstated. He literally impacted millions of lives.

Honored with the presidencies of both the Medical Association of Alabama and the Southern Surgical Association, Noland led the medical community throughout the remainder of his life.

The O'Neal family
Business and government
Jefferson County

He was a bright kid with good ideas. Kirkman O'Neal was also the son and grandson of former Alabama governors, so maybe his bosses at the steel plant in Washington County were a little envious. Whatever the reason, they ignored Kirkman's carefully prepared plans to make the steel plant more efficient.

Leadership was clearly in his genes, as Kirkman's grandfather Edward O'Neal was a Confederate general and then Alabama Governor. Kirkman's father Emmet was governor and president of the Alabama State Bar. When Kirkman's ideas were not considered, he moved to Birmingham and ultimately borrowed $2,000 to invest in the company now known as O'Neal Steel in 1921. Kirkman's son Emmet guided the company for decades, reaching even greater success.

Thankfully for the company, the tradition continues. Craft O'Neal, grandson of Kirkman and son of Emmet, leads the company that has restructured and broadened the scope of its operations and its footprint in the industry. Craft became the first and current CEO of O'Neal Industries, founded in 2008 as the parent company for O'Neal Steel and other subsidiaries.

Nearing its 100th year, the company became and remains a giant of Alabama industry.

Joy O'Neal, wife of Emmet O'Neal III, has made her impact in the state by founding and operating The Red Barn. O'Neal and her team succeed in using this Shelby County farm facility to help children and adults with physical, cognitive, and emotional disabilities or special circumstances.

Jimmy Parnell
CEO of ALFA Insurance Companies
Chilton County

For no less than five generations, the Parnell family has farmed the land of Chilton County. Now a leading family in the cattle and timber businesses, the Parnell name has become synonymous with the traditions that have Alabama's agriculture industries second to none. Continuing in his family's footsteps, Jimmy Parnell was named Alabama Logger of the Year by the Alabama Forestry Association in 2006.

Parnell has expanded that tradition, taking the lessons of his family legacy to Montgomery as head of the state's most prominent farming organization.

Parnell serves as chairman, president and CEO of ALFA Insurance Companies and Alabama Farmers Federation. In that role, he leads organizations that affect almost every Alabamian. From auto insurance, to the foods we consume, to the choices of whom to elect as our leaders, ALFA has become the leading advocate for all issues arising from farmers, their property, their interests, and their success.

Did You Know???

A giant of American education was once an illiterate slave?

——————

Booker T. Washington might have been born a slave, but he spent his life empowering people through education.

After he and his family were freed, he worked at a college in Hampton to fund his own education. When he co-founded the college now known as Tuskegee University, he let his first students build the academic buildings to pay for their tuition. The faculty and students grew their own food.

While some critics said he didn't fight hard enough for civil rights, he secretly raised funds for anti-lynching groups and other organizations while letting those critics unknowingly provide public cover for his activities. Washington also recruited George Washington Carver to Tuskegee.

Joe Perkins
Political strategist
Montgomery & Tuscaloosa Counties

He has quietly spent decades devising winning strategies and tactics for political candidates and interest groups. He has become a legend among those who follow Alabama politics. Neither his clients nor his opponents question his ability or intellect.

Joe Perkins came from Holt High School in Tuscaloosa County, part of the Perkins family that has been a pillar of the Holt community for generations. He became prominent, sought, and feared simply by becoming the best. His brother, Mark, was a rising star in politics, serving as Democratic Party Chairman and a member of the Tuscaloosa County Board of Education until his tragic passing in his thirties.

Perkins became a chief strategist and sage for Democrats across Alabama and beyond, and especially for groups like the Alabama Education Association that typically supported Democrats. Even after the demise of the Democratic Party, Perkins has remained a top player in Montgomery politics. He reportedly played a significant role in the winning strategies for the election of Doug Jones to the U. S. Senate.

Joe L. Reed
Political operative, university trustee
Conecuh & Montgomery Counties

Joe Louis Reed was born in the Conecuh County of the 1930s, and then left to see the world.

He literally saw much of the world, as he was stationed in South Korea with the United States Army. According to published accounts, Reed was deeply disappointed to return to the segregated Deep South, after serving in the army where everyone dined and lived in the same facilities.

After the war, Reed graduated from Alabama State University and became an activist in the Civil Rights Movement. Within two years of his college graduation, he became executive secretary of the all-black Alabama State Teachers Association.

For Joe Reed, with the background of an integrated military, an all-black teachers group was intolerable. He worked to join forces with the white group, the Alabama Education Association and its dynamic young leader, Paul Ray Hubbert.

Reed and Hubbert developed a meeting of the minds, and the result became a political juggernaut that defined most of the state's campaigns, elections, and legislative agendas for the next generation.

On its editorial page, the *Columbus Ledger-Enquirer* offered the following description of Reed and his political acumen:

"Joe Reed has wielded power in his own way as skillfully and relentlessly as did Wallace -- and like the former governor, he did so to the delight and admiration of his allies and the fuming exasperation of his foes."

In addition to his service to the state's educators, Reed also became a longtime leader on the board of trustees of his alma mater, Alabama State University.

Frederick Douglas Reese
Civil Rights leader
Dallas County

We could learn much from Frederick Douglas Reese. He became one of Selma's "courageous eight," who worked hard for increased voting participation by black citizens, notwithstanding court orders that slowed those efforts. He spent over 50 years as the pastor of the Ebenezer Missionary Baptist Church, and used his standing in the community to push support of the Civil Rights Movement while teaching Christian nonviolence, similarly to the message preached by the Dr. Martin Luther King, Jr.

And it was Reese who first invited Dr. King to Selma to support local efforts in the Civil Rights Movement. As the president of the Dallas County Voter's League, he was the one who had the authority to officially request King's assistance.

While some grew impatient with the movement's progress and supported violence or property destruction, Reese joined with King in seeking permanent harmony between the races. It was a bumpy road, especially in his hometown of Selma, but Reese carried himself with the dignity and class appropriate for a minister. Reese passed away in his beloved Selma in 2018.

The Wild West

Three of the Wild Wests' most famous gunfighters had Alabama connections

------

Pat Garrett, the sheriff famous for shooting Billy the Kid, was born in Chambers County and lived there for the first few years of his life.

If he had returned to Alabama as an adult, he might have run across two of the most famous outlaws in American history. Jesse James and brother Frank, while hiding out from law enforcement, spent a significant time living in rented rooms in the elegant St. James Hotel. The St. James sits majestically in Selma, on a bluff overlooking the Alabama River.

Jake Reiss
International booksmith
Jefferson County

He has been called the best book promoter in America. On any given day, he might receive book orders from California, Wisconsin, London, or Sydney.

This is clearly not your typical bookstore. You can see it from Highway 280 in Homewood but still have trouble getting there.

The national media has indeed figured out how to find Jake Reiss and his unique store in downtown Homewood. The Alabama Booksmith has appeared on lists of the best bookstores in America, and in the world. *Southern Living, NPR, Readers Digest, C-SPAN*, and even *Atlas Obscura* have featured it.

So what makes it different? What distinguishes The Alabama Booksmith from the countless other stores carrying similar inventory?

Therein lies the answer; no one else carries a similar inventory. Jake Reiss and his bookstore feature First Edition books, signed by the author, and nothing else.

"Let's face it; most people are not interested in whether a book is signed or whether it is a first-edition," Reiss explained. "But a small percentage of the population wants exactly that. Some search them out because they are serious collectors. But for a great many people, they make excellent gifts. Books signed by the author can transform an average gift into a thoughtful gift that people will remember."

"Jake Reiss has cleverly taken the one thing that hurts bookstores, the internet, and turned it into his best tool," explained Dr. Wayne Flynt, an acclaimed author who has seen Reiss in action.

Dr. Flynt has cracked the case; The Alabama Booksmith thrives because the internet allows shopping by collectors and thoughtful gift-givers from around the world.

Reiss didn't originally establish The Alabama Booksmith as a boutique-type business. In fact, he didn't plan on going into the business at all. Reiss volunteered to help his son, who was a bookseller in California and now does the same in Atlanta, with acquiring books. Soon, he began to love both the business and the books.

This unique business attracts media attention, which captures the attention of publishers and agents. That means Reiss can schedules signings with top-level authors. From President Jimmy Carter, to novelist Pat Conroy, to Tracy Chevalier, to just about anyone else without regard to genre, Jake Reiss sports some of the best book signings of any independent bookstore.

Pulitzer Prize-winning author Rick Bragg has become one of his good friends, as have many other authors. That's probably not unusual for the winsome Reiss. "This is the owner a lot of folks asked if I'd met yet," wrote Marc Fitten on his nationwide tour of the Indie 100.

So what was his favorite memory from a book signing? "There have been so many," he explains with his trademark, deliberative cadence. "But my favorite would probably be a private lunch with President Jimmy Carter on the day of his book signing here. Lunch was sent over from a local deli, and President Carter and I shared chicken salad at our own private table after the signing."

So whether it's a retired head of state or someone searching for a last-minute birthday gift, Reiss enjoys providing a service that makes a visit to his bookstore, in person or online, a memorable experience.

Chief John Ross
Cherokee Nation
Cherokee County

For forty years, John Ross served as the principal chief of the Cherokee Nation. He led his tribe through some of its darkest hours and helped rebuild after disaster.

The name John Ross might not seem like a typical Native American name, and Ross was never a typical person in any respect.

Ross' mother was a member of the Cherokee tribe, and his father was a Scottish trader. Ross was raised in Turkey Town, a Cherokee area near the current location of Centre (Cherokee County). His father arranged for a formal education, so Ross was comfortable dealing with both white people and his fellow tribesmen.

After operating a business in Chattanooga (then called Ross's Landing), he acquired a farm in nearby Georgia and bought slaves to handle the workload. Again, he was not the stereotypical Native American.

Ross rose through the ranks and ultimately became the Cherokee Nation's principal chief.

His tenure covered some of the critical-mass moments in the tribe's existence. The expulsion from the southern United States and the Trail of Tears exodus to the Oklahoma Territory brought intensive grief and serious danger. Ross' own wife died during the journey.

The American Civil War brought an agonizing decision as to whether to remain neutral or side with the Union or Confederate governments. While Ross remained cryptic about his true intent, the majority of Cherokees wanted to side with the Confederates (because of pro-slavery sentiments) and that was exactly what happened.

Chief Ross was actually held by Union troops as a prisoner of war, although he claimed that he had supported the Union side all along. To his credit, Ross had an almost impossible task of trying to navigate the Civil War crisis.

Despite the two existential crises, John Ross remains one of the most revered leaders in the rich history of the Cherokee Nation.

The Samford family
Leaders of government and business
Jefferson County

One of Alabama's oldest and most prominent families has been known, for over 150 years, for their devoted public service, zealous support of education, and generous contributions to charitable causes.

The Samford family arrived in Alabama in 1846, when Emory University professor William Flewellyn Samford (and wife Susan Lewis Dowdell Samford) moved to Chambers County, Alabama. Foreshadowing the leadership and public service of future generations, William F. Samford quickly became editor of multiple Alabama newspapers and a prominent leader. He ran for governor in 1857 as a Democrat and in 1859 as an Independent, advocating a stronger stance on states' rights than his opponent, Andrew B. Moore.

Samford's writing ability, combined with his zealous advocacy of the secessionist cause, earned him the monicker of the "penman of the Civil War."

His son, William J. Samford, enlisted in the Confederate Army during the Civil War, was captured, and held as a prisoner for 18 months. After the war, he resumed his studies and ultimately became an attorney. He was elected to the U.S. Congress in 1878, then returned home and was elected to the Alabama House of Representatives and later to the Alabama Senate. In 1900, Samford was elected Governor of Alabama.

Due to an increasingly serious heart condition, Samford was unable to attend his own inauguration, and was instead sworn in by his son. The leader of the Alabama Senate, William Jelks, became acting governor until Samford was able to assume the duties of the office.

It seems fitting that the 20th century began with Samford and Jelks working together, as the Samford descendants and the Jelks descendants (the Cabiness family) would continue leading roles in the state over the entire century and beyond.

Samford passed away on June 11, 1901, after a meeting of the University of Alabama Board of Trustees. His seven-month-long tenure as governor was too brief for many accomplishments, but he did call for a constitutional convention and establish the Alabama Department of Archives and History.

Governor Samford's son, William Hodges Samford, became a leader in the state's legal community and judicial system, serving as a Justice of the Alabama Court of Appeals.

Despite a full century of leadership and public advocacy, the family's most notable accomplishments still lay ahead.

The governor's grandson, Frank Park Samford, built Liberty National Life Insurance Company (now Torchmark Corporation) into the state's largest life insurance company. Samford left a lasting impact on the state's insurance industry and in the business community.

Like the generations before him, Samford was also a devoted public servant. Instead of running for public office, he used his standing as a leading citizen to improve the state, especially in the realm of education. Samford served, for decades, on the Board of Trustees for both Auburn University and Howard College. He led the effort to move the Howard College campus from Birmingham's East Lake area to Homewood.

In 1965, Howard College was renamed Samford University, memorializing the indescribable impact of Frank Park Samford and his family on the university, the city of Birmingham, the state of Alabama, and the education of countless students.

As Alabama begins its third century as a state, the Samford family continues its leadership, generosity, and advocacy for great causes that has defined the state and their lineage.

Richard Scrushy
Founder of HealthSouth
Dallas and Jefferson Counties

Richard Scrushy of Selma became best known for the wild ride of first becoming fabulously wealthy, and later losing his empire. The most remarkable story, however, just might be his brilliantly conceived journey from a Selma bricklayer to the founder of a multi-national corporation.

Scrushy grew up in Selma, and enjoyed many of the traditional activities of youth such as little league baseball, the Boy Scouts, and his church youth group.

Even at a young age, Scrushy had a type of sixth sense for innovation. He taught himself piano and guitar, and earned money playing at events and parties. He worked at a hamburger joint and as a bell hop at a local hotel.

He found a better job as a apprentice to a bricklayer, but aspired to more. Much more. As legend has it, Scrushy, while living in a trailer park, held aspirations to become wealthy and cultured, so he often served wine and cheese to guests in his home.

Scrushy sought a degree in respiratory therapy, and studied at Wallace State, Jefferson State, and ultimately the University of Alabama at Birmingham to earn his degree. After school, his impeccable work ethic converged with his aggressive leadership, and he became the leader of the UAB's respiratory therapy program and the founder of a similar program at Wallace State.

In 1979, he took a job with LifeMark Corporation in Texas, and within a year was running three departments within the company.

The meteoric rise of Richard Scrushy had begun.

In 1983, LifeMark was sold, and Scrushy pursued his idea of a outsourced rehabilitation services company. The next year, he founded HealthSouth in Arkansas and soon moved the company to Birmingham.

By the turn of the century, HealthSouth had clinics in all 50 American states and in the United Kingdom. Over 50,000 employees worked for the company in its 2,000 clinics.

The end of the Scrushy era began when accounting and government reporting irregularities caused a national scandal. Scrushy was found "not guilty" at a highly publicized trial that became a national spectacle. A later conviction for bribery, arising from dealings with the state government resulted in his incarceration. Later, a judge found him liable, under the recently enacted Sarbanes-Oxley Act, for over two billion dollars in damages caused by stock value and revenue misreporting by HealthSouth.

Despite the personal and financial fall, the vast charitable contributions by Scrushy during his HealthSouth years have benefitted the state's people, educational institutions, and children.

Dr. Annette N. Shelby
Internationally renowned professor
Tuscaloosa and Coffee Counties

In a word, she is extraordinary. Dr. Annette Nevin Shelby became the first tenured female professor in the history of the Georgetown University School of Business, while teaching advanced classes, publishing highly acclaimed academic articles, lecturing at Ivy League schools and European universities, playing a critical role in her husband's national political success, and raising two young sons in a new city.

A common description of her, by people who know her well, and casually, is that she is the smartest person they have ever met.

Dr. Shelby had settled in for a successful career as a business professor at the University of Alabama, raising their sons in Tuscaloosa with her husband, Richard. Both graduated from the university, and Richard was a successful attorney and Alabama State Senator. Their life seemed settled.

Then came the campaign for Congress in 1978, which Richard Shelby won by a wide margin. Ironically, as he began his ascent in the Congress, Annette Shelby became nationally known in her field even before her husband did in the world of politics. She also played a substantial role in his success; sources close to Shelby's 1986 campaign for the U.S. Senate believe that her work in that election was critical. After the victorious Senate campaign, she was diagnosed with lupus, a chronic, autoimmune disease that can damage any part of the body. Thankfully, Alabama had one of the world's great hospitals, at the University of Alabama in Birmingham, where Dr. Shelby received the type of elite care for which the institution has become famous. This ongoing health issue inspired Senator Shelby to become a major supporter of funding advanced and innovative biomedical research.

Despite any challenges imposed by lupus, Dr. Shelby continued lecturing at Georgetown University and on the campuses of foreign universities. She continued contributing works for publication and remained an important advisor to Senator Shelby, who no doubt appreciated having her expertise available while serving as Chairman of the Senate Banking Committee.

In gratitude for her service, impact, and life of excellence, the City of Tuscaloosa named Annette Shelby Park in her honor.

Arthur Shores
Attorney, activist
Jefferson County

The man was a giant.

That might seem like a surprising description, as Arthur Shores stood only five-foot-three and weighed only 145 pounds, but as his daughters explained to *AL.com*, he was a giant in life.

Arthur Shores certainly stood taller than most in both the legal profession and in the Civil Rights Movement. After graduating from Talladega College, Shores then pursued a legal education to fulfill his longtime dream of practicing law. He graduated from the LaSalle Extension University, and passed the Alabama Bar examination in 1937.

His law practice thrived, and his clients included Dr. Martin Luther King, Jr., Autherine Lucy, Vivian Malone, and James Hood. Future U.S. Supreme Court Justice Thurgood Marshall stayed in the Shores home while he and Shores handled the Lucy case together. Later, that same family home was bombed twice within a few weeks, not long before the nearby 16th Street Baptist Church bombing claimed the lives of four young girls. The area of town where the Shores family lived was called "dynamite row," after the many bombings, and Birmingham was becoming known as "Bombingham."

Transcending the violence and threats, Shores spent his legal career leading the races together. Maybe serving as a leader came naturally for the oldest of nine children growing up in Wenonah. Maybe it was also the high-profile cases that he tried as a young attorney, including one case arising from a rogue policeman's assault of an innocent civilian.

Thankfully, things did improve during the 1960s in Birmingham, and Shores went from an attorney living in constant danger to the first African-American appointed to the Birmingham City Council in 1968. Just a few years later, he was awarded an honorary doctorate degree from the University of Alabama at Birmingham, and was honored with a listing in the *Encyclopedia of Alabama*.

Fittingly, his daughters (Helen Shores Lee and Barbara Shores) wrote a book about the remarkable career of their legendary father, titled: *The Gentle Giant of Dynamite Hill.*

Milton "Bubba" Smith
Business leader, developer
Jefferson County

First, he grew up in downtown Homewood. Later, he transformed it.

Between those two events, Milton "Bubba" Smith quietly became a giant of commercial real estate in Birmingham and beyond. Early in his career, he became the leading producer at Daniel Realty Corporation. He then became an integral part of Harbert Properties, until John M. Harbert purchased Smith's ownership interest in the company.

Continuing his ascent into the world of commercial property development, Smith joined AIG Baker Development. becoming president in 1998. Once again, his superior performance vaulted him up the corporate ladder and he became the company's president. He retired, effective in October of 2007, from Baker Shopping Center Properties, LLC.

For almost anyone else, that would have ended a highly successful career. For Smith, it was merely time for the next challenge. That challenge, as it turned out, was the transformation of his childhood hometown of Homewood.

He developed the $36 million Soho Square, a mixed use facility with condominiums, retail, restaurants, and government buildings that was the first of its type in Alabama.

Next came the W Hotel, a $20 million project with street-level retail that has become the #1 occupancy hotel in Birmingham. It was also named Best Hotel by the *Birmingham Magazine*. More projects have followed, including the Broadway Park development.

Even with all of the other successes, Soho Square stands as an innovative project that changed the face of Homewood. "Soho has many unique features other than great architecture and location," he explained. "It was the first true Public/Private Commercial Mixed Use project in the state of Alabama, the development team, every professional, was the best of the best."

And it all began around a campfire.

"The craziest feature is hard to believe, the project concept was conceived on a Saturday night in 2002 over a fire pit conversation in Greene County, Alabama, by Scott Bryant and myself," Smith explained. "Personally, I am blessed to have had the opportunity to participate."

And Homewood has been blessed by its transformation by one of its own.

James Spann
Television star and meteorologist
Jefferson County

Wherever he goes, people want his autograph. Children dress up like him for Halloween. If he speaks at an event, the crowd is invariably good. People ask him to pose for selfies.

Shipt

How a grocery store trip in Birmingham gave birth to a national company

It all started with two fussy children.

Most parents have been there and done that. Bill Smith had both of his small children inside a Birmingham grocery store, and the kids began to cry and fuss. It was nothing unusual, but it inspired an idea. When he returned home, he told his wife that he was going to follow the suggestion of many and open an on-demand grocery shopping service.

Smith, who had previously opened a reloadable credit card business, had the capacity to fund the company and revolutionize the world of grocery shopping.

In 2018, Smith's creation, the national online grocery shopping Shipt, announced that it will hire 881 new Alabama workers as it expands its operations.

Already serving over 160 markets across America, Shipt has become the future of grocery shopping, allowing customers to order their groceries online and receive them the same day.

In 2017, the Target store chain purchased Shipt for $550 million.

Although the company has become a national name and a tech giant, Shipt has remained loyal to Alabama, keeping its company headquarters in its hometown of Birmingham and hiring local workers whenever possible.

Thanks to Smith, many parents will enjoy staying home with small children as someone else shops for their groceries.

No, it's neither a rock star nor a football coach. Actually, James Spann, one of the world's most successful meteorologists, is like a rock star in Alabama. He has been named national Broadcaster of the Year by the National Weather Association (2012). Spann has won two Emmy Awards (2001 and 2014). In 2013, he was elected to the National Academy of Television Arts and Sciences Silver Circle.

Clearly, the national organizations have learned what the people of Alabama have known for decades: James Spann has built a sterling reputation as an elite broadcaster who cares about the safety of his viewers. For over four decades, Spann has provided viewers of ABC 33/40 the best of weather coverage. His earlier stops included WBRC Channel 6 in Birmingham, and his time as a popular radio disc jockey in Tuscaloosa.

But there's much more to the success of James Spann than the classic baritone pipes and the energetic delivery. The man truly cares, and not just abstractly about the safety of his viewers, although that's important. Spann cares and learns about the communities themselves. When he describes the path of a storm, he goes beyond using major highways or towns that are county seats. He'll tell everyone near the Top Hat Barbecue restaurant in Blount County to take cover, or he'll let the people in Ranburne know that they might be in the path of a potential funnel cloud. Spann doesn't have to find a map to know where Sayre is, or how good the cobbler is at the *Twix & Tween*.

That's because he knows the communities, traveling the state of Alabama to speak and to teach how to prepare for, and remain alert for, severe weather or dangerous travel conditions.

And that's how a weatherman became a rock star.

The St. John family
Leaders, legislators, literary star
Cullman County

Over the past five generations, the St. John family has produced leaders in Alabama government, the state's education system, and the *New York Times* bestseller list.

When the Alabama General Assembly (that later became the Legislature) created the state's first public education system, William P. St. John was part of that effort.

Finis St. John, Jr., served as Speaker Pro Tem of the Alabama House of Representatives and Chairman of the House Ways and Means Committee. His son, Finis St. John, III, followed in his family's tradition, serving as President Pro Tem of the Alabama Senate.

"Fess" St. John (Finis St. John, IV,) showed his leadership skills at a particularly young age when he was elected Key Club International President while a student at Cullman High School. He left the prestigious St. John and St. John law firm in Cullman to serve as Chancellor of the University of Alabama System.

Cousin Warren St. John is a native of Birmingham who now lives in New York. He has authored numerous successful works, including a book about the culture of Alabama Crimson Tide football, *Rammer Jammer Yellow Hammer: A Road Trip into the Heart of Fan Mania*, that made the *New York Times* bestseller list. Warren St. John now serves as CEO of *Patch,* a national network of hyperlocal news sources.

Frank Stitt
Nationally honored chef
Jefferson and Cullman Counties

The James Beard Awards have become known as "the Oscars of dining." No recognition of restaurants or chefs carries more prestige.

In 2018, the *Highlands Bar & Grill* was named most outstanding restaurant in America, receiving the James Beard medallion at the James Beard Foundation awards ceremony, held at the Lyric Opera of Chicago.

Frank and Pardis Stitt have seen their work nationally recognized before, as *Highlands* is a ten-time finalist for the award. However, they now stand at the pinnacle of accomplishment in the industry. Over 35 years ago, Stitt opened *Highlands*, featuring a blend of French fine dining and Southern delicacies such as specially prepared recipes for grits.

Stitt's vision for that blend of French and Southern cuisines arose from his youth. He grew up in Cullman, and as the son of a surgeon, he was exposed to extensive travel and fine dining by his parents. He learned his craft while working in several elite restaurants.

Highlands launched an entire scene, in the Southside area of Birmingham, that includes the other Stitt restaurants, *Chez Fonfon, Bottega*, and *Bottega Cafe*.

Dolester Miles, the *Highlands* pastry chef and longtime friend of the Stitts, was named the Best Pastry Chef in America by the James Beard Foundation as well.

While Frank handles the culinary vision of the restaurants, Pardis has created her own art form with her management of the atmosphere and business that makes every visit to a Stitt restaurant an event, rather than merely a meal.

John Turner
CEO, Regions Bank
Jefferson County

John Turner stands tall as one of the top business leaders in Alabama. His career, and the institution he leads, bring some pretty daunting numbers.

By the Numbers

1...Regions is the one and only Fortune 500 company headquartered in Alabama.

3...John Turner had leadership experience with three different prestigious financial institutions before taking the helm of Regions. He served in a variety of positions with AmSouth. He served as president of Whitney National Bank, and he served with Regions as president of the south region that included Alabama, Mississippi, south Louisiana and Florida Panhandle.

$125 billion...Regions Bank holds a whopping $125 billion in assets, making it one of America's most important financial institutions.

200...In Alabama alone, Regions operates more than 200 branches, making it user-friendly and easily accessible to the customers who have made it a great institution.

Vulcan
Statue and park
Jefferson County

Vulcan stands tall, literally, as the iconic image of Birmingham and its iron and steel industries. Companies have been named after it, as have a professional football team and the presidential war cabinet in 2003.

By the numbers

56...Vulcan stands 56 feet tall. Originally designed for a height of 50 feet, the plans were changed to make it the world's largest cast iron statue, exceeding a 52-foot tall statue in Japan.

1904...Vulcan was created for the 1904 World's Fair in St. Louis. Originally, the state government planned to construct and transport it for exhibit in St. Louis as a promotion for Birmingham's steel industry. When financial problems at the state level made the venture cost-prohibitive, private citizens stepped in and made it happen. The idea for a statue was proposed by Birmingham Chamber (then called the Commercial Club) president Frederick M. Jackson and state fair director J.A. MacKnight.

40...as in an incredible 40 days.

As the *Encyclopedia of Alabama* explained: "MacKnight commissioned Italian sculptor Giuseppe Moretti. Moretti agreed to complete a plaster cast in 40 days, as the World's Fair opening day loomed on April 30, 1904." In just 37 days, using the cast from Moretti, the Birmingham Steel and Iron Company, led by its president, James R. McWane, cast the statue from pig iron.

30...For just short of 30 years, Vulcan was displayed at the state fairgrounds, until the Kiwanis Club of Birmingham lobbied the U.S. Works Progress Administration to move it to its current site on Red Mountain. The site was purchased for $5, thanks to the generosity of its owner, the Tennessee Coal, Iron, and Railroad Company.

Did You Know?

The Givhan family will soon begin its 10th decade of leadership in Alabama

The family's public service began almost 90 years ago, in 1930, when Selma's Walter Givhan was elected to his first term in the Alabama House of Representatives. In 1954, he was elected to the first of six terms in the Alabama Senate. Senator Givhan was known as the "father of the soybean movement in Alabama," helped create the Alabama Milk Control Board and Alabama Dairy Commission, according to the Auburn University agriculture department website.

Maj. Gen. Walter D. Givhan, the namesake of the Senator, also grew up in Selma and blazed his own trail in the U.S. military and civilian realms. Givhan served as Deputy Assistant Secretary of State in charge of U.S. global assistance programs and as Commandant of the Air Force Institute of Technology in Dayton, Ohio. He serves as Senior Vice Chancellor for Advancement and Economic Development, and has been named Chairman of the Alabama Historical Commission.

In 2018, the family tradition was renewed, as Sam H. Givhan, Selma native and attorney in Huntsville, was elected to the Alabama Senate, serving in the same body in which his grandfather rose to prominence over half a century ago. In addition to his law practice, Givhan also served as a leader in the Alabama Republican Party before his election to the Alabama Senate.

Warrior Met Coal, Inc.
Tuscaloosa County

As Alabama's bicentennial year approached, an event in Brookwood, Alabama, revealed how one of the state's signature industries had sprung back to life. In May of 2018, Warrior Met Coal, Inc. and Alabama Governor Kay Ivey joined in a ribbon cutting, celebrating the completion of Warrior Met Coal Company's new No. 7 Mine North portal facility.

The ceremony brought the announcement of a 33,000-plus square foot portal featuring a bathhouse, two kitchen areas, 40 offices and training rooms in addition to a hoist system which is double the capacity of the hoist currently in use at No. 7 West Mine. The new 7 North hoist features a 40-ton capacity, utilizing the latest technology and operates at a speed of 900 feet per minute to traverse the 1,451-foot-deep shaft. The hoist will accommodate 70 people.

Warrior Met Coal is a leading producer and exporter of metallurgical coal for the global steel industry from underground mines located in Brookwood, Alabama, southwest of Birmingham and near Tuscaloosa. These underground coal mines are 1,400 to 2,100 feet underground, making them some of the deepest vertical shaft coal mines in North America.

Throughout the rich history of Tuscaloosa County, coal mining has played a central role in the communities and their people. Coal companies helped construct the first Brookwood school, and have contributed in countless ways through the decades.

In Brookwood, Warrior Met has found the perfect location for a superior product. Metallurgical coal mined from the Blue Creek coal seam contains very low sulfur and has strong coking properties, making it ideally suited for steel makers. Warrior Met Coal's cost-efficient operations serve markets in the United States, Europe, Asia, and South America via convenient barge and rail access to the Port of Mobile. The company currently has the operational capacity to mine about eight million tons of coal per year from more than 300 million tons of recoverable reserves.

"The opening of our new portal speaks strongly to Warrior Met Coal's commitment to maintaining safe working conditions for all of our employees, as well as our confidence in the Met Coal market in the months and years to come," said Walt Scheller, CEO of Warrior. "Today's celebration comes on the heels of our second anniversary as a company operating in the great state of Alabama. And it was also just a year ago in April that we became a publicly traded company on the New York Stock Exchange.

"Our investment in this company has not only been in buildings and infrastructure," Mr. Scheller noted. "Our investment has also been in people. When we look back over the past year, the statistics show we've added 1,000 new people to our operations roster, and we are still hiring."

"Our commitment to the industry and to the people who work in it does not end with the opening of the new portal facility," said Jack Richardson, Chief Operating Officer of Warrior. "Our Board has committed significant capital of $100 to 120 million to reinvest in our mine infrastructure and equipment needs this year, positioning us well for future growth and improvement."

Fitzgerald Washington
Secretary of Labor
Tuscaloosa County

As the scorching summer sun pounded the asphalt parking lot, Fitzgerald Washington joined in the opening ceremony for a multi-million-dollar business expansion in Tuscaloosa County. After the ribbon cutting, as the cameras circled around Governor Kay Ivey, the first question from the media was about Washington's success as Alabama's Secretary of Labor.

"Secretary Washington does an outstanding job, and he has made a tremendous impact as Alabama's Secretary of Labor," she explained.

For Washington, the work of the past five years has yielded a harvest of success, with Alabama earning the largest drop of unemployment percentage in the entire nation. That has become one of the signature accomplishments in a tenure marked by victories in the labor market, and in the development of the state's workforce. Not too long ago, that would have been unheard of for a state saddled with a reputation for an undertrained and undereducated population.

In theory, public service should be a sacrifice of time from the best and brightest in our communities. For Washington, that was precisely what happened when he gave up an elite corporate career when asked to head the Alabama Department of Labor. Since 2002, he had served as General Sales Manager of Buffalo Rock, one of the Deep South's most successful corporations. Founded in 1901, Buffalo Rock is the largest independent single shareholder-owned Pepsi bottler in the United States, the 3rd largest Sunkist; the 6th largest Dr Pepper and the 10th largest Canada Dry bottler in the nation. Buffalo Rock manufactures and sells almost a billion containers of its products annually, and its local facilities include 14 distribution centers that encompass over 1.4 million square feet on approximately 190 acres.

In no small part, sustaining that success has arisen from not only recruiting businesses, but actually bringing the jobs to the people. In 2017, the Department of Labor's regional job fair initiative drew more than 7,000 jobseekers. Over 600 employers participated in these events, including a first-ever Governor's Disability Job Fair, held in Birmingham.

Thanks in part to Washington and his team, the state's bicentennial celebration has also become a celebration of low unemployment and new jobs pouring into the state.

Edgar Welden
Author, business leader
Elmore and Jefferson Counties

Although he was a good high school athlete in his hometown of Wetumpka, Edgar Welden's extraordinary career and hall of fame inductions have come from his achievements off the field. He also used a tragedy to refocus his own life and inspire others.

Along with his brother, Charles, Edgar Welden developed one of the Deep South's premier businesses in the realm of real estate development, mortgage, and property management companies in the Southeast. Turning his attention to state government, he led as Director of the Alabama Development Office (ADO) and the Alabama Department of Economic and Community Affairs (ADECA) and as Special Assistant to the Governor for Economic Affairs. Welden was selected as Alabama's Citizen of the Year for 1987 by the Alabama Broadcasters Association.

In December of 1996, his world was shaken when tragedy struck. Welden's good friend and Birmingham business leader Frank A. Nix was tragically killed in a plane crash on December 16th of that year. Welden and Nix were roughly the same age, and shared similar career paths by founding their own companies and achieving enormous success. Both had graduated from the University of Alabama, and each had been an outstanding athlete in their day.

After Nix passed away, Welden felt inspired to enjoy life more than he had. The result was *Time Out!* a book authored by Welden that chronicled his year of attending the greatest sporting events of that time. According to the amazon.com description of the book, "Welden attended 250 different sporting events, 35 different kinds of sports, and traveled over 120,000 miles. Welden saw the blockbusters - the World Series, the Superbowl, the Final Four, The Masters, but he also saw the less publicized events - the X Games, the Triathalon, the Iditarod and the Nine ball pool championship."

Welden's charitable and civic contributions have continued through the years, including the Birmingham Athletic Partnership, providing Birmingham city schools with millions of dollars in support. He was inducted into the Alabama Academy of Honor, the Alabama Sports Hall of Fame, and the Alabama High School Athletic Association Hall of Fame. In 2010 he received the Alabama Humanities Award and the 2010 Distinguished Alumni Award from the University of Alabama.

Leland Whaley & A.J. Johnson
Political talk show hosts
Jefferson County

When Leland Whaley and A.J. Johnson on the Leland Live Show hit the airwaves each day, they bring the unusual combination of politics, media, and humor that can entertain supporters and opponents alike.

Politics has been Whaley's career, which is fitting since he came from a politically active family in Randolph County. The political path has taken him from Republican Party activism, to the campaign and later staff of Governor Bob Riley, to the media, where he brings a natural ability to explain difficult issues.

A.J.'s path to the broadcast booth in Birmingham has taken a more circuitous route, but that's nothing new to the son of a military family. While his mailing address might have changed from time to time, his path of developing expertise in broadcasting and video production has remained consistent. That, along with the fact that he's really funny, make him a blessed balance for the news and politics of the day.

The show brings the unusual combination of great humor and the format of taking on the toughest and most highly charged issues of the day.

Hattie Hooker Wilkins
Activist, suffragist, legislator
Dallas County

Selma's Hattie Hooker Wilkins ran for the Alabama House of Representatives in 1922, the first election after the 19th Amendment gave women the right to vote.

Wilkins stood as a natural candidate for the position, as a native of Selma, a community leader, the child of a prominent family, and a leader in the women's suffrage movement. She was a founding member of both the Alabama Equal Suffrage Association and the Alabama

Russell

The name that says it all

It all began in Tallapoosa County, in a small, wooden building. At first, Benjamin Russell ran his family's mercantile company, but in 1902 a fire in Alexander City destroyed that business. At the mere age of 24, he decided to rebuild the business but become a garment manufacturing company. When Russell opened in 1902, it had six knitting machines and 10 sewing machines... and no electricity. For the first ten years, the company relied on steam to power their machines.

The company's fortunes rose and fell with the economy and world wars, but the 1920s decision to focus on athletic apparel set the company on its course of legendary success. In 1962, it became Russell Mills, and in 1973, it became the Russell Corporation. Both changes in international trade and the advent of companies like Nike and Under Armour might have dethroned Russell as the king of sports apparel, but its place in Alabama history remains secure.

Thankfully, the story doesn't end there.

The Russell family and the Russell Corporation continued the innovative planning that marked their family patriarch and company founder, Benjamin Russell. Russell and its associated groups became the primary catalyst for beautiful development on Lake Martin, the area from which the Russell family and the company originated.

Both the family and the corporation also continue their enormous generosity through charitable giving. Hospitals, university and college facilities, and other entities bear the Russell name because of their love of Alabama and its people.

League of Women Voters.

She succeeded as a legislator, becoming head of the committee on public health. She worked hard, especially on issues involving education, health care, and children. She decided against seeking re-election. At the end of her term, her colleagues honored her with an inscribed cup, reading: "To Mrs. Wilkins, the First Woman Member of the Alabama House of Representatives, a Token of Esteem From Her Fellow Members, 1923."

Charles Woods

War hero, business leader
Henry and Houston Counties

The story of Charles Woods stands beyond belief. Abandoned by his mother, he was raised in an orphanage until his adoption by the Woods family of Headland. He joined the U.S. Army Air Corps and bravely served and sacrificed during World War II.

When their plane exploded on December 23, 1944, Woods and the crew were departing Kurmitola, India, carrying tons of fuel to China. An inexperienced pilot botched the takeoff and crashed, causing 28,000 pounds of fuel to explode. Woods was the crash's only survivor, but suffered burns on over 70 percent of his body.

The fuel-fed inferno melted his face away, requiring 24 different surgeries to reconstruct.

Fighting unspeakable pain, mental anguish, and the stigma arising from his disfigured face and body, Woods set out to rebuild his life.

Could he ever live a normal life? No; he did much, much better.

Woods married, became the father of 12, and built a business empire. He owned companies in the worlds of construction, television, and radio.

Woods ran for lieutenant governor of Alabama and won the most votes in the 1974 Democratic Party primary, but narrowly lost the runoff to Jere Beasley. He made an impressive showing in two different U.S. Senate elections (one in Alabama, and the other in Nevada). Undeterred by the odds, he ran for President of the United States in 1992, and again received an impressive number of votes.

Charles Woods sacrificed more for America than most people could even imagine, but never let that interfere with his life of achievement and continued patriotic service. Upon his passing, he was buried in the Arlington National Cemetery.

Tom & Allen Young

Husband and wife founders
Kord Technologies
Madison County

In many ways, the idea for Kord Technologies arose from the tragedy of September 11, 2001. Allen and Tom Young lived in Washington then, and saw the damage, lost lives, and terror begat by the terrorist attack.

Moreover, they had a friend killed in the attack on the Pentagon, a place with which Tom was highly familiar. As the former chief of staff to Senator Richard Shelby, Tom had assisted Shelby with work on the Senate Select Committee on Intelligence and the Senate Armed Services Committee.

Allen was already an accomplished professional in the field of communications. Her leadership and creative background, combined with Tom's experience and connections, made them well equipped to start their own business.

Ten years ago, Tom and Allen Young decided to do exactly that. Recalling the suffering on September 11, they decided that keeping America safe would become the focus of their new business.

Accordingly, Kord Technologies was born.

Naturally, they chose Huntsville as the site of their space and defense contracting company. With Allen as CEO and Tom as president, they have built their company into a seamlessly integrated team that includes 170 employees. Kord handles a variety of space and defense missions, including core transportation capabilities for NASA's journey to Mars on the Space Launch System. The company plays a pivotal role in the intersection of communication systems, intelligence analysis, and cybersecurity. Kord was awarded a five-year, $114m contract to provide training support, aircraft and ground vehicle maintenance, and logistics services to the 120th Multi-Functional Training Brigade.

Top, left: Pardis and Frank Stitt. Top, right: Dr. Jane N. Geiger. Second row: Doug Marshall (center) and children of the Presbyterian Home for Children. Third row, left: Bicentennial Ambassador Bobby Joe Seals. Third row, middle: Marillyn Hewson. Third row, right: Amelia Boynton Robinson. Bottom row, middle: Arthur Shores.

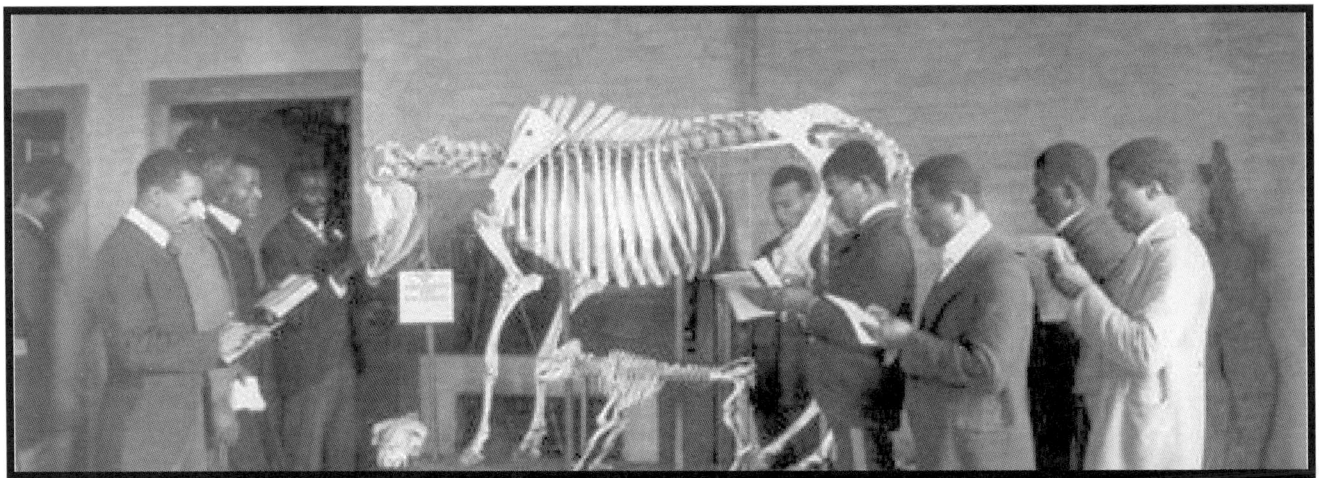

Pictured (top) George Washington Carver instructs students at Tuskegee Institute; (middle left) this photo was taken during the conversation in which someone exclaimed that the equipment "eats bushes like a hog," giving name to the "Bush Hog" company; (middle right) Maj. Gen. Walter Givhan served his country as Assistant Secretary of State and has returned home to Alabama; (above) Helen Keller and Anne Sullivan; (right) Vicki Hollub, CEO of Occidental Petroleum.

Miss America

Three Alabama girls have won the coveted title

The iconic words of the pageant's theme say it all: "There she is, Miss America." Nothing else is necessary for the world's most pretigious pageant.

As the Miss America website explains, "For the past 97 years, Miss America has been one of the country's most recognizable household names and has been at the center of everything from national trends to social movements to the birth of television. The young women involved have made a significant difference in people's lives through their charitable and community service endeavors, using the national platform to educate millions of Americans on issues facing the nation."

Three Miss America winners have hailed from Alabama, and their stories stand as diversely situated as the history of the pageant itself.

Along with the three Miss Americas, the Miss Alabama pageant has routinely produced Top Ten finishers in the pageant, including four girls in the last two years.

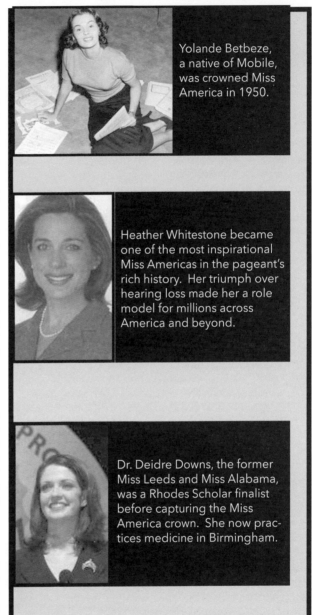

Yolande Betbeze, a native of Mobile, was crowned Miss America in 1950.

Heather Whitestone became one of the most inspirational Miss Americas in the pageant's rich history. Her triumph over hearing loss made her a role model for millions across America and beyond.

Dr. Deidre Downs, the former Miss Leeds and Miss Alabama, was a Rhodes Scholar finalist before capturing the Miss America crown. She now practices medicine in Birmingham.

Yolande Betbeze

The Mobile native was crowned Miss America in 1950, and was indirectly responsible for the creation of the Miss USA pageant when she refused the request of a sponsor to wear a swimsuit at public appearances. Betbeze was an accomplished opera performer.

Heather Whitestone

When Heather Whitestone won the Miss America Pageant in 1994, one can only imagine the journey her parents had traveled to Atlantic City from that hospital, long ago, with their 18-month-old daughter suffering from a dangerously high fever. It ultimately cost Heather her hearing, but never defeated her. Just as Helen Keller inspired her, she has challenged and motivated countless others.

Deidre Downs

Deidre Downs became one of the great intellectuals in the pageant's history. When she was crowned Miss America in 2005, she already had a degree from Samford University (magna cum laude) where she earned distinction as a Rhodes Scholar finalist. Downs later graduated from the UAB medical school. She practices medicine in Birmingham.

The tradition continues...

The past two years have seen two Alabama girls finishing in the Miss America Top Ten. In 2017, the past two Miss Leeds Area winners amazingly finished in the Top Ten, Miss Alabama Jessica Procter, and Miss District of Columbia Briana Kinsey. In addition to the two Miss America success stories, the Miss Leeds Area winner had won the Miss Alabama pageant in four of the previous seven years.

In 2018, the state of Alabama once again placed two contestants in the Miss America Top Ten, with Allison Farris from Jasper (Miss District of Columbia) and Miss Alabama Callie Walker.

ALABAMA PIONEERS

The Lee family
Business leaders, benefactors
Jefferson County

For four generations, the Lee family has served as a pillar of the Alabama community as they have run their family business. The family has enjoyed the taste of success, and you have probably tasted their success as well.

That family business is Buffalo Rock, one of the largest privately-held, single-family owned Pepsi-Cola franchises in the United States.

But it all began when a grocery guy and a chemist invented something special.

In the late 1800s, the Alabama Grocery Company was founded by Sidney W. Lee. Along with a chemist from Selma, Ashby Coleman, Lee developed a great tasting Ginger Ale. Lee named the new drink "Buffalo Rock Ginger Ale," and by the late 1920s, his grocery company had become a soft drink company.

Sidney Lee was succeeded by his son James, who continued the innovative leadership of his father by growing and expanding the company. His son, James Lee, Jr., changed the company forever by acquiring the bottling rights to Pepsi products in 1951.

James "Jimmy" Lee, III, wasted no time in preparing to lead his family's company, beginning his work career at age 12. Continuing the tradition into which he was born, Lee has invested himself in the family business and his community ever since.

Under his leadership, Buffalo Rock has soared to new heights, employing over 2,100 people in three states.

In addition to leading the company, Lee has served on the Board of Directors of the National Center of Sports Safety, as Director of the Birmingham Business Alliance, Past Chairman of the Board of Children's Hospital of Alabama, Past President and Current Member of the Alabama Beverage Association, Past Board Member of the American Beverage Association, Past President of the Vestavia Park Foundation, Past President of Children's Hospital Foundation Board, and Past President of the Auburn University Athletic Development Council.

The Koikos family
The Bright Star restaurant
Jefferson County

When The Bright Star's doors first opened in 1907, the small establishment in Bessemer sat only 25 diners. By 1914, the restaurant had already outgrown three different venues and moved to its current location.

Over 100 years later, brothers Jimmy and Nick Koikos still succeed with the restaurant their dad and uncle acquired way back in 1923. Thanks to their dynamic leadership and vision for growth, The Bright Star has become a top destination, and more of an event than merely a meal.

The decor, including murals by a European artist, reminds the diners that they have ventured to a historic location. Through the years, dining at The Bright Star would not only bring a delicious meal of Greek snapper or Greek tenderloin, but might also include a sighting of repeat customers such as Bear Bryant, Richard Shelby, Gene Stallings, Howell Heflin, or even actress Sandra Bullock.

The restaurant's history is compelling and the reputation unmatched, but the consistently savory food, along with the Koikos flair for service, stands as the real reason for The Bright Star's success since 1907.

Trivia

Which insect is honored by a statue in an Alabama town?

An Alabama town built a statue to honor a bug

In 1919, the town of Enterprise (Coffee County) erected a statue honoring the boll weevil, a pesky insect that decimated cotton crops across the Deep South. In fact, the boll weevil caused such harm to local economies that it was credited with helping cause the massive migration of African-Americans from the Deep South to urban areas in the Northeast and Rust Belt.

So why the statue?

The farmers and leaders of Enterprise wisely refused to play the role of victims. They diversified their crops, planting peanuts and various vegetables. They planned well, and used the destruction of cotton crops to create an economy no longer dependent on one major commodity.

The inscription on the monument to the boll weevil says it all:

In profound appreciation of the boll weevil and what it has done as the herald of prosperity, this monument was erected by the citizens of Enterprise, Coffee County, Alabama.

Making history

Rosa Parks, Rev. E.D. Nixon, and the Montgomery Bus Boycott

Rosa Parks became globally famous after she refused to give up her seat to a white person on a Montgomery bus. Her courage, poise in the face of hostility, and personal class have made her an inspiration to countless people.

She became one of the most famous people ever produced by Alabama in its 200-year history. The Montgomery Bus Boycott lasted 381 days, hurting the Montgomery bus system economically and creating a national movement, now represented by human faces, against a systemic wrong that had to go.

The Montgomery Bus Boycott also propelled Martin Luther King, Jr., to fame as a leader of the Civil Rights Movement.

And then there was Rev. E. D. Nixon.

On that fateful day when Rosa Parks was arrested, Rev. Nixon, a Lowndes County native pastoring in Montgomery, bailed her out of jail. Parks had worked with Rev. Nixon in the NAACP, so Nixon fully understood that Parks was a person of high character. He arranged for prominent attorney Clifford Durr, who also knew Parks, to represent her in the criminal case.

As the driving force behind the boycott, Nixon wanted a young leader to serve as its public face, along with Rosa Parks. He decided to ask the pastor at the Dexter Avenue Baptist Church, Rev. Dr. Martin Luther King, Jr., to accept the challenge. When Nixon first called and pitched the idea, King did not immediately agree, but wanted to discuss with his congregation first.

Ultimately, King accepted the challenge, and Nixon's choice altered the course of American history.

Pictured, top, Rosa Parks (right) visits with her old friend and Civil Rights Movement activist Virginia Durr (left). Pictured, bottom, Rev. E. D. Nixon was the driving force behind the Montgomery Bus Boycott, and personally asked the young Dr. Martin Luther King, Jr., to become the public face of the boycott.

Alabama Pioneers

Jan Hess
President, Teledyne Brown
Madison

As Teledyne Brown celebrates its 65th anniversary as the leading defense and space contractor, a Huntsville native leads the way.

Jan Hess has served as President of the Engineered Systems Segment of Teledyne Technologies Incorporated comprised of Teledyne Brown Engineering, Teledyne Energy Systems, Teledyne Turbine Engines and Teledyne CML.

In 2018, Hess was named to the prestigious listing of the Yellowhammer Women of Impact, for her role in the Huntsville business community and the defense and space industries.

Hess holds a Bachelors of Science in Accounting from Auburn University, and holds a Certificate in Management from Darden Graduate School of Business Administration, University of Virginia.

According to the company's website, Hess "has created a solutions-based company culture, fostering continuous improvement, yielding enhanced efficiencies for Teledyne and its customers."

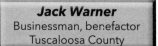

Jack Warner
Businessman, benefactor
Tuscaloosa County

Jack Warner led a remarkable life in which he succeeded grandly, and then spent time and resources helping Tuscaloosa succeed as well.

By the Numbers

50...During his 50 years at the helm of Gulf States Paper Company, Warner led the business to enormous success and expansion into six different states.

1...The North River Yacht Club stands as one of Alabama's greatest facilities, with stunningly beautiful scenery, an excellent golf course, tennis courts, and other recreational areas surrounded by an equally impressive residential development. When Alabama officials began recruiting Mercedes officials, their first event was held at North River.

2011...In 2011, the Metropolitan Museum of American Art in New York unveiled its Jack and Susan Warner Hudson River Gallery. Like everything else he did, Warner compiled an art collection second to none.

Pictured, bottom left: Tuscaloosa'a Jack Warner, who founded the North River Yacht Club, a multi-state paper company, two museums, and countless other assets he shared with the community and beyond.

Dr. Carl Marbury
President, Alabama A & M University
Jefferson County

As a young student, Leeds native Carl Marbury received historic career advice that changed his life. While career advice is common and usually not life-changing, the source of that advice made it special.

While interning with a church in Detroit, Michigan, Marbury had the opportunity to meet Rev. Dr. Martin Luther King, Jr., a former classmate of the senior pastor of the church. Dr. King learned that Marbury had been accepted into Harvard, Yale, and Princeton to pursue his doctorate, and offered some advice to the youngster from Alabama.

"Dr. King asked me to please consider Harvard, because it sat in Boston, where the American Revolution began and where I would come to a greater understanding of American history and the role that African Americans can play by making the American dream accessible to everyone."

Not surprisingly, Marbury chose Harvard.

The other advice from King was equally compelling. "Dr. King asked what I wanted to do right now, and I told him that I wanted to go to work for him," Marbury explained.

Then, Martin Luther King, Jr., spoke words that would change Marbury's life.

"He told me I could make a greater impact in another way. Dr. King said he had plenty of people working for him, but the one thing we needed most were more young academics. He told me that I could be president of a university one day, and I could make a greater impact on more lives that way."

Dr. King called his shot; the young Carl Marbury, who later became Dr. Marbury, ultimately served as President of Alabama A & M University. Even in retirement, Dr. Marbury has spent his time working tirelessly for a variety of causes, including the long-range planning for the state of Alabama and for his beloved hometown of Leeds.

Pioneers of college football

Top row (L-R): Wallace Wade, Frank Thomas, and John Heisman (photos courtesy of the *Encyclopedia of Alabama*.

Bottom (left) Harlon Hill (photo courtesy of *RoarLions.com*).

When it comes to sports, many Americans associate the Deep South with college football. That reputation has been well earned through national championships, Heisman Trophy winners, and elite players.

But it didn't start out that way.

Until the 1925 season, many Americans and most of the national media didn't take football seriously if it was played below the Mason-Dixon Line.

Enter ***Wallace Wade*** and the University of Alabama Crimson Tide.

Wade had recruited and trained a highly talented and prepared group of players. At the end of the 1925 season, Wade's team was set to face the University of Washington in the Rose Bowl. The Huskies stood as the prohibitive favorites to claim the national championship, which a Rose Bowl victory meant in that era.

Then a funny thing happened on the way to Washington's coronation as champs. The team ran into a mighty Alabama defense and the dashing Johnny Mack Brown. The Washington defenders found him dashing through their attempted tackles, and the Hollywood talents decided he should spend the next many years dashing to defeat the bad guys in cowboy movies.

Famous as he became, Johnny Mack Brown wasn't the lede emerging from the Rose Bowl. The biggest winner was Southern football. The media learned it, and the Deep South celebrated it with multitudes turning out in various cities to greet the train bearing the Alabama players during the return trip home.

Wade won three national championships at Alabama (1925, 1926, and 1930) establishing the program as the gold standard of Southern football.

Frank Thomas succeeded Wade and won two national championships of his own (1934 and 1941), as well as four conference titles.

Thomas was a disciple of legendary Notre Dame coach Knute Rockne, and made his alma mater proud during his 15-year tenure in Tuscaloosa. Thomas also recruited the greatest player in the program's history, Don Hutson, as well as future coaching legend Paul "Bear" Bryant. He compiled a record of 115 wins with just 24 total losses in 15 years, along with 7 ties.

If the name ***John Heisman*** sounds familar, it might be because the most famous individual award in American sports bears his name.

Heisman coached the football team in Auburn from 1895 to 1899, launching the university's legacy into college football lore before the twentieth century began. Known then as the Alabama Polytechnic Institute, the future Auburn University reaped benefits even beyond the realm of football. Heisman founded the API (Auburn) Dramatic Club at the university, providing cultural advancement as well as athletic success.

Heisman Trophy winners Pat Sullivan, Bo Jackson, and Cam Newton have each renewed the intertwined legacies of a university and its most famous coach.

Just as the Heisman Trophy honors the outstanding Division I player, the ***Harlon Hill*** Trophy celebrates the top player in Division II.

Hill graduated from Lauderdale County High School, and played his college football for his hometown school, Florence State Teachers College (now the University of North Alabama).

Passed over until late in the 1954 NFL draft, Hill was finally taken in the 15th round by the Chicago Bears.

Hill quickly made teams regret their mistake in not choosing him, as he burst onto the NFL scene, setting team records and earning the Rookie of the Year award.

According to legend, professional scouts had never noticed Hill, and became aware of his ability when the Jacksonville State University coach mentioned his name during a conversation.

Because of his college football success and his remarkable professional career, the Harlon Hill Trophy now recognizes the outstanding player in Division II football, and renews the pride of Lauderdale County and the University of North Alabama each year.

PIONEERS

Teaching the world

Jimmy Wales: founder of Wikipedia
Madison County

If you have ever used Wikipedia to research something, anything, you're in good company. It has become the world's largest encyclopedia. Its founder, Jimmy Wales, has been named to The 100 Most Influential People in the World by *Time* magazine. Wales grew up in Huntsville, graduating from the prestigious Randolph School. After earning degrees from both Auburn University and The University of Alabama, he taught briefly before entering the business world.

After other ventures, he founded Wikipedia on January 15, 2001, as an open-source encyclopedia.

Every single day, countless millions of people across the globe have Jimmy Wales to thank for making information and enlightenment easily accessible.

A life well lived...

Rod Bramblett: the voice of Auburn sports
Lee County

When he was chosen to replace a legend in 2003, Rod Bramblett succeeded grandly. As the voice of Auburn University sports, he not only replaced Jim Fyffe, but carved his own legacy into the rich history of the Auburn Tigers. Bramblett's uninhibited energy and smooth delivery converged to entertain fans through riveting victories and heartbreaking losses alike.

Perhaps no one moment captured the essence of Rod Bramblett's style and success than the "kick-six" play in the 2013 Iron Bowl against the University of Alabama. As it became one of the most famous plays in college football history, Bramblett's classic call of the moment also became a part of sports lore. The game-winning field goal to defeat the University of Oregon Ducks for the 2010 national championship wasn't too bad either.

His talent and likability were surpassed only by his love for his family and his Auburn Tigers...in that order. When Bramblett and wife Paula were tragically killed in a motor vehicle accident in May of 2019, the outpouring of grief and tributes knew no bounds of geography or sports loyalty.

The unlikely legend

Dwight Stephenson
The University of Alabama

One of the great careers in football history almost never happened.

Dwight Stephenson is considered by many to be the best center in the game's history. The NFL Hall of Fame website conservatively described him as the "premier center of his time." Coach Paul "Bear" Bryant reportedly said that Stephenson was the greatest player he ever coached at any position.

Were it not for a decision by a Virginia real estate agent, Stephenson might never have played football.

Today, Greg Garrett is a well known, highly successful realtor on the Virginia peninsula, in Hampton, Newport News, Yorktown, and Poquoson. Decades ago, he was the starting center on the Hampton High School Crabbers, and the legendary Mike Smith. Smith stands as the third winningest coach in American high school history and sports 12 state championships, so when Garrett told coach Smith that he would not play his senior year of football, it was a seismic event for the team. Smith explained to the young Garrett that there was not yet a backup center for the team, but Garrett had decided that he wanted to pursue other activities and would not play.

So Smith went looking for a Hampton High student, outside the football program, whom he could quickly teach to become the team's center. He found Dwight Stephenson, and the rest is history.

Despite an injury-shortened professional career, Stephenson was named to five consecutive Pro Bowls and helped lead the Miami Dolphins to two Super Bowls.

A Bright Future

Massive solar energy project brings dynamic partnership for Alabama cities

In its bicentennial year, Alabama businesses have introduced a seemingly endless number of innovative new products and projects.

Fred Clark, CEO
Alabama Municipal
Electric Authority

For the Alabama Municipal Electric Authority, that includes a solar energy project that will change the way many Alabamians receive their household energy.

Led by Fred Clark, a longtime energy executive and former aide to Senator Richard Shelby, the AMEA has partnered with energy company Lightsource BP for this dynamic project.

-- By the Numbers --

350,000...The solar energy production facility will feature a whopping 350,000 solar panels, harvesting clean, affordable, renewable energy.

800...The facility will be located on 800 acres in Montgomery County.

20,000...Over 20,000 homes in 11 municipalities will receive energy from this facility.

$125 million...The investment will total $125 million and include an agreement by the municipalities to purchase energy for at least 20 years.

$5 million...Montgomery County schools will receive over $5 million in property tax revenue over the life of the project.

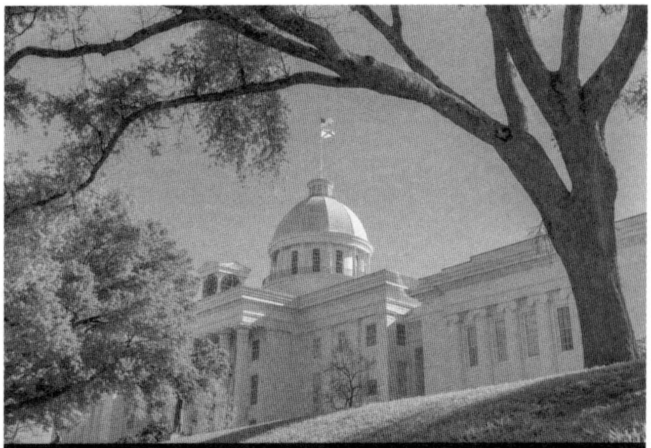

Alabama State Capitals

St. Stephens

Before Alabama became a state, St. Stephens served as the capital of the Alabama Territory from 1817 to 1819. Located in Washington County, less than 70 miles from Mobile, the town was beautifully postured on a bluff above the Tombigbee River. The Spanish originally established the settlement because of its strategic importance, and named it Fort San Esteban. The United States ultimately acquired the territory, and when Mississippi became a state in 1917, St. Stephens because the first Alabama capital.

Huntsville

As the state's leading area of population and politics, Huntsville was chosen as the first temporary capital of the newly formed State of Alabama during 1819 and 1820. The state's first constitutional convention was held there, as was the inauguration of the first governor, William Bibb.

Cahawba

When the first Alabama Territorial Assembly met in St. Stephens, the battle to decide the permanent capital was already underway. One group favored Tuscaloosa, but the other group, advocating Cahawba, included the governor. Using his vast national connections, Governor William Bibb secured a grant of free land to establish the capital, and the Cahawba group won. The group in Tuscaloosa was able to limit the original term of the capital's time in Cahawba, and was ultimately able to move it to Tuscaloosa.

Despite the economic damage of losing the capital, Cahawba made a comeback in the 1840s when Dallas County became the wealthiest area of the state because of cotton production. However, the Civil War and changes in railroad routes devastated the city and it became a ghost town by 1900.

Tuscaloosa

Tuscaloosa served as the capital from 1826 to 1846. During those years, the state university was established in 1831 and became a leading area for professionals, academics, and intellectuals.

Montgomery

Since 1846, Montgomery has served as the capital of the state, and also served as the first capital of the Confederate States of America.

More Alabama Trivia

Question: Which great American author began writing to impress his high school baseball coach?
Answer: Gay Talese hoped to earn playing time by writing game summaries for the local newspaper. However, his talent was unmistakable, and he was quickly hired by the newspaper. After sharpening his skills at The University of Alabama, Talese became one of the greatest modern American writers.

Question: Which Alabama business leader became the namesake for a major city and founded a famous company?
Answer: Prattville is named after ***Daniel Pratt,*** one of the great businessmen in the state's history. His company sold cotton gins as far away as Russia and Germany. With his massive wealth, Pratt acquired ownership of railroads and steel interests. His son in law, ***Henry F. DeBardeleben***, ultimately succeeded Pratt and brought even greater success.

Question: Which native of Tuscaloosa became the WBC heavyweight boxing world champion?
Answer: In 2015, ***Deontay Wilder*** became the first American heavyweight champion in almost a decade. A native of Tuscaloosa, he won a bronze medal in the 2008 Olympic Games.

Question: Which future judge stood beside the teenage Bill Clinton as he famously shook hands with President John F. Kennedy?
Answer: ***Judge Pete Johnson*** attended Boys Nation with Clinton, and became the face of Boys State in Alabama for over four decades. Judge Johnson has inspired and influenced generations of future leaders.

Question: Which Alabamian founded the Black Jacket Symphony, which has become one of the great Southern musical traditions?
Answer: Birmingham's ***Jay Willoughby*** has spent his life creating and performing music at an elite level. In his youth, he was the lead singer for the Newboys, one of Alabama's most popular acts in the 1980s, best known by their hit song *Dramatics of Love*. Willoughby founded the Black Jacket Symphony, in which one of the great modern albums is precisely recreated.

Question: Which Auburn University football coach defeated the Alabama Crimson Tide six years in a row?
Answer: Coach ***Tommy Tuberville*** defeated his rival six consecutive years, went undefeated (13-0) in 2004, and was named national Coach of the Year in 2004.

Question: Who was the Revolutionary War hero whose visit to the state capital inspired the state to spend more money celebrating him than on constructing the capitol building itself?
Answer: In 1825, the ***French General Marquis de Lafayette*** visited Cahawba. He remained revered in the U.S.; were it not for his fleet's timely arrival for the battle of Yorktown, America might have remained a British colony. Alabama had spent $10,000 constructing the capitol in Cahawba, and over $17,000 hosting the hero.

Question: Which Alabamian became the all-time sacks leader for the Dallas Cowboys?
Answer: ***DeMarcus Ware***, from Troy University, racked up more sacks than any player in the history of the Dallas Cowboys. He also became one of only three players in NFL history to record at least 10 sacks in seven straight seasons.

Question: Which 100-year-old restaurant has been a favorite of Elvis Presley, Franklin Roosevelt, Hank Williams, Harry Truman, and countless others?
Answer: The ***Katechis family*** and ***Chris' Hot Dogs*** have already celebrated their 100-year anniversary. It remains famous for the delicious hot dogs and hamburgers that are somehow ready almost as quickly as you place your order. When the presidential train would pass through Alabama, Roosevelt liked to order boxes of the world-famous hot dogs.

Question: Which Alabamian once served in the White House as a Russian interpreter for President Reagan?
Answer: Today, people know Walker County's ***James "Jay" Snow*** as an American Legion leader or retired attorney. In the Reagan White House, he was a Russian language interpreter during the height of the Cold War, when every communication with the Soviet Empire carried great potential importance.

Question: Which Alabama golfer won the PGA Championship, the FedEx Cup, four other PGA tour wins, a college national championship and the college player of the year, all before his 25th birthday?
Answer: In 2017, ***Justin Thomas*** of The University of Alabama became only the fourth modern golfer to win five PGA tournaments before his 25th birthday (with Jack Nicklaus, Tiger Woods, and Jordan Spieth). He played on the 2013 Crimson Tide national championship team.

Question: Which football star became a renowned surgeon and the author of over a dozen books?
Answer: ***Dr. Gaylon McCollough*** excelled at college football and as a successful plastic surgeon. Despite writing many books, he is not the most creative member of his family. His wife, ***Susan N. McCollough***, has achieved international acclaim as an artist.

Question: How did Jones Valley become a leading part of modern day Huntsville?
Answer: Engineer and farmer ***Carl Jones*** purchased a 2,500 acre farm in 1939, when Huntsville only had 12,000 people. He wisely planted Kentucky grass and replaced cotton with cattle. The family, led by son ***Ray Jones***, developed it as a leading area of modern Huntsville.

Question: Which Childersburg basketball star became the national player of the year and played 14 years in the NBA?
Answer: ***Gerald Wallace*** won the Naismith Prep Player of the Year as America's best high school player, played at The University of Alabama, and then starred for 14 years in the NBA.

INDEX

Profiles and Names